JAPAN

— IN —

WAR

AND

PEACE

Japan

— in —

War

and

Peace

—

Selected Essays

John W. Dower
New Press · New York

Published in the United States by The New Press, New York
Distributed by W.W. Norton & Company, Inc.,
500 Fifth Avenue, New York, NY 10110

Library of Congress Cataloging-in-Publication Data

Dower, John W.
Japan in war and peace / John Dower. — 1st ed.
p. cm.
Includes index.
ISBN 1-56584-067-4
1. Japan—History—Showa period, 1926–1989.
2. Japan—Economic conditions—1918–1945.
3. Japan—Economic conditions—1945– 4. Japan—
Relations—Foreign countries. I. Title.
DS888.2.D68 1993
952.03'3—dc20 92-50821
CIP

Established in 1990 as a major alternative to the large, commercial
publishing houses, the New Press is the first full-scale nonprofit
American book publisher outside of the university presses. The
Press is operated editorially in the public interest, rather than for
private gain; it is committed to publishing in innovative ways
works of educational, cultural, and community value that, despite
their intellectual merits might not normally be "commercially"
viable. The New Press's editorial offices are located at the City
University of New York.

Printed in the United States of America.

HC 93 94 95 96 9 8 7 6 5 4 3 2 1
PB 95 96 97 98 9 8 7 6 5 4 3 2 1

For Yasuko

Contents

Tables (all appear in Chapter 4)

1. Peace Preservation Law Violations (1928 through April 1943)
2. Tenancy Disputes, 1917–1944
3. Labor Disputes, 1897–1945
4. Labor Disputes by Industry and Sector (Jan. 1943–Nov. 1944)
5. Displacement of Personnel in Wartime Japan
6. Incidents Involving Koreans in Japan (Jan.–Nov. 1944)
7. Absenteeism in Japanese Industry, 1943–1945
8. Ratio of Paid-in Capital of Companies under the Control of the Principal *Zaibatsu* (1937/1946)
9. Japanese War Casualties
10. War Damages in Japan
11. Rumors Investigated by the Military Police during the Pacific War
12. Lèse Majesté Incidents (1936–April 1943)

AUTHOR'S NOTE

In citing Japanese names, I have followed the proper order of surname first for Japanese nationals, including all authors of writings in Japanese cited in the end notes. Where the writings of Japanese authors appear in English, I have consistently placed surnames last, as they usually appear for the convenience of bibliographers and general readers.

Introduction

FOR IDEOLOGICAL REASONS, the Japanese calculate time differently than do other peoples. They tie it to the emperor's reign. Thus 1993, the year this introduction is being written, is Heisei 5 in the Japanese reckoning, the fifth year of the reign of Akihito, the Heisei emperor. Prior to Emperor Akihito's ascension to the throne in 1989, it was the reign of his father Hirohito, the Shōwa emperor, by which Japanese marked time. Accordingly, 1926 was the first year of Shōwa. The year 1931, when the Manchurian Incident took place and Japan seized China's three northern provinces and turned them into a puppet state, was Shōwa 6. All-out war against China began in Shōwa 12 (1937), and the attack on Pearl Harbor took place in Shōwa 16 (1941). Emperor Hirohito personally informed his subjects of Japan's capitulation on the fifteenth day of the eighth month of Shōwa 20 (1945), his reedy voice crackling over the airwaves; and he continued to reign as august sovereign for forty-four years thereafter. Until Emperor Hirohito died on January 7, 1989, that momentous year was identified as Shōwa 64.

This marriage of calendar to sovereign is not a traditional way of counting time in Japan, but rather a highly modern way of engaging in

1

symbolic politics. Until 1868, the year upstart warriors overthrew the ancien régime of rule by feudal shoguns and samurai, the Japanese did indeed identify years by "era names," but ones that usually had little to do with imperial rule. Ruling authorities simply selected through divination and other rites an auspicious name made up of two ideographs (such as "Tempyō," or "Heavenly Peace"), and started counting from then until famine, drought, inflation, gross corruption, peasant insurrection, or some comparably unpleasant development dictated choosing a new era name, hoping for better luck, and counting from scratch again. The emperor was peripheral to all this. Indeed, most Japanese were unaware of his existence, or at least indifferent to it.

This changed when the "modernizers" and "Westernizers" assumed authority after 1868, for Japan's new leaders soon concluded that they needed a counterpart to God and Christianity in the West to hold their emerging nation together ideologically. They found this in the long-neglected imperial family, and in ancient mythohistories about the divine origins of the imperial line. This shrewd reinvention of tradition, rather than abiding old beliefs, accounts for why the Japanese count modern and contemporary time as they do. The Shōwa emperor was only the third monarch in memory whose reign was coterminous with an "era name," known as *gengō* in Japanese; and in 1979, Japan's conservative government ensured that the emperor-centered calendar would carry on indefinitely by passing legislation that mandated continued use of the *gengō* practice.

The two ideographs used to write Shōwa literally mean "brightness" and "harmony," hardly the most accurate signifiers for a reign that encompassed in its early decades so much repression, aggression, atrocity, misery, and plain dark conflict. Yet in a curiously happenstance way, this monarchic construct of a "Shōwa era" is more meaningful to the historian than is the conventional Euro-American way of designating time in the mid twentieth century. For obvious reasons, we Westerners tend to cut the century with a great watershed at 1945, and think of "prewar" and "postwar" periods. This is reasonable but misleading, for it tends to obscure the dynamic continuities between our prewar and wartime and postwar experiences, not only in Japan but elsewhere in the world. In this regard, the embracing concept of Shōwa—serendipitously linked to the early coronation and prolonged good health and good luck

2

of a Japanese man with the bluest of bloodlines—is more suggestive. "Shōwa" threads the critical decades of the mid twentieth century together, and reminds us of how closely past and present, "prewar" and "postwar," war and peace are interwoven.

To a degree still not fully appreciated, we can thank a conservative American, General Douglas MacArthur, for the survival of this uniquely Japanese way of reckoning time: for as Supreme Commander of the victorious forces that occupied Japan from August 1945 to April 1952, it was primarily MacArthur who not only preserved the imperial institution as "symbol of the State and of the unity of the people" but also summarily dismissed the possibility of having Emperor Hirohito abdicate and write *finis* to the disastrous two-decade-old Shōwa era. Such proposals emerged even from within the emperor's own entourage on three conspicuous occasions in postsurrender Japan—in the wake of defeat in 1945–46, after the conclusion of the Tokyo war crimes trials in late 1948, and in the final stages of the Occupation in 1951—and on each occasion MacArthur dissuaded the emperor's advisers, and Emperor Hirohito himself, from pursuing the option of abdication. Had the other course been taken, the political psychology and mythology of postwar Japan would have been significantly altered, and basic questions of political and moral responsibility as well as of democracy itself would have been less easily ignored. Here, as so often in the decades since Commodore Matthew Perry forced Japan to abandon its feudal seclusion in 1853, a substantial chapter of modern Japanese history was written by an American hand.

All this is by way of prelude to introducing the essays collected here, which deal with Japan of the Shōwa period and the tangled history of mutual hatred and respect, conflict and cooperation, which has characterized U.S.-Japan relations over the last half century. The essays were written over the course of the last fifteen years or so. Some were published in well-concealed academic places. Some appeared only in Japanese translations. One long and central piece (Chapter 4, "Sensational Rumors, Seditious Graffiti, and the Nightmares of the Thought Police") comes from some two hundred pages in an old manuscript that was boiled down to a mere fifteen pages in a book published in 1979. Most, but not all, of the essays have been touched up for this present volume.

There was no grand plan in the writing of these pieces, but in

3

retrospect they reflect certain preoccupations that, as time has passed, have attracted me as a historian. Working on mid-twentieth-century Japan and U.S.-Japan relations is, of course, an ideal field in which to wrestle with impossibly grand dichotomies (past and present, war and peace, "East" and "West") and issues (racism and capitalist models among them). At the same time, and at the other extreme, there is plain satisfaction in excavating and reconstructing the gritty detail of the past and thereby gaining insight into other people in other places at other times. We can, among other things, learn a great deal about ourselves this way. Be that as it may, in the middle ground where these essays reside, I have tried to address, or at least to evoke, several themes.

One is the dynamism of transwar legacies in Japan—the extent, that is, to which the great accomplishments of postwar Japan, not only economically but also in the vigor of antimilitary sentiments among the general populace, are rooted in the war years. This is spelled out in the opening essay on "The Useful War," and also in Chapter 5, which weighs Yoshida Shigeru, the conservative old diplomat who led Japan through the Occupation into independence, in the "scales of history."

A second pervasive theme—the heretical ground bass, as it were, of a number of these explorations—is the heterogeneity of modern Japanese society and extraordinary turmoil and internal tension that has characterized the modern Japanese experience. This challenges the popular emphasis in Japanese as well as non-Japanese literature on harmony, consensus, the "group model" as the central axis of Japanese thought and practice. In other writings I have dealt with Japanese indoctrination (and atrocities) in World War II, as well as with the increasing regimentation that appears to have accompanied the "takeoff" into high economic growth beginning around 1960. The essays in this present volume offer a counterpoint to this, being more attentive to political, social, and ideological tensions in Japan, even during the war years.

Thus Chapter 2, "Japanese Cinema Goes to War," analyzes one of the great cultural resources of the war years which has been little seen since 1945, and finds ambiguous and even humanistic strains amidst the crass propaganda. The essay that follows this, on Japan's wartime atomic-bomb research, finds major tensions and conflicts (and plain disorder) within the society Japanese ideologues extolled as "one hundred million hearts beating as one." Chapter 4, on wartime rumors and graffiti, uses

4

the secret records of the Thought Police to help explain why militarists as well as antimilitarist conservatives feared that the losing war might lead to revolution in Japan. And Chapter 7 introduces a corner of the grass-roots antiwar movement in postwar Japan through three kinds of artwork dealing with the atomic-bomb experience: drawings by survivors, children's books, and the collaborative mural art of Maruki Iri and Maruki Toshi. It is entirely true that the conservative Japanese government, led by the Ministry of Education, has long been engaged in a campaign to sanitize accounts of Japanese aggression and atrocity in World War II. My interest here, in addition to seeing Hiroshima and Nagasaki through Japanese eyes, is to introduce a small sample of that largely antimilitary Japanese populace whom the government is trying to brainwash.

Tension and conflict of a different order, between Japan and the United States, is another focus of the essays. It would be absurd to say that America has been preoccupied with Japan over the course of the six decades of Shōwa, but the reverse is essentially true: Japan has been obsessed with the United States, and its fate has been inextricably linked to the colossus across the Pacific. For tens of millions of Japanese, the Shōwa era has been powerfully defined, for better or worse, by relations with the United States—through war and Occupation, through decades of ambiguous client-patron relations, and in recent decades through the bizarre and unchoreographed dances of contemporary capitalistic cooperation and conflict.

Chapter 5, on "Occupied Japan and the Cold War in Asia," is a close-knit and rather conventional policy analysis of early postwar U.S.-Japan relations, based primarily on hitherto-secret official U.S. documents. By placing postsurrender U.S. policy toward Japan in a global context, this essay goes against the grain of an earlier generation of American scholarship, which treated the Occupation essentially as an isolated and purely idealistic experiment in "social engineering," a test-tube baby for democratic American reformers, as it were. Chapter 6, on Yoshida Shigeru, approaches the Occupation from the Japanese side, highlighting through the conservative postsurrender prime minister how vigorously change was resisted at elite levels in defeated Japan—and suggesting also what a heavy psychological burden the legacy of "subordinate independence" has been for postwar Japan. We can never hope to understand current tensions between the United States and Japan if we neglect not merely the bitter legacy of World War II but also the ambiguous legacy of the Occupation and the ensuing decades of profitable but psychologically debilitating Japanese acquiescence to America.

Such considerations lead to a different level of inquiry than can be accommodated by conventional analyses of policymaking and of political economy. They call attention to the central place of emotion and irrationality in history, sheer visceral attractions and (more often) animosity; and also to the power of unwitting as well as witting symbolic manipulation—the patterns of perception, the tropes, the visual and verbal formulas by which we commonly define ourselves and others. Where Japan and U.S.-Japan relations are concerned, this visceral and symbolic dimension is exaggerated and often extreme, for obvious reasons. Racism is involved; so too is power, hegemony, domination in the only game left since the collapse of communism and socialism—capitalist competition. These issues emerge, often in very vernacular idioms, in the comparative essay on "Race, Language, and War in Two Cultures" (Chapter 8), which examines Japanese and American perceptions of self and other in World War II, and a complementary article titled "Fear and Prejudice in U.S.-Japan Relations" (Chapter 10), which links the racial idioms of war to those of contemporary conflict (or "trade wars"), and relates this to competing models of capitalism and the profoundly disorienting acceleration of technological change in our contemporary world.

When I began research as a historian a little more than two decades ago, we did not think of using informal or mass-based materials such as rumors and graffiti, films and popular drawings, or crude colloquial expressions as legitimate documentation for our craft. Now we understand better how much insight into consciousness and culture—and mass psychology and consumer society—can be gained by utilizing such materials. The "graphic essay" of Japanese and Anglo-American cartoons and other visuals which appears between Chapters 8 and 10 lays out some of the raw stuff itself, in a structured way, to suggest how certain archetypical images persist in Japanese and Western perceptions of themselves and each other—in Japanese perceptions of a threatening West and a poor, pure self, for example, and Western perceptions of the Japanese as simultaneously "little people" and ominous yellow supermen.

6

That such images abide through war and peace, and through seemingly cataclysmic changes, does not say a great deal that is encouraging about our imaginations and ability to transcend prejudice. We ignore these quick, impressionistic images at our peril. Such cultural artifacts cannot replace more traditional scholarly concerns with institutions, policy processes, and the like (as in Chapters 1 and 5), but the latter no longer can be addressed in isolation from the visceral, the symbolic, the ideological. And, alas for the scholar, in this imagistic age such simplistic, subjective, impressionistic constructs tend to be more influential than wheelbarrows full of academic books.

Both the formal histories and more popular images can be easily exploited, of course, and here we confront the issues of uses of history and manipulation of symbols. This emerges in more than just the essays that directly address U.S.-Japan relations. Chapter 3, on Japan's A-bomb research, for example, is actually a two-level essay, concerned with what we can learn about science and society in wartime Japan from this project, on the one hand, and with how information about these long-ago activities was disingenuously presented in the mainstream U.S. media in the late 1970s to reinforce an image of Japanese duplicity, on the other. The final two essays in the book return us to the acme of playing with history and symbols, for they address the death of Emperor Hirohito in 1989 and the ensuing struggle to capture the meaning of the Shōwa era's end. These short pieces, published in Japan at the time of the emperor's death, have been left untouched. The reader will see here, perhaps more transparently than elsewhere, my own clear engagement not merely in doing history but also in using it. That, as I see it, is not merely both a pleasant avocation and challenging task, but also a responsibility that requires constant rethinking.

My debts in preparing these essays over the years are many, and some are acknowledged precisely in the notes. Here I wish to express particular thanks to David Bordwell, Hirano Kyoko, Ishikawa Yasuo, Katō Yōko, John Russell, Sodei Rinjirō, Takemae Eiji, and Charles Weiner. And, with a deep sense of loss, to the late Howard Schonberger, with whom I shared materials over the years. At the New Press, I am grateful for the assistance of Ted Byfield, Dawn Davis, and Akiko Takano.

I also thank my daughter Kana, who typed some of the more drastically revised essays; and Yasuko, my wife, who saw all these pieces in the making and helped in ways beyond counting. This book is for her.

Boston, Massachusetts
April 14, 1993

The Useful War

OF THE MANY descriptive phrases associated with Shōwa Japan, three are especially popular and evocative. The first, well known in Japan, is "the dark valley" (*kurai tanima*), referring to the decade and a half of militarism and repression that preceded Japan's surrender in 1945. The other two phrases refer to the postwar years. One, closely associated with early Occupation-period (1945–1952) policies of demilitarization and democratization, is "the new Japan." The other, popularized when Japan attained high growth rates in the 1960s and emerged as an economic superpower in the early 1970s, is "the Japanese miracle."

It is easy to see where all three phrases come from, but they are not equally accurate. For the peoples of Asia who suffered from Japanese aggression, and for most Japanese themselves, the period from 1931 to 1945 was indeed dark and tragic. Although far-reaching reforms were carried out in the years that followed, however, it is misleading to speak of a "new Japan" risen out of the ruins of the old. And the notion of a postwar "miracle" belongs to mythology rather than serious history. In fact, many of the characteristics and accomplishments of postwar Japan are deeply rooted not merely in the prewar period, but more precisely

9

in the dark valley of early Shōwa. In ways we only now are beginning to understand, developments that took place in conjunction with Japan's fifteen-year war proved to be extremely useful to the postwar Japanese state.

This is not a popular argument, and it easily can be misunderstood. That the policies and practices of the early Shōwa state brought misery to countless millions of people is beyond dispute, just as it is beyond dispute that postwar Japan has been a more democratic and obviously less militaristic nation. That the early, militaristic decades of the Shōwa era also were a period of immense complexity and diversity that influenced the nature and dynamics of postwar Japanese society in positive as well as negative ways is more difficult to comprehend. In many ways, however, the dark valley of early Shōwa resembles a tumultuous earlier period that preceded an epoch of dramatic renovation and change in Japan: the Bakumatsu era of 1853–1868 that began with the forced opening of feudal Japan to the West and ended with the Meiji Restoration and overthrow of the ancien régime.

In both Bakumatsu and early Shōwa, we see not merely the "deep" legacies of the past but also the accelerated processes of change that occur in periods of acute crisis. The wide-ranging reforms and accomplishments of the Meiji period (1868–1912) are inexplicable without an understanding of Bakumatsu dynamics—and much the same argument holds for the relationship between postwar Japan and the dynamics of the decade and a half before Japan's surrender, when the entire country was mobilized for total war in a comparable crisis atmosphere. In the twentieth-century case, as in the nineteenth, the linkages and influences are apparent almost everywhere one looks: in continuities of personnel and institutions, in technological and economic legacies, in bureaucratic and technocratic activities, and in the permutations and transformations of consciousness and ideology at both elite and popular levels. The Japanese of the postwar era, like their Meiji predecessors, may have undertaken to reinvent themselves; but they necessarily did so with the materials at hand.[1]

<hr>

Some of these linkages, such as continuities in personnel and institutions, are fairly obvious. In retrospect, apart from the military officer corps, the purge of alleged militarists and ultranationalists that was conducted under the Occupation had relatively small impact on the long-term composition of men of influence in the public and private sectors. The purge initially brought new blood into the political parties, but this was offset by the return of huge numbers of formerly purged conservative politicians to national as well as local politics in the early 1950s. In the bureaucracy, the purge was negligible from the outset, apart from the temporary removal from public office of hundreds of former Home Ministry officials who had been intimately involved in running the apparatus of the police state. In the economic sector, the purge similarly was only mildly disruptive, affecting less than sixteen hundred individuals spread among some four hundred companies. Everywhere one looks, the corridors of power in postwar Japan are crowded with men whose talents already had been recognized during the war years, and who found the same talents highly prized in the "new" Japan.[2]

Such continuity of influential personnel was facilitated by the fact that, at almost every level, the postwar state rested on organizational pillars that were firmly planted in the past. Much of this institutional continuity was readily apparent, as seen in the preservation of the imperial throne, the revival of prewar political party lineages across the ideological spectrum, and the straightforward carryover of powerful public institutions such as the Ministry of Finance and Bank of Japan. More often, however, the institutional genealogies are more complex than is apparent at first glance. The powerful Economic Planning Agency established in 1955, for example, traces back to the Economic Stabilization Board that was created in 1946 in the midst of the rampant inflation that followed Japan's surrender; and this in turn was the successor to the major bureaucratic superagency of the war years, the Cabinet Planning Board established in 1937. Similarly, the Ministry of International Trade and Industry (MITI), established in 1949, is not merely the successor of the former Ministry of Commerce and Industry (1922–1943, 1945–1949), which functioned as the Munitions Ministry between 1943 and the end of the war. MITI also absorbed trade functions of the Occupation-period Board of Trade, which was the successor to the semiautonomous Trade Bureau established for war purposes in 1937— thus combining authority over industrial and trade policy to a degree not even attained under the militarists.[3]

In the private sector, institutional continuities are similarly more complicated than they usually appear to be at first glance. Keidanren, the immensely influential Federation of Economic Organizations, for example, was established in 1946 but actually traces its genealogy not merely to the prewar Japan Economic Federation (Nihon Keizai Renmei, founded in 1922), but also and more suggestively to some of the "control associations" (*tōseikai*) established by the government in the final stages of the war in a desperate last attempt to bring state and private economic interests in line. In analogous ways, the contemporary Japanese business world includes not only major corporations that had their origins in the war economy but also older concerns that predated the Shōwa era but increased their scale and market share enormously in the 1930s and early 1940s. Even the mass media, often ignored in such analyses, reflects this phenomenon. Of the five great national newspapers in contemporary Japan, two (*Nihon Keizai*—often referred to as "Japan's *Wall Street Journal*"—and *Sankei*) are by and large offspring of wartime mergers, while the other three (the *Yomiuri, Asahi,* and *Mainichi*) date from the nineteenth century but greatly increased their circulation and influence during the war.[4]

More important than examples of individual organizations, however, is the dynamic legacy to the postwar economy of war mobilization in general. The picture of ruined Japanese cities and a run-down productive system that became etched in popular consciousness at war's end is not wrong. Rather, it is misleading. Sixty-six major urban centers including Hiroshima and Nagasaki were heavily bombed in the last year of the war, and the Japanese government later calculated that the war in its entirety destroyed one-quarter of the nation's wealth. This was equivalent to wiping out the tangible assets created during the whole decade prior to surrender—and this estimate did not include some $20 billion in overseas assets that also were lost through defeat. As John Stuart Mill noted long ago, however, from the perspective of economic production it does not matter greatly if a country is laid to waste "by fire and sword," for in a few years one can expect wealth to be reproduced. What matters is not the physical goods destroyed, but rather the population that remains—or, more precisely, the skills of the population and the resources available to them. The Japanese economy was collapsing even before the U.S. air raids began, but what the rubble and exhaustion of 1945 obscured was the rapid growth that had taken place throughout the 1930s and for several years after Pearl Harbor.[5]

In the 1930s, when much of the world was struggling to recover from the Depression, for example, Japan's annual growth rate averaged 5 percent of GNP (the United States, by contrast, was still attempting to regain the level of 1929 in the late 1930s). Growth was particularly rapid in metals, chemicals, and engineering: the index for consumption goods rose from 100 to 154 between 1930 and 1937, while that for investment goods rose from 100 to 264. By 1937, Japan was constructing most of its own plants, including many kinds of machine tools and scientific instruments, and was largely self-sufficient in basic chemical products. The British economic historian G. C. Allen estimated that Japan's industrial production at this time was twice as great as the rest of Asia's combined (excluding the Soviet Union). As a trading nation, Japan had become a major exporter of manufactured products (although still over half textiles) and a major importer of raw materials. Its merchant marine was the third largest in the world, and it was surpassed as an exporter only by the United States, the United Kingdom, and Germany. These accomplishments, moreover, reflected developments within Japan proper —that is, not including growth in the Formosa and Korea colonies, or in the rapidly industrializing puppet state of Manchukuo.[6]

On the eve of Pearl Harbor, Japan was thus one of the most rapidly growing economies in the world. As the government intensified its controls following the initiation of open war with China in July 1937 and then with the Allied powers in December 1941, moreover, many of the newly emerging industrial sectors continued to experience accelerated growth. Between 1937 and 1944, for example, production indices showed increases of 24 percent in manufacturing, 46 percent in steel, 70 percent in nonferrous metals, and 252 percent in machinery. By another calculation, paid-in capital invested in machinery (including shipbuilding and machine tools) rose from 7 percent of total investment in 1937 to 24 percent in 1945. In metals, the comparable figures were 5 percent in 1937 and 12 percent in 1945. The labor force in manufacturing and construction increased from 5.8 million in 1930 to 8.1 million in 1940 and 9.5 million in 1944, and this was accompanied by a dramatic alteration in the percentage of workers employed in light and heavy industry. In 1930, only 27 percent of the industrial work force was in heavy industry; this rose to 47 percent in 1937 and 68 percent by 1942.[7]

Japan was still a late developer in comparison with the United States, and by war's end—after the colossal war boom experienced by the United States—the gap was greater than ever. Nonetheless, between the Depression and 1945 Japan underwent a "second industrial revolution" that carried with it profound changes in the basic structures of both capital and labor. After the war, the Japanese were called upon to play catch-up economics in a very different milieu, but they had a strong base of experience and knowhow from which to do so. In the long view, the Japanese even may be said to have benefited by losing. In the Cold War context, they quickly became a favored client of the United States, rewarded for acquiescence in the "containment" of communism with access to advanced U.S. technology (much of which also represented breakthroughs of the war years). In certain instances, moreover, the destruction of physical plant in the air raids actually hastened the construction of more up-to-date factories after the war. And the dismemberment of the old empire that was one of the prices of defeat forced the Japanese to devote concerted effort to planning new market strategies in a world that was, in its own way, about to move slowly and painfully into an era of decolonization. One of these strategies, it soon became clear, was to promote the export of manufactured goods other than textiles—that is, to convert the new wartime technologies into peacetime trade advantages. This began to be emphasized in Japanese planning papers within a few years after surrender, and it became a reality in the 1950s.

From the perspective of postwar development, then, what is important about the increasingly militarized economy in this critical decade and a half is not that it was militarized, but that it was diverse and sophisticated in ways that facilitated conversion to peacetime activity. The automobile industry illustrates this. Of the eleven major auto manufacturers in postwar Japan, ten came out of the war years; only Honda is a pure product of the postsurrender period. Three of these ten firms—Toyota, Nissan, and Isuzu—prospered as the primary producers of trucks for the military after legislation passed in 1936 had driven Ford and General Motors out of the Japanese market. For the seven other manufacturers, postwar auto production in most instances was a spinoff from wartime activity in such fields as aircraft, tank, and warship manufacture, precision machinery, and so on. Even the major postwar lobby for the automakers (the Japan Automobile Manufacturers Association), which was founded in 1948 and played a major role in persuading the government to support protectionist policies and low-cost loans in the 1950s and 1960s, was obliquely connected to wartime organizations. Its precedents were to be found in two "control associations" established in 1941 and 1942 to coordinate the production and distribution of vehicles; both wartime associations were headed by company executives who worked closely with the government.[8]

Other corporate giants on the postwar scene gained comparable competitive advantage during the war years. Nomura Securities, for example, which is now the second wealthiest corporation in Japan after Toyota, was founded 1925 as a firm specializing in bonds. Its great breakthrough as a securities firm, however, came through expansion into stocks in 1938 and investment trust operations in 1941. Hitachi, Japan's largest manufacturer of electrical equipment, was established in 1910 but emerged as a comprehensive vertically integrated producer of electric machinery in the 1930s as part of the Ayukawa conglomerate, which also included Nissan. Similarly, Toshiba, which ranks second after Hitachi in electrical products, dates back to 1904 but only became a comprehensive manufacturer of electrical goods following a merger carried out in 1939 under the military campaign to consolidate and rationalize production. Dentsu, described as the world's largest advertising agency in the 1970s, took its present name only in 1955. Yoshida Hideo, the leading figure in its postwar success, however, had been intimately involved in the wartime consolidation that reduced the number of Japanese advertising companies from 186 to 12. In a good example of personnel continuity, moreover, Dentsu recruited so many ex-military officers and former Manchukuo bureaucrats after the war and Occupation that its corporate headquarters became known as the "Second Manchurian Railway Building."[9]

Whole sectors were able to take off in the postwar period by building on advances made during the war. Japan's emergence as the world's leading builder of merchant shipping by 1956, for example, is directly related to the almost frantic development of a capacity to turn out

15

warships (and superbattleships such as the *Yamato* and *Musashi*) in the previous decades. Other manufacturing sectors that Japan relied on during the early stages of its postwar recovery—such as cameras, binoculars, watches, and the like—were similarly grounded in technologies given priority during the war. In some cases, the swords-to-plowshares transformation was so thoroughgoing as to border on the maudlin: in one instance, for example, sewing machines were produced by factories converted from making machine guns.[10]

Examples such as these give substance to John Stuart Mill's sensible observation that it is the capabilities of the population that matter most. It is well known that manpower policy under the Japanese militarists was often inefficient, and that by the final two years of the war the labor market was near chaos. Nonetheless, the nonagricultural work force was not merely larger but also conspicuously more skilled in 1945 than it had been fifteen years earlier. Almost four million new workers were brought into the industrial labor force between 1930 and 1945—while millions of males who had been exposed to military discipline survived to be reintegrated into the postwar economy. The number of technical schools increased from eleven to over four hundred between 1935 and 1945, while at the same time in-firm technical training designed to create a highly skilled cadre of blue-collar workers became a widespread practice.

Science and engineering also were stimulated by war. University students in these fields became exempted from the draft, and the number of graduates between 1941 and 1945 was triple what it had been a decade earlier. While isolation from interaction with Western scientists was a grievous blow to first-rate researchers, moreover, the other side of the coin was the expansion of indigenous research facilities in both basic and applied science, centering on such institutions as the prestigious "Riken" laboratory. At the same time, the military's need for mass-produced goods of reliable quality led to the establishment of uniform standards. Although the "QC" (quality control) ideals that have become so famous in contemporary Japan were decisively influenced by postwar American technical consultants such as W. Edwards Deming, even in the mid 1980s the formal guideline for quality maintenance used by MITI remained the Industrial Standardization Law introduced by the military government in 1940.[11]

As Nakamura Takafusa and other economic historians have demonstrated, the expansionary pressures of the wartime economy also brought about fundamental changes in the interweave of industrial and financial capital, as well as in labor-management relations. Mobilization for war stimulated a spectacular concentration of capital. As military orders came to play an increasing role in the economy, the hegemony of the four "old *zaibatsu*"—Mitsui, Mitsubishi, Sumitomo, and Yasuda—was challenged by the emergence of a group of so-called "new *zaibatsu*" (*shinkō zaibatsu*) more exclusively dependent on military contracting. Six conglomerates dominated the new *zaibatsu*: Asano, Furukawa, Ayukawa, Okura, Nomura, and Nakajima. In 1937, these ten largest *zaibatsu* controlled 15 percent of total paid-in capital in Japan; by the end of the war, this had risen to over 35 percent.[12]

These big capitalists did not evaporate after Japan surrendered. Although the *zaibatsu* concentrations were weakened by the dissolution of holding companies and diversification of shareholding in the early Occupation period, many of the key enterprises have remained close through a variety of formal and semiformal relationships. The vaunted "big six" enterprise groups (*kigyō shūdan*) and related "financial enterprise groups" (*kinyū keiretsu*) of postwar Japan, for example, consist of three old-*zaibatsu* groupings (Mitsui, Mitsubishi, and Sumitomo) and three groups headed by giant banks (Fuji, Dai-ichi Kangyō, and Sanwa). The Fuji Bank is in fact the former central bank of the old Yasuda *zaibatsu*, and its so-called Fuyō group includes many former Yasuda enterprises. Corporations affiliated with the "big six" accounted for 23 percent of the assets of large corporations in 1955, and almost 30 percent in 1970. In the early 1980s, more than 17 percent of all corporate assets were associated with these six enterprise groups.[13]

The central role played by a highly concentrated banking structure in the postwar economy is itself a conspicuous legacy of the war years. Prior to a severe banking panic in 1927, there were approximately fourteen hundred ordinary commercial banks in Japan. By the end of 1931, the number had declined to 683. At the end of 1936, it stood at 418. Between then and the end of the war, the number of banks was drastically reduced by mergers and absorptions to sixty-one—and there has been little change since. Moreover, the powerful "city banks" (actually national banks) that stand at the hub of the postwar enterprise groups were in most instances greatly strengthened by critical legislation introduced between 1942 and 1944, which designated a small number of "authorized financial institutions" to receive special support from the government and Bank of Japan in providing the great bulk of loans to over six hundred major producers of strategic war materials. Even the famous "overloan" or "leveraging" policy that has characterized postwar Japanese lending practices had its genesis in the war economy. As Sakakibara Eisuke and Noguchi Yukio have shown, the figures here are quite striking. Thus, in 1931 the ratio of direct (equity) to indirect (bank loan) financing of industry was roughly 9:1. By 1935, the ratio had become 7:3, by 1940 it was 5:5, and in 1945 it was exactly the opposite of what it had been in 1931—and almost exactly the same as what it would be during the high-growth 1960s—that is, 1:9.[14]

In the nonconcentrated sector of the economy, the war years witnessed the emergence of tens of thousands of small and medium-sized enterprises, which also greatly influenced the dynamics of postwar growth. The negative side of this industrial "dual structure" became widely criticized in the 1950s and 1960s, for it was associated with gross wage and income differentials and recognized as being a primary facilitator of dumping abroad. Such legitimate criticism, however, should not obscure the dynamism of the nonconcentrated sector. Many small enterprises flourished as subcontractors as well as independent entities under the war economy and continued to do so after the war. In the late 1960s, for example, over 40 percent of the ancillary firms supplying parts to Toyota traced their subcontracting relationship back to the war years. And in certain critical sectors such as the machinery industry, small-scale firms frequently were responsible for a major portion of relatively high-skill output. During the war, small entrepreneurs developed effective networks of political and bureaucratic patronage, and they generally responded with strong support for the militarist government. In the postsurrender period, their support was successfully cultivated by the conservative politicians who eventually merged to form the Liberal Democratic Party in 1955. Much of the genuinely innovative entrepreneurial energy that lies behind Japan's postwar economic takeoff, moreover, has come from such smaller enterprises.[15]

18

Inevitably, the war-stimulated "second industrial revolution" altered not merely the size, composition, and competence of the labor force, but also the basic nature of industrial relations. In recent decades, a great deal of attention has been given to the existence of a purportedly unique "Japanese employment system," and commentators both in and outside Japan delight in finding deep, peculiar cultural explanations for this. Japanese industrial relations, this thesis goes, reflect old Confucian values of harmony and hierarchy, or the master-apprentice relationships and lifelong loyalties of feudal merchant houses, or "familial" values that transcend Confucianism and reflect some quintessentially Japanese consciousness of the *ie*, or "household." In fact, the three distinct features associated with labor-management relations in contemporary Japan—lifetime employment, seniority-based wages, and company or enterprise unions—apply not to the majority of industrial workers but primarily to workers in large enterprises. They reflect the peculiarities of a dualistic labor force, rather than some old cultural legacy. And they did not become fixed in their present forms until the 1950s. Like the dual structure itself, however, all three distinctive features of labor relations in large enterprises have strong roots in the war years.

At no time prior to the postwar period is it possible to speak of a stable labor market in Japan. Surveys conducted by the government between the 1937 China Incident and the attack on Pearl Harbor four years later disclosed alarmingly high rates of employee turnover in critical industries, and job jumping actually continued until the very end of the war. It was in response to this instability that the military government intervened to try to bring the industrial labor force under greater discipline and control. Thus, between 1939 and 1942 the authorities sponsored a series of ordinances prohibiting unauthorized changes in places of employment. Between 1939 and 1943, an equally dense and detailed series of laws and regulations was introduced aimed at stabilizing the wage structure in a manner that would likewise hold workers to their jobs; this included fixed starting salaries and clearly defined raises at regular intervals. As a result of these government actions, two of the three pillars of "the Japanese employment system"—permanent employment and wages pegged to seniority for skilled and semiskilled employees—came into general practice. With them came other practices that also characterize postwar labor relations in large firms, such as greater reliance on on-the-job training, as well as certain supplemental in-company benefits such as family allowances.

The genesis of the third feature of the postwar employment system in large firms—enterprise unionism—is more controversial among Japanese industrial-relations specialists, some of whom stress the decisive influence of early postwar developments. Here, however, it is in any case impossible to ignore the organizational and ideological influence of the wartime mobilization of labor under the notorious "Sampō" organization (Sangyō Hōkokukai, or Industrial Patriotic Association). Established under government auspices in 1938, Sampō brought some six million employees in eighty-seven thousand companies under a nationwide umbrella distinguished by corporatist ideals, a company-focused modus operandi, and "enterprise family" (jigyō ikka) rhetoric. Such ideological fixations had much more of a future in Japan than they did a past.[16]

While mobilization for war accelerated trends in the modern sector, it simultaneously undermined one of the most basic and retrogressive features of the prewar economy: the extensive prevalence of landlordism in the countryside, where over 40 percent of the total national work force was engaged in agricultural production. At the time of Pearl Harbor, only 36 percent of Japanese peasants owned all the land they farmed, and 46 percent of all cultivated land was worked by tenants. Rents for riceland commonly were paid in kind, at a rate of slightly more than half the average crop, thus perpetuating a large "semifeudal" sector within the developing economy. Although some landlords may have been paternalistic, poverty and unrest were widespread in rural Japan. The militarists came to power after the Depression promising, among other things, to rectify the rural crisis; and, wittingly and unwittingly, their policies rang the death knell for the landlord class.

The land reform carried out between 1946 and 1948 dispossessed the landlords and virtually eliminated tenancy. This was a critical step in achieving an expanded domestic market and mature bourgeois capitalism in Japan, and that it was accomplished so swiftly and smoothly is due almost entirely to the exceptional circumstances of war and defeat. The land reform was a central part of the "demilitarization and democratization" agenda introduced by the victorious Americans, and it is indisputable that the authority wielded by the victors was essential to ensuring that the reform was implemented thoroughly. As the Americans themselves acknowledged, however, success ultimately depended on circumstances beyond their control. That the vast majority of the rural population welcomed such a drastic transformation of relations was of course essential, but the reform also was facilitated by two additional circumstances. First, there existed a cadre of Japanese academics and former wartime bureaucrats who were themselves committed to land reform and possessed the technical and administrative expertise to carry it out. And second, it quickly became apparent that wartime developments, especially after 1940, had severely eroded the traditional power of the landlords.

The second point frequently is overlooked. The precipitous decline in landlord authority can be dated from 1941, when the government introduced a "food administration system" designed to increase agricultural production and to expedite delivery. By paying tenants directly for their produce, the government essentially undercut the landlords economically and destroyed their direct relationship with their tenants. Andrew Grad, who was involved in planning the postwar Japanese land reform, acknowledged the profound ramifications of this in an early resumé of what had been accomplished. "The separation of the landlord from the land was far-reaching in its consequences," Grad wrote concerning the war years. "As the produce of his land was not permitted to reach him, as the price paid him for rice was considerably lower than the price paid to the tenant, and as he was not permitted during the war to evict his tenants, the bond between the landlord and his land was all but severed. In the eyes of the government he became little more than a good-for-nothing rentier—a view that paved the way for the postwar land reform. It became much easier to take land from the landlords when they could not claim it, its produce, or even its rent." Grad concluded that "it is doubtful that, even with the support of the Occupation authorities, land reform could have been carried out by a conservative government as successfully as it was, if the way had not been smoothed during the war."[17]

In most of these developments, there was a visible hand. More accurately, there were many visible hands, and the most blatantly manipulative of them came from the military and civilian bureaucracy. These were years of extraordinary intervention and experimentation on the part of the Japanese state, and the practice and ideology of technocratic control which emerges so vividly here is certainly among the most conspicuous and controversial of the wartime legacies to contemporary Japan.

War strengthened the bureaucracy, and the nearly seven-year Occupation that followed strengthened it further. Each in its own way, both war and peace fostered an overwhelming sense of crisis and an intense preoccupation with national security. Both stimulated renovationist thinking among the bureaucrats—a deep commitment to the necessity of guided change—and in this sense there was no real break between the presurrender and postsurrender periods. Immediate tasks changed drastically, of course, from "war" to "peace." What remained was a deep dissatisfaction with the status quo and an abiding commitment to top-down, long-range planning to create a strong state in a new world order.

Nor was there any break in the elite status and intellectual élan of the civilian bureaucracy. Before 1945 as well as after, huge numbers of the brightest university graduates gravitated to careers in the bureau-cracy. This was the elite course, and during the war it attracted thousands of ambitious young planners who drew eclectically and voraciously on intellectual and ideological thinking outside Japan—meaning Nazi and fascist and national-socialist thought, to be sure, but also Marxism, Lenin-ism, and Stalinism, and also Fordism, scientific management, and New Deal interventionism where these seemed to offer solutions to the crisis of economic depression and war. These "new bureaucrats" (*shin kanryō*) or "renovationist bureaucrats" (*kakushin kanryō*) had allies among the intelligentsia and even in certain corporate circles, as well as within the military. In contrast to the United States, wartime government service was not a temporary diversion from normal career paths for most of these flexible young technocrats. Sharp and agile, they stepped lightly across the surrender and continued to administer the postwar state.

One of the less abstract and more neglected legacies of the presurren-der renovationist bureaucrats lay in the area of social-security and social-welfare legislation. For some bureaucrats, a genuine populist idealism may have lain behind this. More often, social reform was rationalized as being essential to the creation of a strong defense state, for the Depression and war crisis exposed how physically unfit and psychologically demoralized the Japanese populace as a whole really was. A nation-wide survey of draft-age men conducted by the army in 1936, for example, revealed a shockingly high percentage of males who were unfit for military service because of malnutrition, communicable diseases, or job-caused disabilities. The Japanese were in much poorer physical condition than their American or European counterparts, and the army attributed this to conditions such as low income, poor nutrition, excessive working hours, and hazardous job conditions. Such exploitation was not new, but its scale and implications were greater than ever before. Military conscription was hampered, the civilian work force enfeebled. The morale of parents and elders, as well as that of young servicemen and workers themselves, was undermined. The possibility of communist upheaval—always a fear of the ruling groups after 1917—was strengthened. Because for decades the private sector had failed to ameliorate such conditions, the task devolved upon the bureaucracy.

Such reports merely confirmed what had been apparent earlier, and the bureaucratic response to this social crisis was intense. A new Ministry of Health and Welfare was created in 1938. That same year, in the wake of the invasion of China, medical insurance coverage was expanded. By war's end, over half of all Japanese were covered by these entitlements, which became the basis of the postwar medical insurance system. Similarly, the postwar pension system was built upon a series of laws enacted between 1939 and 1944, which originally were designed to hold workers to their jobs while simultaneously creating a capital fund that the government could tap to help finance the war.[18]

After Japan's surrender, the "social bureaucrats" who had been involved in formulating such reformist wartime legislation played a complex role. On the one hand, they helped draft such progressive legislation of the early Occupation period as new fundamental labor laws (the Trade Union Law of 1945 and the Labor Standards Law of 1947), a revised civil code, and a drastically reformed educational system. They also played an important role in implementing the land reform. On the other hand, former wartime social bureaucrats also were able to temper some of the early drafts of reformist legislation introduced by the U.S. Occupation authorities—without, however, ever attempting to gut them entirely. This occurred in such basic reforms as the new constitution and legislation aimed at promoting greater local autonomy. Once the Cold

War intensified and U.S. Occupation priorities turned from reform to economic reconstruction, the Japanese technocrats and their American counterparts found common cause in antileftist activities such as the McCarthyist "Red purges" of 1949 and 1950, which resulted in the firing of over twenty thousand employees in the public and private sectors. Many of the former Home Ministry officials who had been purged after Japan's surrender were depurged before the Occupation ended in 1952, and quickly rose to important and conspicuously reactionary "social control" positions under the conservative Liberal Democratic Party, America's new ally in Asia. All along the line, "convergence" made for unexpected bedfellows.[19]

Even more far-reaching than the influence of the social bureaucrats, however, was the postwar impact of their colleagues who had been directly engaged in managing the war economy. The postsurrender dissolution of the military and Home Ministry removed two of the strongest institutional rivals to the economic bureaucrats. At the same time, the early Occupation policy of dissolving *zaibatsu* holding companies and introducing antimonopoly legislation placed the private sector at a temporary disadvantage. In the chaos of the early postsurrender transition, the United States even transferred to the bureaucracy some of the economic regulatory functions that the private sector had struggled to maintain all the way through the war. The rule-from-above style of the U.S. Occupation staff reinforced the acceptability of bureaucratic direction; the policy of running the Occupation "indirectly" through the Japanese government enhanced the real power of the career bureaucrats; and the truly stupendous economic disorder and confusion that prevailed until almost the very end of the Occupation in 1952 placed economic and technocratic expertise at a premium. It is generally acknowledged that the economic bureaucrats had even more influence under the Americans than they did under their own military leaders during the war.

Even after 1952 the rigidly Cold War nature of the peace settlement with Japan helped perpetuate the preeminence of the economic bureaucracy. Because the country was so thoroughly subordinated to the United States militarily and diplomatically, it really had no foreign policy of its own. As a consequence, even the proud Ministry of Foreign Affairs found itself overshadowed by MITI, which is the most conspicuous example of the long ride of the economic bureaucrats. Until the mid

1970s, all top officials in MITI came out of the presurrender bureaucracy; and their memories, clearly, were excellent. As Chalmers Johnson has shown, for example, the controls over trade and foreign exchange that enabled MITI to orchestrate a successful industrial policy from the 1950s to the 1970s were first codified in the 1930s and then perpetuated, almost willy-nilly, in the 1949 Foreign Exchange and Foreign Trade Control Law enacted while Japan was still under U.S. direction. Another feature of the MITI modus operandi, its ability to target specific industries for official guidance and support, can be traced back not merely to organizational arrangements introduced in the late 1930s but also to a panoply of industry-specific laws introduced between 1934 and 1941— many of which were "resurrected" during the 1950s and 1960s, when MITI power was at its zenith.[20]

The economic bureaucrats, whether managing war through such organs as the Munitions Ministry and Cabinet Planning Board, or managing peace through MITI and the Economic Planning Agency, pose a challenging question for political analysts: What sort of capitalism have the Japanese been practicing since the 1930s? Clearly, it is not laissez-faire in the manner associated with Adam Smith. On the other hand, state ownership is not the issue, for in fact this is minimal in Japan. The question is really one of laissez-faire in a box—that is, how (and how much) control is imposed on the market—and in recent years numerous phrases have emerged which all suggest that the box is very intricately constructed indeed. Japan is said to be a plan-rational as opposed to a market-rational nation, a mixed capitalist state, a capitalist development state, a technocratic state, a neomercantilist state, a "smart" state, a network state, a corporatist (or corporatist-without-labor) state. It practices industrial policy, administrative guidance, "window" guidance, patterned pluralism, canalized pluralism, bureaucracy-led mass-inclusionary pluralism, administered competition, compartmentalized competition, guided free enterprise, managed capitalism, quasi-capitalism, state-directed capitalism. In Chalmers Johnson's phrase, since the 1930s Japanese development has been powerfully guided by an "economic general staff"—a most effective metaphor for conveying both the historical and the ideological mesh of war and peace that lies behind the so-called Japanese miracle.

These catchphrases are lively and useful, but they can be misleading if taken to mean that Japan is first and foremost a bureaucratic state. More pertinent is the fact that it is a strong capitalist state, and its version of capitalism is brokered by conservative interests in a manner that retains the market while controlling "excessive" competition and promoting nationalistic goals. The economic bureaucrats are indeed influential actors in this grand enterprise, but so also are big business and the conservative politicians. This brokered capitalism is neither very new nor very old. It is not simply a postwar phenomenon—a "Japan, Inc." or "new Japanese capitalism" that emerged out of the ashes in the 1950s. On the other hand, neither is it a traditionally "closed" system rooted in the economic nationalism of the Meiji period or in the insular and consensual values of an even earlier time. Japan's brokered capitalism is fundamentally a transwar phenomenon. The conservative elites that work the system now are no longer militaristic. As we have seen, however, a great many of their institutions, ideas, practices—and leaders— were formed in the crucible of war.

In peace as in war, this brokering of power has been fierce and costly. Even in the most desperate years of World War II, Japan's leaders never succeeded in establishing a totalitarian state, or a consensual polity, or a harmonious body politic. Contrary to the popular image of a fanatically loyal populace resolutely united behind the war effort, intense competition and conflict took place within as well as among different constituencies—the military, the civilian bureaucracy, old *zaibatsu* and new *zaibatsu*, political parties, small and medium-sized enterprises, rural versus urban interests, and so on. Like the myth of the "enterprise family," the wartime slogan "one hundred million hearts beating as one" was an illusive goal rather than a description of reality, and this internal tension and competitiveness is as important as any other legacy to the postwar years. It helps explain both high levels of achievement and what often appears to be indecisive and even two-faced behavior, especially in the international arena in recent years. The curious image that Japan acquired in the 1980s of being a powerful but seemingly decapitated state, especially when it comes to assuming the responsibilities that should accompany economic eminence, can be partly explained by this internal conflict.

Many observers would agree that nationalism and a paternalistic elitism have held Japan's brokered capitalism together ideologically since the war. If this is so, then what can we say about postwar Japanese democracy? We can say that this too has been brokered, in ways that respect the form but often kill the spirit of democracy.

The intellectual and ideological legacy of the war is contradictory. On the one hand, shattering defeat left the Japanese people as a whole with an almost visceral aversion to military activity. The mass media have helped to keep memories of the "dark valley" of early Shōwa alive in numerous ways, and such memories entail not only recollection of suffering at home and abroad, but also an abiding wariness toward the sort of authoritarianism and muscular nationalism that contributed to the disastrous war. The early Occupation ideals of "demilitarization and democratization" struck a resonant chord in Japan because the Japanese already were sick of repression and death long before the war ended. Even after the Cold War intensified and the Americans themselves backed away from their initial reformist agenda, millions of Japanese continued to cherish these twin ideals and to regard them as inseparable.

The most dramatic expression of antimilitarism and democracy in postwar Japan is the liberal "peace constitution" adopted under the Americans in 1946. Three features distinguish this national charter: the famous "renunciation of war" in Article Nine (buttressed by strongly expressed antimilitarist ideals in the constitution's preface); sweeping guarantees of human rights (including the equivalent of a feminist "ERA" article); and relegation of the emperor to the status of being merely "the symbol of the State and of the unity of the people." Although the ruling conservative party has been openly dedicated to revising the constitution since the mid 1950s, and although the original sweeping antimilitary intent of Article Nine has been distorted to permit incremental Japanese rearmament (with strong U.S. support), for almost half a century popular sentiment has prevented any amendment whatsoever of this unusually progressive charter. Even if the conservatives eventually succeed in breaking this taboo against constitutional revision, as seems likely in the foreseeable future, it is predictable that their efforts will focus on modifying Article Nine to legitimize remilitarization within certain limits, including dispatch of fighting forces abroad under United

Nations auspices. Other basic constitutional ideals—including the separation of powers, bicameral elective parliament, symbolic status of the emperor, and clear provision of human rights—retain strong support even in conservative circles. Appreciation of not merely the "virtues" but also the practical efficiency of parliamentary democracy is yet another of the abiding legacies of the lost war.

At the same time, however, it cannot be denied that regimentation and susceptibility to certain forms of soft indoctrination also survive as legacies from the war years. Loyalty to the firm and sacrifice for the country remain effective appeals. In some instances, acquiescence to such appeals may reflect a real sense of reciprocal obligation; in many instances, it reflects plain weariness and existential resignation on the part of the average employee and citizen. Whatever the case, the ethic of self-denial has depended on the maintenance—even the reinvention—of immense pressures ranging from carefully nurtured social taboos to overtly paramilitary rituals such as company drills and corporate "boot-camp training." By the 1980s, as international tensions rose in response to Japan's new economic eminence and economic nationalism, moreover, more strident ideological legacies of the war years had emerged in the form of disturbing neonationalistic appeals to the homogeneity and superiority of the "Yamato race."

The nature of Japan's brokered postwar democracy is a subject that still awaits its historian. In suggestive ways, however, it returns us to an observation made at the outset of this essay, namely, the resonance between Japan's mid-nineteenth-century transition from feudalism to industrialization and "Westernization," and its mid-twentieth-century transition from war to peace. In both cases, far-reaching and even revolutionary transformations took place. And in both cases, these were revolutions "from above." Where democratic ideals are neither defined nor won by the general populace, they are relatively weak. From the perspective of Japan's civil elites, this too was a useful legacy of the war.

NOTES

1 If one defines "postwar" Japan as equivalent to the latter part of the Shōwa period (1945–1989), a popular and reasonable equation, the comparison between Bakumatsu-Meiji (1853–1868, 1868–1912) and wartime-

postwar (1931–1945, 1945–1989) is remarkably close in terms of years. There is a danger of falling into numerology here, but the parallels should not be dismissed out of hand. That the period of crisis lasted a decade and a half, or roughly half a generation, in both cases helps explain the intensity as well as the incompleteness of the processes put in train. The longer duration of the renovationist aftermath (four-plus decades in both cases) permits a clearer picture of how these processes unfolded in the long run—but is still short enough to retain the visibility of personal, institutional, and behavioral linkages.

2 For basic coverage of the purge, see Hans H. Baerwald, *The Purge of Japanese Leaders under the Occupation*, vol. 12 of University of California Publications in Political Science (Berkeley: University of California Press, 1959), esp. pp. 78–98. On the negligible effect of the purge in bureaucratic and business circles, see T. J. Pempel, "The Tar Baby Target: 'Reform' of the Japanese Bureaucracy," in Robert E. Ward and Yoshikazu Sakamoto, eds., *Democratizing Japan: The Allied Occupation* (Honolulu: University of Hawaii Press, 1987), p. 160; Eleanor M. Hadley, *Antitrust in Japan* (Princeton: Princeton University Press, 1970), pp. 87–99.

3 See Chalmers Johnson, *MITI and the Japanese Miracle: The Growth of Industrial Policy, 1925–1975* (Stanford: Stanford University Press), ch. 4.

4 Ishikawa Ichirō, one of the founders of the postwar Keidanren, actually was nicknamed "god of the control associations"; see Karel van Wolferen, *The Enigma of Japanese Power* (New York: Knopf, 1989), p. 354. On the press, see Gregory J. Kasza, *The State and the Mass Media in Japan, 1918–1945* (Berkeley: University of California Press, 1988), p. 281.

5 For the basic 1949 government assessment of war damage, see Table 10 in this present volume, as well as Arisawa Hiromi and Inaba Hidezō, eds., *Shiryō: Sengo Nijūnen Shi*, vol. 2: *Keizai* (Tokyo: Nihon Hyōronsha, 1966), pp. 2–5. See also Takafusa Nakamura, *The Postwar Japanese Economy: Its Development and Structure*, trans. Jacqueline Kaminski (Tokyo: University of Tokyo Press, 1981), p. 15; T. F. M. Adams and Iwao Hoshii, *A Financial History of the New Japan* (Tokyo: Kodansha International, 1972), p. 17 (for overseas assets). Paul Sweezy called attention to Mill's observation (from *Principles of Political Economy*, bk. 1, ch. 5, sec. 7) in a review article on Japan in *Monthly Review* (Feb. 1980): 6.

6 The best concise summary of the economic legacies of the war mobilization appears in Nakamura, *Postwar Japanese Economy*, ch. 1, esp. pp. 14–20. For an earlier general overview, see G. C. Allen, *Japan's Economic Recovery* (London: Oxford University Press, 1958), ch. 1, esp. pp. 4–6. Hugh Patrick and Henry Rosovsky estimate the 1930s growth rate at 5

percent in "Japan's Economic Performance: An Overview," in Patrick and Rosovsky, eds., *Asia's New Giant: How the Japanese Economy Works* (Washington, D.C.: Brookings Institution, 1976), pp. 8–9. The paucity of close analysis of the war years in basic economic overviews of modern Japan borders on the scandalous and is reflected in the slight attention to this period in the standard "Long-Term Economic Statistics" (LTES) of Japan on which most recent scholarship is based.

7 Nakamura, *Postwar Japanese Economy*, p. 12; Michael A. Cusumano, *The Japanese Automobile Industry: Technology and Management at Nissan and Toyota* (Cambridge, Mass.: Council on East Asian Studies, Harvard University, 1985), p. 14; Jerome B. Cohen, *Japan's Economy in War and Reconstruction* (Minneapolis: University of Minnesota Press, 1949), pp. 296–97. It should be kept in mind that productivity in many sectors began to decline conspicuously by 1944, and economic data that singles out 1945 as a key point for comparison or generalization can be extremely misleading.

8 Cusumano, *Japanese Automobile Industry*, pp. 1–72; Konosuke Odaka, Keinosuke Ono, and Fumihiko Adachi, *The Automobile Industry in Japan: A Study of Ancillary Firm Development* (Tokyo: Kinokuniya Company and Oxford University Press, 1988), esp. pp. 1–39, 89–100, 107–19, 251–55.

9 Company and institutional information is generally available in standard reference works such as the nine-volume *Kodansha Encyclopedia of Japan* (henceforth *KEOJ*), (Tokyo: Kodansha, 1983). On Dentsu, see also van Wolferen, *Enigma of Japanese Power*, pp. 386–87.

10 Masataka Kōsaka, *A History of Postwar Japan* (Tokyo: Kodansha International, 1982), p. 220; Nakamura, *Postwar Japanese Economy*, p. 15. For an effusive comment on the technological legacies of "the *Yamato* and the Zeros," see *U.S. Naval Institute Proceedings* 105 (Sept. 1979): 86.

11 On manpower mobilization (and chaos), see Cohen, *Japan's Economy*, ch. 5, and Andrew Gordon, *The Evolution of Labor Relations in Japan: Heavy Industry, 1853–1955* (Cambridge: Council on East Asian Studies, Harvard University, 1985), pp. 314–17. On science and engineering, see Christopher Thorne, *The Issue of War: States, Societies, and the Far Eastern Conflict, 1941–1945* (London: Hamish Hamilton, 1985), p. 309; Thomas R. H. Havens, *Valley of Darkness: The Japanese People and World War Two* (New York: W. W. Norton, 1978), pp. 30, 139, 213. The basic 1940 standardization law is noted in David A. Garvin, "Japanese Quality Management," *Columbia Journal of World Business* 19, no. 3 (Fall 1984): 9.

12 In critical sectors of the modern economy, the influence of the "big ten" *zaibatsu* had become truly awesome by 1945: 49 percent of paid-in capital in mining and heavy and chemical industries, 50 percent in banking, 85 percent in trust funds, 60 percent in insurance, 61 percent in shipping, 30 percent in real estate and warehousing. The "big four" old *zaibatsu* alone controlled 10.4 percent of paid-in capital in 1937 and 24.5 percent at the end of the war. See Table 8 in the present volume.

13 Richard E. Caves, with the collaboration of Masu Uekasa, "Industrial Organization," in Patrick and Rosovsky, *Asia's New Giant*, p. 499, for 1955 and 1970 percentages; *KEOJ*, 2:221, for early 1980s.

14 *KEOJ*, 1:137–41; Eisuke Sakakibara and Yukio Noguchi, "Dissecting the Finance Ministry–Bank of Japan Dynasty," excerpted in Daniel I. Okimoto and Thomas P. Rohlen, eds., *Inside the Japanese System: Readings on Contemporary Society and Political Economy* (Stanford: Stanford University Press, 1988), pp. 43, 61.

15 Odaka, Ono, and Adachi, *Automobile Industry in Japan*. David Friedman, *The Misunderstood Miracle: Industrial Development and Political Change in Japan* (Ithaca, N.Y.: Cornell University Press, 1988), presents the argument for the viability of small and medium-sized enterprise in detail through analysis of the prewar and postwar machine tool industry.

16 For general overviews of the industrial relations system, see Gordon, *Evolution of Labor Relations*, esp. chs. 7 and 8; Solomon Levine's essays "Labor" and "Labor Laws" in *KEOJ*, 4:343–49, 351–53; Taishirō Shirai, "A Theory of Enterprise Unionism," in Shirai, ed., *Contemporary Industrial Relations in Japan* (Madison: University of Wisconsin Press, 1983), pp. 117–43; Ernest J. Notar, "Japan's Wartime Labor Policy: A Search for Method," *Journal of Asian Studies* 44, no. 2 (Feb. 1985): 311–28; Sheldon Garon, *The State and Labor in Modern Japan* (Berkeley: University of California Press, 1987), pp. 187–227.

17 Andrew J. Grad, *Land and Peasant in Japan: An Introductory Survey* (New York: Institute of Pacific Relations, 1952), pp. 34, 39–40. See also Ronald P. Dore, *Land Reform in Japan* (London: Oxford University Press, 1959); and Tsutomu Takizawa, "Historical Background of Agricultural Land Reform in Japan," *The Developing Economies* 10, no. 3 (1972).

18 See Notar, "Japan's Wartime Labor Policy," pp. 314–15, for the 1936 survey. For welfare problems and projects in general, see Yoshida Kyūichi, *Gendai Shakai Jigyōshi Kenkyū* (Tokyo: Keisō Shōbō, 1979), pp. 271–401; *KEOJ*, 5:144–45, 6:172–73, 7:209–11; Havens, *Valley of Darkness*, pp. 46–49; Garon, *The State and Labor*, pp. 203–5, 236; Kōseishō

Nijūnen Shi Henshū Iinkai, ed., *Kōseishō Nijūnen Shi* (Tokyo: Kōsei Mondai Kenkyūkai, 1960), and Kōseishō Gojūnen Shi Henshū Iinkai, ed., *Kōseishō Gojūnen Shi* (Tokyo: Kōsei Mondai Kenkyūkai, 1988), esp. pp. 339–572.

19 On labor, see Takemae Eiji, *Sengo Rōdō Kaikaku: GHQ Rōdō Seisaku Shi* (Tokyo: Tokyo Daigaku Shuppankai, 1982), pp. 102–11; Sheldon M. Garon, "The Imperial Bureaucracy and Labor Policy in Postwar Japan," *Journal of Asian Studies* 43, no. 3 (May 1984): 446–48; Garon, *The State and Labor*, pp. 235–37. For the Japanese role in revision of the civil code, see Kurt Steiner, "Reform of the Japanese Civil Code," in Ward and Sakamoto, *Democratizing Japan*, pp. 188–220. On educational reforms, see *Senryōki Nihon Kyōiku ni kansuru Zai-Bei Shiryō no Chōsa Kenkyū* (Tokyo: Sengo Kyōiku Kaikaku Shiryō 6, Kokuritsu Kyōiku Kenkyūjo, March 1988). For the U.S.-Japan interplay in reforms involving local autonomy and the national charter, see Akira Amakawa, "The Making of the Postwar Local Government System," in Ward and Sakamoto, *Democratizing Japan*, pp. 253–83, and Kenzō Takayanagi, "Some Reminiscences of Japan's Commission on the Constitution," *Washington Law Review* 43, no. 5 (June 1968): 961–78. On the role of the former Home Ministry officials in "reverse course" policies, see Garon, "The Imperial Bureaucracy," 448–53. The "Red purges" are covered in J. W. Dower, *Empire and Aftermath: Yoshida Shigeru and the Japanese Experience, 1878–1954* (Cambridge, Mass: Council on East Asian Studies, Harvard University, 1979).

20 See Johnson, *MITI and the Japanese Miracle*, on these various aspects of MITI. Another recent historical study that identifies transwar influences as central to understanding postwar and contemporary Japan is Richard J. Samuels, *The Business of the Japanese State: Energy Markets in Comparative and Historical Perspective* (Ithaca, N.Y.: Cornell University Press, 1987), esp. ch. 5.

2

Japanese Cinema Goes to War

W AS W ORLD W AR II in Asia, as some would have it, essentially a clash of cultures?

No. It was a clash of national interests, in which Japan waged war against adversaries of extremely diverse cultural backgrounds—China, colonial Asia, and the Anglo-American powers including Australia and New Zealand. Westerners, accustomed to thinking in terms of Pearl Harbor and the "Pacific War," often neglect the broader context of the great cataclysm in Asia: the global depression and subsequent trade wars beginning in the late 1920s; the strategic fears and armaments controversies that intensified after the failure of the London Naval Conference in 1930; the devastating "fifteen-year war" between Japan and China that began in 1931; the colonial dimension of the struggle in South and Southeast Asia.

Culture was not the critical issue here. Power, wealth, and security were.

Yet "culture" in the broadest sense still mediated this multifaceted conflict. In the cauldron of war, participants on all sides labored to define their national destiny and assert their special qualities as a people. They

33

refurbished old cultural values, created new myths, expounded appealing ideologies, and lifted the techniques of mass-oriented propaganda to previously undreamed-of levels.

In the United States, no one did this more brilliantly at the popular level than the moviemakers. It is simply unthinkable to talk about wartime America today without dwelling on Hollywood's evocative images and the slick documentaries prepared by the military services. Japan's wartime cinema similarly captured the passions and tensions of these times as seen through Japanese eyes, but suffered a different fate and became all but forgotten after Japan's defeat. Losers do not get reruns.[1]

The disappearance of Japan's war films from popular consciousness has left a hiatus in our understanding of the cultural and emotional milieu in which the Japanese were mobilized for war. That these films were subtle and skillful was recognized by a handful of Americans after Pearl Harbor. A group of Hollywood directors who in the spring of 1943 reviewed some twenty Japanese films made between 1937 and 1941 unanimously agreed that they compared favorably with the best films produced in Europe and the United States. One of this group, Frank Capra, who produced the U.S. Army's famous "Why We Fight" series, has been widely quoted for the grudging admiration he expressed upon viewing *Chocolate and Soldiers*, one of the most popular Japanese films of 1938. "We can't beat this kind of thing," Capra exclaimed. "We make a film like that maybe once in a decade. We haven't got the actors."[2]

What Capra meant was that Hollywood, with its reliance on a stable of charismatic superstars, could not match the Japanese in presenting a cast of appealing character actors with whom the audience could immediately empathize. Why democratic America worshiped stars while nondemocratic Japan had mastered the common touch was a paradox upon which Capra did not dwell.

In an insightful study prepared for both the U.S. Office of War Information and the Office of Strategic Services in March 1944, the anthropologist Ruth Benedict similarly praised Japanese war films for their artistic excellence and found them to be extremely sophisticated vehicles of psychological warfare. Benedict concluded that "the spirit of sacrifice or the subjection of self to pattern" was the dominant theme in these films. She also offered another tantalizing but undeveloped comparison between the Japanese and American cinema by contrasting the realism of Japan's offerings to Hollywood's exaggeration and contrived endings. "The Japanese films," Benedict found, "have a propaganda courage which American films have usually lacked." For scores of U.S. intelligence personnel being trained as Japan specialists, such captured Japanese films were an integral part of learning to "know your enemy."[3]

This neglected celluloid world where art, ideology, and propaganda commingled offers numerous surprises that run counter to the usual Western stereotypes of the Japanese at war. For a starter, there is a minimum of rhetoric about why Japan was at war, and astonishingly little reference to the emperor apart from perfunctory phrases or gestures. Heroes are innocent. Enemies are amorphous. Interracial love is less of a taboo than it was in Western cinema at the time. There are no roller-coaster rides between the agony of defeat and joy of victory. Fanaticism is tempered, and for every suicidal mission on the Japanese screen one can surely point to one or two similar Hollywood episodes. Life is far more precious than Westerners nurtured on a vision of "banzai charges" would expect.

The films are propaganda first and last, but they contain strains of humanism and even pacifism that bespeak the filmmakers' roots in less militaristic and repressive times and constitute strong legacies to the years following Japan's defeat. Technically—and this, at least, comes as no surprise—there are innumerable moments when the movement is supremely natural, or when one could freeze a frame almost at random and find a perfect composition.

———

To most non-Japanese, the first shattered expectation probably will be the nature of Japan's cinema war heroes. They resemble neither Hollywood's supermasculine heroes nor the swashbuckling samurai types we often think of as constituting Japan's own traditional culture heroes. Rather, the archetypical Japanese man at war is a young officer or humble conscript who performs his duty without question and is distinguished by an appealing lack of guile.

"Purity" is the supreme character trait of the hero of these years. Americans have their own analogue to this in the pervasive myth of

American innocence, but the Japanese elevate the mystique of national, cultural, and individual purity to extraordinary levels. As a personal quality, purity subsumes all other virtues: duty and loyalty, simplicity and sincerity, bravery and self-sacrifice. This is the common thread that joins the plain but attractive foot soldiers in the 1938 classic *Five Scouts*, the lower-class father who sends his son chocolate-bar wrappers from the China front in *Chocolate and Soldiers*, the idealistic tugboat captain in *China Night* (1941), the innocent pilot in *Our Planes Fly South* (1943), and even the passionate young martial arts expert in Kurosawa Akira's 1943 period drama *Sugata Sanshirō*. It goes without saying that purity is expected of all Japanese women; but the virtue is genderless and really attains its apotheosis in males at war.

Turned about: war purifies. This is true for women as well as men, and on the homefront as well as the battlefield. Thus, as Japan's situation deteriorated and the homefront was called on to endure increasing privation and sacrifice, this too became presented as a purifying and ennobling experience. In the print media, ideologues ransacked the cultural lexicon of the past for an appropriate term that would turn such suffering into a uniquely Japanese virtue, and they came up with such phrases as *yase gaman*, or "emaciated endurance" (the official English rendering). In the cinema, the attainment of spiritual purity through deprivation and misery received consummate expression in *The Most Beautiful*, Kurosawa's 1944 film about the hardships of women workers in an optical-instruments factory. As Donald Richie has suggested, by this date the message and the medium had become almost inseparable. The stringent conditions under which Japanese moviemakers had to work by the end of the war made a film such as *The Most Beautiful* in itself an example of how a rare and pristine "truth" could emerge out of conditions of scarcity.[4] The film, like its heroines, represents beauty born of hardship. It also represents a conspicuously more austere world than the U.S. homefront genre of "Rosie the Riveter"—which the U.S. propaganda machine romanticized with catchy songs and pink-cheeked poster-girl graphics.

Even where the Japanese filmmakers eulogized a real-life war hero, they eschewed the Hollywood style of battlefield hagiography. In *The Story of Tank Commander Nishizumi*, one of the most acclaimed films of

1940, for example, audiences were introduced to a young officer who had been killed in China in 1938 and subsequently received one of the Japanese government's highest posthumous honors: he was designated a *gunshin*, or "military god." The film opens with scenes from Nishizumi's hometown, including his boyhood schools and his grave, while the voice-over informs us that he was remembered in his native place as a modest and straightforward youth. Those same qualities characterize the man whom we follow to his death in China.

The Story of Tank Commander Nishizumi contains dramatic battle scenes, including some stunning night fighting; and the film takes pain to portray Nishizumi as a brave man who repeatedly takes risks he might easily have ordered his men to take instead. In the end, however, it is clear that what makes the young officer a "military god" is his calm and utterly steadfast devotion to both his country and his men. His death, like his personality, is simple. Shot by a dying Chinese soldier while testing the depth of a stream with a stick, Nishizumi bleeds to death. Although he lingers a while before expiring, he makes no flowery farewell speech, nor does he die with the emperor's name on his lips. We do not even see the moment when he actually dies. At the close of the film, Nishizumi's commanding officer, seated with a candle by the dead man's head, murmurs, "He is sleeping well . . . he was a good man . . . he looks just as if he were alive."

The American counterpart to such "military gods" presumably would be fighting men awarded the Congressional Medal of Honor. By contrast, however, such American heroes almost always earned their laurels by single acts of exceptional bravery which usually entailed killing a conspicuous number of the enemy.

Nishizumi's plain life and unexceptional death exemplify what Ruth Benedict had in mind when she spoke of the realism of Japanese war films, and their ability to strike a resonant chord in the heart of Japanese viewers. Nishizumi's men weep—indeed, sob—when they learn he is gone; and such tears not only make the scene credible, but simultaneously epitomize the pure emotions of all other Japanese men at war. Tears flow copiously on the homefront too. When someone attempts to comfort the youngster in *Chocolate and Soldiers* at his father's funeral service by telling him his father was a brave man, the boy replies, "Yes, but I can't go fishing with him anymore." At such a point, it is easy to imagine sobs racking the entire audience—and also easy to imagine Frank Capra tipping his hat to the Japanese filmmakers.

The "realism" of these films takes other forms as well, in some instances beyond the bounds of what was tolerated by Japan's military authorities. The exhausting, seemingly endless nature of the China campaign, for example, could be conveyed by slow pans of China's vast landscape and by long holds of the camera on men marching along seemingly interminable roads. Kamei Fumio's extraordinary 1939 documentary *Fighting Soldiers* (*Tatakau Heitai*) is so relentless in portraying the tedium and emotional drain of the Japanese invasion of China that it was nicknamed "Exhausted Soldiers" (*Tsukareta Heitai*) and banned by the government. Somewhat surprisingly, a comparable on-location portrayal of the unceasing miserableness of the China War that was produced the same year—Tasaka Tomotaka's *Mud and Soldiers*—escaped the censor's wrath and became a prize-winning film.

While Kamei's gritty documentary style reflected his personal left-wing sympathies, as well as the lingering influence of traditions of humanism and social realism that had been gaining ground in Japanese film circles in earlier years, a more naive and almost unwitting sort of "realism" provoked official ire against a Shōchiku film five years later. For most of its course, the film, Kinoshita Keisuke's *Army*, follows the most platitudinous formulas concerning the sacrificing mother and idealistic son. Its final long sequence, however, collapses into a wrenching portrait of a mother's despair at sending her son off to become cannon fodder. There is a startling impression here of myths crumbling before one's very eyes as the war enters its final years.

Other war films offer realism of a more conventional sort. *The Story of Tank Commander Nishizumi* was sponsored by the Ministry of War partly to introduce Japanese citizens to "the importance of mechanization of the military" by new units such as the tank corps, and some of its combat scenes are so realistic that they appear to be documentary footage. *China Night*, although the most unabashed of propagandistic soap operas (it depicts the romance and marriage of a Japanese man and Chinese woman), nonetheless contains sobering scenes of sections of Shanghai that have been turned to rubble in the war. Tōhō's 1942 "national policy film" *The War at Sea from Hawaii to Malaya* contains such effective mock battles (done in miniature in the studio) that U.S. Occupation authorities spent time after the war searching for the original footage in the belief it was actually shot on the scene.

Combat footage, however, plays but a small part in the total oeuvre of Japanese war films. And, indeed, so does the enemy. Many Japanese war films have no explicit enemies at all; the focus remains almost exclusively on the pure self. Others portray enemies only abstractly, in the form of a distant plane, a running figure, the chatter of a machine gun or boom of field artillery. The foe often simply is identified as "they" (*karera*), or as a vague "enemy" (*teki*), or "enemy soldier" (*tekihei*), or "enemy force" (*tekigun*). Chinese or Korean communists are dismissed as "bandits" (*hizoku*). *Our Planes Fly South* makes passing reference to "American aircraft." *The Story of Tank Commander Nishizumi* identifies the enemy as "the Chiang Kai-shek army," behind whom lurk other "big powers" (Great Britain and the Soviet Union). In *Nishizumi*, when we do actually see the Chinese enemy (they are identifiable by their battle helmets), they are expressionless and almost robotlike figures—albeit unmistakably brave.

Hollywood films, by contrast, were notorious for their consistent depiction of the Japanese as a peculiarly despicable and atrocious enemy. The caricature rarely varied, but rather became part of a ferocious crusade for vengeance. Typical here is a famous scene in *Operation Burma* in which an American comes upon the mutilated bodies of GIs. "Degenerate, moral idiots," he curses. "Stinking little savages. Wipe them out, I say. Wipe them off the face of the earth. Wipe them off the face of the earth."

It often is said that there is no real counterpart to such venomous hatred in Japanese war films. As Ruth Benedict put it, "There is no personalization of the enemy and therefore no hatred of him." This is generally true, but it is misleading to let the matter rest there. In other forms of propaganda, after all, the Japanese did dehumanize the enemy and call for their extermination. In wartime cartoons as well as popular colloquialisms, for example, it was commonplace to depict the Americans and British as demons (*oni*), devils (*akki, akuma*), and monsters (*kaibutsu*). Exhortations to kill the "devilish Anglo-Americans" (*kichiku Ei-Bei*)

The ideal of the sincere and selfless fighting man was firmly established in Tasaka Tomotaka's pioneer 1938 film *Five Scouts*.

were uttered with mounting fervor as the Allied powers closed in on the home islands.

Despite this, such violent images of the enemy rarely carried over to film—or, for that matter, to popular songs or even (although here the exceptions are greater) to the bulk of popular Japanese war literature. The propaganda message varied subtly with the medium; and for whatever reason, for the Japanese the cinema message was softer. There is simply no "enemy" counterpart in Japanese films comparable to the atrocious and subhuman "Jap" beloved of Hollywood. Even when the Japanese undertook to produce explicit "hate-the-enemy" films, they generally did this in the form of historical dramas depicting the onerous behavior of earlier generations of Western imperialists in Asia. *The Opium War*, released in 1943, is a classic example of such propaganda; and it is noteworthy that many of these "historic" hate-the-enemy films attack Great Britain rather the United States.[5]

Kamei Fumio's 1939 documentary *Fighting Soldiers,* nicknamed "Exhausted Soldiers," was commissioned by the army but never shown to the public.

It would be a mistake, however, to conclude that Japanese war cinema as a whole was so preoccupied with romanticizing what it meant to be a "good Japanese" that enemies were of relatively little concern. Whether implicitly or explicitly, the defense of the pure self entailed constant struggle against a formidable array of hostile forces. More than just enemy armies and navies were arrayed against Japan. The country and "national polity," it was believed, confronted powerful cultural and psychological threats as well. Indeed, if "enemies" are construed in the broadest sense, it is arguable that they make an appearance in the Japanese war films in at least five guises.

> *First* is the amorphous, depersonalized, enemy—who is often invisible—to which Ruth Benedict and others called attention.
> *Second* is the redeemable enemy, the antagonist who can be won over to Japan's side.

41

Interracial love was depicted in the 1940 classic *China Night,* directed by
Fushimizu Osamu and starring Hasegawa Kazuo and the captivating
Japanese actress Yamaguchi Yoshiko, who was known at the time by the
Chinese name Li Hsiang-lan or (in Japanese rendering) Ri Ko-ran.

Third is the cultural enemy—or, more precisely, the perception of Anglo-American values (or "Westernization") as the
real threat to Japan and the Japanese.

Fourth is the enemy or potential enemy within the heart
and mind of each Japanese, the human emotions that Japan's
ideologues always feared might corrupt the self-sacrificing
"purity" they touted so passionately.

Finally—and most suggestive to the transition to postwar
Japan and a more antimilitarist cinema—in many Japanese
films of the 1930s and 1940s, war itself is the ultimate enemy.

The first of the five enemies certainly remains the most engrossing,
for it amounts to a phantom foe. As such, it may be best explained by
its opposite. In American films about the same conflict, war was a cause

Uesugi Ken as a humane "military god" killed on the
China front, in Yoshimura Kenzaburō's acclaimed 1940
film *The Story of Tank Commander Nishizumi.*

("fighting for democracy," etc.), and the enemy was clear (Japan, "the
Japs"). For Japanese filmmakers, by contrast, war was more like a natural
disaster (like a storm or earthquake, Benedict suggested; like fire or
flood in the metaphor of Joseph Anderson and Donald Richie). What
mattered was not whom one fought but how well. In this regard, U.S.
intelligence analysts found especially revealing the pre–Pearl Harbor
film *The Japanese*, which opened with scenes from the civil wars in Japan
in the 1870s, and moved on through the Sino-Japanese War of 1894–1895,
the Russo-Japanese War of 1904–1905, the Manchurian Incident of 1931,

A climactic scene from Imai Tadashi's 1942 action film about Japanese-Korean collaboration against "bandit" (guerrilla) resistance, *Suicide Troops of the Watchtower*.

and the China Incident of 1937. Japanese rebels, Russians, Chinese—all of the enemies, the Americans concluded, "remain shadows. Their character, nationality, or race are quite incidental to the business of war. Who they are is immaterial."

Much the same conclusion can be drawn from any number of Japanese war films, including a lavish extravaganza mounted jointly by the Imperial Army and Navy to rally popular spirits in the desperate final years of the war. In *The Divine Wind Blows*, released by Daiei in 1944, the enemy does indeed appear on the screen—in the form of the Mongol forces who twice attempted to invade Japan in the late thirteenth century. The cast for this costume drama was huge; leading roles were played by some of the country's most famous film actors; the film includes stirring cavalry scenes, as well as effective recreations of the Mongol fleet; and much of the cinematography is impressive and clearly costly—all evidence of a major investment at a time when Japan was desperate

Mizoguchi Kenji's 1942 version of *The Loyal 47 Ronin,* the classic account of feudal honor and revenge, fared poorly at the box office.

for resources. The parallel between Mongol invaders seven centuries earlier and the Allied threat at the time obviously was lost on no one—but the main point of the film lies elsewhere, and is explicitly inner-directed. Japan is a special land, indeed, a "divine land," it is stated, but this does not mean its people can expect divine support as a matter of course. "Only after everyone has exerted himself to the very utmost," the film intones, "does the divine wind (*kamikaze*) of Ise blow." Such reference to deity actually is rare in the Japanese war films (God was cast far more frequently by Hollywood), but even here the emphasis is on self-sacrifice. Enemies come and enemies go—but they will continue to go only so long as the Japanese spirit remains indomitable.

While the main enemy remained generally amorphous and deperson-alized, the filmmakers nonetheless did find good story lines in the portrayal of a redeemable enemy—antagonists, that is, who could be converted to the Japanese cause. The redeemable enemy was invariably

Tanaka Kinuyo as an anguished mother seeing her son march off to war in the controversial closing scene of Kinoshita Keisuke's 1944 *Army*.

Asian. In Tōhō's 1942 *Suicide Troops of the Watchtower*, for example, it is a Korean "bandit" (that is, guerrilla fighter) who recognizes the righteousness of the Japanese cause and turns his gun against his former comrades. In *Vow in the Desert*, released in 1941, a Chinese communist assassin is converted to Japanese-style Pan-Asianism by the magnanimity of his dying Japanese victim.

The Chinese were the favorite redeemable enemy of the Japanese filmmakers, and the most fascinating movies on this theme used the allegory of interracial love between a Japanese man and Chinese woman. Beginning in 1939, the captivating bilingual and quadrinamed Japanese actress Yamaguchi Yoshiko (alias Li Hsiang-lan in Chinese, Ri Ko-ran in Japanized Chinese, and Shirley Yamaguchi in her postwar American incarnation) starred in several such films. The great classic of the series was 1940's *China Night*, which may well be the most shameless and fascinating propaganda exercise of the war years. The story of an idealistic Japanese seaman who wins the confidence and eventually love of a

Yaguchi Yoko leads a fife-and-drum corps made up of young female factory workers in Kurosawa Akira's 1944 homefront film *The Most Beautiful*.

Chinese war orphan, *China Night* was a semi-musical (its theme song became immensely popular in Japan) which actually was produced with three different endings for three different audiences. For the Chinese audience, the film ends with a wedding ceremony. In the Japanese version, the hero is called on a dangerous mission moments after the wedding and killed by Chinese communists; his bride, heartbroken, drowns herself. For export to Southeast Asia, the wounded groom returns from his brush with death just in time to save his bride from killing herself.

Interracial love was in itself a daring theme. Americans shied away from it (Twentieth-Century Fox's *China Girl* is one of the few Hollywood films that dared touch on the subject, and then only gingerly). And the Japanese government, as concerned about racial purity as it was about spiritual purity, opposed miscegenation. The symbolic potential of

47

interracial romance was irresistible, however, and as bald and transparent as can be imagined. Japan is the strong, disciplined, rational, patient, dominant, protective, firm but compassionate male. China, by contrast, is feminine, weak, dependent, misguided, suspicious, mildly hysterical and irrational—but exceedingly attractive and ultimately capable of being won over. The mix of race and gender, moreover, was actually less iconoclastic than might appear at first glance. Only in *China Night* do the Japanese hero and Chinese heroine actually marry, and even there, in the version shown in Japan, the marriage is never consummated. In none of the other interracial love stories (there were several involving Japanese and Germans as well) does love end in marriage. Invariably, duty demands otherwise.[6]

The third or "cultural" enemy perceived as threatening Japan was Westernization itself, particularly the corrosive influence of Anglo-American values. This was a target of all forms of Japanese propaganda. In the consistent vocabulary of the times, Anglo-American attitudes "polluted" the pure spirit of Japan; and the list of values that consequently needed to be purged was quite specific. It included, in most recitations: individualism, egoism, selfishness, materialism, hedonism, extravagance, money-worship, liberalism, democracy, and "Anglo-American ideas" in general.

"Westernization" of a scientific or technological sort was of course a different matter. In this the Japanese took pride, and the propaganda films take pains to display the country's modern might. Planes, guns, and ships are not just part of the war scene. They are also symbols of Japan's technological accomplishments, to be admired not only by the Japanese themselves but also by the non-Japanese Asian audiences to whom these films also were shown. The more foppish accouterments of Western civilization, however, became contrary symbols of the general spiritual decadence of the West. The twist in the propaganda films, where actual Westerners rarely appear, is to present weak and dissolute Asians as surrogate Westerners—that is, as conspicuously "Westernized" individuals. Admirers of Kurosawa will recognize this in the villain in the sequel to *Sugata Sanshirō*. Ruth Benedict and her colleagues found that the cowardly and degenerate Asians in *every* film they analyzed were given over to Western ways.

In the eyes of the ruling groups, Westernization threatened all Japanese. It was, after all, something to which the populace already had been exposed and attracted. In their most pernicious form, moreover, Anglo-American ideas were perceived as reinforcing the greatest threat "from within" of all—namely, longing for personal and privatized happiness. This was the fourth of the five enemies. As the propagandists well knew, there really was little joy in sacrificing oneself for the state. By far the more natural emotion was to seek personal comfort and cherish intimate personal relationships within the family. The conflict between duty (*giri*) and emotion (*ninjo*) which had given such tension and vitality to the dramas of the late feudal period was to a very considerable degree replayed in the war films. Duty demanded that wife give up husband; that mother give up son; that husband, father, and son give up their lives if called on to do so. Duty demanded, in essence, that the natural bonds of family love be forsaken.

It is in this context that we can best understand the persistent imagery of the state or military as a surrogate family, an implicit theme that pervades so many of the Japanese war films. Officers are father figures, or elder brothers. Soldiers are like brothers to each other. On those occasions when he is evoked (as in *Five Scouts*), the emperor, remote and awesome, is the great pater familias. Why, in the final analysis, was this overpowering mystique of the "family state" necessary? Because the authoritarian and militarist state had all but destroyed the nuclear family.

On the surface, this tension between duty and emotion, state and family, is resolved by the pure heroes of the war films, who achieve transcendence through suppressing their personal attachments. In fact, the tension is rarely resolved at all. Sacrifice and duty are onerous. The camaraderie of the battlefield is bittersweet. As the critic Satō Tadao has observed, even the smile of a "military god" such as tank commander Nishizumi is melancholy. Almost none of the Japanese war films can be seen as a glorification of war—and some are transparently at war within themselves. This is especially apparent in the films of the China War made prior to Pearl Harbor, such as *Chocolate and Soldiers* and *Five Scouts*, where humanistic and antiwar sentiments frequently threatened to override the propagandistic message. In *Army*, released by Shōchiku in 1944, the suffering breaks through with startling and unexpected intensity—almost as if unplanned by the filmmakers—as we encounter a mother who in the end finds it impossible to "bear the unbearable" and send her son off to war with stoic pride. When the young man finally marches off to war, as his mother repeatedly has encouraged him to do, she literally claws her way through the crowd of bystanders cheering off the departing troops, desperate to prolong the sight of her doomed offspring. War may be a duty for every mother and mother's son, but it is also the final, ultimate enemy.

It is surely this latter fixation on the misery of war and self-sacrifice that helps explain (more than theories of ideological convenience or shallow faddishness) the quick emergence after Japan's surrender of films of a decidedly antimilitarist and even pacifist and communist cast. The year 1946 saw several outstanding productions of this sort, led by Kurosawa's *No Regrets for Our Youth*, Mizoguchi Kenji's *Victory of Women*, Kinoshita Keisuke's *Morning for the Osone Family*, and Imai Tadashi's *Enemy of the People*. In 1947, Kamei Fumio and Yamamoto Satsuo codirected an intense antiwar drama, *Between War and Peace*, which actually incorporated footage from Kamei's censored 1939 documentary *Fighting Soldiers*. In a most suggestive turnabout, these and later Japanese antiwar films actually carried on the fixation on "purity" by simply redirecting the process of purification against a new set of corrupting influences—"militarism," for one, and "feudalism" or "feudal legacies" for another.

▬

None of this should be construed as implying that war films made prior to Japan's surrender were fundamentally honest and benign. They were not. Recent renewal of interest in them in the United States, for example, has provoked protest by Chinese and Chinese-Americans, who see this as yet another attempt to sanitize the true nature of Japanese aggression in China. Their anguish is understandable. There are no real Chinese in these films. The amorphous, depersonalized enemy is a dehumanized enemy, virtually an abstraction—and consequently easy to kill, or ignore. To the viewer of such "humanistic" films as *Five Scouts*, *Chocolate and Soldiers*, *The Story of Tank Commander Nishizumi*, even *Fighting Soldiers*—all set in China—Nanking would simply be a place where Japanese soldiers met hardship. One would never know that hundreds of thousands of Chinese soldiers and civilians were wantonly slaughtered there.

50

There are other areas in which the grossly propagandistic nature of the films also is notable. The physical brutality and mental abuse that were a now-notorious part of prewar Japanese military training, for example, were totally ignored. On the contrary, major productions such as *Our Planes Fly South* and *Flaming Sky* (1940) present the training of young officers as an almost idyllic exercise. While the misery and tedium of war does emerge in many Japanese war films, moreover, the full horror of the conflict was suppressed by Home Ministry production codes prohibiting footage of close-up fighting or truly grisly scenes. Needless to say, the corruption and oppression of the "family state" went unrecorded by the camera's eye.

All this is more or less what we would expect of the propaganda of any nation at war, but there is a final, pernicious legacy of Japan's war cinema that calls attention, once again, to the extraordinary preoccupation with Japanese "purity." The overriding image that any viewer of these films will retain is of the Japanese as an innocent, suffering, self-sacrificing people. It is the image, in the end, of the Japanese as eternal victims—victims of war, of fate, of noble commitments, of vague enemies, of misguided antagonists, of whatever one might choose to imagine. The perversity of such an image is obvious: it is devoid of any sense of individual or collective responsibility for war, or of any recognition that, at every level, the Japanese also victimized others.

To see ordinary Japanese in World War II as simultaneously victims and victimizers offends our conventional sense of morality, but is nonetheless an important step toward recognizing that the great war in Asia was a tragedy for everyone involved. The war films in and of themselves fail to convey this, but they contribute to our own ability to fashion such a tragic and still critical perspective. They show us, with unusual vivacity, how the war was represented and distorted in Japan, how sacrifice and death for the country were ennobled. And they offer, time and again, moments of artistic brilliance which remind us of the creative talents that were being preserved even in the midst of destruction and death. No history of wartime Japan—political and ideological, as well as social and cultural—can really be complete without close attention to these powerful evocations of the time. And no serious history of Japanese cinema can any longer ignore what was produced in that terrible cauldron of war.[7]

NOTES

1 The first major retrospective on Japanese wartime cinema was sponsored by the Japan Society of New York in 1987 and featured twenty-seven films made between 1937 and 1947. Most of these were provided by the U.S. National Archives and still are exceedingly difficult to obtain for public viewing. For an excellent concise description of these films, see the Japan Society's booklet *Japan at War: Rare Films from World War II*, issued as a guide for this retrospective. The present article was written in conjunction with this presentation and originally published in the *Japan Society Newsletter* of July 1987.

   For a general English-language overview of wartime Japanese films, see Joseph L. Anderson and Donald Ritchie, *The Japanese Film: Art and Industry* (expanded ed., Princeton: Princeton University Press, 1982); see also Chapter 1 ("From War to Occupation") in Kyoko Hirano, *Mr. Smith Goes to Tokyo: Japanese Cinema under the American Occupation, 1945–1952* (Washington: Smithsonian Institution Press, 1992), pp. 13–46. In Japanese, see Imamura Shōhei, Satō Tadao, Shindō Kaneto, Tsurumi Shunsuke, and Yamada Yōji, eds. *Sensō to Nihon Eiga* [War and Japanese Films], vol. 4 in the eight-volume series, *Kōza—Nihon Eiga* [Japanese Films Series] (Tokyo: Iwanami Shoten, 1986). Kamei Fumio's reminiscences were published as *Tatakau Eiga: Dokyumentarisuto no Shōwa Shi* [Fighting Films: A Documentary Filmmaker's History of the Shōwa Period] (Tokyo: Iwanami Shoten, 1989).

2 Capra is quoted in the Japan Society's *Japan at War* booklet.

3 See, for example, *Japanese Films, A Phase of Psychological Warfare: An Analysis of the Themes, Psychological Content, Technical Quality, and Propaganda Value of Twenty Recent Japanese Films*, Office of Strategic Services, Research and Analysis Branch Report no. 1307, March 30, 1944 (available at the National Archives, Washington, D.C.).

4 Donald Richie, *The Films of Akira Kurosawa* (Berkeley: University of California Press, 1965).

5 One of the most graphic cinematic depictions of the Caucasian enemy appears not in a regular feature film but rather in a pioneer feature-length animated film entitled *Momotarō—Divine Troops of the Ocean*. Produced at considerable expense in collaboration with the Imperial Navy, completed around December 1944, and released in April 1945, this seventy-four-minute Shōchiku black-and-white cartoon turns the folktale of Momotarō the "Peach Boy" into a contemporary fable of pure Japan (Momotarō) and its capable loyal people (Momotarō's domesticated animal retainers)

leading the less developed peoples of Asia (charming jungle creatures) against the rapacious Westerners who have violated the peace of Asia.

One extraordinary "historical" flashback in the film diverts to the style of a silhouette play, somewhat in the manner of Indonesian shadow shows, to depict the early rape of a paradisal Asian kingdom by scheming, mercenary Europeans. Eloquently narrated, with a sophisticated tension between the unctuous words of the European "merchants" and visual scenes of their true piratical and rapacious nature, this sequence concludes with a stone monument in the jungle, all that is left of the once-peaceful kingdom. Engraved on this is a prophesy: "On a night when the moonlight is bright, there will come from an Eastern land of the Son of Heaven [*Tenshi*] a divine soldier on a white horse, who is destined to liberate the people."

Momotarō and his "divine troops" fulfill this prophesy in dramatic fashion, parachuting into a white man's stronghold whose absurd human figures betray their demonic nature by small horns on their heads. (Their maps confirm this with place names like Ogre's Island, Lake Devils, Devil's Strait, and so on). In a fleeting scene that is especially shocking because it contrasts so sharply with the lyric tone of the film to that point, one of the charming Japanese paratroopers runs a bayonet into the chest of a white soldier. In the more prolonged depiction of the utterly routed enemy, however, the characterization is one of utterly craven and cowardly men. They stutter and stammer in English (with Japanese subtitles at this point), fall to their knees at one point when Momotarō threatens to renew hostilities, and eventually agree—this in 1945!—to "unconditional surrender" to the Japanese. In the cartoon's final frames, youngsters back in Japan (charming and innocent little animals) emulate the divine heroes by pretending to parachute out of a tree and onto an outline of the United States drawn on the ground.

Momotarō—Divine Troops of the Ocean probably stands with *China Night*, the musical feature film about interracial love in war-ravished China, as one of the two most remarkable cinematic renderings of the enemy in wartime Japan.

6 The other Japanese films in which Yamaguchi Yoshiko played a Chinese woman involved with a Japanese man were *Song of the White Orchid* (1939), *Vow in the Desert* (1941) and *Fighting Street* (1942).

7 The Japanese titles of films cited in this essay are: *Army* (Rikugun); *Between War and Peace* (Sensō to Heiwa); *China Night* (Shina no Yoru); *Chocolate and Soldiers* (Chokorēto to Heitai); *The Divine Wind Blows* (Kakute Kamikaze wa Fuku); *Enemy of the People* (Minshū no Teki); *Fighting Soldiers*

(Tatakau Heitai; usually rendered "Soldiers at the Front"); *Fighting Street* (Tatakai no Machi); *Five Scouts* (Gonin no Sekkōhei); *Flaming Sky* (Moyuru Ōzora); *The Japanese* (Nihonjin); *Momotarō—Divine Troops of the Ocean* (Momotarō—Umi no Shinpei); *Morning for the Osone Family* (Ōsone-ke no Asa); *The Most Beautiful* (Ichiban Utsukushiku); *Mud and Soldiers* (Tsuchi to Heitai); *No Regrets for Our Youth* (Waga Seishun ni Kuinashi); *The Opium War* (Ahen Sensō); *Our Planes Fly South* (Aiki Minami e Tobu); *Song of the White Orchid* (Byakuran no Uta); *The Story of Tank Commander Nishizumi* (Nishizumi Senshachō-den); *Sugata Sanshirō* (Sugata Sanshirō); *Suicide Troops of the Watchtower* (Borō no Kesshitai); *Victory of Women* (Josei no Shōri); *Vow in the Desert* (Nessa no Chikai); *The War at Sea from Hawaii to Malaya* (Hawai Marē oki Kaisen).

"NI" and "F":
Japan's Wartime
Atomic Bomb Research

ON JANUARY 7, 1978, the front page of the *New York Times* carried a headline reading JAPANESE DATA SHOW TOKYO TRIED TO MAKE WORLD WAR II A-BOMB. The story also was featured in the *Washington Post* and sent out on the wire services of both the *Post* and the *Times*, thereby ensuring worldwide coverage. The two newspapers, together with National Public Radio in the United States, based their stories on a forthcoming article in the journal *Science* by staff writer Deborah Shapley, who had provided her essay to them as an advance scoop. Shapley's article as well as the broader media coverage that accompanied her purported exposé conveyed the misleading impression—one among many misrepresentations, as it turned out—that this information was based on a study being prepared by two distinguished American academics.

This was history as news, but history of a politically consequential sort nonetheless, although it could be used in different ways. The Japanese A-bomb project was of interest to students of science, technology, and the state who were concerned with controlling nuclear proliferation, for example. At the same time, and quite predictably, it proved to be grist for the mill of anti-Japanese sentiment, which for economic reasons has been grinding with ever-greater momentum in the United States since the early 1970s.

The former concern was of greatest interest to Herbert York of the University of California at San Diego, who was prominently quoted at the time. Professor York, the chief scientific adviser to the Defense Department during the Eisenhower administration, is a noted expert on weaponry and well-known spokesman for arms control. In commenting on the significance of the Japanese project, he drew two conclusions: that in Japan, as in all other nations with World War II A-bomb projects, the initial impetus came from scientists and engineers rather than from the highest ranks of the military and government; and that the Japanese project, which "completes the set" for World War II (the United States, Soviet Union, Britain, Germany, France, and now Japan), constitutes yet another demonstration of "technological momentum," or "a general technological imperative."

Shapley, on the other hand, drew a specifically anti-Japanese lesson:

> [T]he historical importance of the project lies not in the fact that Japan failed but that she tried, and that Japan's postwar attitude, that she, as the one nation victimized by atomic weapons, is above seeking to acquire them for herself, is not historically accurate. The historical record shows—on the basis of the eagerness of her military and the willing coopera-tion of her scientists—that if other factors had made a bomb possible, the leadership—which by the end of the war were placing their own youth in torpedoes to home them on the advancing U.S. fleet—would not have hesitated to use the bomb against the United States.

Where the York thesis places technology in command and thereby diminishes the significance of national or sociopolitical considerations, the interpretation reflected in *Science* returns state, national, and, indi-rectly, racial considerations to the fore, although it also minimizes the social and political context.[1]

It is no doubt true that Japan would have used the A-bomb if it had been available, and this may be comforting to those Americans who bear, however lightly, a sense of guilt for Hiroshima and Nagasaki. The potential anti-Japanese thrust of the argument lies elsewhere, however—namely, in the impression that for over three decades the Japanese deliberately and effectively concealed their own wartime engagement in A-bomb research, and in doing so assumed a hypocritical posture of moral superiority. The publicity concerning what *Science* labeled Japan's "social secret" easily became metamorphosed into a notion, a "confirmation" for those so inclined, of Japanese duplicity.[2]

Both the technological and xenophobic responses were misleading. As a consequence, one really confronts here a "double" topic. There is the core story of what actually took place in the way of nuclear research in wartime Japan. And now, superimposed upon this, is the related story of how contemporary societies, in this particular case the United States more than Japan, manipulate history to construct modern myths and reinforce national, cultural, and racial prejudices.

It may be helpful to begin with several observations. Japan's wartime research on an atomic bomb was not really "news" in 1978; it was an old story that had been rediscovered and refurbished. Also, while the Japanese research may complete the "set" of nuclear research in World War II, the national pieces in this set remain grossly, almost grotesquely, unbalanced. Japan's activities in this area were puny and almost pathetic. Moreover, while the thesis of a technological imperative is attractive, it is not a conclusion one could emphasize from studying the Japanese case alone.

Certainly the intimation of a "social secret," a postwar conspiracy of silence on the part of the Japanese, must be qualified at the outset. In one of the earliest postwar survey histories of Japan, first published in 1949, Chitoshi Yanaga of Yale University, discussing the destruction of Hiroshima, noted that "Japanese scientists knew immediately that it was the atomic bomb, for they too had been working on it for years."[3] Ten years later, a RAND Corporation study of atomic energy in the Soviet Union included a general but quite accurate paragraph on Japan's futile wartime project, and cited an article in Japanese entitled "Japan's Uncompleted Atomic Bomb."[4] Subsequently the research was mentioned, although not always completely accurately, in a number of more popular English sources.[5]

That this information did not make a great impression upon Americans—and that it subsequently evaporated from standard Western histories of Japan—cannot be attributed to a Japanese conspiracy. In fact, Japanese scholars and publishers have acknowledged the wartime work on the atomic bomb *in English* in a number of places. It was mentioned well over a decade before the 1978 "exposé" by several Japanese historians of science.[6] And it was described in considerable detail in a 1972 book, *The Day Man Lost*, written by a group of Japanese scholars and published in the West by a major Japanese publishing firm. The "revelations" published in *Science* and the *Times* and *Post* added only minor details to this latter account.[7]

Where Japanese-language sources are concerned, moreover, considerable data was available long before the American media discovered the subject. The Japanese government apparently has not spoken publicly on the matter (as will be seen, it did brief U.S. officials secretly after the war), but discussions of Japan's wartime research on a nuclear weapon had appeared in Japanese before the U.S. Occupation ended in 1952. At the very end of 1949, for example, Nishina Yoshio, the leading physicist involved in the wartime project, was interviewed in *Kingu*, a major mass-circulation magazine, and frankly acknowledged that Japanese scientists had done research on a nuclear weapon but concluded this would be impossible for Japan to make.[8] Taketani Mitsuo, an outspoken left-wing theoretical physicist who had worked with Yukawa Hideki on the meson theory in the 1930s, discussed his wartime bomb-related calculations concerning the critical mass for fission in various places beginning around 1951.[9]

For most of the Occupation, discussion of the atomic bombs was in fact sharply curtailed by U.S. authorities in Japan. This policy began to ease around 1949, but it was not until after Japan regained independence in April 1952 that graphic materials such as photographs of Hiroshima and Nagasaki could be shown in Japan, or that scientific studies of the human effects of the bombs could be freely disseminated.[10] Thus, the popular "discovery" by ordinary Japanese of their own secret A-bomb research really took place in the 1950s, while they were reencountering the trauma of actually having suffered nuclear destruction. As these revelations unfolded in the 1950s and 1960s, moreover, it also became apparent that they contributed in a small way to ongoing debates of a practical nature. Understanding why Japan had failed to make an atomic

bomb, that is, could be seen as a little case study which helped to illuminate some of the fundamental scientific, technological, and technocratic weaknesses that made Japan so conspicuously inferior materially
to the United States.

It is fair to say that a general picture of Japan's wartime A-bomb
research had become available in Japanese by the end of the 1950s; that
by the late 1960s, this had been fleshed out with both reminiscences and
technical data; and that the topic was standard fare by the 1970s. The
article on "Japan's Uncompleted Atomic Bomb" that later made its way
into the previously mentioned RAND study, for example, appeared in
the well-known monthly magazine *Kaizō* in November 1952.[11] The
following year, a popular book about "secret weapons" of the war years
included a reminiscence by Itō Yōji, a navy officer who coordinated
some of the earliest deliberations on the military application of atomic
energy.[12] Also in 1953, Yamamoto Yōichi, a former army officer who
had been involved in the search for uranium ores, published a long,
detailed, and highly opinionated article that, among other things, defended the U.S. use of the atomic bombs against Japan (war is war, he
said) and severely criticized civilian scientists such as Nishina for being
preoccupied with pure science (*kagaku*) and failing to understand or
respect applied theory and technology (*gijutsu*) in organizing Japan's own
A-bomb project.[13] In 1959, coinciding with the fourteenth anniversary of
Hiroshima and Nagasaki, the popular weekly magazine *Shukan Bunshun*
published a sober article on the failure of Japan's wartime attempts to
build an atomic bomb. The magazine did not engage in moral hand-
wringing, but rather posed the interesting question of why it was that
the democratic United States and Great Britain were able to mobilize
talent and resources to address this tremendous scientific challenge while
dictatorial Imperial Japan and Nazi Germany were not. (The answer,
much as Yamamoto Yōichi had argued six years earlier, was to be found
in the psychological as well as material gap between world-class scientists
and a weak technical and industrial base).[14]

Certainly by 1970, the subject had been quite thoroughly explored
and exposed in Japan. The original Japanese version of *The Day Man
Lost* appeared in 1968, while a volume in a heavily promoted popular
history of the Shōwa period published that same year devoted over 150
pages to "Japan's atomic bomb," consisting almost entirely of accounts

by participants in the wartime project.[15] In 1970, a volume in an encyclo-pedic new multivolume history of science and technology in Japan in-cluded an entire chapter of commentary plus technical documentation and excerpts from earlier references pertaining to the A-bomb project.[16] Four years after that, Kigoshi Kunihiko, one of Nishina's key research-ers, published a frank and entertaining essay about his wartime experi-ments with uranium hexaflouride.[17] By 1976, these activities were such common knowledge that a book about Nishina in a series of biographies written for school-age Japanese contained a chapter about Nishina's wartime military activities, including a section on "NI-go," the code name for his A-bomb research.[18]

Between Japan's capitulation on August 15, 1945, and the arrival of U.S. Occupation forces two weeks later, Japanese military and civilian officials engaged in the wholesale destruction of potentially incriminating documents. Basic records pertaining to A-bomb research were included in this massive (and well-known) act of camouflage, and in this regard it is correct to speak of a Japanese cover-up.[19] In the light of subsequent public attention to the subject in Japan beginning around 1949 and ranging from mass-circulation publications to scholarly reference sources, however, the accusation of a Japanese "social secret" really tells more about the accuser than the accused. Unfamiliar languages and societies are themselves "secrets" to those who do not know them; and the impression that information and ideals not rendered in English are at best irrelevant and at worst duplicitous has become a familiar aspect of American parochialism. One of the anomalies of the 1978 "exposé" concerning Japan's A-bomb research was that the supposedly secret data all came from Japanese sources that had been in the public domain for many years. *Science* magazine obtained these from an American scholar who in turn had received them from Japanese colleagues specializing in physics and the history of science.[20]

One of the major sources upon which *Science* relied was in fact the texts and commentaries contained in the 1970 history of Japanese science and technology mentioned above, and a short document included in this source places the notion of secrecy in yet another light. This is the Japa-nese version of a memorandum dated October 10, 1945, and originally presented in English to the U.S. military in Japan, in which the Japanese briefly described that aspect of their wartime research which involved the navy and Kyoto Imperial University. This calls attention to the usually forgotten fact that after the war U.S. intelligence systematically and in utmost secrecy debriefed the Japanese on an immense range of military-related matters, nuclear research (as well as lethal medical and biological experiments) among them. Following the surrender, Japanese scientists in nuclear-related fields were placed under restraint and close supervision. Japanese stockpiles of uranium compounds and other minerals pertinent to nuclear research were carefully inventoried, and information about such potential resources in Japan's former colonies and occupied areas in China and Southeast Asia was gathered. To the extent that there was a "social secret" about these matters at the state level in the Cold War milieu, that secret was in considerable part binational.[21]

There is thus a great deal to be learned both about and from the Japanese A-bomb project, but as this was presented to the public in 1978 the most conspicuous lessons were about Yellow-peril journalism and American ideology. As an instructive exercise in the popular uses of history, it must be emphasized that the "news" solemnly presented in *Science*, the *Times*, and the *Post* was old; the details offered were not notably new even to the English-language record; and the spadework was done by the Japanese themselves, who then proceeded to be accused of burying the subject. Japan's wartime A-bomb research is not really of great interest as an example of postwar cover-ups, and it most certainly does not indicate that there was some sort of race between the United States and Japan to develop the bomb. On the contrary, the Japanese project was an erratic endeavor and conspicuous failure, and as such is of primary interest because of the insights it can provide concerning science and society in wartime Japan.

▬

Above all else, Japan's failure to develop nuclear weapons reflected a paucity of human and physical resources, compounded by the confusion and material drain of a losing war. The failure also exposed constraints within the scientific community, however, as well as conflicts in the overall structure of wartime authority. These tensions and conflicts are of no little interest, for they contradict the image of Japanese harmony and group solidarity which both Japanese ideologues and anti-Japanese critics have been fond of evoking ever since the war years. The wartime

Japanese state was as conflict-ridden as any other complex bureaucracy and society—possibly more so than many others, including the United States—and the disorganized A-bomb research is but one illustration of this.

Upon close examination, moreover, the Japanese project does not seem to confirm Professor York's conclusion that "the cadre of scientists and engineers" took the lead in promoting the A-bomb in Japan as elsewhere. On the contrary, the most readily identifiable initiatives came from the military, many of the country's leading scientists approached the project with ambivalent feelings at best, and in the end no one really took much of a lead at all. This is not meant to deny that Japanese scientists as a whole were mobilized behind the war effort, or to imply that those approached about developing a nuclear weapon addressed moral questions more squarely than did their Western counterparts. The situation in Japan contrasted sharply with that in the West, however, and evidence is scant for suggesting, as the account in *Science* did, that Japanese scientists were either driven by "blind patriotism" or drawn irresistibly to what Robert Oppenheimer called the "sweet problem" of the explosive potential of the atom.

Scientific research in wartime Japan was bittersweet at best. There was certainly a nationalistic imperative. There was also a practical, financial imperative: it took the military crisis (and eventual severance of the Japanese scientific community from the rest of the world) to bring in the funds, bring about the restructuring, and begin to approach the scale that had long been necessary for first-rate research in general, and for solid basic research in particular.[22] In certain areas, wartime exigencies and military support actually gave researchers more freedom than they enjoyed previously—or even subsequently, under the U.S. military aegis during the period of Occupation.[23] In addition, there was often a simple personal and opportunistic imperative at work: good scientists rarely were sent to the front. For younger scientists, participation in the war effort of the laboratories was thus a form of self-preservation unavailable to students in the humanities and social sciences. For older scientists, collaboration at a higher organizational level was a way of saving younger colleagues from probable death. This appears to have been one consideration in the A-bomb project, and it can be taken at two levels: the bond of human affection, and the desperate desire to save the future of science—in this case, the future of physics—in Japan.[24]

For some Japanese scientists, the war years were undeniably good years. Some of the intellectual challenges *were* intrinsically attractive, and the unprecedented support for advanced research was a bonanza. Indeed, one of the many ironies of World War II for Japan is that—at a cost of devastation and close to 2.7 million Japanese lives—militarism and aggression forced the breakthroughs, not least in scope and scale of scientific research, that provided a base for postwar economic "miracles." In the crisis context of a disastrous war, however, the prospects for epochal leaps in the militarized new science were limited to certain areas (Japan, albeit belatedly, did develop radar and penicillin), and the new priorities often were disruptive of promising ongoing research (for example, on cosmic rays).

Japanese scientists who had occasion to comment on the A-bomb project appear to have been almost unanimous in believing that this was a hopeless task for the immediate future—certainly for Japan, but for every other belligerent country as well, including the United States.[25] They immediately recognized what the Hiroshima bomb represented, but they had not believed it possible before Japan's defeat. Thus it is difficult to detect any esprit in the Japanese undertaking, any genuine sense of a race against time or a race against the enemy or a race toward an imminent scientific threshold. The Allied A-bomb project marshaled an international cadre great in numbers and superlative in expertise at every level, all giddy with anticipation and all fearful almost to the end that Werner Heisenberg and his German colleagues would beat them to the wire. The Japanese worked in isolation, deeply and realistically pessimistic concerning their prospects but naively sanguine in their sense that it did not really matter. For sound reasons, Allied intelligence dismissed the possibility of an atomic threat from Japan.[26] But for these same reasons, and for others suggested below, the Japanese work on a potential nuclear or uranium bomb presents qualitative as well as quantitative differences from the research in other countries.

In most general terms, the point is this: for economic, technological, and material reasons, Japan proved incapable of mounting anything remotely comparable to the American, British, or German A-bomb efforts. Beyond this, even after it had been decided to investigate the feasibility of a nuclear weapon, the country was unable effectively to mobilize and coordinate the limited resources available. The Japanese endeavor was badly fragmented, inadequately staffed, indifferently pursued, and plagued by doubt and ambivalence at the individual level. In various respects, it thus repudiates some of the most cherished stereotypes commonly applied to Japan: of a "consensus" society, a robotlike "efficiency," a wartime solidarity of "one million hearts beating as one," and a tightly regimented prewar "totalitarian" regime.

Among the several contradictions that the nuclear project illuminates, one concerns the nature of prewar and wartime science in Japan. On the one hand, Japanese scientists were capable of pioneer theoretical work; on the other hand, their community was vulnerable to severe institutional and economic constraints. The former observation can be illustrated by a few chronological highlights in the development of nuclear physics in Japan:[27]

- In 1903, Nagaoka Hantarō proposed a detailed "Saturnian" model of a nuclear atom. (The existence of the atomic nucleus was confirmed by Lord Rutherford in 1911, although Nagaoka had overestimated the probable number of electrons).

- The theoretical physicist Ishiwara Jun introduced relativity theory to Japan after studying in Europe from 1911 to 1915 under Albert Einstein among others.

- "Riken," the Institute of Physical and Chemical Research (*Rikagaku Kenkyūjo*), which is regarded as the first great step in the advancement of pure research in prewar Japan, was established in Tokyo in 1917—in response to the economic boom *and* economic challenges of World War I.

- Nishina Yoshio, later a key figure in the wartime A-bomb work, studied under Rutherford from 1921 to 1922, and under Niels Bohr from 1923 to 1928, and established the famous Nishina Laboratory within Riken in 1931. Einstein himself had visited Japan in 1927, and serious research in quantum mechanics and nuclear physics in Japan is commonly dated from around 1931–1932. Historians of Asia will note that this coincides with the global depression, the Manchurian Incident and beginning of Japan's "fifteen-year war" with China, and the gearing of the economy toward a "total war" capacity. Historians of science might emphasize that 1932 was the year of great breakthrough, the so-called *annus mirabilis*, in the field of nuclear physics itself— and that Japanese physics thus approached maturity at the moment that international physics embarked upon the path that culminated in the controlled release of nuclear energy.

- In this setting, in December 1932, the Japan Society for the Promotion of Scientific Research was founded, with both government and private subsidies. This became a major vehicle for the funding and rationalization of research.

- Yukawa Hideki proposed the meson theory in 1934. (The meson particle was discovered in 1937, and Yukawa received the Nobel Prize for this early work in 1949.)

- In 1935 the Nuclear Research Laboratory was founded at Riken, and the institute began work on a huge cyclotron in 1937 (obtaining a sixty-inch magnet through Ernest O. Lawrence, seven years after Lawrence had built the prototype of the first cyclotron). Major research on cosmic rays had begun in 1935, largely under Nishina, and in March 1937 this project was reorganized to include research on the atomic nucleus.

By the time of the China Incident in 1937—and prior to the discovery of nuclear fission in late 1938—Japan thus had made substantial progress in physics, and several of its leading scientists were of international stature. Nishina is credited with assembling a talented corps of young researchers and running his laboratory in a democratic manner unusual for Japan; approximately 110 scientists, mostly physicists, were associated with the Nishina Laboratory when war broke out with the United States in 1941.[28] After 1933, moreover, considerable funds for research in cosmic rays and nuclear physics were made available through the Japan Society for the Promotion of Scientific Research and from private business circles.

Despite such advances, the level of expertise remained uneven and scientific progress was impeded by restraints inherent in both the archaic structure of the academic system and the relative underdevelopment of the economy. Experimentation still was largely carried out by fragmented small groups. Research still was not well coordinated nationally, and the scale of funding was low by international standards. The several levels of a truly coherent program, moreover—theoretical research, experimental research, technological adaptation, and manufacture— remained out of phase and uncoordinated.[29]

In all countries, scientists making the break with classical physics encountered a certain professional and social resistance. In Japan, such resistance took peculiar forms and may have lasted longer. Nagaoka, who advanced the nuclear model of the atom in 1903, was accused of practicing metaphysics rather than science by his Japanese colleagues, and turned to another field of study (magnetism) in the face of this discouragement, although he remained the venerable elder statesman of Japanese physics into the war years. Ishiwara, who introduced quantum theory to Japan, was fired from Tohoku University because of his love affairs.[30]

Even after World War I, and notwithstanding the considerable collegiality and accomplishments of the leading physicists, the community of scientists remained plagued by institutional rivalry and elitism (the notorious *gakubatsu*, or "academic cliques"), and by what is commonly described as the "feudalistic" *kōza* or professorial-chair system, which granted virtually dictatorial power over funding and research to the single senior professor in each tightly defined university unit. Where *gakubatsu* rivalry and elitism impeded interuniversity collaboration, the *kōza* system sometimes stifled creativity and initiative on the part of younger scholars.

Sakata Shōichi—another of the great prewar physicists, who also was known for his radical political views—later commented that truly serious theoretical work had been possible only at Osaka Imperial University, where Yukawa was based for a period.[31] Even the Osaka nexus did not hold, and Sakata eventually moved to the new Nagoya University. It is symbolic of the internal university pressures of prewar—and, indeed, much of postwar—Japan that Sakata is still famous for "democratizing" the physics department at Nagoya. At the same time, however,

66

the hiatus between the advanced theoretical and experimental work of the scientific vanguard and the applied research being developed under the auspices of private enterprise and the military establishment also reflected to some degree an elitist detachment and proud "academism" on the part of the leading scientists themselves.

In looking back upon the prewar physics community, it also is appropriate to consider a further problem that can be only briefly and tentatively suggested here. This involves the relationship between science, politics, and ideology, and evokes the "externalist-internalist" debate among historians of science. It is well known that Marxism influenced both the political and scientific thinking of some of the leading Western theoretical physicists; Einstein is perhaps the best-known example. This also was true of some of Japan's leading nuclear theorists in the 1930s, for one of whom, Taketani Mitsuo, there is available an illuminating semiautobiographical essay in English.[32] Taketani collaborated closely with Yukawa and Sakata in refining the meson theory in the mid 1930s, while at the same time he was involved with a radical group of young scientists in Kyoto, who "engaged in lively discussion about resistance movements." In early 1935, the group began publishing a journal called *Sekai Bunka* (World Culture), which included articles dealing not only with science and methodology, but also with popular-front movements against fascism in Europe. These discussions were construed as an attempt to create a basis for resistance against Japanese imperialism—the journal was suppressed in 1937, and Taketani was imprisoned from September 1938 to April 1939—but Taketani also applied his immersion in Marxist thought directly to his theoretical work on the meson, ultimately to great effect: "Throughout these thrusts in the dark it was the three-stage theory of materialistic dialectics that guided our research and fortified our resolution to overcome difficulties."

Shortly after the war, Sakata also published an article arguing that the development of postclassical physics in the twentieth century confirmed the validity of dialectical materialism—and Sakata's own progressive attitudes and activities already have been noted.[33] Such vivid, concrete examples of the integration of political consciousness and theoretical natural science at the highest level are obviously provocative. The more limited question that arises here is how pervasive and important the political dimension may have been in influencing the nature of collaboration between the scientific community and the state as Japan mobilized for war-related research and production. While many dissident and persecuted European scientists were able to escape to the Anglo-American countries, for example—and while participants in the A-bomb projects in the Allied countries were sustained by a strong sense of mission—Japan's scientists did not or could not flee, and in at least some instances clearly did not identify with the goals and practices of their government and society.

It thus seems possible that political and ideological considerations also may have contributed to the haphazard mobilization of scientific talent which characterized Japan's wartime A-bomb research. That proof of this thesis will not be easy is suggested by the case of Taketani himself, who near the end of the war was visited in succession by Nishina and the Special Higher Police, or Thought Police (*Tokkō*). The former asked him to apply his theoretical talents to the floundering research on the bomb; the latter placed him in jail, once again, for his subversive thoughts. Taketani then proceeded to work out his equations—and indeed discover the error in prior calculations—under surveillance in a police interrogation room. It was better than being at the front, he observed. It was a nice intellectual challenge. And he experienced no crisis of conscience, for he firmly believed there was no possibility of Japan actually being able to manufacture an atomic bomb.[34]

These vignettes convey an impression of constraints and ambiguities within the prewar community of physicists. In the case of the A-bomb project, such internal problems meshed with tension, factionalism, and disorganization at the governmental level. To wrest a metaphor from the field under discussion, it can be said that at both the scholarly and official levels there were numerous forces operating against the creation of a critical mass of expertise and efficiency.

This is a tedious point to document, but relatively simple to state. Recent scholarship on Japan has shown increasing awareness of the pervasiveness of conflict within Japanese society, and it is clear that this persisted—may even have been exacerbated—during the supreme test of national unity, World War II. As in the case of prewar science, here on the side of government and bureaucracy, of power and authority, there also was a great contradiction: after 1937, and especially after 1941, the mechanisms of centralized control were tightened, but factionalism remained bitter and particularism remained intense in Japan. In the midst of global war, this was a country beset by internal skirmishes.

Military historians, for example, point to tensions between the army general staff and field officers; between the Control Faction (*Tōsei-ha*) and the Imperial Way Faction (*Kōdō-ha*); among the various naval commands; and, with extraordinary ferocity, between the army and navy. Economic historians of these years must deal with the "dual structure" of a handful of giant oligopolies, on the one hand, and tens of thousands of small and medium-sized enterprises, on the other; the conflict between old *zaibatsu* (*kyū zaibatsu*) and "new *zaibatsu*" (*shinkō zaibatsu*); the controlled-economy theorists (*tōsei keizaironsha*) versus the apostles of capitalist "free enterprise." Students of bureaucratic politics must come to grips not merely with normal interministerial and inter-agency infighting, but also with the phenomenon of a cadre of so-called new bureaucrats (*shin kanryō*) or "renovationist bureaucrats" (*kakushin kanryō*), who defined their role in terms antithetical to those of the traditional technocrats. Diplomatic historians emphasize an ongoing squabble between the advocates of autarky and Pan-Asianism, on the one hand, and the proponents of cooperative imperialism in collusion with the Western powers, on the other. Intellectual historians wrestle with the potentially explosive paradoxes of National Socialism (how nationalistic? how socialistic?) and right-wing radicalism (how conservative? how radical?). Those who follow the spies find the Special Higher Police of the Home Ministry dogging the army's military police (*Kempeitai*), and vice versa, with scant exchange between the two. And on, and on.

This was, to be sure, factionalism within a system of overriding authoritarianism, and as the Pacific War drew to a climax, the channels of control were increasingly clarified and narrowed. It was not until 1945, however, that scientific research was more or less coordinated under a single agency (the Japan Scientific Research Council), and even then, until Japan's surrender, competition and disunity on research priorities persisted among such groups as the army, the navy, the Ministry of Munitions, the Ministry of Education, and so on.[35]

In this situation, it comes as little surprise to discover that it really is misleading to speak of *the* Japanese A-bomb project. The army appeared, retreated, then reappeared to sponsor research on the problem under Nishina in Tokyo. The navy showed early interest in nuclear weapons, then sank from sight, then resurfaced under a different command as the patron of an A-bomb project in Kyoto. Within the scientific community itself, there was no unanimity at all on whether it was worthwhile to commit scarce resources to nuclear weapons research, and individuals brought in as participants at one point might turn their backs on the project at another. Such disagreement actually surfaced publicly in a rather astonishing way in October 1944, when Nagaoka Hantarō—the elderly dean of the physics community, who at the time was president of the Imperial Academy (*Teikoku Gakushiin*), Japan's most prestigious honorary academic society—used the pages of a military journal to call for abandoning nuclear research and committing resources to more feasible weapons systems. In Japan's present circumstances, Nagaoka declared, atomic weapons were "castles in the sky," and those who urged trying to make them were "grasping at clouds." He himself had lost patience with "stupid arguments" about making an atomic bomb, and urged other scientists and planners to likewise concentrate on more practical military-related objectives.[36]

It was in the context of such bureaucratic disorganization and academic disarray that Nishina requested coordination and clarification of government demands and priorities ("unification" in one document, "one window" in another account). This never materialized, but it appears to be on the basis of such slight phrases that, in U.S. accounts, the thesis of initiative emanating from the scientific community (the "technological imperative") was grounded.[37]

■

The German scientists Otto Hahn and Fritz Strassmann discovered atomic fission, the breaking up of the uranium nucleus, in the closing weeks of 1938. The possibility of an explosive avalanche of fission, a chain reaction caused by emitted neutrons, was recognized soon thereafter, and Hahn later claimed that upon confronting the awesome military implications of this he contemplated committing suicide. As it turned out, he stayed his hand, participated in Germany's nuclear research through the war, and learned a few months after Hiroshima and Nagasaki that he had been awarded the Nobel Prize for his pioneer work on fission.[38]

German scientists moved swiftly in investigating the military potential of atomic fission, and their activities were observed elsewhere and, in some instances, replicated. In Japan in August 1939, for example, a scientific article appeared under the title "A New Super-Weapon Utilizing the Energy of the Uranium Atom—the Ominous Silence of the German Academic World."[39] The sensational prospect of an "atom bomb" (*genshi bakudan*) also quickly became part of Japanese popular culture and consciousness. Shortly before Pearl Harbor, for example, a distinguished scientist sitting in the appointive House of Councillors warned of a world in which undreampt-of explosive power could be contained in a bomb the size of a matchbox. Science-fiction writers appropriated this doomsday vision, and in the very midst of the Pacific War a popular boys' magazine actually published a story titled "Atom Bomb."[40]

In the United States and Great Britain, the German accomplishments were perceived with more intimate foreboding. Great refugee physicists who had fled Nazism and fascism, such as Einstein and Enrico Fermi, called for an Anglo-American counterproject to Germany's potential nuclear menace. Here could be seen a deep personal and political imperative (transcending technological momentum), but that is another issue. It is, however, instructive to set Japan's activities against the A-bomb research undertaken elsewhere in the world at this time.

Although many of the most eminent physicists and chemists who remained in Germany collaborated in exploring the military potential of nuclear fission, they never received the full support of the Nazi government. Hitler was hostile to "Jewish science," and the Blitzkrieg mentality of Germany's military strategists was not receptive to the uncertain and long-term prospects of nuclear weaponry. The German scientists themselves, moreover, were not all equally committed to reaching the point of actual manufacture of a nuclear weapon. Heisenberg, Germany's most eminent theoretical physicist, for example, concluded at an early date that a nuclear weapon was entirely beyond Germany's reach in the near future, and apparently never even seriously attempted to calculate the critical mass necessary to produce a chain reaction. Progress was impeded further by factors seen also in the case of Japan: gross underestimation of American capabilities; competing centers of interest and authority; an academic fascination with pure over applied research; and the necessity, in the end, of working amidst falling bombs under a dying regime. All in all, Germany committed approximately ten million dollars and less than one hundred researchers to the development of nuclear weaponry. Although the Western powers had been genuinely alarmed by the possibility of a German A-bomb, these fears turned out to have been unfounded; as the head of the postwar U.S. investigation into the matter observed, "the whole German uranium setup was on a ludicrously small scale."[41] It is a measure of the "relativity" of these undertakings, however, that the Japanese effort was in turn ludicrous in comparison to the activities of the German nuclear scientists.

In contrast to the Anglo-American powers, and the refugee scientists in the West, the Soviet Union did not take the German nuclear threat seriously, and actually ceased serious nuclear research in the summer of 1941, when Hitler invaded Russia. Prior to this date, nuclear physics had attained a high level of sophistication in Russia, and the decision to abandon this reflected the dire exigencies of immediate life-or-death struggle in the homeland (and the absence of strategic bombing as part of Soviet military strategy), as much as any sanguine intelligence evaluation of the improbability of a nuclear threat from Germany. Nuclear research was resumed in 1943, after the defense of Stalingrad and turn of the military tide against the Germans. In the wake of the recent collapse of the Soviet Union, it has become known that this was prompted in major part by Soviet penetration of the U.S. Manhattan Project by a still unidentified agent code-named "Perseus." Based on ultrasecret data provided by Perseus, the Soviet project led by nuclear physicist Igor Kurchatov was able to leapfrog ahead on crucial technical issues such as using plutonium as a basic element in the bomb. "If it had not been for the information that other people were developing a bomb," a former Soviet spy handler involved in this observed in 1992, "we would not have started our own effort until the end of the war."[42]

In contrast to the Soviet Union, Great Britain, also confronted by the Nazi menace, moved decisively to investigate and develop the military potential of the atom. British scientists and officials initially were skeptical concerning the feasibility of a nuclear superbomb—in April 1939, for example, the chairman of the Committee on the Scientific Survey of Air Defense put the odds against such a weapon at 100,000 to one—but by spring of 1940 the British had become essentially convinced of the practical possibility of building a "uranium bomb." The famous MAUD Committee, composed of several of Britain's most eminent scientists, was formed in April 1940 with the urgent charge of reporting on the possibility of developing an atom bomb during the present war. Simultaneously, major research was initiated, involving first-rate physicists and chemists from a number of institutions, who addressed the many problems involved from a variety of methodological approaches. By the end of 1940, the British had made impressive progress at minimal cost; they were further along in many areas of atomic research than the United States, and had accomplished far more in a matter of months than the Japanese were to accomplish over the course of several years.

By July 1941, the MAUD Committee had completed a report that was effusive concerning the happy prospects of the uranium bomb ("the destructive effect, both material and moral, is so great that every effort should be made to produce bombs of this kind"), and extremely optimistic concerning when the first bomb could be available (by the end of 1943). In every respect—speed, coordination, breadth, imagination, and unblinking zeal—the British pursuit of the bomb contrasted dramatically with the Japanese situation, and indeed with any other country as of 1941. "There is no doubt," the official history of Britain's wartime atomic policy observes, "that the work of the MAUD Committee had put the British in the lead in the race for a bomb. . . . Without the work of the MAUD Committee, the clarity of its analysis, its synthesis of theory and practical programming, its tone of urgency, the Second World War might well have ended before an atomic bomb was dropped."[43]

Despite this head start and heady optimism, for numerous reasons Britain found it necessary to pass the baton to the United States, which soon became the only serious participant in the race. The scale of the Manhattan Project is well known: it involved, in the end, 150,000 persons, an estimated 539,000 man-years of effort, a physical plant covering tens of thousands of acres in numerous states as well as Canada, and an outlay of roughly $2 billion. Here it may suffice to note merely that the Japanese "A-bomb project" was minuscule even when compared with U.S. experiments and accomplishments prior to the formal inauguration of the Manhattan Project in September 1942.[44]

———

Japan's atomic bomb activities can be divided into four segments, or four somewhat overlapping stages: (1) preliminary, and rather desultory, inquiries by the military, from 1940 to 1942; (2) evaluation of feasibility by a committee of scientists, under naval auspices, from July 1942 to March 1943; (3) the "NI Project," carried out with army support in Tokyo from late 1942 to April 1945; (4) the "F Project" in Kyoto, sponsored by the navy from possibly as early as mid 1943, but barely underway at the time of Japan's surrender.[45]

EARLY INQUIRIES

The first serious inquiries concerning a nuclear weapon for Japan appear to have come from Lieutenant General Yasuda Takeo, chief of the Army Aviation Technology Research Institute, who in April 1940 ordered Lieutenant Colonel Suzuki Tatsusaburō to investigate the matter. Suzuki consulted Sagane Ryōkichi, his former professor at Tokyo Imperial University, and in October produced a twenty-page report which concluded that manufacture of an atomic bomb was possible, and that Japan might be able to obtain adequate uranium resources to pursue this. The report was not treated with great confidentiality but was circulated quite widely in military, academic, and industrial circles. Around April 1941, Yasuda, through Suzuki, approached the head of Riken, Ōkōchi Masatoshi, and formally requested expert advice. Ōkōchi turned the problem over to Nishina, whose response to the army certainly appears on the surface to have been languid and informal. More than a year elapsed before a committee of experts actually was convened to render a considered opinion, and this committee was sponsored by the navy rather than army.[46]

The navy had approached the scientific community for an opinion on nuclear weaponry in late 1941, as relations with the United States neared the breaking point. Their approach tended to parallel that of the army. The navy's inquiries were directed by Captain Itō Yōji, who was affiliated with a subsection of the Navy Technology Research Institute. Initial advice was solicited from Sagane and another Tokyo professor, Hino Juichi, through Lieutenant Commander Sasaki Kiyoyasu. Both professors agreed on the necessity of investigating the problem, and this led eventually to the creation of a Committee on Research in the Application of Nuclear Physics (*Kakubutsuri Ōyō Kenkyū Iinkai*). The committee's investigations were subsidized by a modest grant of two thousand yen from the navy.[47]

THE COMMITTEE OF EXPERTS

The committee of experts, comprised of eleven prominent scientists under the chairmanship of Nishina, did not hold its first meeting until July 18, 1942, over half a year after the first serious contact between the navy and the scientific community. "Ten plus" meetings followed, ending on March 6, 1943. In 1953, Itō Yōji published the following summary of the committee's conclusions:

(a) Obviously it should be possible to make an atomic bomb.

(b) The question was whether or not the United States and England could really do this in time for this war, and whether or not Japan could do so ahead of them. The venerable Professor Nagaoka Hantarō studied this carefully. Dr. Nishina Yoshio also gave it serious consideration.

(c) It emerged that the basic mineral does not exist in Japan. There were some prospects in Korea but they had not been developed. Among the territories occupied by the Japanese, Burma was most hopeful.

I remember that Burma was old Dr. Nagaoka's idea. The professor explained that a heavy substance like uranium is likely to appear where there are wrinkles in the earth. Since earlier, the Army had already been pursuing this research in collaboration with Riken. The Navy had not the slightest intention of initiating a rival project, and only had in mind doing their own investigation and, based on the results, entering into collaboration with the Army. In the committee, problems concerning nuclear fission and the critical mass for a chain reaction were discussed, and the sending of a mineral investigation group to Burma was taken up.

(d) The general line of thought, however, led to the conclusion that it would probably be difficult even for the United States to realize the application of atomic power during the war.

These observations convinced the Navy Technology Research Institute that its resources were best concentrated elsewhere (notably in radar research), and it withdrew from the picture.[48] Subsequent navy interest in a nuclear weapon was to emanate from a different command and to be pursued by a different group of scientists.

NI PROJECT

Prior to the end of 1942, it remains unclear precisely what studies Nishina initiated in response to the separate inquiries of the army and navy. Several scientists prepared data for him, but apparently none on a serious full-time basis until the very end of the year. Around October, Nishina asked a young Riken researcher named Kigoshi Kunihiko if he would be interested in running experiments to produce uranium hexaflouride. As Kigoshi later recounted the story, Nishina's approach was extremely casual ("If you fuss around with that, you won't have to go to war"). Kigoshi accepted, was indeed excused from the draft, and essentially spent the next several months "wandering around" looking for potential uranium compounds in storehouses. At one point in February 1943, he even purchased one hundred 450-gram bottles of chemicals used in glazing ceramics with the hope that these might eventually lead to uranium. Until well into the summer of 1943, it was Kigoshi's impression that Nishina did not take the project seriously.[49]

In late December of 1942—the same month that Fermi created the first chain reaction in a uranium pile in the now-famous squash court at the University of Chicago—Nishina tapped another young researcher, Takeuchi Masa, to work on isotope separation. Takeuchi was no Japanese Fermi—and, indeed, no nuclear physicist. He was a specialist in cosmic rays, and he responded to Nishida's summons with much the same puzzled goodwill that Kigoshi did.[50]

Takeuchi discussed the general problems of isotope separation with Nishina and other scientists for several months. In mid March of 1943— almost immediately after the committee of experts conveyed its pessimistic conclusions—a basic experiment was initiated under Nishina at Riken and pursued until April 1945, when the single building housing it was destroyed in an air raid. All this was subsidized by the army and, from around May 1943, designated NI Project (*Ni-go Kenkyū*). Army research projects were often identified by symbols from the katakana syllabary, and in this instance it was generally understood that NI stood, conveniently, for Nishina.[51] NI Project—which was accompanied by a largely futile search for uranium in Japan, Korea, and the territories under Japanese military occupation—constituted Japan's major A-bomb research.

NI Project ran on a single, modest track: it was aimed at developing a method for isolating the rare and critical uranium-235 isotope, and it explored only one of the four possible methods of separation, thermal diffusion. The decision to pursue this method alone was reached by Nishina on March 17, 1943, and conveyed to the army two days later.[52] For technical and financial reasons, the Tokyo project excluded a priori any experimentation in the other three potential methods of isotope separation (electromagnetic, ultracentrifuge, and gaseous diffusion), and no attempts ever were made to create a uranium pile. Although actual production of U-235 by the thermal diffusion process would require construction of elaborate, multistage "cascade" plants, the Japanese never advanced to the point of seriously planning these. And, since NI Project never transcended the rudimentary technical problems of U-235 separation, the Japanese never got to the point of actually designing, let alone attempting to manufacture, a uranium bomb.

A personnel roster for the NI Project lists thirty-two individuals (twenty-five associated with Riken, six scientists from Osaka Imperial University, and one military coordinator).[53] This is misleading. Some of these persons appear to have contributed little to the project, while on the other hand it is possible to cite a number of scientists, technicians, and military officers not listed who had at least a partial and passing relationship with these activities. The more significant figures, however, are these: until March 1944, NI Project was entrusted primarily to Kigoshi and Takeuchi. In March 1944, they were joined by ten recent graduates in physics who were assigned to assist them by the army. These young scientists had joined Riken upon graduating, but were drafted soon thereafter; they were assigned to the NI Project after completing officer training. When the project was destroyed by bombs in early 1945, its full-time work force was less than fifteen persons—all young, none distinguished, and none a recognized expert in nuclear physics.[54]

Beginning in June 1943, NI Project was housed in "Building No. 49" in the Riken complex, a two-story wooden structure that had been built in 1942 to serve, in part, as a dining room. The total floor space was 330 square meters (roughly 3,000 square feet), with five rooms on each floor. On the first floor, Takeuchi—who was in his early thirties when Nishina recruited him in December 1942—devoted himself to designing and constructing an isotope separator. On the second floor, Kigoshi, in his mid twenties, ran a laborious series of experiments to produce uranium hexafluoride, which had a notorious reputation for devouring metal, glass, and human patience. This uncongenial compound was to be introduced into Takeuchi's separator, turned into a gaseous state, and heated with such precision that it began to surrender its precious U-235.

Kigoshi labored for well over a year before producing, in early 1944, what he described as a single lovely crystal of uranium hexafluoride the size of a grain of rice. Along the way, he nearly lost his eye in a laboratory experiment. Takeuchi completed his separator almost simultaneously, in March, and tested it with argon in mid May. The argon test was a failure, but it was decided to push on nonetheless and test Kigoshi's uranium compound, which by now was being produced in small quantities. For six months, beginning in July 1944, the small group in Building No. 49 ran Kigoshi's handiwork through Takeuchi's handiwork. In the interim, the Allied bombing of Japan began, and several vials of the precious product of the thermal diffusion run were lost in the process of being secured; they simply disappeared from a bomb-proof storage place. By February 1945, the group had a small amount of *something*, which they wished to analyze on a mass spectrometer, but they were unable to get access to such equipment. They used Riken's small cyclotron instead, which indicated that the experiment was a failure. U-235 had not been isolated. As Kigoshi later put it, the task was hopeless—but this came as no surprise to him or Takeuchi.[55]

On April 13, 1945, bombs fell on Tokyo, and part of the Riken complex was destroyed. Building No. 49 appeared to have survived the air raid, but hours later, in the darkness after midnight, it burst into flame.

Takeuchi's modest and as yet unsuccessful separator was destroyed. Even before this had occurred, Kigoshi had attempted to relocate his project in a presumedly safe high school building in nearby Yamagata prefecture, and plans had been broached to make use of separation devices at both Osaka Imperial University and a Sumitomo factory in Amagasaki. Kigoshi accomplished very little in rustication (much of his time in Yamagata was spent bartering with local farmers for food for himself and his family), and the proposed moves to Osaka and Amagasaki remained paper proposals. For all practical purposes, NI Project was dissolved in May 1945.[56]

THE SEARCH FOR URANIUM

While Takeuchi and Kigoshi and their ten draftees were running these discouraging experiments, the army and navy were combing the old and new empires for uranium-bearing ores and compounds. They were guided in their search by Iimori Satoyasu, an eminent Riken expert on rare elements who had studied under Frederick Soddy at Oxford from 1919 to 1922; Soddy had collaborated with Rutherford in the famous experiments on the atom in the early twentieth century.

The futile quest in the field complemented the abortive quest in the laboratories quite nicely. It was hoped that abundant and high-quality ore could be obtained from the Ishikawa mine in Fukushima prefecture, and 150 middle school students wearing straw sandals were mobilized to help explore this. But the Ishikawa deposits proved to be sparse and coarse. High expectations were placed in a mine near Seoul, but it turned out that the mine was closed, and that it would take around one thousand miners working every day for one year with rudimentary equipment to produce ten kilograms of refined uranium. An investigation team from Tokyo visited China and the southern theater. All with negligible results. Promises of several tons of uranium-bearing ore from Manchuria failed to materialize. Burma's wrinkles proved to be just wrinkles. Residues of tin ore containing monazite and zircon were located in Malaya, and around 1943 the Japanese prepared to ship this home; some 4,500 tons arrived before U.S. submarines began to decimate the transport ships. Black sand was sought in Korea, but most of what was discovered turned out to have a uranium content of less than one-tenth of one percent. In early 1945, plans were made to ship monazite from China to Japan, but the Chinese deposits were in areas where the anti-Japanese resistance was strong, and the war ended before much was accomplished here.[57]

In the midst of this ride on the mineralogical merry-go-round, the Japanese even pumped up the moribund Axis Pact and requested pitchblende from Germany (Marie Curie had used this in her experiments on radium, and the Germans had control of deposits in Czechoslovakia). Ambassador Ōshima Hiroshi reportedly succeeded in conveying the urgency of the request to the Nazi high command in late 1943, and Japan was promised two tons of the ore, to be sent by two submarines. Nothing ever arrived. Reportedly one submarine was sunk, and the other never left.[58] A more melodramatic abortive mission took place in May 1945, when a U-boat destined for Japan with a reported 560 kilograms of uranium oxide in its cargo surrendered to the United States in the Atlantic upon learning of Germany's surrender. With a fine if unwitting comic-opera touch, the submarine's identification number was U-234.[59] This essentially commercial transaction, incidently, seems to be the only point of contact between the Japanese and Germans involving, however peripherally, potential development of an atomic bomb. There appears to have been no contact whatsoever between the scientists of the two countries, and development of nuclear weaponry was never discussed at the official level. Here, as in so many other areas, it is obvious that the concept of a "front" or "camp," which does have meaning in the case of the Allied powers, merely distorts the realities of relations between the Japanese and German "Axis powers."

F PROJECT

Although the Navy Technology Research Institute bowed out of the picture following the discouraging report of the committee of experts in 1943, a different naval command, the Fleet Command, emerged as a sponsor of A-bomb research in the latter stages of the war—when there was, of course, virtually no navy left upon which to devote attention. This project centered upon a research team under Professor Arakatsu Bunsaku of Kyoto Imperial University, and bore the designation "F Project" (*F-go Kenkyū*), the "F" standing for "fission."[60]

In the recollections of Arakatsu's wartime colleagues, there is quite a bit of ambiguity concerning the actual date of origin of F Project, but the formal record (the navy's memorandum of October 10, 1945, to the United States) indicates that Arakatsu received naval funding for "research on the utilization of nuclear energy" beginning in May 1943. This seems entirely plausible, and the differing starting dates suggested by participants—which range from late 1942 to early 1945—merely reflect the rather casual beginnings and leisurely early pace of the Kyoto project. The first and last formal meeting between F Project scientists and their navy sponsors took place on July 21, 1945—over two years after the "official" start of the project, and twenty-five days before Japan's surrender.

There was no close collaboration between the navy and army projects, although some data was exchanged. The basic technical difference was that the Kyoto group decided to try to separate the U-235 isotope by the ultracentrifuge, rather than thermal diffusion, method (still relying, however, on uranium hexafluoride). It was calculated that a centrifuge capable of at least 150,000 revolutions per minute would be necessary. The speed of the existing machines in Japan was one-fourth or one-fifth of this, and consequently much of the activity of F Project was devoted to *designing* an ultracentrifuge. The design was completed in July 1945. The machine was never built.[61]

On paper, there were nineteen scientists in Arakatsu's team. In practice, there appear to have been five major contributors in addition to Arakatsu himself. Kobayashi Minoru, working under Yukawa, addressed theoretical problems, including the critical mass of U-235 necessary to produce a chain reaction. Kimura Kiichi and Shimizu Sakae, the associate professor and lecturer under Arakatsu, concentrated on the centrifuge design. Chemical problems, especially the handling of gaseous states, were entrusted to Sasaki Shinji. Okada Takuzō of the engineering department dealt with the production of metallic uranium, essential to any actual manufacture of a bomb.[62]

The concrete accomplishments of F Project consisted of several theoretical papers, plus success on the part of Okada in producing a stable sample of purely metallic uranium for the first time in Japan; it was about the size of a postage stamp, three centimeters on each side and one millimeter thick.[63]

The preceding summation derives largely from the retrospective accounts of Japanese participants, most of which were collected by an editorial team affiliated with the newspaper *Yomiuri* in the latter half of the 1960s. Although Nishina died in 1951, and left no known account, other major participants spoke freely and often at considerable length to the *Yomiuri*. They included Takeuchi, Kigoshi, Iimori, Taketani, and several of the "ten draftees" from NI Project; Arakatsu, Kimura, Shimizu, Kobayashi, and other participants in F Project; and a number of the former army and navy officers who acted as key liaison on the A-bomb research. These accounts are not always precise or consistent, and the familiar perils of relying upon reminiscence obviously apply here. There is, however, some corroborating material and also a pattern in the recollections which suggest several concluding observations.

First, the impetus to build a uranium bomb appears to have come from the military rather than from civilian scientists and engineers. Both the army and navy began to explore the possibility of military adaptation of nuclear energy on their own around 1940. The Army Aviation Technology Research Institute approached Riken in early 1941. The Navy Technology Research Institute requested a feasibility study in late 1941 or early 1942. The Navy Fleet Command took the initiative in urging Arakatsu to explore the possibilities of a uranium bomb, probably in mid 1943. According to Kawashima Toranosuke, a former army colonel who is hyperbolically described as the "General [Leslie] Groves" of the Japanese project in the *Yomiuri* publication, the creation of NI Project was strongly supported by Prime Minister Tōjō Hideki himself.[64] Several accounts also indicate that the emperor's brothers, Princes Mikasa and Takamatsu—shadowy uniformed figures in much of Japan's wartime activity—knew of the project and encouraged it, taking special interest in the search for uranium ore.[65]

Second, data concerning the projects can be played like a concertina, and when figures concerning personnel and subsidies are stretched to the limit, it may appear that Japan's commitment to developing an atomic bomb was fairly substantial. The total number of scientists on the formal rosters for NI Project and F Project comes to fifty. To this one can add the committee of experts which met in 1942–1943, plus other physicists and chemists who were consulted at one point or another. Takeuchi estimated that in the long course of building his thermal diffusion apparatus, he borrowed the services of probably thirty or forty engineers and technicians at Riken.[66] In addition, numerous military officers and industrialists became involved with aspects of the two projects.

The amount of money spent on Japan's wartime A-bomb research also may have been relatively large—although the sums suggested are unconfirmed and extremely difficult to place in perspective. According to Koyama Kenji, a key army figure at the time, a total of two million yen was allotted to NI Project, but one-quarter of this was not actually disbursed to Riken until immediately after Japan's surrender.[67] There are conflicting figures given concerning support of F Project. One version has it that upon being approached by the navy, Arakatsu requested an annual grant of three thousand yen, with which the navy readily complied. This is the type of small subsidy that would be granted for theoretical work rather than actual experimentation. Although F Project made little progress beyond theory, however, the October 1945 memorandum that the Japanese navy prepared for U.S. authorities indicates that the Kyoto group received a total of 600,000 yen in two installments between May 1943 and the surrender.[68] These figures are great or small depending upon the point of comparison. The round sum of 2.6 million yen, for example, is equivalent to one-quarter of the total research expenditures of the Japan Society for the Promotion of Scientific Research from 1942 to 1945. On the other hand, it amounts to less than one-half of one percent of the total army and navy research expenditures from 1942 to 1945.[69]

In the final analysis, however, it seems indisputable that the scale of Japan's wartime work on the uranium bomb was so small as to be virtually meaningless. The number of persons employed in this research full-time was never more than a few score. The Tokyo project, which involved a single preliminary isotope separation experiment, ended in failure. The Kyoto project never got to the experimental stage. In the end, Japan could show for its pains a few theoretical papers and a wafer of metallic uranium.

The haphazard organization of these projects, their leisurely pace, their negligible size, and their failure to effectively mobilize or coordinate available expertise lead to a third general observation, already suggested earlier: the project was of relatively low interest to the scientists themselves. It should be kept in mind that over one hundred physicists were associated with the Nishina Laboratory alone at the time of Pearl Harbor, but little interest was shown in applied nuclear energy—and virtually none in the bomb—until the military requested such studies. This was true also of the Kyoto Imperial University group, which included Yukawa and Sakata at this time and had long been engaged in advanced theoretical and experimental work on the atom. The Japanese record simply does not reproduce those British, German, and American scenes of scientists carrying the case for the bomb to the government.

On the contrary, there emerges in the Japanese case an almost antithetical impression: the best physicists and chemists indicated disinterest in working on the bomb—or, alternatively, approached the problem once assigned to it in a manner quite contrary to the military, namely, as *gakumon*, a purely scholarly exercise. This is a common word in the reminiscences of the participating scientists, and there seems no reason to doubt it, for its connotations are pragmatic rather than moral. It is difficult to cite a scientist who believed that Japan had a serious chance of actually manufacturing an atomic bomb. When pressed to a timetable, they rolled out decades as metaphors of impossibility: ten, twenty, fifty, one hundred years would be necessary before Japan, in its present state, could make a nuclear weapon. As a result, the Japanese never progressed to the stage of actually working seriously on the theory of the bomb itself, and were thereby spared hard questions of both a practical and moral nature.

This led to an often ambivalent and ambiguous situation. When the navy approached the Kyoto group, for example, they were told flatly that for reasons of research structure, industrial capacity, materials, and resources, Japan could not hope to have an atomic bomb during the present war. The navy's purported reply revealed a new appreciation of long-range planning: "If it's not ready for this war, then it can be ready for the next war." This was a catchy riposte, but it does not accurately convey the atmosphere in the research centers themselves. Kimura Kiichi, who recounted this comment in his account for the *Yomiuri*, for example, went on directly to suggest that Arakatsu and Nishina—like Kimura himself and his colleagues in F Project—regarded the bomb as a catchphrase that could be "borrowed" to keep nuclear physics going and young researchers alive. But at the same time, Kimura acknowledged, he felt guilt at being relatively safe on the homefront while his peers were giving their lives; and thus he gave himself to the bomb project with devotion and diligence.[70]

Nishina can be taken as an example of the complexity of this general question of motivation and imperatives. He was, to begin with, *ordered* to work on the bomb. But he was also, without question, a patriot, and it is easy to illustrate both his dismay at Japan's insane military quest and his commitment to help his country. Thus he gave rousing speeches to his staff, and told the army and navy to shape up. What is striking about NI Project, however, is that in concrete practice Nishina did not really do much at all. He did not promote the applied use of nuclear energy on his own. He did not respond at all quickly to army or navy importunement concerning a uranium bomb. And even after he had committed himself to the A-bomb project, he did not put the best men on it, and indeed left it all but unstaffed. Neither of his two major researchers, Takeuchi and Kigoshi, had outstanding credentials, and Takeuchi was not even a specialist in isotope separation. One of the most valuable basic documents on NI Project is a chronicle that Takeuchi assembled after the surrender, based on his diary and research notes. At one point he refers to himself as a "blank page" in the area of atomic energy, and at another point, at the very beginning of his assignment, he asks rhetorically why the order did not go to certain scientists actually engaged in research on the atom. "In the first place," he writes, in answer to his own question, "they all wanted to do their own work."[71]

Indeed, one of the most striking aspects of Japan's A-bomb research is that there never occurred anything remotely approaching a serious nationwide mobilization of talent. Experts came and went, and more often went than came. Even the two projects that were sponsored tended to remain cabined in their respective Tokyo or Kyoto-Osaka institutional bailiwicks, rarely communicating with each other and never even seriously tapping all the talent available to them locally. Takeuchi and Kigoshi did have access to the expertise available within the great complex of the Nishina Laboratory and the Institute for Research in the Physical and Chemical Sciences (Riken), as well as the outside academic community. They often took advantage of this, and also occasionally made use of outside facilities and equipment, but the effort was not really systematic. Advice from Riken colleagues frequently appears to have been solicited during lunch breaks, and assistance on critical basic problems was not always readily forthcoming. In his diary-memoir, for example, Takeuchi wrote that while he could undertake construction of an apparatus for thermal diffusion, fundamental theoretical calculations concerning "probability" and neutron behavior simply had to be done by others: "I strongly urged that this be given to the nuclear people, but the nuclear people apparently had no desire to do it, and this situation continued up to the end of the experiment [October 1944]." At one point, Takeuchi sought advice from Takeda Eiichi, a physicist at Osaka Imperial University, and then urged that Takeda be brought in as a member of NI Project. Neither Nishina nor Takeda, however, showed any interest in this proposal.[72]

There was a kind of casual desperation in these activities which suggests the larger tragicomedy of the enterprise as a whole. Takeuchi and Kigoshi were clearly on a doomed solo flight in Building No. 49. Kigoshi estimated that for want of expert advice on one aspect of his experiment he probably wasted a whole year in working out the preparation of uranium hexafluoride,[73] and there is no question that he and his colleague on the floor below also wasted an immense amount of time by being forced *personally* to scrounge for materials. Both men have left some memorable vignettes of their activities as scavengers, not least of which is Kigoshi's account of attempting to obtain *sugar* from the army for a heating experiment ("We would like to obtain an extra ration of sugar to build an atomic bomb"). When the military did not immediately come up with the sugar, Kigoshi resorted to pilfering from his own household ration, thereby incurring the wrath of his mother. When, in May 1944, he eventually obtained twenty kilograms of sugar from the army, he found himself suddenly a popular man at Riken, as colleagues ("large ants in clothes," Kigoshi called them) dropped by to ask for a tiny taste of the stuff, which by then was a rare and almost decadent treat.[74]

By late 1944 and early 1945, the absurdity of the situation had assumed a Kafkaesque quality. Kigoshi was producing small quantities of the noxious uranium hexaflouride on the second floor. Takeuchi's separation apparatus was running night and day downstairs without ever having proved it could separate anything important. The military officer-scientists were sleeping around the clock in the rickety building to observe the behavior of an invisible gas. On the way to the lunch room, Riken's exhausted researchers routinely kept their eyes peeled for edible grasses, to improve the soup; and after relocating his project in the high school building in Yamagata, Kigoshi spent part of his days cutting grass, which he then bartered for milk to make cheese for his family. By 1945, he recalled, he was so hungry that he could neither concentrate on his work nor hold a test tube steady. Meanwhile, Nagaoka, the grand old man of Japanese physics, was publicly denouncing A-bomb research as a waste of precious time and resources, while Taketani, the left-wing theorist, was working out complex formulas in a jailhouse interrogation room belonging to the Thought Police and belatedly proving that basic prior calculations were wrong. Geologists were combing the empire and tearing their hair. The navy was sunk; the air forces were replacing bombs with young men in one-way aircraft; the army was girding for a bamboo-spear defense of the homeland—and it was calculated that a serious A-bomb project would require one-tenth of the electricity and one-half of the critical military stock of copper in Japan.[75] There was very little uranium to work with anyway. The saturation firebombing of Japan's cities was commencing, in the name of peace and democracy.

And, contrary to what the scientists believed possible, nuclear destruction was about to be realized in Japan.

NOTES

1 Deborah Shapley, "Nuclear Weapons History: Japan's Wartime Bomb Projects Revealed," *Science* 199 (Jan. 13, 1978), pp. 152–57. Professor York, quoted in *Science*, repeated his views in a radio interview on "All Things Considered," National Public Radio (Washington, D.C.), on January 9.

Shapley, in her *Science* article, and the media conveyed the impression that the exposé of a Japanese A-bomb project was based on a study being prepared by York and Charles Weiner, a historian of science at MIT with particular expertise in the early history of nuclear weapons research and development. However, according to Weiner, there was no such study. Shapley based her story primarily on published Japanese-language materials Professor Weiner had received from Japanese colleagues in 1974, along with rough summaries and translations a non-Japanese graduate student had made of their contents. York learned of these materials and talked about them informally with Weiner on a single occasion in 1976. Shortly thereafter, Shapley contacted Weiner and proposed doing a brief "news note" in *Science*. Weiner told her he had done nothing with the Japanese materials, but it was clear that the Japanese project had never gotten off the ground; he also expressed concern that such a story could easily be distorted and sensationalized. He provided Shapley with copies of the raw materials with the understanding that these were for her personal interest.

Over a year later, on January 6, 1978, Shapley called Weiner to tell him she had done a story on the project and sent it to the *Times*, the *Post*, and NPR, along with his name. He was never asked about or shown the article itself, and when the journalists called he explicitly repudiated the anti-Japanese spin Shapley and the media obviously wished to put on the story. Weiner pointed out that he had not worked with York, that there was no research report, that the Japanese had made negligible progress on their A-bomb project, and that the project has been public knowledge in Japan for decades. The journalists virtually ignored these observations, although the *Post* (which began its page-one article with a paragraph stating, "Two historians of the Atomic Age have turned up the first evidence that Japan tried to develop an atomic bomb during World War II") did quote Weiner saying that the project did not go far. Neither the *Times* nor the *Post* published critical letters Weiner sent them after the misleading stories appeared.

I am indebted to Charles Weiner for providing me with this background information.

2 A comment by Professor Derek de Solla Price of Yale University which accompanied the *Science* article carries this undertone: "Japan's attempt to acquire an atomic weapon during World War II changes the moral and ethical relationship between Japan and the United States that has grown up over the use of the atomic bomb against Japan. The story has been that the Americans were guilty and the Japanese were innocent and blameless; that the Americans developed this terrible new weapon and proceeded to commit an atomic rape of the then-helpless Japanese. But the fact that the Japanese were trying to develop the bomb, too, means that America was in an arms race with Japan as much as she was with Germany." Professor Price's interest in the nationalistic and "moral" implications of a Japanese A-bomb project had been expressed many years previously in a letter written (with Eri Yagi Shizume) to the *Bulletin of the Atomic Scientists* 18, no. 9 (Nov. 1962), p. 29.

The specious argument that the United States had been involved in an arms race with Japan, or even believed there was a remote possibility of this being the case, was repudiated by no less an insider than Lieutenant General Leslie R. Groves, the U.S. military coordinator of the Manhattan Project. In his well-known memoirs, Groves wrote this:

> We did not make any appreciable effort during the war to secure information on atomic developments in Japan. First, and most important, there was not even the remotest possibility that Japan had enough uranium or uranium ore to produce the necessary materials for a nuclear weapon. Also the industrial effort that would be required far exceeded what Japan was capable of. Then, too, discussions with our atomic physicists at Berkeley, who knew the leading Japanese atomic physicists personally, led us to the conclusion that their qualified people were altogether too few in number for them to produce an effective weapon in the foreseeable future. Finally, it would have been extremely difficult for us to secure and to get out of Japan any information of the type we needed. I hoped that if any sizable program was started, we would get wind of it from one of the various intelligence-collecting agencies with which we maintained liaison. In that event, we would have immediately done everything we could to interfere with their operations.

See *Now It Can Be Told: The Story of the Manhattan Project* (New York: Harper, 1962), p. 187.

The 1978 account in the *Times*, which begins "Documents have come to light ...," reinforces the notion of a Japanese conspiracy of silence, although in a confusing manner. After mentioning Japanese sources on the subject dated 1970 and 1973, the article notes elsewhere: "The American scholars currently studying the period suggest that a conspiracy of silence on the part of Japanese atomic physicists had been so effective that the truth had come close to being obscured forever. But accounts in the last two years [*sic*] by various Japanese scientists have disclosed some information about the project." As indicated in the preceding note, American scholars (presumably York and Weiner) had merely obtained materials previously published in Japanese, and Weiner explicitly had rejected this interpretation when journalists from the *Times* and the *Post* contacted him. Moreover, as will be seen, public Japanese mention of the project actually became common from the 1950s.

The original version of the present essay was written in response to these misrepresentations in *Science* and the press and published in the *Bulletin of Concerned Asian Scholars* 10, no. 2 (April–June 1978), pp. 41–54. For a lengthy journalistic presentation, see also John W. Dower, "Japan's Atomic Weapons Research," in the English-language *Daily Yomiuri*, August 11, 1978. The Japanese-language *Yomiuri Shimbun* carried an abridged version of the latter essay with complementary materials, also on August 11.

Science published letters responding to its original article in its issues of February 17, March 24, April 21, and May 5, 1978. A brief summary of the ensuing debate is given in Phillip S. Hughes, "Wartime Fission Research in Japan," *Social Studies of Science* 10 (Aug. 1980), pp. 345–49. Professor Weiner's criticism of the misuse of the Japanese data appears in a letter to *Science* on February 17 and in "Retroactive Saber Rattling?" *Bulletin of the Atomic Scientists* 34 (April 1978), pp. 10–12. Although the *New York Times* and *Washington Post* did not publish Weiner's letter of protest, other papers that picked up the story from them (the *Los Angeles Times*, *Boston Globe*, and *Miami Herald*) also were sent copies of the letter by Weiner and did print it.

The major extended response to the article in *Science* was a rambling popular book by journalist Robert K. Wilcox, with an apocalyptic introduction by Derek de Solla Price and a predictable conspiracy–theory title: *Japan's Secret War: Japan's Race against Time to Build Its Own Atomic Bomb* (New York: Morrow, 1985). Professor Price went so far as to declare that, "Now I, for one, cannot escape the possibility that the atomic bombing of California (with the bombs delivered by kamikaze pocket submarines) might have been an actuality if the war had continued and Truman had not made the decision to end it all with the American bombs" (p. 8). He also used Wilcox's speculations concerning possible Japanese A-bomb related activities in northern Korea to venture the further speculation that this may have contributed to the postwar Soviet development of nuclear weapons (p. 9). My critical appraisal of the Wilcox book appears in a review in *Bulletin of the Atomic Scientists* 43, no. 1 (Aug.–Sep. 1986), pp. 61–62.

3 Chitoshi Yanaga, *Japan Since Perry* (first ed., Hightstown, N.J.: McGraw Hill, 1949), p. 618.

4 Arnold Kramish, *Atomic Energy in the Soviet Union* (Stanford, Calif.: Stanford University Press, 1959), p. 56.

5 In 1959, Yanaga's reference was incorporated in the adapted translation of a popular Japanese military history: Saburō Hayashi (in collaboration

with Alvin D. Coox), *Kōgun, the Japanese Army in the Pacific War* (Quantico, Va.: Marine Corps Association, 1959), pp. 162, 216. The original Japanese version of Hayashi's study, published while Japan was still under occupation, had noted that "the Army high command was interested in the military adaptation of uranium, and research was being pursued. They accepted at face value, however, the opinion of the nuclear scientists, *viz.*, that 'No country whatsoever will be able to perfect an atomic bomb during World War Two' " (*Taiheiyō Sensō Rikusen Gaishi* [1951: Iwanami Shinsho 59], pp. 261–62).

Passing mention of wartime research on the bomb in Tokyo appears in John Toland, *The Rising Sun: The Decline and Fall of the Japanese Empire, 1936–1945* (New York: Random House, 1970), p. 795. Fairly frequent mention of an aspect of these activities is made in Thomas M. Coffy, *Imperial Tragedy* (New York: World Publishing, 1970); see the index citations under Nishina Yoshio. An article in the August 12, 1977, issue of *New Statesman* referred to the Kyoto side of Japan's wartime work on the A-bomb as if this were common knowledge (p. 199).

6 Chikayoshi Kamatani, "The History of Research Organization in Japan," *Japanese Studies in the History of Science* 2 (1963), p. 63; Tetu Hirosige, "Social Conditions for the Researches of Nuclear Physics in Pre-War Japan," ibid., pp. 87–88. Hirosige's article was reprinted in Shigeru Nakayama, David L. Swain, and Eri Yagi, eds., *Science and Society in Modern Japan, Selected Historical Sources* (Cambridge, Mass.: MIT Press, 1974; originally Tokyo University Press). In a 1965 article, also in English, Hirosige again referred in passing to the fact that Japanese "nuclear physicists began the study of the atomic bomb" around 1943: "The Role of the Government in the Development of Science," *Cahiers d'histoire mondiale* 9, no. 2 (1965: special issue on "Society, Science and Technology in Japan"), p. 335.

7 The Pacific War Research Society, *The Day Man Lost: Hiroshima, 6 August 1945* (Tokyo: Kodansha International, 1972); see especially the data within pp. 18–49, and also pp. 93–94, 126–27, 183–84, 201–202, 293. The original Japanese version of this popular account was published in 1968.

8 Suzuki Bunshirō, "Nishina Yoshio Hakushi to Kataru" [A Conversation with Dr. Nishina Yoshio], *Kingu*, 1950 New Year special issue (Dec. 1949), pp. 134–43, esp. p. 138. For this and several other articles cited below, I am indebted to Kurauchi Hitoshi of TV Man Union, who assembled them in preparing a television documentary on Nishina.

9 Yukawa Hideki, Sakata Shōichi, and Taketani Mitsuo, *Shinri no Ba ni Tachite* [Standing on the Place of Truth] (Tokyo: Mainichi Shimbunsha, 1951), pp. 222–27.

10 Committee for the Compilation of Materials on Damage Caused by the Atomic Bombs in Hiroshima and Nagasaki, *Hiroshima and Nagasaki: The Physical, Medical, and Social Effects of the Atomic Bombings* (New York: Basic Books, 1981), pp. 5, 503–13, 564, 585.

11 Yamashita Nobuo, "Ma ni Awanakatta Nihon no Genbaku" [Japan's Uncompleted Atomic Bomb], *Kaizō*, November 1952, pp. 162–65.

12 Itō Yōji, *Himitsu Heiki no Zembō: Waga Gunji Kagaku Gijutsu no Shinsō to Hansei* [The Full Story of Secret Armaments: Reflections and Truth Concerning Our Military Science and Technology] (Tokyo: Koyosha, 1953). Itō's account is excerpted in *Shōwashi no Tennō* (note 15, below), vol. 4, pp. 177–82, and contains some of the data "revealed" in *Science*.

13 Yamamoto Yōichi, "Nihon Genbaku no Shinsō" [The Truth About Japan's Atomic Bomb], *Daihōrin*, August 1953, pp. 6–40.

14 *Shukan Bunshun*, August 10, 1959, pp. 11–19.

15 Yomiuri Shimbunsha, ed., *Shōwashi no Tennō* [The Emperor and Shōwa History] (Tokyo: Yomiuri Shimbunsha, 1968), vol. 4, pp. 78–229 (hereafter referred to as *SST*). Much of the account in *The Day Man Lost*, which is poorly annotated, derives from this volume.

16 Nihon Kagakushi Gakkai, ed., *Nihon Kagaku Gijutsushi Taikei* [Outline of the History of Japanese Science and Technology] (Tokyo: Daiichi Hogen, 1970), vol. 13, pp. 441–47 (hereafter referred to as *NKGT*). This volume, with its "documents," accounts for three of the four major sources mentioned in *Science*. The fourth is a 1973 "social history of science" by Hirosige Tetu, which has not been consulted here, but which apparently represents the book form of a series of articles published by Hirosige in *Shizen*, where Japan's bomb project was discussed in the March 1972 issue (pp. 97–98). I am grateful to Professor Edward Daub for identifying these sources.

17 Kigoshi Kunihiko, "Nihon no Genbaku Seizō Jikken Zasetsu Nōto" [A Note on the Breakdown of Japan's Experiments to Make an Atomic Bomb], *Hōseki*, September 1975, pp. 162–73.

18 Tamaki Hidehiko and Iwaki Masao, *Nishina Yoshio* (Tokyo: Kobudosha, 1976).

19 Some of the reports pertaining to Japan's wartime A-bomb research that were supposed to have been destroyed surfaced in the hands of a Japanese scientist on the faculty of the University of Arkansas in 1983. To judge

from journalistic accounts, these materials add little to the information already available by this date; see "Genbaku Kaihatsu no Uchimaku Namanamashiku" [Vivid Inside Account of Developing an Atomic Bomb], *Yomiuri Shimbun*, August 13, 1983.

20 See note 1, above.

21 *NKGT*, pp. 468–69; *SST*, pp. 172–74. Postsurrender Japanese reports on "wartime research" which were submitted to U.S. Occupation authorities are collected under the papers of the Scientific and Special Projects Group (formerly Scientific and Technical Division) of the Economic and Scientific Section (ESS) of the Supreme Commander for the Allied Powers (SCAP) in the National Archives in Suitland, Maryland. See especially materials in Record Group 331, Boxes 7416 and 7431.

The immediate U.S. concern with Japan's nuclear potential became an international cause célèbre in late November 1945 when U.S. Occupation authorities, acting on instructions from the War Department, seized and destroyed the five existing cyclotrons in Japan, causing heartbreak among Japanese researchers, outrage within the international scientific community, and of course a major setback to the pursuit of peaceful nuclear research in postsurrender Japan. This followed a swift succession of acts undertaken by U.S. authorities to control nuclear research in occupied Japan. A directive (SCAPIN 47) of September 22, 1945, prohibited all research "which has as its object effecting mass separation of Uranium-235 from Uranium, or effecting mass-separation of any other radio-actively unstable elements." An order from Washington dated October 30, 1945, reaffirmed this ban, and ordered all persons engaged in such research to be taken into custody and all atomic energy research facilities to be seized; the scientists were not released from custody until mid December. A "Scientific Intelligence Survey in Japan," which completed its report on November 1, apparently concluded that "the Japanese had made little progress on the release of atomic energy up to the time of the Surrender"—but in the furor that arose upon destruction of the cyclotrons, the U.S. War Department intimated that its actions had been based upon certain, unspecified, intelligence findings. The issue requires further research; as will be seen, the cyclotrons played almost no part in the A-bomb-related work which the Japanese did undertake during the war. Some general comments appear in Supreme Commander for the Allied Powers (Japan), General Headquarters, Statistics and Reports Section, *History of the Non-Military Activities of the Occupation of Japan* (1952): monograph 54, "Reorganization of Science and Technology in Japan,

1945 – September 1950" (available on microfilm from the National Archives), pp. 1–5, and p. 1 of the Appendix. See also Y. Nishina, "A Japanese Scientist Describes the Destruction of His Cyclotrons," *Bulletin of the Atomic Scientists* 3, no. 6 (June 1947), pp. 145, 167; Groves, *Now It Can Be Told*, pp. 367–72; Charles Weiner, "Cyclotrons and Internationalism: Japan, Denmark and the United States, 1935–1945, "*Proceedings of the XIVth International Congress of the History of Science* (Tokyo, 1975), pp. 353–65, esp. 360–61; Weiner, "Retroactive Saber Rattling?" (note 2, above). The ongoing U.S. investigation and control of Japanese nuclear-related activity was systematically reported in the top-secret "SWNCC 52 Series," conducted by the State-War-Navy Coordinating Committee and titled "Control and Surveillance of Atomic Nuclear Energy Research and Development in Japan."

The most notorious U.S. cover-up of Japanese wartime experiments involved the use of POWs in lethal medical experiments, especially by the top-secret "Unit 731" based in Harbin. This atrocity was covered up by U.S. authorities in exchange for full debriefing by the Japanese scientists involved. See John W. Powell, "Japan's Germ Warfare: The U.S. Cover-Up of a War Crime," *Bulletin of Concerned Asian Scholars* 12, no. 4 (Oct.–Dec. 1980), pp. 2–17; Powell's "Japan's Biological Weapons, 1930–1945: A Hidden Chapter in History," *Bulletin of the Atomic Scientists*, October 1981, pp. 43–53; and Peter Williams and David Wallace, *Unit 731: Japan's Secret Biological Warfare in World War II* (New York: Free Press, 1989). The Soviet Union tried certain lesser members of Unit 731 after the war, and published the "Khabarovsk trial" proceedings in English: *Materials on the Trial of Former Servicemen of the Japanese Army Charged with Manufacturing and Employing Bacteriological Weapons* (Moscow: Foreign Languages Publishing House, 1950).

22 See Kamatani, "History of Research Organizations," and Hirosige, "Social Conditions." Japanese historians of science, many of whom work within a rather neo-Marxist framework, are acutely sensitive to the relationship between development of scientific research and the stage of economic growth and military demand. Thus the relative backwardness of the Japanese research structure vis-à-vis the West prior to World War II is placed firmly in the context of the comparative underdevelopment of Japanese capitalism. Among other considerations, this backwardness and comparative disadvantage led the Japanese to attempt to remain competitive by relying upon cheap wages and *borrowed technology*, rather than development of original technology through costly research investment.

23 Yamamoto, "Nihon Genbaku no Shinsō," pp. 19–20, cites interesting postsurrender commentary to this effect from a June 1948 discussion in the science journal *Shizen* [Nature] and a 1951 questionnaire circulated among scientific researchers.

24 See *SST*, pp. 103–4, 171, 189–90, 219; also Kigoshi, " 'Nihon no Genbaku,' " pp. 164–65.

25 The theme of fundamental pessimism concerning the prospect of making an atomic weapon before the current war had ended is almost universal in Japanese recollections. See, for example, the interview with Nishina in *Kingu* (note 8, above); Yukawa et al., *Shinri no Ba ni Tachite*, pp. 222, 224; Yamamoto, "Nihon Genbaku no Shinsō," pp. 23, 33; *Shukan Bunshun*, August 10, 1959; Kigoshi, " 'Nihon no Genbaku,' " pp. 167–68, 171; and the reminiscence of another insider, former Imperial Army officer Suzuki Tatsusaburō, "Nihon Genbaku Keikaku" [Project for a Japanese Atomic Bomb], in Tokyo Channel 12, ed., *Shinpen—Watakushi no Shōwa Shi* [My Shōwa History—Supplementary Edition] (Tokyo: Tokyo Channel 12, 1973), pp. 113–24. Suzuki's reminiscence comes from a television presentation broadcast in July 1972.

26 Thus the famous Smyth Report, which was completed in July 1945, noted that "most of us are certain that the Japanese cannot develop and use this weapon effectively"; Henry DeWolf Smyth, *Atomic Energy for Military Purposes: The Official Report on the Development of the Atomic Bomb under the Auspices of the United States Government, 1940–1945* (Princeton, N.J.: Princeton University Press, 1947), p. 224. See also Arthur Holly Compton, *Atomic Quest: A Personal Narrative* (London: Oxford University Press, 1956), p. 225; and General Groves's observations in note 2, above.

27 See Nakayama et al., *Science and Society*, especially the articles by Taketani Mitsuo, Itakura Kiyonobu and Yagi Eri, Hirosige Tetu, and Kaneseki Yoshinori.

28 *SST*, pp. 88–89.

29 See *NKGT*, p. 443; also Kamatani, "History of Research Organizations," p. 56.

30 Nakayama et al., *Science and Society*, pp. 25–26.

31 Ibid., p. 213.

32 "Methodological Approaches in the Development of the Meson Theory of Yukawa in Japan," in Nakayama et al., *Science and Society*, pp. 24–38; this originally appeared in Japanese in 1951.

33 Tetu Hirosige, "Studies of History of Physics in Japan," *Japanese Studies in the History of Science* 1 (1962), p. 28.

34 *SST*, pp. 163–71. The *Tokkō* operated under the Home Ministry. The

army, which was sponsoring the bomb research and had its own police arm (the *Kempeitai*), apparently was not concerned by Taketani's leftist associations.

35 Cf. Kamatani, "History of Research Organizations," esp. pp. 48–57.

36 Cited in Yamamoto, "Nihon Genbaku no Shinsō," p. 23. The military journal was *Gunji to Gijutsu* [Military Affairs and Technology]. This suggests that the wartime engagement in nuclear weapons research was an open secret, an impression reinforced by the casual manner in which researchers such as Takeuchi and Kigoshi solicited advice from other scientists.

37 *NKGT*, p. 442; *Yomiuri Shimbun*, August 13, 1983. In the *Science* version, "Nishina managed to keep the Riken atomic research going by suggesting that the research sponsorship be unified"—but the article itself goes on to note that no unification of sponsorship ever occurred.

38 David Irving, *The German Atomic Bomb: The History of Nuclear Research in Nazi Germany* (New York: Simon and Schuster, 1967), p. 33. Hahn's moral distress can be seen in the recently declassified transcripts of the response of German nuclear scientists interned by the British to the news of Hiroshima; see Jeremy Bernstein, "The Farm Hall Transcripts: The German Scientists and the Bomb," *New York Review of Books*, Aug. 13, 1992, pp. 47–53.

39 *NKGT*, pp. 441–42.

40 Yamashita, "Ma ni Awanakatta Nihon no Genbaku," p. 162–63. The magazine was *Shin Seinen* [New Youth], and the story dealt with an atomic bomb utilizing uranium-235.

41 The quotation is from Kramish, *Atomic Energy in the Soviet Union*, p. 51. For general commentaries on the German project see Irving, *The German Atomic Bomb*; Bernstein, "The Farm Hall Transcripts"; Thomas Powers, *Heisenberg's War: The Secret History of the German Bomb* (New York: Knopf, 1993); and Rudolf Peierls's review of Powers, titled "The Bomb That Never Was," in *New York Review of Books*, April 22, 1993, pp. 6–9.

42 The Perseus story is reported in the *Washington Post National Weekly* of October 12–18, 1992 (pp. 10–11), and quotes a KGB officer maintaining that this unidentified American agent's motives were purely ideological, being based on the belief that the United States intended to use the bomb not against Germany but against the Soviet Union. He quoted Perseus as saying that "America will destroy socialism by means of the uranium bomb." The earlier Western understanding of the Soviet project is described in Kramish, *Atomic Energy in the Soviet Union*, chs. 1–8.

43 Margaret Gowing, *Britain and Atomic Energy, 1939–1945* (New York: Macmillan, 1964), part I. The quoted passage appears on p. 85.

44 The standard account is Richard G. Hewlett and Oscar E. Anderson, Jr., *The New World, 1939/1946*, vol. 1 of *A History of the United States Atomic Energy Commission* (Pennsylvania State University Press, 1962).

45 The discussion that follows derives primarily from *SST*, the most detailed single source, and *NKGT*. *The Day Man Lost* also reproduces much of the information in *SST*. The 1978 *Science* article relied primarily on selectively culled data from *NKGT*, while ignoring *SST* (although an excerpt from *SST* appears in *NKGT*), and contained a number of errors including incorrect dates, misplaced attributions, and mistranslations.

46 *SST*, pp. 78–81 (account of Suzuki Tatsusaburō). In another version, Nishina was commissioned to study the problem by the army around September 1940; *Shizen*, March 1972, p. 97.

47 *SST*, pp. 177–80 (account of Itō Yōji). The members of the committee were Nagaoka Hantarō and Nishina Yoshio from Riken; Ishikawa Masaharu, Sagane Ryōkichi, Hino Juichi, and Mizushima Sanichirō from Tokyo Imperial University; Asada Tsunesaburō and Kikuchi Masashi from Osaka Imperial University; Watanabe Satoshi and Nishina Tamotsu from Tohoku Imperial University; and Tanaka Masamichi from Tokyo Shibaura Electric Company.

Here, as on many points, there is some ambiguity on dates. Coffey (*Imperial Tragedy*, pp. 333–38), apparently relying on an interview with Asada Tsunesaburō, states that the decision to form the committee was made in a very formal setting on December 17, 1941, in a meeting attended by over a dozen high-ranking naval officers and at least five members of the subsequent committee of experts (Asada, Sagane, Watanabe, Kikuchi, and Nishina). Coffey depicts Nishina as a scientist long interested in the military application of science, and even has him suggesting that the navy might obtain uranium from Africa. He gives the navy title for the study ordered at this time as "Project A." *The Day Man Lost* has it as "B-research" (p. 26).

48 *SST*, pp. 180–81.

49 Kigoshi, " 'Nihon no Genbaku,' " pp. 164–68.

50 *NKGT*, pp. 442, 445; *SST*, pp. 86–88 (account of Takeuchi Masa). *Science* unaccountably gives the key date as December 1940 instead of December 1942.

51 *NKGT*, p. 442; *SST*, p. 85.

52 *NKGT*, pp. 446–47; *SST*, pp. 92–93. *Science* interprets the decision of

March 19, 1943, as evidence of Nishina's vision of, and hope for, a large-scale project. This interpretation was facilitated by a mistranslation of the phrase "several hundred kilograms" as "several hundred tons" (the ideographs are similar)—in reference, presumably, to the amount of uranium the Japanese might hope to process once preliminary thermal diffusion experiments had been completed. It also rested on one of Nishina's cryptic notations to the effect that "whether the explosion will be successful or not will be determined by experiments parallel to and separate from thermal diffusion." This was, of course, an official army project to build an atomic bomb, and one would indeed expect Nishina to talk in terms of ideal postpreliminary objectives. As the Japanese accounts make clear, however, the practical meaning of the March decision was restrictive, and there were no significant parallel experiments. As will be seen, Nishina in practice appears to have been content to keep NI Project on a minuscule scale.

53 *NKGT*, p. 465.

54 There were actually eleven officer-scientists assigned to the project in March 1944. Five assisted Takeuchi, five worked with Kigoshi, and one was assigned to assist Professor Iimori Satoyasu, noted below in connection with the search for uranium; *SST*, pp. 99–101. One of the draftees assigned to work with Kigoshi at this time, Ishiwatari Takehiko, actually had been involved in the uranium project before being drafted.

55 *SST*, pp. 101–37; this includes both Takeuchi's and Kigoshi's accounts of the experiments. A close technical summation is given in Takeuchi's diary-memoir in *NKGT*, pp. 444–64. See also Kigoshi, " 'Nihon no Genbaku,' " p. 171.

56 *SST*, pp. 156–64; Kigoshi, " 'Nihon no Genbaku,' " pp. 172–73.

57 *SST*, pp. 141–56. The middle school students mobilized to work at the Ishikawa mine are mentioned in Yamamoto, "Genbaku no Shinsō," pp. 26–31. A precise estimate of uranium compounds exported to Japan remains impossible, although U.S. military authorities looked into this carefully after Japan's surrender. One intelligence report refers to an unspecified number of fifty-kilogram boxes of "uranium ore" being shipped to Tokyo from Manchuria; Edwin W. Pauley, *Report on Japanese Assets in Manchuria to the President of the United States* (July 1946), p. 152. Another report calculates that some 250–300 pounds of uranium oxide were exported through the navy to Professor Arakatsu Bunsaku at Kyoto Imperial University; SWNCC 52/17 (June 3, 1946), p. 57, in box 120, Record Group 218, National Archives. Yet another U.S. military report indicates that as of August 1946, 3,400 pounds of "uranium compounds"

and 15,200 pounds of "thorium compounds" had been located in Japan, along with over 5,100 tons of "thorium and uranium-bearing ores" (consisting primarily of black sand from Korea); JCS 1380/33 (August 14, 1946), p. 240, in box 121, Record Group 218, National Archives.

58 *SST*, pp. 146–48.

59 Wilcox, *Japan's Secret War*, pp. 102–4, 141–44, 155–60.

60 *SST*, p. 221. An alternative and improbable interpretation associates "F" with the fluoride in the critical uranium hexafluoride compound; *SST*, p. 204.

61 *SST*, p. 183–205. Only four Kyoto scientists attended the July 21, 1945, meeting: Arakatsu, Yukawa, Kobayashi Minoru, and Sasaki Shinji. Yukawa gave a report surveying "International Research on Nuclear Power," based on information from neutral countries, in which he reiterated the belief that no nation was capable of harnessing the atom to military uses in the immediate future.

62 *NKGT*, p. 468; *SST*, p. 191.

63 *SST*, pp. 191, 201, 203, 228; *NKGT*, p. 468.

64 *SST*, pp. 84, 142, 145.

65 *SST*, p. 155; Yamamoto, "Nihon Genbaku no Shinsō," pp. 18–19. The role of the princes was also picked up by *Science*, which identified them as "sons" of the emperor.

66 *SST*, p. 120.

67 Ibid., p. 206.

68 Ibid., pp. 182, 173; *NKGT*, p. 469.

69 For 1942–1945, research expenditures were approximately as follows:

Japan Society for the Promotion of Scientific Research	¥ 10,417,000
Ministry of Education	46,550,000
Agency of Science and Technology	70,027,000
Army	462,166,000
Navy	281,516,000

See Kamatani, "History of Research Organizations," pp. 58–61; *Shizen*, March 1972, pp. 97–99. Suzuki Tatsusaburō, who coordinated the army's initial feasibility study, estimated that all told Japan spent around ten million yen on the bomb, half of which went to the search for uranium-bearing ores; *Shinpen—Watakushi no Shōwashi*, pp. 122–23. The highest available estimate—twenty million yen—comes from Yamamoto Yōichi and, like a number of Yamamoto statements, does not appear to be reliable; "Nihon Genbaku no Shinsō," p. 16.

Precise comparison to U.S. expenditures is impossible, but a general monetary sense of the vastly different orders of magnitude of the Japanese and U.S. projects can be suggested. If one takes the very rough estimate of one wartime U.S. dollar being equivalent to four yen, the Japanese expenditure of 2.6 million yen amounts to $650,000. The $2 billion expended on the Manhattan Project amounts to over three thousand times that.

70 *SST*, pp. 190–91; *NKGT*, p. 468. *Science* uses the quote in this manner: "So it seems that the scientists viewed the project as extremely long term at best, or, as one of them would later write, 'if not for this war then in time for the next one.' " As noted, the scientist who said this was derisively quoting a navy officer's comment uttered during the war.

71 *NKGT*, p. 445.

72 Ibid., p. 447.

73 *SST*, pp. 107–108.

74 Ibid., pp. 97–99, 114; Kigoshi, " 'Nihon no Genbaku,' " pp. 169–70.

75 *NKGT*, p. 442; *SST*, pp. 122, 208.

4

Sensational Rumors, Seditious Graffiti, and the Nightmares of the Thought Police

DURING WORLD WAR II, there flourished within Japan, and among Japan's Allied enemies as well, a mystique about the "Yamato spirit." Unlike the purportedly discursive West, it was said, the Japanese possessed intuitive ways of understanding one another: they did not depend much on words. They were, in addition, unusually harmonious as a race, culture, and society. And they fought to the bitter end.

In fact, throughout the war years Japanese ideologues, publicists, and so-called men of culture almost fell over one another coining phrases, propounding slogans, telling their countryfolk what to think. For months on end after Pearl Harbor, to give but one example, one popular magazine managed to run a different patriotic slogan in the margin of every page of every issue.[1] A collection of the official and semiofficial slogans of wartime Japan would fill an entire book—and, indeed, has done so.[2] Although the Allies also had their patriotic rhetoric, they managed to march to war without the same incessant drumbeat of slogans and catchphrases.[3]

Part of the cleverness of this Japanese wordiness was that it projected the image of a community of intuitive Shintōists, nondiscursive Zenists—and, most important, inherently sincere patriots and emperor worshipers. The overriding impression of harmony and homogeneity was captured in a single resonant phrase: *ichioku*, "the hundred million." This was a literal exaggeration (Japan's population at war's end was around seventy million), but it evoked a powerful sense of common purpose grounded in racial and cultural solidarity. "One hundred million hearts beating as one." "The hundred million as a flaming jewel." "The hundred million as one family."

And also: "The hundred million as a shattered jewel" (*ichioku gyokusai*). This particular suicidal slogan was coined by the Imperial government in the last stage of the war, as Allied forces closed in on the homeland, but it tapped a rhetoric of collective self-sacrifice which ideologues had emphasized all along. *Gyokusai* (the shattered jewel) was a classical phrase, as were many other death-inviting war slogans. The most common version of "fight to the bitter end," for example, was *uchiteshi yamamu*, also exhumed from an ancient text. In a similar manner, Japan's most evocative martial song, *Umi Yukaba* (Across the Ocean) took its lyrics from lines written by the great eighth-century poet Ōtomo Yakamochi and preserved in the *Manyoshū*, the earliest and greatest of all Japanese anthologies:

> Across the ocean, corpses soaking in the water;
> Across the mountains, corpses covered by the grass.
> We shall die by the side of our lord.
> We will never look back.

This was adroit propaganda, for it evoked an idealized premodern past in a manner conducive to contemporary national mobilization: the archaic ring of such slogans and lyrics conveyed the impression that collective self-sacrifice was a deep and abiding Japanese tradition. This was untrue, for the old language reflected ideals that pertained to a small warrior elite and had been honored more often in the breach than in actual practice. Like all good propagandists, however, the Japanese ideologues hoped that constant reiteration of the warrior ideals of loyalty and self-sacrifice would help make those ideals come true.[4]

To some degree, this happened. Japanese soldiers and sailors fought tenaciously and astonished the world with their ethic of no-surrender.[5]

When, beginning in October 1944, the desperate Imperial forces adopted *kamikaze* suicide tactics as a formal policy, it appeared that this was indeed a people prepared to fight to the bitter end. Only a handful of Western intelligence specialists, led by individuals in the Foreign Morale Analysis Branch of the U.S. Office of War Information, argued that this was not so. By 1945, these analysts concluded, Japanese morale was cracking badly and the country was beset by serious internal tensions.[6]

The secret Japanese war record confirms this impression of seriously deteriorating morale. Indeed, contrary to the public rhetoric of one hundred million hearts beating as one, police records from as early as 1942 convey a picture not merely of demoralization and mounting defeatism, but of growing contempt for existing authority extending even to the emperor himself. In the view of the Home Ministry's notorious Thought Police (*Tokkōtai*, literally Special Higher Police), as defeat drew closer and closer, Japan faced impending chaos and possibly even revolutionary upheaval.

Police state minions thrive on exaggeration, but the dire vision of Imperial Japan teetering on the verge of revolution also was entertained by many conservative Japanese critics of the militarist regime. In these circles, the apocalyptic thesis received its consummate expression in the now famous "Konoe Memorial" of February 1945, in which Prince Konoe Fumimaro, who had served as prime minister between 1937 and 1941, personally urged the emperor to effect a surrender quickly in order to save Japan "from a communist revolution." Konoe's alarming memorial was neither impetuous nor brief. It reflected gossip and intelligence that the prince had collected over the course of several years from his sprawling web of personal and professional contacts. And it spelled out in detail for the emperor the precise manner in which Japan seemed ripe for revolutionary transformation.[7]

In the view of Konoe and his circle, as well as that of the Thought Police, Japan was threatened by revolutionary upheaval from three directions: outside, above, and below. The first, external, threat emanated from the international communist movement, which had reached into Japan soon after the Bolshevik revolution of 1917, and which, in the current chaos of war, appeared to be growing by leaps and bounds in Asia (witness China) and in Europe. As prime minister, Konoe himself had delivered the "New Order" speech of November 1938, in which

Japanese aggression against China was justified as being essential to protect Japan against the dual menace of white imperialism and Red bolshevism in Asia. By 1944, the prince and many other Japanese had concluded that communism now posed a far greater danger to Japan than capitulating to the Americans. Doyens of the old guard—former prime ministers, for example, and members of the House of Peers— were treated to alarmist lectures on "world communism."[8] Shortly before the surrender, the emperor himself attended intelligence briefings warning of the Soviet threat to Japan.[9]

That there existed in Japan a fifth column ready to embrace the Soviets was brought home to the ruling groups on the eve of Pearl Harbor, with the sensational exposure of a Soviet spy ring headed by Richard Sorge. More shocking than the uncovering of Sorge himself was the revelation that his key Japanese contact was Ozaki Hotsumi, a respected journalist and China specialist who moved easily among high-level think tanks and advisory groups, and had been one of Konoe's own trusted advisers.[10] It was Ozaki's forecast—explained in almost spellbinding detail for his police interrogators over the course of several years, before he was executed in November 1944—that "social revolutions" (shakai kakumei) would occur in those countries which were defeated in World War II. This was certainly true of Japan, Ozaki declared, and to the moment of his death he expressed pride in his contribution to the creation of a "Red" Japan: "Japan is plunged in the Great War, the country is in chaos, and revolution is just around the corner. Nine-tenths of my work is done and my only regret is that I shall not live to see its completion." In the postwar era, Ozaki explained, this new Japan would join the Soviet Union and a communist China in leading a "New Order of Society in East Asia" (Tōa Shinchitsujo Shakai). "Needless to say," he happily told his inquisitors, this radical new order in Asia would constitute "one link in the world revolution."[11]

Ozaki's dreams were the Imperial state's nightmares, of course, and were taken seriously because two further developments within Japan seemed to give them credence. The first was the presence of radical young reformers in the officer corps and civilian bureaucracy—"Red fascists" to some of their critics, "emperor-system communists" to others. The deliberate contradiction in such labels aptly conveys the ideological confusion and fear of subversion prevailing at the time. Here, as it were, the revolutionary threat was seen as emanating "from above"—from ostensibly loyal servants of the state who desired to create a genuine national *socialism*.

The other development, and ultimately the most alarming of all, was the emergence of popular exhaustion and cynicism, which seemed to suggest that the people as a whole were indeed ready to support radical change. Their lives were truly being shattered, but no one was so brainwashed as to find this jewel-like. They did not desire to fight to the bitter end, but they did desire an end to the bitter death of loved ones, the bombing of homes, the disappearance of food, the absence of personal security or even of simple joy. In such disillusion, the hundred million seemed ripe for radical upheaval from below.

Where apprehension of revolution from above was concerned, the police and other watchdogs of the state could call attention to numerous concrete examples of "renovationist" officers and bureaucrats who seemed determined to destroy the status quo. The puppet state of Manchukuo, for example, attracted large numbers of ex-communists and clandestine Marxists who embraced the notion of "Manchukuo as ideology" and regarded this new frontier as an ideal locale in which to create a model of "state capitalism." The Imperial bureaucracy at home was being infiltrated, almost flamboyantly, by cadres of "new bureaucrats" (*shin kanryō*) and "reform bureaucrats" (*kakushin kanryō*), who similarly regarded classical laissez-faire capitalism as bankrupt and desired to impose ever more extensive governmental controls over the private sector. Left-wing intellectuals (such as Ozaki) found temporary security in fashionable think tanks such as the Shōwa Research Association (Shōwa Kenkyūkai), where new mixes of the private and public sectors could be explored. In the military, the brightest proponents of mobilization for "total war" inevitably found themselves confronted with fundamental questions concerning the role of the state in economic development— and likewise answered on the side of enhanced state control. It was not mere happenstance that the military faction with which General—later prime minister—Tōjō Hideki was associated was called the Control Faction (*Tōsei-ha*).

Such a milieu was conducive to black humor, and a good sample of this occurred in 1944 when word circulated among the elites that a Soviet officer in Tokyo had joked that Japan was so communistic already that the Soviet Union, in confronting Japan, might have to engage in anticommunism.[12] So far as can be told, no one laughed. Like most political and ideological issues, however, the specter of revolution from above crystallized in Japanese consciousness by becoming intensely personalized. This took place, as it happened, before Pearl Harbor—in the so-called Cabinet Planning Board Incident of April 1941, in which the Thought Police announced that they had uncovered a nest of Reds in the highest reaches of government, after an investigation that had consumed two and a half years.

The Cabinet Planning Board (Kikakuin), one of the more conspicuous spawn of the war state, was a "superagency" created in 1937 to coordinate military and civilian policy at the highest level. From the outset, its members were, to put it mildly, disenchanted with Anglo-American style capitalism, a common sentiment through much of the world in the wake of the Great Depression. As the Thought Police unraveled the situation, for example, they found that as early as 1937 boardmembers had proposed a plan for Manchukuo which, in their own words, would inevitably involve "total change in the capitalistic industrial system."[13] Bureaucrats in this superagency, the police were shocked to discover, routinely talked about "inevitable stages in history" in which capitalism was transcended; about the intensification of capitalist contradictions under conditions of war; and about the inevitable and desirable "realization of a socialist society."[14] Befitting thought police, the gendarmes even became bibliographers and itemized the various Marxist texts that boardmembers took seriously: two works by Lenin (*The Development of Capitalism in Russia* and *Capitalism and Agriculture*), Rosa Luxemburg's *The Accumulation of Capital*, Karl Kautsky's *The Agrarian Question*, Stalin's *Foundations of Leninism*, and seminal Japanese Marxist texts such as Yamada Moritarō's *Nihon Shihonshugi Bunseki* (Analysis of Japanese Capitalism).[15]

As the Thought Police saw it, members of the Cabinet Planning Board embraced a "left-wing progressiveness" that did not necessarily conform to the platform of the Communist Party, but nonetheless "meshed" with it. "Thus it is clear as day," they noted in their final report, "that should this situation continue—with one group [the Cabinet Planning Board] working within the state structure and hastening the destruction of the state from above, and the other [bonafide Communists]

106

operating from outside and inciting change from below—the consequences will be frightening indeed."[16] As a consequence of this investigation, seventeen members of the board were arrested. After the war, the most famous of these, the agrarian economist Wada Hiroo, became a major figure in implementing the epochal land reform enacted under the U.S. Occupation, which almost completely wiped out the presurrender landlord class. The premonitions of the police and fears of the old elites were not, after all, entirely irrational.

When all is said and done, however, the most fascinating aspect of the wartime counterrevolutionary and anticommunist hysteria lies in the premonition that "revolution from above" would be abetted—indeed, made possible—by revolution from below. This was not an idle prediction, for changes that were radical though not communistic did take place in postsurrender Japan, and they survived the Occupation largely because ordinary Japanese desired and supported them. The Thought Police and Konoe-type conservative elites may well have been mildly paranoid in their intimations of a communist revolution. They were not at all out of line, however, in perceiving that the misbegotten losing war had created an almost open-ended receptivity to drastic change among the hundred million.

This is essentially what Ozaki Hotsumi had concluded, and Ozaki's revolutionary ardor was actually fairly typical of leftist polemics in the 1930s and early 1940s. The most important theses of the Japan Communist Party, for example, issued with Comintern approbation in 1928 and 1932, anticipated "spontaneous mass protests and struggles in the near future."[17] And the grand apostle of continuing revolution himself, Leon Trotsky, predicted throughout the 1930s that the stress of war would be the cauldron in which revolutionary upheaval occurred in Japan. Following the Manchurian Incident of 1931, for example, Trotsky grandly declared that the "hasty mixture of Edison with Confucius" had created tensions that surely made revolution imminent in Japan.[18] Within weeks of the China Incident of July 1937, he analyzed the situation in these terms:

Japan at present represents the weakest link in the capitalist chain. Its military-financial superstructure rests on a foundation of semi-feudal agrarian barbarism. The periodic explosions of the Japanese army simply reflect the unbearable tension of social relations in that country.... The probable military successes of Japan against China will be of significance only as historical episodes. China's resistance, closely linked with the rebirth of that nation, will grow stronger from year to year. Japan's growing difficulties will end in military catastrophe and social revolution.[19]

Subsequently, Trotsky turned the screw tighter by comparing Japan's situation with that of Imperial Russia on the cusp of revolution:

Under the circumstances, the danger of a proletarian revolution in Japan is beyond doubt and arises from fundamentally the same sources as in other countries—from the domination of monopoly capitalism. Survivals of feudalism in Japan, sharpening as they do the antagonisms of interests between the peasantry and the landlord class, create the danger of revolutionary peasant movements and thus create conditions for the support of a proletarian revolution by a peasant war.[20]

Comparable intimations of revolution occurring in a Japan strained by war came from a gamut of outside observers including Mao Tse-tung, the communist theoretician Karl Radek, Comintern Japan specialists O. Tanin and E. Yohan, and a variety of anticommunist Western commentators.[21] At the January 1945 Hot Springs conference of the Institute of Pacific Relations, the leading international academic group specializing in Asia, participants called attention to the possibility that the postsurrender Japanese working class might attempt "to copy the U.S.S.R.," and that Japanese peasants "represented a double-barreled gun," historically both "stable" and "revolutionary," and thus potentially capable of following the course of radical agrarian protest so evident elsewhere in the contemporary world.[22] The historical and comparative perspective evident here was characteristic of the most persuasive arguments concerning the possibility of popular upheaval in Japan. Such a perspective treated Japan as neither more nor less "unique" than other countries, and called attention to a history of domestic conflict that traced back to peasant rebellions of the premodern period and the persistence of both rural and urban conflict throughout the course of Japan's rapid "modernization" and industrialization.

The Home Ministry, which took responsibility for domestic stability, was scrupulously attentive to the numerous potential sources of discontent and agitation in Japan. As the country prepared for possible war with the United States in mid 1941, for example, the Home Minister spoke reassuringly about public morale at a top-level government meeting (the Liaison Conference of July 29), but then proceeded to observe that a vigilant attitude had to be maintained and particular attention paid to clandestine communist activities, Koreans, ex-soldiers, persons engaged in small- or medium-size business, and the "peasant movement." In an illuminating comment that reveals one side of the increasing fear of class conflict even before Pearl Harbor, he noted that, "the rich have become richer because of the China Incident, while small and medium businessmen are in difficulties because they went to the front."[23] On the very eve of the Pacific War, Tōjō spoke in similar terms at a policy conference that included the emperor, warning that the populace would face inevitable food and monetary problems. To the Home Minister's catalog of potential sources of resentment and agitation, he specifically added laborers and religious leaders.[24] Over three years later, when impending defeat was undeniable, the emperor was politely informed that "our people possess loyalty in their hearts and the spirit to resist enemy invasion and the like, but on the other hand there is a mood that seeks a change in the situation. Criticism against the military and government is steadily becoming more active, and there is a tendency for the feeling of trust toward the ruling class [shidōsō] to begin to waver. . . ."[25]

By mid 1944, even before the air raids began, a high official of the Thought Police privately was describing the social situation as "like a stack of hay, ready to burst into flame at the touch of a match."[26] His alarm reflected close familiarity with the dossiers maintained by the Home Ministry on potentially disruptive "social movements." These secret reports, circulated internally on a regular basis, covered both "left-wing" and "right-wing" or "ultranationalist" activities, and commonly were divided into the following categories: communists; other radical leftists (such as social democrats, anarchists, and the proletarian movement); labor; the peasantry; intellectuals; racial minorities (notably Koreans, but also Chinese); religious groups (particularly Christians, but also certain new religions); and patriotic societies (that is, groups whose ultranationalism went beyond officially sanctioned norms and promoted right-wing radicalism). Surveillance also was directed at "liberal" elements within business and professional circles, and to the rural and urban middle class who suffered as a consequence of forced mergers demanded under the mobilization for war. Exceptional care was taken to track down "negative gossip" (*ryūgen higo*) and "sensational rumors" (*zōgen higo*) deemed injurious to popular morale, and the official compilation of graffiti or "public scribbling" (*rakugaki, rakusho*) was so meticulous as to leave the impression that it was a rare toilet or factory wall or lamppost that escaped official scrutiny while the holy war was in progress.

The situation in Japan naturally was not comparable to that in the occupied countries of Europe and Asia, where partisan and resistance movements emerged to oppose foreign invaders and their collaborators through armed opposition coupled with increasingly radical political ideologies. No organized resistance or concerted protest was possible, and as a consequence the impression of widespread discontent came to the police in an essentially scattershot or pointillistic manner. At the same time, however, it was possible to find a range of data, including numbers, which suggested how easily popular resentment might be channeled into potent movements directed against the status quo.

There was, to begin with, the question of clandestine communists. The Japan Communist Party had been dissolved in 1932, and many of its former members had engaged in dramatic public "recantation" (*tenkō*). Nonetheless, it remained uncertain how many of these apostasies were bonafide and how many individuals still remained loyal to Moscow or at least sympathetic to Marxism. Home Ministry figures up to this point certainly provided little comfort, for beginning in 1928 over sixty thousand arrests of "leftists" had been made under the notorious Peace Preservation Law (see Table 1), with actual prosecutions numbering in the several thousands. Accused leftists continued to be arrested throughout the war years, but the imponderable question was how many people might rally behind communist or socialist appeals in the wake of shattering defeat.

Such concerns were reinforced by other considerations where statisti-

TABLE 1 PEACE PRESERVATION LAW VIOLATIONS

(1928 through April 1943)

	1928	1929	1930	1931	1932	1933	1934	1935	1936	1937	1938	1939	1940	1941	1942	1943 (1–4)
APPREHENDED	3,426	4,942	6,124	10,422	13,938	14,822	3,994	1,785	2,067	1,312	982	722	817	1,212	698	159
1. Left-wing	3,426	4,942	6,124	10,422	13,938	14,822	3,994	1,718	1,207	1,292	789	389	713	849	332	87
2. Religious	–	–	–	–	–	–	–	67	860	13	193	325	33	107	163	19
3. Other	–	–	–	–	–	–	–	–	–	7	–	8	71	256	203	53
TOTAL CASES DISPOSED OF	713	368	809	838	2,198	3,850	1,986	581	562	529	674	874	568	659	1,054	166
PROSECUTED	525	339	461	307	646	1,285	496	113	158	210	240	388	229	236	339	52
1. Left-wing	525	339	461	307	646	1,285	496	113	97	210	237	163	128	205	217	18
2. Religious	–	–	–	–	–	–	–	–	61	–	–	225	89	2	60	19
3. Other	–	–	–	–	–	–	–	–	–	–	3	–	12	29	62	15

SOURCE: Okudaira Yasuhiro, *Chian Ijihō* (vol. 45 of *Gendaishi Shiryō*, Tokyo, 1973), pp. 646–49. The discrepancy between the number of individuals apprehended (*kankyo jin-in*) and the number of cases actually formally disposed of (*shori jin-in*) presumably reflects the extent of harassment through arrests or police roundups which did not result in actual litigation. Cases formally disposed of, but not resulting in prosecution or indictment, fall into the categories of stay of prosecution, disposition postponed, no accusation, and "other" in this tabulation. Cases disposed of in a given year do not necessarily involve only persons apprehended that same year, but include cases pending from an earlier date.

cal as well as more impressionistic data conveyed a disturbing sense of deep-rooted popular grievance. This seemed true no matter where the police or queasy conservatives looked—in the rural and urban sector, across class strata, among young and old, men and women. In the countryside, for example—supposedly the very repository of traditional values and selfless patriotism—apprehension about "social movements" reflected a problem that traced back to the late nineteenth century and involved the more "feudalistic" side of the modern economy: the prevalence of extensive tenancy, often involving exploitive rents. At the time of Pearl Harbor, 46 percent of arable land was cultivated by tenants, and only 30 percent of the peasantry owned all the land it farmed.[27] Beginning around 1917 (the year of the Bolshevik revolution), disputes between landlords and tenants began to rise precipitously—often with a flamboyant communist coloration. These peaked in the mid 1930s, but the basic problems never were ameliorated and rural confrontations continued through the war years (see Table 2).[28]

Certain wartime measures—such as rent control, conversion from rent-in-kind to money rents, and fixed rice prices—adversely affected the landlords, and some tenants also benefited by wartime inflation, which effectively lessened their debts. In the final stages of the war, the countryside also was spared the ravages of being bombed, and urban food shortages enabled many farmers to profit on the black market.[29] Basic landlord-tenant friction remained, however; and war also created new rural grievances, such as resentment against government production quotas (which cut into family food and resources to sell on the black market), as well as resentment against the sudden intrusion of urban kinfolk forced out of the cities by the air raids.[30] As the war approached its denouement, rural burdens also were increased by the mobilization of some 2.4 million soldiers for a projected defense of the homeland, because rural residents were expected to provide for these militia in their own homes.[31] It was in this context that the watchdogs of the Home Ministry confidentially expressed concern about mounting selfishness and self-centeredness among the rural population. As one secret midwar report put it, "we also fear that the very agrarian soul [nōkon] of the rural community, which is the sustaining source of the Yamato race, may be disintegrating at the root."[32] Another report on the rural situation, dated April 1945, observed that even though one could not say

	TABLE 2 TENANCY DISPUTES, 1917–44			
Year	Number of Disputes	Number of Landlords Participating	Number of Tenants Participating	Cultivated Land (ha) Involved
1917	85	–	–	–
1918	256	–	–	–
1919	326	–	–	–
1920	408	5,236	34,605	27,390
1921	1,680	33,985	145,898	–
1922	1,578	29,077	125,750	90,253
1923	1,917	37,712	134,503	89,080
1924	1,532	27,223	110,920	70,387
1925	2,206	33,001	134,646	95,941
1926	2,751	39,705	151,061	95,652
1927	2,053	24,136	91,336	59,168
1928	1,866	19,474	75,136	48,694
1929	2,434	23,505	81,998	56,831
1930	2,478	14,159	58,565	39,799
1931	3,419	23,768	81,135	60,365
1932	3,414	16,706	61,499	39,028
1933	4,000	14,312	48,073	30,596
1934	5,828	34,035	121,031	85,838
1935	6,824	28,574	113,164	70,745
1936	6,804	23,293	77,187	46,420
1937	6,170	20,236	63,246	39,582
1938	4,615	15,422	52,817	34,359
1939	3,578	9,065	25,904	16,623
1940	3,165	11,082	38,614	27,625
1941	3,308	2,037	32,289	21,898
1942	2,756	11,139	33,185	25,544
1943	2,424	6,968	17,738	11,442
1944	2,160	3,778	8,213	5,096

SOURCE: Tsutomu Takizawa, *The Developing Economies* 10, 3 (1972), p. 295. See also Tōyama Shigeki, Imai Seiichi, and Fujiwara Akira, *Shōwa Shi* [Shōwa History] (rev. ed., Tokyo: Iwanami Shinsho, 1959), pp. 23, 65, 142, 220.

that mounting tensions in the countryside necessarily were rooted in a background of subversive thought, "the germination of an impending class struggle is a real matter for anxiety."[33]

If developments in the rural sector were unsettling, the effects of the war on the urban and industrial scene were by comparison many times more alarming. Here, to begin with, officials were acutely aware of a conspicuous recent tradition of labor agitation. Contrary to managerial slogans about the "beautiful customs" of the Japanese enterprise system, industrialization in Japan had been accompanied by a rising incidence of labor conflict, which, like the rural tenant disputes, was curbed by wartime controls but nonetheless carried on even into the years of the Pacific War (see Table 3). These were most prevalent, moreover, in the most strategic sectors: machine and tool manufacture, transportation, mining, and metals. Between January 1943 and November 1944, for example, the Home Ministry counted a total of 740 disputes in the industrial sector, with another 612 potential disputes being thwarted (see Table 4).

Overt worker agitation, moreover, seemed but the tip of the iceberg, for by 1943 or 1944 the labor force in general presented a spectacle bordering on chaos. Some ten million men were drafted for military service; millions of others were transferred from their regular employment to war-related industries; new cadres of women (beyond the traditional female employees in textiles and other light industry) were recruited for factory work; students were uprooted from their classrooms to work in industry and agriculture; and many of the most onerous jobs, such as mining and other heavy manual labor, were turned over to conscript foreign labor (see Table 5). Korean workers, who numbered over one million as of 1945, suffered particular abuse and responded with various forms of violent as well as nonviolent protest (see Table 6).

Overt protest in the police state obviously required exceptional courage, but the incidence of these conflicts paled before those numbers which told of exhaustion, defeatism, and eventual physical abandonment of the workplace. This too was evident even before the bombing of urban areas commenced in late 1944. In August 1944, for example, one factory typically reported that 30 percent of the women and boys in its work force were suffering from beriberi.[34] Absenteeism in Japanese industry was running around 20 percent before the air raids, and by July

TABLE 3 LABOR DISPUTES, 1897–1945					
Year	Incidents	Participants	Year	Incidents	Participants
1897 (7–12)	32	3,517	1922	584	85,909
1898	43	6,293	1923	647	68,814
1899	15	4,284	1924	933	94,047
1900	11	2,316	1925	816	89,387
1901	18	1,948	1926	1,260	127,267
1902	8	1,849	1927	1,202	103,350
1903	9	1,359	1928	1,021	101,893
1904	6	879	1929	1,420	172,144
1905	19	5,013	1930	2,290	191,834
1906	13	2,037	1931	2,456	154,528
1907	57	9,855	1932	2,217	123,313
1908	13	822	1933	1,897	116,733
1909	11	310	1934	1,915	120,307
1910	10	2,937	1935	1,872	103,962
1911	22	2,100	1936	1,975	92,724
1912	49	5,736	1937	2,126	213,622
1913	47	5,242	1938	1,050	55,565
1914	50	6,904	1939	1,120	128,294
1915	64	7,852	1940	732	55,003
1916	108	8,418	1941	334	17,285
1917	398	57,309	1942	268	14,373
1918	417	66,457	1943	417	14,791
1919	2,388	335,225	1944	296	10,026
1920	1,069	127,491	1945 (to surrender)	13	382
1921	896	170,889			

SOURCE: Yamazaki Gorō, *Nihon Rōdō Undō Shi* [History of the Japanese Labor Movement] (rev. ed., Tokyo: Rōmu Gyōsei Kenkyūjo, 1966), pp. 25, 28, 34, 37, 45, 53, 62, 71. See also Iwao F. Ayusawa, *A History of Labor in Modern Japan* (Honolulu: East-West Center, University of Hawaii, 1966), p. 154.

1945 had deprived the country of half of its potentially available man-hours (see Table 7).

Part of this monumental disruption could be attributed to the physical destruction of factories, part to illness in the work force. A great portion of such absenteeism, however, came from workers who placed private needs above the demands of the state and abandoned their jobs to forage

TABLE 4   LABOR DISPUTES BY INDUSTRY AND SECTOR JANUARY 1943–NOVEMBER 1944

(as calculated by the Special Higher Police)

Industry or Sector	Total Number of Disputes	Slowdowns, Walkouts, and Lockouts	Number of Disputes Thwarted
1. Machines and tools	231 (108/123)*	150 (64/86)	249 (164/85)
2. Transportation	80 (50/30)	53 (35/18)	78 (55/23)
3. Mining	74 (44/30)	53 (28/25)	49 (34/15)
4. Metals	67 (41/26)	49 (29/20)	64 (35/29)
5. Lumber/wood products	45 (20/25)	28 (13/15)	18 (14/4)
6. Spinning	44 (23/21)	37 (21/16)	32 (23/9)
7. Chemicals	43 (28/15)	31 (20/11)	32 (22/10)
8. Construction	40 (29/11)	24 (19/5)	16 (8/8)
9. Cement/quarrying	26 (13/13)	21 (10/11)	7 (3/4)
10. Business/commerce	19 (15/4)	11 (8/3)	11 (11/0)
11. Public services	14 (9/5)	10 (5/5)	3 (2/1)
12. Fisheries	11 (6/5)	6 (3/3)	2 (2/0)
13. Printing/bookmaking	9 (7/2)	7 (6/1)	5 (2/3)
14. Foodstuffs	6 (5/1)	3 (2/1)	8 (7/1)
15. Gas/electricity/water	5 (3/2)	4 (3/1)	5 (4/1)
16. Agriculture	2 (1/1)	1 (0/1)	0
17. Other industry/ enterprise	24 (16/8)	18 (11/7)	33 (26/7)
Total number of incidents	740 (418/322)	506 (277/229)	612 (412/200)
Total number of participants	26,037 (14,697/11,340)	16,714 (9,634/7,080)	

* Figures in parentheses are subtotals for 1943 and January–November 1944.

SOURCE: Adapted from Naimushō Keihokyoku Hoanbu (Home Ministry, Police Bureau, Peace Preservation Division), *Tokkō Geppō* (Monthly Gazette of the Special Higher Police), December 1943 (p. 71) and November 1944 (p. 45).

for food in the countryside or simply to find jobs with higher pay. Whatever the reason, here once again was imposing evidence of hearts not beating as one, workers far more intent on surviving than on fighting on to the bitter end. To the police, moreover, this clearly was tinder that easily could feed truly radical upheaval once Japan was defeated and the state lost control of its immense apparatus of repression and indoctrina-

TABLE 5 DISPLACEMENT OF PERSONNEL IN WARTIME JAPAN	
(approximate figures)	
Total males drafted for military service	10,000,000
Army-navy strength at time of surrender	7,200,000
Persons drafted from regular employment to serve in war industries	3,000,000
Students mobilized as draft labor (both industry and agriculture)	3,500,000
Women added to factory labor force	3,000,000
Female "volunteer corps" in military industries	470,000
Non-Japanese labor	
Korean "contract labor," 1939–1945	667,000
Total number of Koreans in work force, 1945	1,300,000
Chinese "contract labor," 1943–1945	40,000
Persons displaced by air raids	15,000,000
Individuals unemployed following surrender (including repatriates and ex-servicemen)	13,240,000

SOURCES: Tōyama Shigeki, Imai Seiichi, and Fujiwara Akira, *Shōwa Shi* [Shōwa History] (Tokyo: Iwanami Shinsho, 1959), pp. 220, 246–47; Jerome B. Cohen, *Japan's Economy in War and Reconstruction* (Minneapolis: University of Minnesota Press, 1949), pp. 288–90, 318, 321, 323–26; Yoshida Naikaku Kankōkai (Yoshida Cabinets Publication Association), *Yoshida Naikaku* [The Yoshida Cabinets] (Tokyo, 1954), p. 56.

tion. Even in the Foreign Ministry, one finds an official ruminating on reports of industrial sabotage and passing on rumors about drunken workers shouting "Stalin *banzai!*"[35] Even students recruited for factory work, who were too young to have been exposed to the Marxist exhortations of the 1920s and early 1930s, appeared to have imbibed class consciousness almost intuitively. Thus, the same foreign service officer also passed on the rumor that students conscripted to work in the Nakajima Aircraft Plant had boldly announced that it was useless to work so that big capitalists could profit.[36]

Comparable alarms were raised about trends in the "middle class," and as Japan's situation worsened it even began to be argued that this middle class faced the threat of being wiped out. Several developments fed this concern. While many small- and medium-size entrepreneurs

TABLE 6 INCIDENTS INVOLVING KOREANS IN JAPAN JANUARY–NOVEMBER 1944	Incidents	Participants
Labor incidents		
1. Walkout	32	1,745
2. Slowdown	35	1,926
3. Collective violence	36	3,176
4. Other direct action	1	5
5. Other	53	3,986
Total	157	10,838
Nonlabor incidents		
1. Collective violence	95	3,632
2. Other direct action	27	70
3. Other	25	1,384
Total	147	5,086
Totals		
1. All incidents	304	15,924
2. Incidents involving collective violence	131	6,808

SOURCE: Naimushō Keihokyoku Hoanbu, *Tokkō Geppō*, November 1944, p. 67. Totals calculated from *monthly* statistics provided in this source, which contains numerous errors in its cumulative tabulations.

flourished as subcontractors to the war machine, for example, a great many others were forced into unwelcome mergers or simply swallowed by big capital. This process actually began during the economic downturn of the late 1920s, on the eve of the Great Depression and the Manchurian Incident, and was accelerated throughout the 1930s by mobilization for "total war." Between the outbreak of the China War in 1937 and Japan's capitulation in 1945, the ten biggest Japanese oligopolies (four "old *zaibatsu*" and six "new *zaibatsu*") dramatically increased their share of paid-in capital (see Table 8).

Middle-class resentment at such trends was compounded many times over when the war literally came home to Japan, and tens of thousands of petite workshops, small businesses, and medium-size factories were obliterated. By the time Japan surrendered, the material as well as human costs of the holy war had proven very great indeed (see Tables 9 and

Area	Percentage of Absenteeism Oct. 1943 – Sept. 1944	Percentage of Absenteeism July 1945
TABLE 7 ABSENTEEISM IN JAPANESE INDUSTRY, 1943–1945		
All Japan: plants damaged in air raids	–	56
All Japan: undamaged plants	20	34
All Japan: damaged and undamaged plants	20	49
Tokyo area: undamaged plants	17	40
Kyoto (unbombed)	24	40
Hokkaido (bombed July 1945; second figure is for June 1945)	28	44
Hiroshima (bombed August 1945)	25	40

SOURCE: U.S. Strategic Bombing Survey, *The Effects of Air Attack on Japanese Urban Economy* (March 1947), p. 25; see also Jerome B. Cohen, *Japan's Economy in War and Reconstruction* (Minneapolis: University of Minnesota Press, 1949), p. 343.

10). The guardians of the Imperial state were acutely aware of the psychological consequences of such devastation, and months before the surrender they began to express fear that the air raids actually threatened to wipe out class gradations, pound the fragile middle class into utter destitution and despair, and create a society starkly polarized between haves and have-nots. Thus, in the words of one contemporary observer:

> Through the air raids, the middle class has found its homes burned and businesses destroyed overnight, and has fallen into a lower-class existence. This has given rise to profound changes in the social structure, and demands attention by the leaders of the war.[37]

119

TABLE 8 RATIO OF PAID-IN CAPITAL OF COMPANIES UNDER THE CONTROL OF THE PRINCIPAL ZAIBATSU

(Whole country = 100)

	1937		1946	
	4 zaibatsu	10 zaibatsu	4 zaibatsu	10 zaibatsu
Mining, Heavy and Chemical Industries				
Mining	20.9%	35.5%	28.3%	50.5%
Metal industry	9.2	14.7	26.4	41.8
Machinery and shipbuilding	18.6	27.2	37.5	56.2
Chemical industry	11.3	18.3	31.4	38.5
Total	14.6	24.9	32.4	49.0
Other Industries				
Ceramics	21.5	46.6	28.4	55.8
Textiles	8.2	10.3	17.4	18.8
Paper-making	4.9	12.1	4.5	4.7
Foodstuffs, agriculture and forestry	3.7	12.1	2.7	10.4
Miscellaneous	2.3	8.4	9.7	16.2
Total	7.0	13.5	10.7	16.8
Finance and Insurance				
Banking	21.0	21.8	48.0	50.4
Trust	37.2	43.6	85.4	85.4
Insurance	49.0	50.5	51.2	60.3
Total	22.5	23.6	49.7	53.0
Miscellaneous Enterprises				
Public utilities	3.0	3.6	0.5	0.5
Land transportation	5.4	6.4	4.9	5.6
Shipping	16.2	19.2	60.8	61.4
Real estate and warehousing	16.1	21.2	22.7	29.4
Trading	5.3	6.4	13.6	20.3
Total	6.1	7.5	12.9	15.5
Grand Total	**10.4**	**15.1**	**24.5**	**35.2**

Notes:
4 Zaibatsu—Mitsui, Mitsubishi, Sumitomo and Yasuda.
10 Zaibatsu—The above 4 Zaibatsu plus Asano, Furukawa, Ayukawa, Okura, Nomura and Nakajima (Figures for 1937 exclude Nakajima).

SOURCE: Mitsubishi Economic Research Institute, ed. Mitsui-Mitsubishi-Sumitomo [1955], p. 6, based on the 1950 report of the Japanese Holding Company Liquidation Commission. Companies referred to as under the control of the zaibatsu groups are domestic concerns only, controlled by their holding companies.

TABLE 9 JAPANESE WAR CASUALTIES	
Military fatalities	
China War, 1937–1941	185,647
Imperial Army, 1941–1945	1,140,429
Imperial Navy, 1941–1945	414,879
	1,740,955
Civilian fatalities in air raids	
Tokyo	97,031
Hiroshima	140,000
Nagasaki	70,000
63 other cities	86,336
	393,367
Other fatalities	
Civilians in Okinawa	150,000
Civilians in Saipan	10,000
Soldiers and civilians in Manchuria	
(winter of 1945–1946)	100,000
POWs in Soviet Union	300,000
	560,000
Total Japanese war dead	2,694,322
Servicemen reported ill or injured (1945)	4,470,000
Servicemen receiving disability pensions	300,000

SOURCE: John W. Dower, *War Without Mercy: Race and Power in the Pacific War* (New York: Pantheon, 1986), pp. 297–99 and accompanying annotations. The mix of precise official data and general estimates is unavoidable.

Or again:

> Class consciousness of confrontation between those above and those below is gradually intensifying. General preoccupation with immediate concerns is proliferating, and attitudes of desperation are becoming more pronounced.[38]

TABLE 10 WAR DAMAGES IN JAPAN

Percentage of total national wealth destroyed		25.4%
Shipping	80.6	
Automobiles	36.8	
Industrial machine tools	34.2	
Structures	24.6	
Products	23.9	
All vehicles (autos, rolling stock, etc.)	21.9	
Furniture and household goods	20.6	
Electricity and gas facilities	10.8	
Railway tracks	7.1	
Cities bombed		
Total number	66	
Area destroyed	40%	
Population made homeless	30%	
Urban residences destroyed		
In air raids	2,510,000	(51% of total residences)
For firebreaks	600,000	(13% of total residences)
In Tokyo	1,066,000	(65% of total residences)
Calorie intake per person		
Before December 1941	2,000	
1944	1,900	
1945 (summer)	1,680	

SOURCES: Keizai Antei Honbu (Economic Stabilization Board), *Taiheiyō Sensō ni yoru Waga Kuni no Higai Sōgō Hōkōkusho* [Comprehensive Report on Damage to Our Country in the Pacific War]. This basic 1949 report is reproduced in various sources, including volume 19 in the Ministry of Finance series *Sengo Zaisei Shi* [Postwar Financial History] (Tokyo: Tōyō Keizai Shimbun, 1978), pp. 15–19. See also U.S. Strategic Bombing Survey, *Summary Report (Pacific War)* (Washington, 1946), pp. 17–20; Takafusa Nakamura, *The Postwar Japanese Economy: Its Development and Structure* (Tokyo: Tokyo University Press, 1981), p. 15; Harry Emerson Wildes, *Typhoon in Tokyo: The Occupation and Its Aftermath* (New York: Macmillan, 1954), p. 2 on housing destroyed.

Shortly after the surrender, an officer of the military police (*Kempeitai*) painted a similar picture of polarization, but put a somewhat different construction upon it:

> The upper-class people were very selfish, and the lower-class people just wanted to eat. The Japanese middle class was very large. It was destroyed by fire and they became lower-class people, so both the upper and lower classes began to desire the end of the war. They became anti-government.[39]

In the end, revolutionary upheaval did not occur in Japan, and perhaps it never actually was close. But the people as a whole were changed by their ordeal. Their daily lives were shattered, their beliefs were undermined, and desire for liberation from the existing situation became widespread. At the most elementary level, such liberation might be envisioned merely as a respite from hardship and personal tragedy, but for a great many individuals the meaning of liberation now extended to demands for a change of regime and the creation of a drastically altered society. The state had become discredited and sorely wounded well before Japan surrendered, and popular receptiveness to a new start and new society became a major wartime legacy on which postwar change could be built.

It is in this regard that the nightmares of the Thought Police assume full significance. The dissident "social movements" they spied on, the sensational rumors and seditious graffiti they collected, the workers' desertions from factories they witnessed—all gave lie to wartime propaganda about social solidarity and a collective willingness to die for the Imperial cause. And all, in retrospect, also help us better understand the turbulent, uncertain, *receptive* social milieu that U.S. forces encountered when they arrived in defeated Japan and set about promoting a relatively radical agenda of "demilitarization and democracy."

Thus, although the Imperial state did not allow public expression of private dissent, from the very outset of the Pacific War the police found such expressions scribbled everywhere in the form of graffiti that vividly suggested the tenuous boundaries between hardship and weariness, stoicism and cynicism, pessimism and defeatism, resentment and outright radical consciousness. Here, for example, is a sample of the anonymous writings which the Thought Police collected from the walls of private and public places between December 1941 and early 1944—always wondering, of course, not merely who wrote them, but how many others had read them and nodded their heads in silent assent:[40]

December 1941

Kill the emperor

Japan is losing in China

Why does our fatherland dare to commit aggression?
Ask the leaders why they're waging aggressive war against
    China.

Communism. Communism.
Workers of the world
Revolution now
. . . including the emperor

Look at the pitiful figures of the undernourished people.
Overthrow the government.
Shoot former Prime Minister Konoe, the traitor.

January 1942

Absolute opposition to the imperialist war.
Japan and Germany proclaim their domination throughout the
    world
But that won't make people happy.
True peace will come only when the Soviet Union obtains
    victory.
You laborers in military industry throughout the land—
Now is the time to become aware.

Soon we won't be able to eat.
Those who feel good being called soldiers of industry are big
    fools.

Win or lose, our lives won't change.
End the war (say the workers).
It's just puffing up the bourgeoisie (says the proletariat).

March 1942

End the war.
In the end we'll lose and the people will suffer.

Her Majesty the Empress is a lecher

Sumitomo Metal is a cheating company that wrings the sweat
    and blood out of us workers for a pittance.
Kill those guys who decide on salaries.

June 1942

Soldiers carry weapons to kill.
What's become of things like personal character?
Ridiculous. All the more reason to commit suicide.

Capitalists are thieves, property is the fruit of exploitation
                                            —A Socialist

No rice. End the war.

End the war. Give us freedom.

July 1942

Capitalists ignited the war and are accumulating wealth and
    hoarding it.
Give the people peace, liberty, and bread.

Destroy the aristocracy—those consuming parasites.

People's Revolution.
Japan Communist Party *banzai!*

What we believe in is nothing more than
    Idealism, Liberalism, Individualism.
Become a youth of "originality."

August 1942

Overthrow the government
Raise wages

November 1942

Starvation and war dead.
The imperalist war intensified work.
Turn the war into insurrection.

Marxism *banzai*
Communist Party *banzai*

We demand repeal of the Peace Preservation Law.
We workers and farmers have been exploited as slaves of the
    bourgeois landlords.
Let's throw off our submissive attitudes of the past.
Unite and overthrow Japanese imperialism
    and overthrow the capitalists who have exploited and
    repressed us.
Overthrow capitalism and imperialism.

No prospect of winning the war.
Kill Konoe Fumimaro.

Stop the war

December 1942

Kill the emperor
Bury the politicians, overthrow the capitalists

February 1943

Kill the dumb emperor

Don't make the farmers weep.
Kill the Minister of Agriculture
Kill Minister Ino.

Kill Tōjō

March 1943

Ridiculous to be a soldier—35 *sen* a day

May 1943

Communism *banzai.* Oppose the war.

Rid Japan of the war-mongering military.
The sword that kills one saves many.

End the war

June 1943

2,000 *yen* to whoever lops off the emperor's head.
2,000 *yen* . . . for the empress.

Japan and the United States should cooperate for world peace

The war is no good

July 1943

Kill the rich

Brave men! Carry out a Red revolution!
Soviet *banzai!* Japan Communist Party *banzai!*
Motherland Russia.

Attack the government's running-dog police.
You who have complaints against the government,
Join with comrades and gather under the red flag.
Anarchism. Anarchism.
Stand up, proletariat.
Destroy the bourgeoisie.

For what purpose have you all been fighting for seven years?

August 1943

Communist Party *banzai.*
Comrades of the country, band together under the flag of
    communism.

Do it. It's life.
Advance and overthrow the capitalists.

Concept of mutual help
Concept of joint responsibility
Concept of class struggle
. . . live with these.

September 1943

How long will the Great East Asian War last?
Three and a half years without food.
One after another, starvation. . . .
All the strong ones have perished. . . .

October 1943

Anglo-American victory, Japanese-German defeat

It's the military and bureaucrats who are profiting from the war
  under the beautiful name of "nation."

November 1943

To the Deity of Poverty, the Tōjō Cabinet, Liberty, and
  Equality:
Commoners die for the glory of a few.
For whom are we fighting this war that was started by the
  privileged class and the military group?

December 1943

What's wrong with liberalism and communism?
We have to reconsider this.

March 1944

Even in the Japanese empire,
Something that was bound to come has come.
What is it? Marxism.

A goodly number of these "public scribblings" obviously showed the practiced hand of seasoned leftists, and this also was true of other forms of anonymous writings such as postcards or letters sent to prominent local and national officials. Unguarded statements and sensational rumors also frequently extended beyond plain expressions of war weariness to explicitly antiwar or antimilitary statements deemed in violation of the Military Code, or to "seditious incidents" (*fuon jiken*)—culminating in lèse majesté (*fukei jiken*)—which called for the overthrow of the existing system and were punishable under various ordinances apart from the Peace Preservation Law. Wartime statistics pertaining to these matters are frequently incomplete and even contradictory, but they convey a general sense of the incidence of such offenses. According to one source, for example, between August 1937 and April 1943, authorities investigated a total of 1,603 cases of rumors deemed serious enough to be in violation of the Military Code, and identified 2,139 individuals involved in promoting these rumors; 557 of these cases (involving 646 persons) were actually prosecuted. Between January 1942 and April 1943, some 227 rumors deemed in violation of a new "peace and order ordinance" of March 1941 were investigated, with 87 of these cases (involving 115 persons) being prosecuted.[41]

A secret Home Ministry survey on the eve of Japan's surrender, dealing with "extreme deterioration" in public attitude, indicates a steady quantitative increase in the most serious cases reported:

> As we survey recent occurrences of statements, letters, and wall writings that are disrespectful, antiwar, antimilitary, or in other ways inflamatory, from April 1942 to March 1943 . . . the total number of incidents was 308, an average of slightly less than 25 incidents a month. From April 1943 to March 1944 . . . the total number was 406, an average of 34 incidents a month. Compared to this, from April 1944 to March 1945 . . . the total was 607, an average of slightly less than 51 incidents a month, thus showing a rapid increase.[42]

Elsewhere it was calculated that, between April 1942 and April 1945, a total of 735 cases involving expressions of dissent actually were prosecuted before the courts, a substantial figure when one considers that the vast majority of letters and public scribblings remained anonymous.[43] A fuller indication of the scope of such anonymous expression of grievance was suggested after the surrender by a Kyoto journalist, who reported that his paper received around two hundred letters per day during the war. While initially these tended to be patriotic, the great majority became critical as the war progressed and included "much denouncing of officials and the military for their alleged failure to share the people's hardships." Such letters, of course, were never published.[44] In March 1945, the police were more explicit in their confidential summary:

> Recent rumors, scribblings, and [other] manifestations are numerically increasing.... They say that the Japanese war leaders, or the leading circles, are responsible for the decisive battle against Japan proper, for intensified air raids, shortage of foodstuff, acute inflation, and so on, all of which have made the people's lives hard. This indignation against the ruling class has been shown in criticisms of military strategy and misrepresentation of the attitude of military circles. Others speak ill of government measures and government communiques. They explicitly assume a hostile attitude toward the government circles. Some others dare to speak of class antagonism.[45]

While overtly seditious statements seemed the cutting edge of a broader revolutionary consciousness, this was abetted by the acid seepage of "sensational rumors" in general. Neighborhoods and communities throughout Japan fell hostage to gossip, all the more so as the war came home and the government's mendacity concerning Japan's situation became patent. It was later estimated that one-tenth of the populace believed defeat inevitable by November 1944, one-half by June 1945, and two-thirds by the time the surrender actually occurred. In the urban areas, three-quarters of the people had come to doubt a Japanese victory by July 1945.[46] As the government lost credibility, only gossip and rumor remained as an alternative source of information, and they filled this role with predictable waywardness. Rumors abounded of implausible victories (such as Japan's in Okinawa) and premature defeats; of spies and neighborhood espionage agents; of police mistakenly killing infants while slitting open backpacks in search of black market rice; of persons, typically Koreans, violating women and even killing and eating young girls; and so on.[47]

The very category of "rumor" was itself vague, but this did not prevent the police from attempting to trace each unsettling bit of marketplace chatter to its source. This was not a task for loafers. In Tokyo alone, the metropolitan police investigated 2,020 "rumors" between 1941 and 1945, while the military police found themselves innundated with over six-thousand "sensational rumors" nationwide in 1944 alone, approximately fifteen to twenty cases a day (see Table 11).

When whispered rumors begin to supplant broadcast pieties as the people's touchstone of belief, ruling groups have good reason to feel threatened. Frequently there also was an almost gleeful sense of defiance and ridicule in some of the anonymous gestures that so unnerved the police. Succinct heresies sometimes were scribbled on paper money, for example, and sent off quietly to infiltrate a straining war economy. One such incident involved discovery of a fifty-*sen* note that bore the word "fool" written over the imperial chrysanthemum crest.[48] An election for the Tokyo assembly in 1943 provided yet another outlet for small gestures of protest, as one vote was cast for "our lord Lenin" and another marked "Tōjō—no confidence." Other ballots called for providing rice; ending the war; ending the imperialist war, or the war on behalf of the capitalists; getting rid of the deceitful government; destroying the upper-class society that patronized the black market and hoarded goods; and so on. One *banzai* was written in for victory by the Soviet Union, another for Japan's destruction. Yet another ballot was marked "End the war quickly, stupid militarists." One ballot was dedicated "to Kōtoku Shūsui, pacifist, who decorated with his blood the first page of the history of the Japanese labor movement." Another was signed: "Antiwar believer."[49]

Examined more systematically, these various expressions of discontent and dissent followed several general patterns. Many were antiwar and antimilitary in a superficially simple way: End the war, Oppose the war, This war is no good. At the least complex level, this could be interpreted as exhaustion and defeatism, as typified in such wall writings as "Immediate peace with the United States and Britain—we can't go on fighting any longer."[50] Such defeatism, however, indicated a decline in willing-

131

TABLE 11 RUMORS INVESTIGATED BY THE MILITARY POLICE DURING THE PACIFIC WAR

	1943	1944													1945				
	Dec	Jan	Feb	Mar	Apr	May	Jun	Jul	Aug	Sep	Oct	Nov	Dec	Jan	Feb	Mar	Apr	May
SUBJECT OF RUMOR (in percentage)																		
Military matters	38.2	–	–	–	–	53.1	65.8	53.7	55.3	–	43.5	53.0	55.7	–	–	67.9	65.0	62.3
Politics/diplomacy	3.5	–	–	–	–	2.3	3.9	9.1	6.4	–	7.7	5.0	2.5	–	–	2.9	3.1	3.3
Economy/livelihood	44.3	–	–	–	–	26.8	16.4	12.6	13.1	–	14.6	18.8	11.3	–	–	5.3	4.0	4.0
Law and order	14.0	–	–	–	–	12.8	13.9	24.6	25.2	–	34.2	23.2	22.9	–	–	23.9	27.3	30.4
Other	–	–	–	–	–	–	–	–	–	–	–	–	7.6	–	–	–	–	–
Total percentage	100	–	–	–	–	95	100	100	100	–	100	100	100	–	–	100	99.4	100
Number of cases	343	343	405	401	357	394	445	596	673	636	660	564	760			623	546	579
Increase in cases, taking Dec. 1943 as index of 100	100	100	118	117	104	115	130	174	196	186	193	166	222			182	159	169

SOURCE: Ikeuchi Hajime, "Taiheiyō Sensōchū no Senji Ryūgen" [Wartime Rumors during the Pacific War], *Shakaigaku Hyōron*, June 1951, p. 41. For unexplained reasons, the official figures for two months (May 1944 and April 1945) do not add up to 100 percent.

ness to sacrifice for the war effort, and concrete cases were recorded which seemed to confirm this. A small businessman in Tokyo, for example, was charged with hoarding gold for exchange after Japan had been defeated, while a village councilman in Saitama prefecture was apprehended for stating that it had become ridiculous to obey official exhortations and donate money to a losing cause.[51] (A more enterprising defeatist was caught in the act of exhorting his neighbors to invest their money with *him* rather than with a government about to go down the drain.)[52]

To desire an end to the war, moreover, implied rejection of any higher national purpose in that conflict: "What is so holy about a war that wastes goods and tens of thousands of our countrymen's lives in cruel strife?" "Can there be anyone at all who really wants to be a soldier?"[53] Thus, a parent was arrested after he was overheard saying, "I learned my child was killed in Singapore. However much one may speak of the country, can a parent help but weep?"[54] Others, including young conscripts, were investigated because they had written poems that spoke of sorrow upon being separated from a loved one.[55] A day laborer was overheard relating the decline in agricultural productivity to lack of fertilizer, and proposing a simple solution: "The best thing to do is submit quickly to Chiang [Kai-shek, the leader of the Chinese enemy] and bring in fertilizer from abroad."[56] A farmer in Okayama was prosecuted for delivering a long and rather eloquent talk in which he emphasized the primacy of the individual over the state; he had been infected, the police noted, with "democratic individualism."[57]

To an increasing number of citizens, it appeared, defeat had come to seem no more onerous than protracted misery under war; for some it was actually preferable. A recurrent comment among incidents investigated by the police was that it meant little difference at all to the common person whether or not Japan was victorious. In the words of one company employee, "The war has dragged on so long and the people's lot is so severe, it doesn't matter whether one wins or loses this war. No matter what country's control we come under, it's all the same."[58] A farmer in Nagano was apprehended on similar grounds for publicly observing that farmers would not be adversely affected by Japan's impending defeat; only officials and politicians would be in trouble.[59]

Many such comments came from the working class, and the following,

133

by a young laborer in the shipbuilding industry, is typical of these. After grousing to his coworkers about rising prices, long hours, and stagnant salaries, he suggested that loafing on the job seemed a reasonable response, and went on:

> The management of the company doesn't work, takes it easy, and still gets good salaries, but factory labor like us who work for cheap salaries are only exploited. We're like captives or slaves, and just experience hardship. The longer the war lasts, the more miserable we workers will be, and win or lose, it makes no difference to workers or day laborers like ourselves who live from day to day, or the small businessmen who live day by day. So it will be good if Japan loses and the war ends soon. Then it will only be the rich guys and upper-class guys who will be in trouble, and to us it won't make much difference in any case.[60]

Other workers were more politically articulate, and pessimistic; the outcome of the war was irrelevant to them, this argument went, so long as they remained under capitalism.[61] Yet other individuals accepted the prospect of defeat with equanimity on more positive and philosophical grounds. "Americans too have souls," a farmer in Chiba observed, and thus by their very nature would not make slaves of the Japanese; "to be hated is the war, and the war is a crime."[62] Some actually welcomed defeat with slogans such as "Win, America, win,"[63] and in several localities the police themselves received anonymous letters expressing positive pleasure at the prospect of being conquered by the Allies. "The people are all joyfully waiting to become part of the United States and Great Britain," one of these read; "Lose, Japan! Win, America and Britain!"[64]

Defeatism, cynicism, or despair led some to see the misbegotten war as an act of national wrongdoing, while many others attributed their hard lot to abuse and incompetence by Japan's own military establishment. "Japan is the enemy," concluded one anonymous letter addressed to military officials. Another letter, also sent to the military, read: "Japan is a good country. What's this 'good country'? This Japan is the enemy of the Orient."[65] More frequent, however, were expressions of derision and even hatred toward the military: "The army's generals are by and large fools"; "The military are idiots who stick medals on their chests like big toys"; "Kill Tōjō! What's destroying us is not the external enemy but our own military."[66] Occasionally, such statements attained a fine point of irony, as in this ditty by a factory worker:

Work, work, my fellow warriors
Your toil and sweat will give
The Order of the Golden Kite
To our commander.[67]

Another individual made his point by writing this classical Chinese phrase on a telephone pole by a military highway: "Thousands die for the glory of a single general."[68]

The belief that military leaders profited materially from the war was expressed in such forms as allusions to "nouveau riche" Tōjō having built "a 300,000-yen mansion"; epigrams such as "The Great East Asian War benefits the military clique"; or the accusation that "In Japan today, it's the military, bureaucracy, politicians, 'face,' and the black market, in that order, that lay their hands on things."[69] A sixteen-year-old boy was apprehended writing such statements as "I hate the military" on the wall of a public toilet,[70] and another young man addressed this unsigned letter to Prime Minister Tōjō in March 1943:

I am the child of someone killed in the war in North China. It is the army and navy ministers, starting with Tōjō, who cruelly killed my precious father and elder brother on the battle-field. Fools! What do you mean by holy war and peace? Look at how miserable my family is. My father died in the desolate fields of North China. My brother is unemployed. My grand-mother can barely swallow the wretched rice she is forced to eat. Our baby is skinny as a praying mantis and cries piteously.[71]

Such bitterness occasionally erupted in open antimilitary gestures, as when persons sitting disconsolately amidst the rubble of their just-bombed neighborhood rose in anger when a military vehicle arrived to appraise the damage, shouting that it was the military's fault, and how did they dare come now to inspect the scene.[72]

135

Humanistic concerns as well as catchwords of the more traditional value system also became the basis for criticism of the military regime. A wall writing in Tokyo, for example, which reflected a higher level of education than most such examples, read as follows:

> Overthrow Tōjō. Overthrow militarism.
> Recognize the meaning of the essence of culture and the
>   individual.
> A great realm which has neither individual nor cultural
>   fulfillment
> Will end like a second Mongol race.[73]

In a different direction, as early as March 1942 police dossiers gave unusually extensive coverage to a spate of anonymous letters sent to various authorities by someone in the city of Kochi in Shikoku. These were couched in markedly more conventional and "traditional" terms, and were discomforting to the authorities because of this very fact. The government, this criticism ran, had failed to bestow favor (*onten o atenu*) upon those who deserved it most, namely the families who had sent children to the front. On the contrary, these families received inadequate financial compensation for their deprivation, and were treated like fools. The national polity was being disrupted (*kokutai ga midareru*) by such inequity, and consequently insurrection was just around the corner (*nai-ran okorimasu zo*). Such insurrection, most strikingly, was envisioned as arising not from the left but, rather, from both the undercompensated survivors of the war dead and the exploited families whose sons still fought on the front.[74] The governor of Osaka was treated to a somewhat comparable combination of familyism and radical rhetoric in September 1943, when he received a postcard containing a number of antiwar phrases, including both "draft labor is destroying the family" and "draftees are the slaves of the state."[75] Prime Minister Tōjō himself was the designated recipient of an anonymous letter in May 1943 warning, somewhat ambivalently, of impending domestic upheaval: "Our people cannot endure this anymore. Take note that insurrection will surely come. Be careful, for the preparations are even now underway."[76]

Home Ministry officials and the military police attempted to draw a distinction between straightforward antiwar and antimilitary statements on the one hand and seditious writings or comments on the other. The fine line was crossed when criticism of the military was extended to criticism of the ruling classes and state structure, and when mere prediction of insurrection was replaced by an explicit summons to participate in organized violence. At this level of criticism, the government clearly was confronted with more than a mere problem of declining morale, for even where there was no explicit call to action, the lines of class confrontation were sharply drawn:

> Since food is no problem for the ministers' wives, they are fat. The great mass of people don't have enough food, and their faces grow sallow. . . .[77]

> The farmers' distress, and on the other side—the capitalists.[78]

> It's the military and financial cliques that instigated the war with America and England. Cursed with hardship, the war is nothing less than our own self-destruction.[79]

> The merchants get fat while farmers' sons spill their blood on the battlefield.[80]

> The lower classes are fighting this war for the capitalists and upper-class minority.[81]

To such perceptions, the radical political response was obvious, although sometimes neatly couched in the hallowed rhetoric of the state itself. This letter was addressed to the police in Osaka in 1942:

> In this decisive stage of the war, it is only the privileged classes and military who live extravagantly, leaving the sacrifices to the common people alone. Abolish aristocratic government.
>
> If you truly wish to speak of one hundred million hearts beating as one, then practice communism thoroughly and treat everyone equally. Don't mouth such utter nonsense as the "Yamato movement." The people's hearts are turning more and more against the government.[82]

The official catalog of "seditious incidents" produced a large portion of unmistakably communist rhetoric—of the *zaibatsu* as feudal remnants, the military cliques as running-dogs of capitalism, the "holy war" as an imperialist war and the last stage of capitalism, or as a struggle between "Red thought and the thought of the Rising Sun."[83] World War II was frequently described as the "decisive war" that would pave the way for Soviet-style socialization in Japan.[84] Targets to kill were generously designated—Tōjō, Konoe, the minister of agriculture, the capitalists, the rich, "those guys who decide on salaries," and the emperor himself. To be overthrown or destroyed were the government, militarist cliques, aristocracy, *zaibatsu*, and bourgeoisie. Ultimate goals here were clear and succinctly expressed—revolution, communism, Japan Communist Party.

Interestingly, where it was possible to identify the purveyors of these heresies, they almost invariably were lower-class men, most frequently farmers and laborers,[85] and their grasp of the communist position was often fairly sophisticated. The war, a thirty-five-year-old farmer explained to his neighbors, bore out the prophesy of historical materialism.[86] Several cases investigated by the police also involved analyses of the situation in terms similar to the notion of "revolution from above," which so terrified Prince Konoe and his conservative colleagues, as in this gleeful anonymous letter of January 1942:

> Lenin's esprit is now reappearing within the capitalist system. "A fundamental transformation in the social organization." A mighty revolution is materializing through the hands of the capitalistic bureaucrats, as reflected in the legislation of the Ministry of Commerce and Industry. Ha Ha Ha. Now its true form is appearing and creating countless numbers of the proletariat class. Ha Ha Ha. Lenin *banzai*. Revolution *banzai*. Vice Minister Kishi has been summoned to the prosecutor's office. Ha Ha Ha. Commit *harakiri* and apologize to society![87]

The most shattering premonition on the part of the ruling classes, however, was that the very capstone of their system, the emperor, was becoming a target of ridicule and contempt. "Antiwar thoughts and feelings finally have come to the point where they even curse and bear resentment against His Majesty," a Home Ministry report of 1945 exclaimed.[88] This was actually misleading. As indicated in Table 12, lèse majesté incidents had occurred with some frequency since at least 1936 and increased most markedly in 1941. From 1936 through April 1943, 441 offenses against the throne, involving 622 individuals, were formally investigated. While prior to 1941 these amounted to a fairly steady average of 50 incidents annually, the number of cases investigated rose to 75 in 1941 and 91 in 1942. Although comprehensive statistics are not readily available thereafter, the number of actual prosecutions may have increased.[89]

The various writings, statements, and acts investigated as incidents of lèse majesté do not as a whole reflect the influence of a formalistic radical critique. The latter was not absent, as suggested in the case of a Kyoto city official indicted in 1942 for commenting that "since the Imperial house is the center of the capitalists, the emperor has been exploiting the people."[90] And undoubtedly some of the "Kill the emperor" slogans scribbled in public places came from the hands of clandestine communists. Certainly more sobering to the authorities, however, was the fact that many of the examples of disrespect to the throne came as spontaneous outbursts. One need not search for a communist cell when a twelve-

TABLE 12 LESE MAJESTE INCIDENTS				
(1936 – April 1943)				
Year	Incidents investigated	Persons involved	Incidents prosecuted	Persons prosecuted
1936	50	61	7	7
1937	45	70	6	11
1938	53	96	19	20
1939	47	68	13	13
1940	54	83	21	26
1941	75	106	22	28
1942	91	112	38	39
1943 (Jan.–Apr.)	26	26	8	8
Totals	441	622	134	152

SOURCE: Okudaira Yasuhiro, *Chian Ijihō* (vol. 45 of *Gendaishi Shiryō*, Tokyo: Misuzu Shobō, 1973), p. 653.

year-old boy addressed a postcard reading "stupid emperor" to the imperial residence (signed "enemy");[91] or when a mother whose two sons had been killed in the war cursed the emperor as "heartless" and trampled his likeness underfoot before burning it;[92] or when a nineteen-year-old student in the last year of middle school was discovered to have written this to his mother in Manchuria:

> What's all this about being the emperor's children! If that were so, the emperor would take care of his poor unfortunate children, but he doesn't. This "emperor's children" is just a lie, nothing more than just keeping others below himself. What is the emperor? You hear a lot about him being some kind of living god. I can hardly keep from bursting out laughing when we study ethics [shūshin] at school! The thing that will develop liberalism in the world is our own power. For that, is there anything more essential than to put pressure on the emperor? It would be good if the emperor and all just died off. What's the emperor![93]

It was fairly common, in the cases investigated, to find persons treating the emperor as an ordinary human—sometimes emphasizing that very fact—and a rather hapless and inept one at that. He was most commonly belittled as fool (baka), stupid fool (bakayarō), and big stupid fool (daibakayarō)—but also as a spoiled child (bōchan), figurehead (kazarimono), good-for-nothing (gokutsubushi), icon (gūzō), and "an expensive rubber stamp" (keihi no kakaru ingyō).[94] He could not even carry his own umbrella, one heretic commented, while another observed that the emperor obviously had no eye for people, since he had picked Tōjō to head the cabinet. Even during the war years, it was not unusual in student circles and the like for His Majesty to be referred to flippantly as Tenchan, or "Little Emp"—although the police did not carry their investigations to this level.[95]

They did, however, find some down-to-earth imagery emanating from their purportedly loyal citizenry. A twenty-seven-year-old farmer was sentenced to six months' imprisonment for commenting that Chiang Kai-shek was the greatest man in the world, compared to whom the emperor was nothing but a stick propped up by his high-level supporters.

"If you have someone holding you up," he concluded, "anyone can do the job. He's not so great."[96] And in September 1942 a rather interesting voice from the lumpenproletariat was heard when the police arrested a thirty-four-year-old man with four prior criminal convictions. Characterized as a figure from the "lower levels of society"—he had previously been a store clerk, employee on a boat, dockworker, and dancer, and was repairing fountain pens when arrested—he was described in the police blotter as having imbibed "extreme individualistic and money-oriented ideas," which had led him to the conclusion that the state did not exist apart from the individual. His offense was having told some twenty youths on a public beach that "without the people, the emperor is nothing at all—he's just like an object you place in the *tokonoma*."[97] A number of the so-called lèse majesté cases did involve the assertion that the people did not exist for the emperor, or nation, but vice versa.[98]

The observation that the upper classes lived well while commoners suffered also was extended to include the imperial family. Thus an elderly farmer complained almost ruefully that while the commoners were urged to "work and work," the emperor himself was idle. "If he worked just two or three hours a day," he suggested, "how pleased the people would be. . . . It would be good if the emperor just tried doing a farmer's work."[99] A photographer who had attended a political meeting where citizens were urged to cut the emperor's picture from the newspaper and worship it in their homes responded that the imperial family didn't have to live on rationed rice and so the emperor didn't deserve such veneration.[100] A young farmer turned the paternalistic mystique inside-out by noting that "the expenses of the imperial house consume four million yen and come out of our taxes. We're the ones who are taking care of the imperial family."[101] Another individual used his exemplary sovereign to rationalize his own avariciousness: "Why not be greedy [*yoku*]? Even the emperor is carrying out the Great East Asian War because of his greed. It's only natural that I should be greedy."[102] Indeed, the emperor and his ministers not only ate well while the masses lived on declining rations, but also deprived the elderly of their very source of sustenance: their sons. In one mother's words, "after having raised them with so much trouble, they're taken away as the emperor's children. I'm disgusted. We don't get paid even a penny from the emperor for raising the children; and then to take them away once they're big—even the emperor will be punished for this."[103]

Even more ominously, some individuals expressed the view that the war had occurred precisely because of the emperor,[104] while others began to associate their own personal misery, and Japan's obvious inferiority in the war, to the relative inferiority of the imperial system itself. Such views were not always entirely coherent, and certainly not necessarily radical. Thus in one instance the emperor was compared unfavorably to Hitler and Mussolini, because the latter had risen from below on their own merits; a similarly negative comparison was drawn between the emperor and Chiang Kai-shek.[105] In another case, a rural charcoal manufacturer criticized the emperor because he was not *leading* the people as did the heads of state in the United States and Soviet Union. "Japan with its family system can't handle a war," this critique went on, with somewhat of a leap in logic. "Can one win a war without a collectivist system as in the Soviet Union? When this war is over, it won't be necessary to support this nothing of a monarch. Since he's not indispensable, we should get rid of him completely."[106] A journalist arrested in October 1943 was accused of having made these comments while a student in a police academy in Manchukuo a year earlier:

> This fellow the emperor experiences neither heat nor chill and enjoys the delicacies of land and sea, all the while treating the people like slaves. He has an insolent face. It's infuriating. Someday the political system will change. Rationally, the presidential system is correct. A person who leads a country should be someone with appropriate knowledge and ability. A person whom all the people support should become the president and the president should be changed every year. The emperor is a true do-nothing. . . .[107]

Ultimately, the spontaneous lèse majesté from the masses was expressed in overt acts of disrespect—commonly desecration of the sanctified tabernacles in schools in which the emperor's portrait resided—and in bitter outbursts of hatred toward both the person and institution of the emperor.[108] "Kill the emperor" exhortations were not uncommon, and often were graphic. "The emperor's expendable," one farmer with a reputation as a drunkard exclaimed; "bring me a gun and I'll shoot him." A miner, also drunk, expressed a desire to beat the emperor to death.[109] Ten laborers in the steel industry were apprehended after a conversation in which they reportedly had discussed the emperor at some length, and concluded that when the farmers and workers made their own world they should throw the emperor into the Siberian snow, like the Russian revolutionaries did with the czar and his family.[110]

Neither the rural population nor the elderly, presumably bedrocks of reverence to the throne, could be viewed as secure. Thus a forty-nine-year-old farmer made these chilling comments in several local meetings in Kochi in 1943, at which the government's agrarian policy was discussed:

> I feel no gratitude for having been born in Japan. Being born in Japan is regrettable, I think, and I loathe the emperor.
>
> Soldiers are killers. Students who get orders are embryo killers. They say soldiers die on the battlefield saying *Tennō Heika Banzai* [Long live the emperor], but it isn't so. Invariably they die filled with loathing.[111]

A sixty-eight-year-old woman in a small rural community, whose bitterness outstripped her grasp of comparative political systems, concluded that "if the United States or the like faced this sort of situation, they'd immediately turn the gun on their emperor, and it would be good if Japan did so too."[112] The most celebrated single incident of lèse majesté in wartime Japan also involved the oldest offender, the octogenarian parliamentarian Ozaki Yukio, who in 1942 gave a speech in which he drew an unfavorable comparison between the great Meiji emperor and his Taishō and Shōwa successors, and suggested that historically the Japanese state had always suffered decline under inferior sovereigns.[113]

Other expressions of lèse majesté that graced the dossiers of an increasingly frazzled police read as follows:

> The emperor is photographed as if nothing were wrong, putting on a good face in spite of having killed so many children.[114]

Eliminate the emperor and establish a republic. End the China Incident immediately. Break up the imperial tombs throughout the country and turn them into cultivated land.[115]

After having let Tokyo get burned down like that, to hell with His Imperial Highness. He said we should endure because we'll win the war, but the farmers can't even do what they want with the rice they make. They're just wasting their time.[116]

Every day, donations, donations. As far as I'm concerned, it would be just fine if His Imperial Highness died.[117]

Things are hard-up now. It's because of the war that we can't get enough to eat, but that there's not enough rice isn't the mayor's fault. It's all the emperor's doing.[118]

Even if we lose, we don't have to worry about getting killed. It's only the emperor and big shots like the ministers who'll be killed.[119]

Socialize the means of production.
The emperor is an expensive rubber stamp.
Overthrow the country of the capitalists.
We are bled white with taxes for the military.[120]

If two or three bombs just fell on the imperial palace, that would cause an interesting uproar.[121]

Overthrow the dictatorial emperor. Liberty!
... Liberals unite. Cease being slaves forever.[122]

Even if drafted, I don't want to die for the emperor.
True happiness will not come to Japan until the imperial family is overthrown.
The emperor is a puppet of those Jews, the *zaibatsu*.[123]

The war is a cruel thing where many people and talented people are killed and injured, so we shouldn't wage war. Why are we waging war and who is doing it? The emperor is doing it. If there were no emperor the war wouldn't be necessary.[124]

It's because we're fighting for the emperor that goods are few and people in difficulty.[125]

Those who gave their lives at Pearl Harbor and defended the country were splendid, but looking at the black marketeers and the like on the homefront, those who died look foolish. If people keep dying for the sake of the emperor, there will be no Japanese people left. The emperor is the same human being [as we], isn't he?[126]

I want to see the emperor's face when Japan is defeated and he becomes a prisoner and slave of the United States. The fate of warlike Japan will inevitably be defeat as heavenly punishment. Immediately shake hands with the United States and Great Britain and rescue our one hundred million people from the war—then it won't be necessary to send sons, husbands, and fathers to battle, and there'll be no worry of air raids, and we'll be able to eat until full too. . . . [127]

In the final analysis, such discontent shading into blasphemy and lèse majesté cannot be taken as indicating large-scale disenchantment with the emperor system, for the majority of Japanese still held the throne in respect.[128] Yet at the same time, the risks to those who made such statements were considerable, and for every case uncovered, who knew how many more had gone undetected—or how many others silently harbored such sentiments, or might come to do so if the miserable losing war did not soon end? Lèse majesté was but the most spectacular of many fissures that were becoming visible in popular support for the holy war; and as the police and many others saw it—not only conservatives, but also radical leftists such as Trotsky and Ozaki Hotsumi and a host of secret scribblers—under the stress of devastating defeat, these fissures might easily converge and destroy the Imperial state. Thus, while propagandists and ideologues were extolling the harmony of "the one hundred million" and their commitment to fight to the bitter end and if necessary die as "shattered jewels," the real jewel that they envisioned being shattered was popular devotion to the vaunted "national polity" itself.[129]

If revolution were to occur in defeated Japan, it was understood that the intelligentsia surely would have to assume a vanguard role in guiding such upheavals. Here, of course, the police looked back with great discomfort upon both the leading role of intellectuals in the heyday of the Japan Communist Party a scant decade or two earlier, and also the immense appeal that Marxism had exerted in academic circles through the 1920s and well into the 1930s. As already seen, a fair percentage of the seditious rumors and anonymous writings of the war years conveyed not only a good, formulaic appreciation of Marxism, but also—and more disturbing—the seductive argument that the losing war clearly demonstrated the correctness of Marxist analysis by exposing the cupidity of the capitalist and ruling classes in Japan. The losing war, it was feared, was radicalizing academics and other men of letters who may not necessarily have been previously drawn to the Left—a premonition that proved correct in postsurrender Japan, when a great many intellectuals embraced Marxism.

In June 1945, an Imperial army briefing for the emperor himself hinted at these dangers in characteristically muffled language by referring to an "underlying current of fretfullness and longing for peace" among intellectuals.[130] A far more vivid and accurate sense of the sheer visceral fear that such prospects struck in the hearts of the old guard, however, is to be found in the diary of Hosokawa Morisada, a young aristocrat who served as a gadabout collector of gossip and information for upper-class circles such as those in which Konoe moved. On December 20, 1943, Hosokawa encountered a drunk but "intellectual-looking" man loudly improvising this song on the trolley:

> They started a war
> they were bound to lose
> saying we'll win, we'll win,
> the big fools.
> Look, we're sure to lose.
>
> The war is lost
> and Europe's turned Red.
> Turning Asia Red
> can be done before breakfast.

And when that time comes,
out I'll come.

This seemed so shockingly prophetic to Hosokawa that he committed
the ditty to memory to preserve in his journal and share with upper-
class colleagues.[131]

NOTES

1 *Osaka Puck* carried slogans in the margin of every page from December
   1941 to July 1942. I have not been able to locate the August 1942 issue,
   but the practice is not followed in the September issue.
2 Morikawa Hōtatsu, *Teikoku Nippon Hyōgoshū: Senji Kokusaku Surōgan
   Zenkiroku* [Collected Slogans of Imperial Japan: A Complete Record
   of Wartime Policy Slogans] (Tokyo: Gendai Shokan, 1989). This book
   contains some 240 pages that simply list wartime slogans, averaging
   fifteen to twenty per page.
3 The Japanese spewed out war slogans with numbing regularity, far
   more than did Americans, and they certainly at least matched the
   Americans in patriotic speeches; yet their war songs were romantic and
   often oblique, and their war films did not rely much on stilted patriotic
   rhetoric at all, in this respect offering a sharp contrast to Hollywood's
   overwritten propaganda offerings. The variations in different modes
   of expression are quite striking.
4 In the so-called age of the samurai, from the twelfth to mid nineteenth
   century, the warrior class constituted perhaps 7 to 10 percent of the
   total population, including women and children; fighting men more
   often capitulated or cut deals instead of dying in battle; there were no
   major battles anyway after 1615; and the vast majority of people were
   oblivious to ideals of death in battle or death for one's lord. They
   had no "lord" as such, and indeed, until after the feudal regime was
   overthrown in 1868, virtually no awareness of the emperor.
5 The *Senjinkun* or Field Service Code, issued by the Imperial army on
   January 3, 1941, and carried by all soldiers in battle, set forth the no-
   surrender policy in the sixth section of the first chapter: "In defense,
   always retain the spirit of attack and always maintain freedom of action;
   never give up a position but rather die."
6 The major intelligence reports are to be found in Foreign Morale
   Analysis Division, Bureau of Overseas Intelligence, Office of War Infor-

mation, Record Group 208, National Archives, Washington, D.C. An excellent summary of the division's conclusion that Japanese morale was cracking was later published by the former head of the division, Alexander Leighton, in his *Human Relations in a Changing World: Observations on the Use of the Social Sciences* (New York: Dutton, 1949). See also U.S. Strategic Bombing Survey, *The Effects of Strategic Bombing on Japanese Morale* (Washington, D.C.: Government Printing Office, June 1947).

7 The Konoe Memorial is translated and discussed in J. W. Dower, *Empire and Aftermath: Yoshida Shigeru and the Japanese Experience, 1878–1954* (Cambridge, Mass.: Council on East Asian Studies, Harvard University, 1979), ch. 7.

8 Ogata Shōji, "Shūsen no Hankyōteki Seikaku" [The Anticommunist Character of the End of the War], *Geppō* 3 (Nov. 1953), a detached insert appearing in the multivolume publication *Nihon Shihonshugi Kōza: Sengo Nihon no Seiji to Keizai* [Series on Japanese Capitalism: Politics and Economy of Postwar Japan] (Tokyo: Iwanami Shoten, 1953). See also Mazaki Katsuji, *Nihon wa Doko e Iku—Wana ni Kakatta Nihon* [Where Is Japan Going?—Japan Caught in the Snare] (Tokyo: Jitsugyō no Sekaisha, 1960), pp. 42–46.

9 Gaimushō (Foreign Ministry), ed., *Shūsen Shiroku* [Historical Record of the End of the War] (Tokyo: Shimbun Gekkansha, 1952), pp. 359–60.

10 The Sorge-Ozaki spy ring receives excellent treatment in Chalmers Johnson, *An Instance of Treason: Ozaki Hotsumi and the Sorge Spy Ring* (Stanford, Calif.: Stanford University Press, 1964).

11 Shigemitsu Mamoru, *Japan and Her Destiny: My Struggle for Peace* (New York: Dutton, 1958), pp. 244–45; Misuzu Shobō, ed., *Gendaishi Shiryō: Zoruge Jiken* [Documents on Contemporary History: The Sorge Case], vol. 2, no. 2, p. 128; see also the translation of the second quotation in Johnson, *An Instance of Treason*, p. 191, as well as ibid., pp. 2, 5, 7, 120, 131, 160, 172. This was not a peripheral observation on Ozaki's part, but the very heart of his hopes and expectations.

12 Hosokawa Morisada, *Jōhō Tennō ni Tassezu* [Reports Do Not Reach the Emperor] (Tokyo: Isobe Shobō, 1953), pp. 189, 312–13.

13 Naimushō Keihokyoku Hoanbu (Home Ministry, Police Bureau, Peace Preservation Division), *Tokkō Geppō* [Monthly Gazette of the Special Higher Police], February 1942, p. 22. This was the secret internal monthly report of the Thought Police, and covered the period from March 1930 through November 1944. (Hereafter it is referred to as *TG*.)

14 Ibid., pp. 7–8.

15 Ibid., pp. 15–16, 22, 28, 35.

16 Ibid., pp. 37–38.

17 The various Japan Communist Party theses are reproduced in George M. Beckmann and Genji Okubo, *The Japanese Communist Party, 1922–1945* (Stanford, Calif.: Stanford University Press, 1969).

18 Leon Trotsky, *Writings of Leon Trotsky, 1930–31* (New York: Pathfinder Press; the twelve-volume collected writings, edited by George Breitman et al., were published between 1971 and 1976), p. 356; see also *Writings of Leon Trotsky, 1932–33*, p. 291.

19 *Writings of Leon Trotsky, 1937–38*, p. 101.

20 Ibid., p. 106; see also *Writings of Leon Trotsky, 1932–33*, p. 293.

21 Mao is quoted in Edgar Snow, *Red Star Over China* (New York: Grove, 1961), p. 95; Karl Radek, "Japan and International Fascism," introduction to O. Tanin and E. Yohan, *Militarism and Fascism in Japan* (New York: International Publishers, 1934); see also Tanin and Yohan's *When Japan Goes to War* (New York: International Publishers, 1936). For sample comments by anticommunist observers, see Russell D. Buhite, *Nelson T. Johnson and American Policy toward China, 1925–1941* (East Lansing: Michigan State University Press, 1968), p. 68; Willis Church Lamont, "What of Postwar Japan?" *Asia* (Oct. 1942), p. 575; William C. Johnstone, "Must We Keep Japan Strong?" *Far Eastern Survey* (Nov. 2, 1942), p. 225.

22 Institute of Pacific Relations, *Security in the Pacific* (New York: Institute of Pacific Relations, 1945), pp. 23, 25.

23 Nobutake Ike, trans., *Japan's Decision for War: Records of the 1941 Policy Conferences* (Stanford, Calif.: Stanford University Press, 1967), pp. 111–12.

24 Ibid., pp. 272–74.

25 Gaimushō, *Shūsen Shiroku*, p. 357.

26 Hosokawa, *Jōhō Tennō ni Tassezu*, pp. 250–51; see also pp. 153–54, 164–67.

27 Ronald Dore, *Land Reform in Japan* (London: Oxford University Press, 1959), p. 22; Tadashi Furutake, *Japanese Rural Society* (Ithaca, N.Y.: Cornell University Press, 1972), p. 10.

28 See also Dore, *Land Reform in Japan*, p. 72, for comparable statistics on the number of disputes; also ibid., pp. 78–79, for a vivid description of radicalism in the countryside in the 1920s and early 1930s. *Tokkō Geppō* figures for wartime disputes are more conservative; see *TG*, Dec. 1942, p. 72; Dec. 1943, pp. 91–92; and Nov. 1944, pp. 43–45.

29 Dore, *Land Reform in Japan*, pp. 22, 114, and ch. 4.

30 Frederick S. Hulse, "Some Effects of the War upon Japanese Society," *Far Eastern Quarterly* 8, no. 1 (Nov. 1947), pp. 22–42.

31 Fujiwara Akira, "Taiheiyō Sensō" [The Pacific War], in Iwanami Kōza (Iwanami Lectures), ed., *Nihon Rekishi* [Japanese History], vol. 21 (Tokyo: Iwanami Shoten, 1963), pp. 184–85.

32 *TG*, March 1943, pp. 58–63.

33 U.S. Strategic Bombing Survey, *Effects of Strategic Bombing on Japanese Morale*, p. 112; see also pp. 241–42.

34 *TG*, Aug. 1944, pp. 5, 15–27.

35 Ogata Shōji (see note 8, above). Stalin actually appears to have been evoked rather infrequently by the dissidents; see *TG*, Aug. 1943, p. 26.

36 Ogata (see note 8, above). As a consequence of such tendencies, special investigators were assigned to prevent "dangerous thoughts" among conscripted student workers; see Jerome B. Cohen, *Japan's Economy in War and Reconstruction* (Minneapolis: University of Minnesota Press, 1949), p. 324.

37 *Asahi Shimbun*, Dec. 6, 1971.

38 Ibid.

39 U.S. Strategic Bombing Survey, *Effects of Strategic Bombing on Japanese Morale*, p. 248.

40 The quotations that follow all appear in *Tokkō Geppō* in the issues for the months indicated.

41 Okudaira Yasuhiro, *Chian Ijihō* [Peace Preservation Law], vol. 45 of *Gendaishi Shiryō* [Documents on Contemporary History] (Tokyo: Misuzu Shobō, 1973), pp. 655–57.

42 Cited by Fujiwara, "Taiheiyō Sensō," p. 185; see also Shinobu Seizaburō, *Sengo Nihon Seiji Shi, 1945–1952* [A Political History of Postwar Japan, 1945–1952] (Tokyo: Keisō Shobō in 4 volumes, 1965–67), vol. 1, p. 52.

43 U.S. Strategic Bombing Survey, *Effects of Strategic Bombing on Japanese Morale*, p. 249.

44 Ibid., p. 244.

45 Ibid., pp. 113, 249.

46 Hulse, "Some Effects of the War on Japanese Society," p. 29. See also U.S. Strategic Bombing Survey, *Effects of Atomic Bombs on Hiroshima and Nagasaki* (Washington, D.C.: Government Printing Office, 1946), pp. 20–21.

47 Ikeuchi Hajime, "Taiheiyō Sensōchū no Senji Ryūgen" [Wartime Rumors during the Pacific War], *Shakaigaku Hyōron* (June 1951), pp.

30–42; U.S. Strategic Bombing Survey, *Effects of Strategic Bombing on Japanese Morale*, pp. 249–50.

48 *TG*, Oct. 1943, p. 97. See also April 1942, p. 27; May 1942, p. 25; Jan. 1943, p. 29; Oct. 1943, p. 97.

49 *TG*, Sept. 1943, pp. 20–21.

50 *TG*, March 1943, p. 19. See also Feb. 1943, p. 21.

51 Shinobu, *Sengo Nihon Seiji Shi*, vol. 1, p. 72.

52 *TG*, Feb. 1944, p. 16.

53 *TG*, Dec. 1943, p. 43; Nov. 1943, p. 34.

54 *TG*, Jan. 1942, p. 13.

55 *TG*, April 1942, p. 30.

56 *TG*, April 1942, p. 30.

57 *TG*, June 1944, p. 26.

58 *TG*, Oct. 1943, p. 104.

59 *TG*, July 1943, p. 33.

60 *TG*, March 1943, p. 19. See also Jan. 1942, p. 11; April 1942, p. 30; Oct. 1942, p. 23; April 1943, pp. 29–30.

61 *TG*, Oct. 1944, p. 16.

62 *TG*, Dec. 1943, p. 43.

63 *TG*, Aug. 1943, p. 28.

64 *TG*, Aug. 1944, p. 32. See also July 1943, pp. 29, 33.

65 *TG*, May 1942, p. 25; April 1942, p. 29.

66 *TG*, Oct. 1944, p. 15; June 1942, p. 19; Oct. 1944, p. 16.

67 U.S. Strategic Bombing Survey, *Effects of Strategic Bombing on Japanese Morale*, p. 243 (slightly revised).

68 *TG*, May 1942, p. 25. A slightly revised version of this line appears in *TG*, Nov. 1943, p. 39.

69 *TG*, April 1943, p. 29; March 1943, p. 19; Oct. 1943, p. 102.

70 *TG*, July 1944, p. 18. This particular case suggests signs of neurosis on the part of the young offender, for his wall writings, which were not entirely coherent, continued on: "... don't lose, either side. I want the war to become more severe. I hate them [it?]. ..."

71 *TG*, April 1943, p. 32.

72 Hosokawa, *Jōhō Tennō ni Tassezu*, p. 359.

73 *TG*, Oct. 1943, p. 102. Although recorded entirely in Japanese in the police report, the accompanying commentary indicates that the actual wall writing was a mix of English and Japanese.

74 *TG*, March 1942, pp. 42–45. See also March 1942, p. 40; May 1942, p. 23; Dec. 1942, p. 39; Sept. 1943, p. 19.

75 *TG*, Sept. 1943, p. 28. See also June 1942, p. 20; Sept. 1943, p. 26; Dec. 1943, p. 40.

76 *TG*, May 1943, p. 29. See also Dec. 1943, p. 39.

77 *TG*, May 1943, p. 23.

78 *TG*, June 1943, p. 31.

79 *TG*, Dec. 1943, p. 39.

80 *TG*, May 1942, p. 23.

81 *TG*, May 1942, p. 25.

82 *TG*, Aug. 1942, p. 179.

83 *TG*, Jan. 1942, p. 10; Aug. 1943, p. 26; May 1942, p. 22; Feb. 1944, p. 14.

84 *TG*, Jan. 1942, p. 10; April 1943, p. 30.

85 See Ikeuchi, "Taiheiyō Sensōchū no Senji Ryūgen," p. 39 (chart 4).

86 *TG*, April 1943, p. 30.

87 *TG*, Jan. 1942, p. 10. See also Dec. 1941, p. 30.

88 Fujiwara, "Taiheiyō Sensō," p. 185.

89 *Tokkō Geppō*, which cannot be regarded as comprehensive, itemized a total of 162 incidents of lèse majesté and sedition (*fukei fuon jiken*) in 1943, of which 85 involved lèse majesté. For the seven months of 1944 readily available in the reprint edition of this gazette (culminating in November 1944), the figures are 71 and 40, respectively. The U.S. Strategic Bombing Survey (*Effects of Strategic Bombing on Japanese Morale*, p. 245) cited an official report of spring, 1944, which emphasized the intensification of popular criticism between September. 1943 and February 1944 and gave these figures for exceptionally serious cases:

	Lèse majesté		Antiwar and Antimilitary		Other	
	Cases	Arrests	Cases	Arrests	Cases	Arrests
Feb. 1943–Aug. 1943	39	22	30	5	61	11
Sep. 1943–Feb. 1944	48	38	32	12	23	7
Total	87	60	62	17	84	18

90 *TG*, Oct. 1942, p. 23.

91 *TG*, Oct. 1943, p. 98.

92 *TG*, Sept. 1943, p. 19.

93 *TG*, Sept. 1943, p. 26.

94 For "just a human" comments, see *TG*, May 1942, p. 21; May 1943,

pp. 27–28. The more exotic variations appear in *TG*, Feb. 1944, p. 17; Oct. 1943, p. 98; Dec. 1943, p. 42; Jan. 1942, p. 11; Dec. 1941, p. 29.

95 *TG*, Feb. 1944, p. 6; Aug. 1944, p. 32. The *Tenchan* appellation is frequently mentioned by Japanese who lived through this period.

96 *TG*, Sept. 1943, p. 24.

97 *TG*, Sept. 1942, p. 31.

98 *TG*, Jan. 1942, p. 11; Aug. 1942, p. 179; Dec. 1942, p. 38; Feb. 1943, p. 20.

99 *TG*, April 1942, p. 27.

100 *TG*, Aug. 1943, p. 27.

101 *TG*, Dec. 1943, p. 42.

102 *TG*, March 1943, p. 16.

103 *TG*, Sept. 1943, p. 24.

104 *TG*, Oct. 1942, p. 24; March 1943, p. 17.

105 *TG*, Jan. 1943, p. 29; Sept. 1943, p. 24.

106 *TG*, Dec. 1943, pp. 40–41.

107 *TG*, Dec. 1943, p. 42.

108 See *TG*, April 1942, p. 28; Sept. 1942, p. 31; March 1943, pp. 13–14; Sept. 1943, p. 21; Dec. 1943, p. 41.

109 *TG*, Oct. 1943, pp. 105, 97.

110 *TG*, June 1943, p. 28.

111 *TG*, Dec. 1943, p. 41. Ienaga Saburō quotes the famous Japanese deserter "Tobin" as stating that he never once heard a dying Japanese soldier exclaim *Tennō Heika Banzai*! See his *Taiheiyō Sensō* [The Pacific War] (Tokyo: Iwanami Shoten, 1968), p. 246. Japanese who survived the battlefield experience privately have expressed the opinion that most soldiers died speaking of their families, especially of their mothers.

112 *TG*, Aug. 1943, p. 28.

113 *TG*, May 1942, pp. 19–20.

114 Shinobu, *Sengo Nihon Seiji Shi*, vol. 1, p. 72; Ienaga, *Taiheiyō Sensō*, p. 253.

115 Ienaga, *Taiheiyō Sensō*, p. 247.

116 Shinobu, *Sengo Nihon Seiji Shi*, vol. 1, p. 72.

117 Ibid.

118 Ibid.

119 Ibid.

120 *TG*, Dec. 1941, p. 29.

121 *TG*, April 1942, p. 28.

122 Ibid.

123 *TG*, June 1942, p. 18. Anti-Semitism emerges on occasion in these invectives; see Jan. 1942, p. 11; U.S. Strategic Bombing Survey, *Effects of Strategic Bombing on Japanese Morale*, p. 240.

124 *TG*, Oct. 1942, p. 24.

125 *TG*, March 1943, p. 17.

126 *TG*, May 1943, pp. 27–28.

127 *TG*, Feb. 1944, p. 15; see U.S. Strategic Bombing Survey, *Effects of Strategic Bombing on Japanese Morale*, p. 245.

128 See the treatment of this subject by Kazuko Tsurumi in *Social Change and the Individual: Japan before and after Defeat in World War II* (Princeton: Princeton University Press, 1970), and U.S. Strategic Bombing Survey, *Summary Report (Pacific War)* (Washington, D.C.: Government Printing Office, 1946), p. 21.

129 The masses, as one report put it, were beginning to question the unquestionable: "the responsibility of the war leaders and, indirectly, that of the emperor for the present war situation. . . . [T]here are many cases which advocate the class struggle by extreme expressions of resentment against capitalists and managers of munitions factories, contending that this 'Holy War' is a private war of the militarists and capitalists." U.S. Strategic Bombing Survey, *Effects of Strategic Bombing on Japanese Morale*, p. 245.

130 Gaimushō, *Shūsen Shiroku*, p. 357.

131 Hosokawa, *Jōhō Tennō ni Tassezu*, p. 73–74; also Gaimushō, *Shūsen Shiroku*, p. 291. See Dower, *Empire and Aftermath*, pp. 289–90 for Hosokawa, and pp. 292–303 for the manner in which, in conservative eyes, these fears of revolution seemed to be materializing in the early stages of the U.S. occupation of Japan.

154

5

Occupied Japan and the Cold War in Asia

WHEN HARRY TRUMAN succeeded Franklin Roosevelt as president in April 1945, the United States had just begun the systematic, low-level saturation bombing of Japanese cities. In the third month of his administration, the new president received word of the nuclear test at Alamogordo, thought immediately of biblical prophesies of the apocalypse, and immediately approved the use of the atomic bombs against Japan. As he phrased it in his belatedly discovered "Potsdam diary," written at the time he learned about the successful test, the Japanese were "savages, ruthless, merciless and fanatic." In a personal letter written a few days after Hiroshima and Nagasaki had been destroyed, the president explained that "when you have to deal with a beast you have to treat him as a beast." Following Japan's capitulation in mid August 1945, the United States occupied the country as the overwhelmingly dominant force in a nominally "Allied" occupation and proceeded to initiate a rigorous policy of "demilitarization and democratization."[1]

Less than five years later, the Truman administration had identified Japan as the key to the balance of power in Asia—and Asia as capable

155

of tipping the global balance in the direction of the Soviet Union. Before the outbreak of the Korean War on June 25, 1950, Okinawa had been taken over as the key U.S. nuclear base in the Far East, the runways on airfields in Japan were being lengthened to accommodate the newest U.S. heavy bombers, policy toward occupied Japan had shifted from reform to economic reconstruction, plans were in the air to promote Japanese production of capital goods including military items for export, and the United States was urging Japan to rearm. In addition, policymakers in Washington were in general agreement on the urgent need to integrate Japan and Southeast Asia with one another economically and militarily, as part of a "great crescent" of anticommunist containment in Asia. As a number of contemporary observers noted, some wryly and some bitterly, the Americans seemed to be dusting off Japan's plans of the 1930s and early 1940s to integrate the southern areas in a great "coprosperity sphere," which had brought World War II to Asia in the first place.

In September 1951, the United States and forty-seven other nations signed a nonrestrictive and relatively brief treaty of peace with Japan in San Francisco, thereby (pending ratification by home governments) formally ending the state of war between the Allied Powers and Japan. Simultaneously, as the essential quid pro quo for this "generous" peace treaty on the part of the United States, a bilateral United States–Japan Mutual Security Agreement was signed, permitting the maintenance of U.S. bases throughout sovereign Japan and anticipating future substantial Japanese rearmament. Because of this de facto military rider, the Soviet Union did not sign the peace treaty. Furthermore, because of disagreements among the Allies concerning policy toward China, neither the People's Republic of China nor the Chinese Nationalist regime ensconced in Taiwan were invited to the peace conference. In the months following the San Francisco conference, however, while Japan remained occupied, the conservative government of Yoshida Shigeru was effectively pressured into signing a bilateral peace treaty with the Chinese Nationalists and adhering to the U.S. policy of isolating and economically strangling communist China. In April 1952—eighty months after the end of World War II in Asia—the Occupation of Japan formally ended and Japan reentered the global arena as the key U.S. ally in Asia. The Occupation had lasted almost twice as long as the Pacific War itself.

At the time the Occupation ended, it seemed to most observers, certainly on the Japanese side, to have been an unduly prolonged affair. Indeed, one of the major arguments in Washington for restoring sovereignty to Japan was that further delay would simply erode Japanese goodwill toward the United States and increase the possibility of Japan's sliding toward the Soviet Union. In retrospect, of course, we are inclined to weigh time differently and see this as a relatively short period in which momentous changes took place. In retrospect, too, it is also now apparent that Japan, less than seven years after sacrificing more than two and a half million of its citizens and losing an empire, was about to embark on a period of accelerated economic growth that actually was facilitated by war: by breakthroughs in technology and labor skills that came about in mobilizing for "total war" beginning in the 1930s; by the destruction of old industrial plants in the U.S. air raids of 1944 and 1945, which paved the way for factory reconstruction at more modern and rational levels after 1945; by the stimulation that the Japanese economy received from war-related "special procurements" and "new special procurements" by the United States after the outbreak of the Korean War in 1950; and by the fact that the U.S. policy of incorporating Japan economically as well as militarily into a new Pax Americana in Asia also involved giving Japanese industrialists fairly generous access to U.S. licenses and patents.

This transformation from "savage" enemy to "freedom-loving" ally was breathtaking in many ways. It was not necessarily conceptually or psychologically disorienting to most Americans, however, because much of the basic rhetoric of the World War II years was simply reassigned. Now the communists were portrayed as the savages who were conspiring to conquer the world (U.S. wartime propaganda had insisted not merely that Japan's goal was world conquest but that the Japanese had a "100-year plan" for accomplishing this). More peculiar to the Asian context, the Japanese now donned the "democratic, business-oriented" characteristics that had been assigned to America's wartime Chinese allies, while the Chinese, as communists, suddenly became inherently treacherous and fanatical, robotlike and antlike. The communist Chinese also absorbed much of the racist "Yellow Peril" animosity that had been directed against the Japanese enemy during World War II—now with the overlay, of course, of the "Red Peril" as well.

157

Even before the Truman administration ended, it was apparent that Japan was the only place in postwar Asia where U.S. policy could reasonably claim success. Judged on its own terms, the Occupation had been unexpectedly amicable; and despite the so-called reverse course that marked the shift in U.S. policies from reform to rehabilitation of Japan as a Cold War ally, many of the initial democratic reforms remained intact. The government of Japan was conservative and staunchly anti-communist. And with the conspicuous exception of the left-wing parties and a good portion of the intelligentsia, who opposed the dilution of reformism and abandonment of the early ideals of demilitarization and neutrality, the Japanese people as a whole also appeared to look favorably on the United States. When Americans looked at the rest of Asia—at China, Korea, and Southeast Asia—Japan could not help but bring a sigh of relief. By comparison with the Soviet presence in Eastern Europe, moreover, Japan could be held up as a model of enlightened "free world" occupation policies.

Until perhaps the end of the 1960s, Western scholarship on U.S. policy toward Japan during the Truman administration tended to dwell on these positive accomplishments and was characterized by several lines of emphasis. The focus was on the occupation of Japan per se and, within this frame, on the positive American contribution to "democratization." The Occupation was presented as a model of enlightened red-white-and-blue "social engineering," as suggested by the title of the most popular book on the subject, Kazuo Kawai's *Japan's American Interlude*, first published in 1960. The "reverse course" was not greatly emphasized (except as a necessary way of preserving the democratic reforms by stabilizing the economy), and the decision to remilitarize Japan was presented largely as a response to a Soviet threat to Japan and Asia. Because Japanese rearmament, the decision to maintain post-treaty U.S. bases in Japan, and the policy of trilateral linkage among Japan, Southeast Asia, and the United States all emerged as formal public policies after the outbreak of the Korean War, it generally was implied that they were responses to that conflict.

More recent scholarship on this period, in Japan as well as in the English-speaking countries, has by no means denied the "democratization" that occurred in postsurrender Japan, but in general it has taken a different tack in approaching occupied Japan as history. In good part, the revised approach derives from the opening of the U.S. archives on this period, along with a wealth of private papers, reminiscences, oral histories, and the like. To some extent, the new approaches also reflect the questions asked by a younger and more skeptical generation of scholars in the United States, who began to do archival work on early postwar U.S. policy in the wake of the Vietnam War. To risk some grand generalizations, it can be said that recent scholarship on U.S. policy toward Japan in the late 1940s and early 1950s (1) gives greater emphasis to the Japanese contribution to developments in occupied Japan, positive as well as negative, and at the popular as well as official levels; (2) is more attentive to the contribution of "middle-echelon leadership" on both the U.S. and the Japanese sides, as well as to the influence of special-interest groups; (3) places U.S. policy toward occupied Japan firmly in the context of U.S. global policy; (4) traces almost all key strategic policies (such as Japanese remilitarization, U.S. bases in sovereign Japan, and integration of Japan and Southeast Asia) to before the Korean War; (5) emphasizes economic and not just military considerations in U.S. planning for Asia (such as the "dollar gap" crisis of the late 1940s); (6) deemphasizes the fear of a direct Soviet attack on Japan on the part of U.S. planners while elevating the importance assigned to Japan in balance-of-power thinking; and (7) calls attention to some of the more hysterical U.S. proposals for Japan that emerged after the outbreak of the Korean War, such as the demand for a Japanese army of at least 300,000 men and the anticipation that Japan should and would soon emerge as an arsenal of select military items for noncommunist Asia.

The implications of such reinterpretations are substantial. For example, the repressive aspects of the reverse course within the Japanese body politic have become more apparent to Western students and scholars. (They always have been emphasized in Japanese writings on the period.) Also, the fundamentally benign picture of Japan's being remilitarized in response to mounting tensions in Asia is called into question, because it is now apparent that the U.S. policy toward Japan also contributed to tension and confrontation in Asia in particular and in the Cold War in general, especially from 1949 on (that is, before the Korean War and even before the Sino-Soviet pact of February 1950, which is often cited as evidence of the hostile intentions of the communist powers). Perhaps the single most concrete and consequential point that emerges from the recently opened archives is the extent to which, by the early 1950s, U.S. planners had come to see Japan and Southeast Asia as inseparable parts of the containment strategy. Southeast Asia needed the Japanese "workshop," it was argued, but even more significantly Japan needed secure access to the markets and raw materials of Southeast Asia, especially if it was not going to be allowed to reestablish intimate economic relations with China. When postwar U.S. policy toward Asia is examined from this perspective, Japan emerges as the greatest "domino" of all well before the Geneva Conference of 1954. It is now apparent that the initial U.S. commitment to counterrevolution in Southeast Asia, which eventually proved so tragic, cannot be fully understood without taking Japan into account.[2]

As these observations suggest, a comprehensive study of the policies of the Truman administration toward Japan must move in several directions, encompassing both internal developments in occupied Japan and broader regional and global strategies. In the latter instance, a great deal more is involved than just the projected linkage of Japan and Southeast Asia, for this positive policy naturally developed against the background of reassessing U.S. policy toward China and Korea—developments that have been the subject of a number of recent monographs in English.[3] The regional dimension also involves international considerations of a slightly different order, namely, the response of U.S. allies such as Britain, Australia, and New Zealand to U.S. initiatives involving Japan and the rest of Asia. These countries, too, have opened their diplomatic archives in recent years, and it is more apparent than ever that their cooperation with the U.S. Cold War policy frequently was tempered by grave misgivings. The rearmament of Japan caused shudders throughout noncommunist Asia, to say nothing of the fear provoked in the communist countries. And the unilateral U.S. decision to promote Japanese economic reconstruction was not exactly received gleefully by Japan's former and future economic rivals in Asia. When it became clear that the United States had decided not merely to assist in the economic rehabilitation of Japan but to deflect such projected growth away from China and in the direction of Southeast Asia, the alarm was palpable, especially in London, where such a policy could be seen as yet another potentially devastating blow to the Sterling bloc. From this perspective, U.S. policy toward

Japan also must be seen in the context of the decline of the British empire and the tensions that arose within the Anglo-American camp as the Pax Britannica gave way to a Pax Americana.[4]

Although the transformation of Japan from bitter enemy to Cold War ally may seem natural in retrospect, this reversal of policy did not occur all of a piece; nor was it arrived at without controversy within U.S. decision-making circles; nor was it a policy without ambiguities—including resentment on the part of many Japanese conservatives who felt they were being denied true sovereignty, and lingering doubts on the U.S. side about how far Japan could be trusted. Even as U.S. planners came to assign Japan a crucial role in the global balance of power, in both a negative and positive sense (denying Japan to the Soviet Union's sphere of influence and using Japan against the Soviet "bloc"), they remained nervous about Japan's "ideological" inclinations. Extremists of either the Left or the Right, it was feared, might still assume power in the future. Thus, while the bilateral United States–Japan security treaty signed at San Francisco in 1951 was first and foremost an anticommunist pact, it simultaneously functioned as a vehicle for controlling Japan by perpetuating its military subordination to the United States in every conceivable direction: strategic planning, matériel procurement, technological development, and the continued presence of U.S. forces in and around Japan. Similarly, the security treaties that the United States negotiated with the Philippines and Australia–New Zealand in 1951 also served the double function of assuring these allies of U.S. assistance in the event of either communist or Japanese aggression. At the time they were negotiated, in fact, these parallel security pacts were requested by the Asian nations involved primarily out of alarm at the specter of a remilitarized and revanchist Japan.

From the perspective of Washington, the U.S. relationship with Japan also was plagued by the legacy of one of the early ideals of the Occupation: the pacifist sentiment embodied in the famous "no war" clause (Article Nine) of the new constitution that General Douglas MacArthur and his staff had pressed upon the Japanese in 1946. Although U.S. officials quickly came to lament this dramatic exercise in "demilitarization," the Japanese people as a whole continued to embrace Article Nine, in spirit if not to the letter, and resisted its abrogation or amendment. Their recollection of the hardships and horrors of the war in Asia and the Pacific remained keen, as did their skepticism of overly zealous appeals to remilitarize in the name of "defense." The symbolic significance of Article Nine in postwar Japanese politics cannot be overemphasized, and Japan's conservative government lost no opportunity to use this in resisting the heavy pressure for rapid remilitarization that the United States exerted after June 1950.

In the pages that follow, the fascinating developments that took place within occupied Japan will be mentioned only in passing; primary attention will be given to Japan's place in the strategic thinking of the Truman administration. Recent country-oriented studies of postwar U.S. policy toward China, Korea, and Southeast Asia as a rule point to the year or so before the Korean War as marking a watershed in U.S. planning. Certainly the documents of the time reveal officials as temperamentally diverse as George Kennan, Dean Rusk, and Louis Johnson all lamenting the "country by country" approach toward Asia that existed in 1949 and into 1950, and it is from this time on that the contours of a more integrated, regional approach to Asia become conspicuous.[5] Strategic policy toward Japan not only fits this pattern but can be analyzed more precisely as having evolved through four stages between the end of the war in 1945 and the end of the Occupation in April 1952: (1) concentration on the "demilitarization and democratization" of Japan and projection of a disarmed and "neutral" Japan in the future (August 1945 to mid 1947); (2) a "soft" Cold War policy, in which primary emphasis was placed on denying Japan to the Soviet sphere (mid 1947 to 1949); (3) a "hard" Cold War policy, in which Japan was assigned a positive, active role in the U.S. anticommunist strategy (mid 1949 to September 1951); and (4) an integrated Cold War policy, in which the concrete mechanisms of regional military and economic integration actually were created— including the peace treaty and various security treaties of 1951–1952, the coordination of U.S. military and economic polices, and the firm commitment to containment of China through the creation of a trilateral nexus linking the United States, Japan, and Southeast Asia (beginning in the latter part of 1951). Obviously, the roots of each "stage" can be found in earlier periods.

DEMILITARIZATION AND DEMOCRATIZATION,
1945–1947

Well before World War II ended, it was widely assumed that the United States would maintain strategic control of the Pacific Ocean—an assumption that was blithely captured at the popular level in a wartime American song entitled "To Be Specific, It's Our Pacific." U.S. military planners gave close attention to the key islands in the Pacific over which they desired to maintain unilateral control indefinitely, but such planning did not extend to Japan per se. Until the final stages of the war, plans for postsurrender Japan anticipated an "Allied" occupation in which the United States would play the leading role, but China, Britain, and possibly the Soviet Union (if it entered the war before Japan surrendered) would all have a serious place.[6]

When Japan's capitulation became a reality, however, the Truman administration took a strong stand against a multinational occupation in any meaningful sense. The United States refused to consider dividing Japan into zones of occupation as had been done in Germany, demanded that all of occupied Japan be placed under a U.S. supreme commander, and balked at the creation of a genuinely influential international control commission. There was some grousing at this on the part of other Allied powers, and the creation of an essentially tokenistic superstructure of international supervision was not completed until early 1946, by which time the bureaucratic apparatus of de facto unilateral U.S. control was firmly in place.[7]

Looking ahead to the rise of Cold War tensions between the United States and Soviet Union, it is noteworthy that Stalin did not make a great issue out of the U.S. assumption of a dominant position in Japan and the Pacific. Although the Soviet Union requested a joint U.S.-Soviet supreme command in Japan, and asked that the northern island of Hokkaido be made a Soviet zone of occupation, Stalin accepted Truman's flat rejection of these requests with little more than a shrug. And although legally entitled to send a Soviet military contingent to Japan as part of the nominally Allied occupation force, the Soviet dictator declined to do so on the grounds that this would inconvenience General Douglas MacArthur, who had been designated supreme commander. In the exchanges that took place over the control apparatus for occupied Japan between August 1945 and early 1946, the Soviets gave numerous signals that they hoped the United States would accept their acknowledgment of a legitimate U.S. sphere of interest in Japan and the Pacific as a quid pro quo for American acknowledgment of the Soviet Union's reasonable security concerns in Eastern Europe. This conciliatory stance was consistent with the restraint the Russians displayed in Korea in August 1945, when Stalin held his forces at the thirty-eighth parallel although they could have occupied the entire Korean peninsula easily before the U.S. forces arrived. Stalin's willingness to recognize the Nationalist regime of Chiang Kai-shek as the sole legitimate government of China in August 1945 and to promise eventual withdrawal of Soviet troops from Manchuria also impressed some observers at the time as being unexpectedly conciliatory. As it turned out, the Truman administration was not inclined to acknowledge that there was any comparability in the assumed spheres of influence of the two nations.[8]

Journalistic accounts from the early months of the Occupation often refer to gossip and scuttlebutt concerning Japan as the "staging area for the next war," and it is indeed possible to find U.S. officials who raised the question of Japan's future importance as an anti-Soviet military base at an early date. Navy Secretary James Forrestal turned this matter over in his mind in the early summer of 1945, for example; in the State Department, John Davies introduced the prospect of Japan as a future *place d'armes* in August 1946.[9] The mainstream of U.S. strategic planning for Asia from 1945 to 1947, however, remained grounded in the passions and assumptions of the recent war: notably, hatred and fear of Japan and lingering hope that China would emerge as a strong ally of the United States and capable "policeman" in Asia. Until well into 1946, and in some circles much later, the *place d'armes* men were drowned out by a potent phrase that carried over from the war years, namely, the "permanent and complete" disarmament of Japan. The genealogy of this idealistic rhetoric is beyond the scope of this essay, but it is well to recall how immensely popular it was during the war. President Roosevelt, with characteristic grandiloquence, had declared this to be the Allied goal for both Germany and Japan; Senator Arthur Vandenberg called for "permanently and conclusively and effectively disarming Germany and Japan" in the famous speech of January 1945 in which he announced his support for a bipartisan foreign policy in the postwar era; the Potsdam Declaration of July projected the "complete disarmament" of Japan; and citizens' lobbies and the media readily embraced the prospect of a permanently defanged Axis foe.[10]

The agenda for Japan was in fact much broader than mere disarmament per se. Until the very eve of Japan's surrender, U.S. military planners still expected that the war in Asia might continue for another year or year and a half. Consequently, they were caught somewhat by surprise by Japan's surrender. Due in good part to the impressive activities of a small State Department group led by Hugh Borton and George Blakeslee of the Far Eastern Division, however, planning for postsurrender Japan at the lower levels of the bureaucracy was in fact well advanced when the war ended. Scores of position papers dealing with specific aspects of the Japanese state and society already had been reviewed by the critical intergovernmental committee in these matters—the State-War-Navy Coordinating Committee (SWNCC)—and these became the basis for a wide range of proposed reforms in occupied Japan. As the Borton-Blakeslee group and SWNCC saw it, disarmament was but one aspect of the task of ensuring a peaceful Japan in the future, for true demilitarization required "democratization" as well. The fundamental assumption here was that the repressive structure of the prewar Japanese state had created a "will to war" (as Assistant Secretary of State Dean Acheson phrased it shortly after Japan surrendered), whereas democracies—by which was meant bourgeois democracies with a thriving middle class—did not practice oppression.[11]

The initial U.S. Occupation policy of demilitarization and democratization rested on such sweeping assumptions. In the many instances where the policy directives emanating from Washington were couched in broad and somewhat ambiguous terms, moreover, MacArthur and his staff in Tokyo tended to interpret them as a mandate for genuinely drastic reform, on occasion of a more radical nature than Washington seems to have had in mind. MacArthur's prestige and messianic style, coupled with the Eurocentrism of the Truman administration, gave the Occupation staff in Japan unusual leeway for approximately two years, until the latter part of 1947. And although the general may have fumed about liberal programs in his homeland under President "Rosenfeld," as he reportedly was wont to call his former commander in chief, as a reformer in the Japanese milieu MacArthur proved to be exceptionally receptive to the recommendations of a small coterie of American liberals and New Dealers. Some of the most dramatic and consequential reforms carried out under the early democratization program, such as the sweeping land reform of 1946–47 and the new constitution promulgated in 1946, actually were given their radical edge in MacArthur's headquarters in Tokyo.

By almost every appraisal at the time, the early democratization program as a whole was fundamentally progressive. War criminals were brought to trial. Some two hundred thousand alleged militarists and ultranationalists were purged from public life. On the economic front, in addition to the land reform, laws were enacted in support of labor unionization and the right to strike; the oligopolistic *zaibatsu* holding companies were dissolved; and policies were announced calling for economic deconcentration, industrial demilitarization, and severe reparations to Japan's war victims. Politically, even the Communist Party was made legal, and "grass-roots" democracy was to be promoted through police decentralization, educational reform, and the strengthening of local autonomy. Under the new constitution, which went into effect in early 1947, the emperor became a "symbol" of the state, the country renounced the resort to war as a means of solving disputes, and the people of Japan were granted a broad array of rights that in some instances (such as explicit acknowledgement of the equality of women) went beyond U.S. constitutional guarantees. In the realm of demilitarization more prosaically defined, Occupation authorities moved quickly to repatriate and demobilize the Imperial army and navy, destroy military stocks, and abolish the entire military establishment. Their zealousness was such that, in one of the more notorious excesses of the demilitarization program, apparently on instructions from the War Department, they smashed the great cyclotron in the "Riken" laboratory in Tokyo and dropped the pieces in the ocean.[12]

There were, to be sure, exceptions to the sweeping demobilization program that seem noteworthy in retrospect. Reliance on the Japanese for minesweeping in the waters around Japan, for example, preserved the nucleus around which a future navy could be reconstructed. The military "demobilization boards" themselves kept remnants of the Imperial army and navy employed and provided a body of records that proved useful later when the decision was made to create a new Japanese military beginning in 1950. Certain Japanese staff officers found a new home in the U.S. Occupation bureaucracy itself, especially the Counter-Intelligence Section (G-2), where they were employed in such tasks as preparing historical accounts of the recent war. Many Japanese officers were "debriefed" as a matter of course, and in one appalling instance—involving officers and scientific researchers in the murderous "Unit 731," which had conducted lethal medical and biological-warfare experiments on prisoners of war in Manchuria (killing an estimated three thousand in the process)—blatant war criminals were granted immunity from prosecution in return for disclosure of their special knowledge. Outside Japan, in parts of both China and Southeast Asia (especially the French- and British-controlled areas), the repatriation of scores of thousands of Japanese soldiers was delayed for months and sometimes even years, as many of these unfortunate pawns found themselves enlisted to fight against indigenous communist or national liberation movements.[13]

In the light of Japan's later remilitarization, these exceptions to the demobilization and demilitarization program are suggestive and perhaps symbolic. At the time, however, they did not reflect the main thrust of U.S. strategic policy. In fact, for reasons that still remain somewhat obscure, this first stage of U.S. policy toward occupied Japan witnessed a rare occurrence: the literal putting into practice of rhetorical promises, namely, the promise of imposing "complete and permanent disarmament" upon Japan. This took the form of Article Nine of the new Japanese constitution, which, in its final form (after passing through MacArthur's headquarters, the Japanese cabinet's experts, the Japanese parliament, and a parliamentary committee), read as follows:

> ARTICLE 9. Aspiring sincerely to an international peace based on justice and order, the Japanese people forever renounce war as a sovereign right of the nation and the threat or use of force as means of settling international disputes.
>
> In order to accomplish the aim of the preceding paragraph, land, sea, and air forces, as well as other war potential, will never be maintained. The right of belligerency of the state will not be recognized.

The precise genesis of Article Nine is one of the tantalizing puzzles of the Occupation. At the same time, the whole process of constitutional revision in occupied Japan is an excellent example of the ambiguity of U.S. policy for Asia in the immediate postwar years and of the way this ambiguity often enabled MacArthur and his staff in Tokyo to promote their own ideals. In one of the earliest basic documents sent to Tokyo to guide MacArthur (SWNCC 150/2 of August 1945), the objective of "complete and permanent" disarmament of Japan was reiterated. In a later policy document that suffered some untidy revision at the hands of the multinational Far Eastern Commission sitting in Washington (SWNCC 228 of January 1946), however, the concept of total and permanent demilitarization was muddied by reference to future prerogatives of the *civilian* branch of the Japanese government. MacArthur's command thus received mixed instructions on this critical issue. Indeed, on the issue of constitutional change in general it received no blueprint but only a general mandate for revision. The first draft of the new Japanese Constitution was composed in English in the Government Section of MacArthur's headquarters, in a hectic and heady two-week period at the beginning of February 1946. Specialists on occupied Japan disagree on whether the idea of the "no war" clause originated with MacArthur himself or with one of the key officers in the Government Section (Charles Kades or Courtney Whitney), or possibly even with the then Japanese prime minister, Shidehara Kijūrō. No matter who may have been responsible for the original idea, however, it is clear that Article Nine originated in Tokyo and never would have become part of the national charter of Japan without MacArthur's blessing.

The "no war" clause of the draft constitution caught Washington by surprise and provoked the aforementioned discussion of Japan as a future *place d'armes* in 1946. By and large, however, Article Nine did not cause consternation in Washington, for it not only crystallized wartime promises concerning the complete and permanent disarmament of Japan but also was consistent with plans that were then being drafted in the State Department for the long-term (meaning twenty-five to forty years) international supervision of a disarmed Japan. No major planner in Washington prior to 1947 envisaged the serious rearmament of Japan in the near future, and those few who speculated that this might be desirable later simply assumed that it would be relatively easy to amend Article Nine.[14]

The survival of the "spirit of Article Nine" as an abrasive feature of the subsequent relationship between Japan and the United States is the greatest and most ironic legacy from this first stage of postwar relations between the two countries—the irony lying in the fact that the American-generated "no-war clause" became the symbolic as well as legal rallying point for Japanese who opposed America's later reversal of policy on the issue of Japanese rearmament. At the same time, another major feature of the eventual, bilateral military arrangement also had emerged at a very early date, namely, the decision that the Bonin and Ryukyu islands (including Okinawa) would be treated differently from the rest of Japan. Top-level U.S. planning in 1945–1946 did not project the long-term maintenance of U.S. military bases in the four main islands of Japan, but from the very end of the war the Bonins and Ryukyus were singled out as being of critical strategic importance to the United States, although it apparently was not until 1948 that Okinawa became formally designated as one of the three major bases "from which to launch a strategic air offensive employing atomic weapons."[15]

THE SOFT COLD WAR POLICY, 1947–1949

On the first anniversary of Japan's surrender, General MacArthur announced that the Japanese people already had undergone a "spiritual revolution" that "tore asunder a theory and practice of life built upon two thousand years of history and tradition and legend." If the nation continued to pursue the great middle road of democracy, it soon would emerge as a "powerful bulwark for peace." Six months later, in March 1947, MacArthur informed a press conference that the time had come to end the Occupation and permit Japan to fulfill this destiny. As was often the case, the supreme commander's grand pronouncement had a highly personal and subjective underside, for at this juncture MacArthur had his eye on the impending presidential primary elections in the United States, in which he hoped to emerge as the Republican candidate. The March call for an early peace with Japan coincided closely with the enunciation of the Truman Doctrine for Europe and served as impetus to a flurry of activities that can be described most charitably as the peace-treaty charades of mid 1947. In the course of public and private debate over the prospects of an early peace with Japan, U.S. officials really began for the first time seriously and systematically to consider Japan's future role in the Cold War.

Four aspects of the peace-treaty flurries of mid 1947 seem especially noteworthy. First, it became apparent that State Department planning for a future peace settlement with Japan remained in the mold of World War II thinking. The basic draft peace treaties for Japan that were being worked on within the department at this time (under the direction of Hugh Borton) were extremely long, and bristled with provisions for post-treaty international supervision and controls over "sovereign" Japan. They amounted, in a word, to a "punitive" peace.

Second, despite the cumbersome and still tentative nature of these internal drafts, the State Department responded to public pressure in July 1947 by calling for an international conference on Japan that (1) was scheduled for a time when Britain and the Commonwealth nations already had prior commitments, and (2) was procedurally unacceptable to the Soviet Union, because in the Soviet view it ignored prior understandings that these matters would first be considered by the wartime "Big Four" (the United States, Soviet Union, Britain, and China) before being submitted to a larger multinational forum. These procedural issues became a cause for charges of bad faith on all sides, and in this setting for the first time U.S. officials and politicians considered the notion that it might be appropriate to anticipate a "separate peace" with Japan—that is, a peace settlement on terms that would be unacceptable to the Soviet Union.[16]

In a third related development, the Japanese—including not only government officials but also the presumedly "symbolic" and nonpolitical emperor himself—took the initiative to convey to the Americans their willingness to accept some sort of separate peace arrangement if necessary. These secret Japanese proposals, which in many respects anticipated by roughly four years the broad contours of the San Francisco settlement of 1951, hinted at a bilateral military agreement with the United States and the development of Okinawa as a major U.S. military bastion. To scholars of the Occupation, these activities are of interest for a number of reasons. They call attention to the positive Japanese contribution to the policymaking process; offer an unusually vivid case study of politicking by the emperor through his personal advisers; and reveal that both the Japanese government and Imperial Household were willing from an early date to trade away true sovereignty for Okinawa in exchange for an early end to the Occupation in the rest of Japan. As many Japanese critics see it, the special treatment accorded Okinawa beginning right after the war—its intense militarization and Americanization—makes it proper to see post–World War II Japan as a "semi-divided" country. Moreover, the Japanese ruling groups, as the record now clearly indicates, did little or nothing to prevent this from happening. On the contrary, they were all too willing to use Okinawa and its people, who have always been regarded as second-class citizens, as bargaining chips.[17]

Finally, the peace-treaty issue of 1947 focused attention on Japan and drew a new group of U.S. planners into the picture, many of whom hitherto had been preoccupied with policymaking for Europe. Even as the United States publicly was blaming the Soviet Union for impeding progress on a peace settlement with Japan, these new national-security advisers were arguing behind the scenes not only that the Borton group's draft treaty was totally outdated but also that an early peace with Japan was out of the question. The United States itself was unprepared to talk concretely about a peace settlement with Japan in mid 1947, and it is for this reason that its public gestures to the contrary can only be described as a charade.

Over the course of the next several years, the vision of a disarmed and neutral Japan remained a potent one in the public arena, partly because of General MacArthur's continued reaffirmation of this ideal. Although the supreme commander's presidential aspirations had been dashed by a stunning defeat in the Republican primary election in Wisconsin in April 1948, he remained very much in the public eye and as zealous a proselytizer as ever concerning the dream of turning Japan into a unique symbol of peace in the modern world. In his scenario, Japan's "disarmed neutrality" would be protected by the positioning of United Nations forces in key Pacific islands, including Okinawa. MacArthur's famous description of Japan as the "Switzerland of the

Pacific" actually was made as late as March 1949, but by then time had passed him by. Still, whether out of pacifist ideals or, more commonly, lingering fear and mistrust of Japan, few American officials were ready to rush pell-mell into the wholesale rehabilitation of Japan as a Cold War ally.[18]

In Washington, the most articulate spokesmen for the new vision of Japan included the State Department's George Kennan and high civilian bureaucrats in the Department of the Army led by Secretary Kenneth Royall and Under Secretary William Draper. The "Kennan touch" was first applied to Japan policy in a decisive way in October 1947 in a paper on the peace-treaty issue for the State Department's Policy Planning Staff (PPS 10). The position set forth there became the basis for the National Security Council documents that governed Japan policy in 1948 and into 1949 (the NSC 13 series), and covered a wide range of sensitive policy issues. Kennan and his aides opposed an early end to the Occupation, partly on the grounds that Japan's present economic instability made it ripe for communist penetration, and they foresaw the possibility of having to impose peace terms "unilaterally" later. While recognizing the necessity of long-term U.S. military control of certain islands peripheral to Japan, as well as of at least the northern part of Okinawa, PPS 10 indicated that the long-term presence of U.S. forces in the main four islands of Japan might not be necessary. The paper also proposed that any future peace treaty with Japan should avoid post-treaty supervision but at the same time reaffirm the principle of complete Japanese disarmament. The Kennan group also recommended that the reparations program should be terminated quickly to end uncertainty and to stimulate capital investment and economic recovery.[19]

By June 1948, this policy had evolved into NSC 13 ("Recommendations with Respect to U.S. Policy toward Japan"). This called for a brief, general, and nonpunitive peace treaty in the indefinite future; reaffirmed the necessity of maintaining long-term military control over not only Okinawa but also the great naval facilities at Yokosuka (south of Tokyo) as well, but deferred decision on post-treaty bases throughout the four main islands; advocated strengthening the Japanese "police"; and announced a shift in Occupation priorities from reform to economic recovery.[20]

While this broad policy directive was worming its way to the surface in the National Security Council, numerous economic studies and proposals that addressed the economic reconstruction of Japan in more concrete terms were piling up on the desks of the national-security managers. As early as March 1947, an important internal State Department report known as the Martin Plan called attention to the changing nature of the world economy and the impending "dollar gap" crisis in Asia. With this in view, the report argued, it was desirable to promote Japan's future economic stability by actively developing its capacity to export capital goods to the nondollar markets of Asia.[21]

The Martin Plan was important as an early intimation of many economic considerations that would emerge as dominant over the course of time: recognition of Japan's heavy dependence on U.S. aid, fear that the dollar-poor countries of Asia would collapse unless more sophisticated patterns of interregional integration were developed, and the perception that in the future Japan would have to rely more on the export of machine goods and the like than on the export of textiles and light-industrial products as in the prewar period. In return for such exports, Japan would import raw materials and cheap manufactures from the less developed countries of Asia.

Similar arguments came from other directions. Almost simultaneously with the Martin Plan, for example, the army received an economic report from MacArthur's Economic and Scientific Section in Tokyo that also recommended curbing inflation and attaining a "balanced Japanese economy" by cutting down the reparations program and promoting Japanese production of capital goods earmarked for export. These prospects were thrown into the arena of public debate in a famous speech by Dean Acheson on May 8, in which the then–assistant secretary of state, with his gift for the sharp aphorism, linked Europe with Asia while separating the Cold War from the old war—all in a single stroke. There was no getting around the fact, Acheson declared, that Japan and Germany had to be developed as the "workshops" of Asia and Europe, respectively. How this was to be done, and how extensively and how rapidly, was debated within both the civilian and military bureaucracies in the months that followed, resulting in a small flood of reports and position papers that became the basis for swinging Congress behind the policy of promoting Japanese economic reconstruction in 1948. In June 1948, under the new Economic Recovery in Occupied Areas program, Congress appropriated $108 million that, for the first time, could be used specifically for economic recovery in occupied Japan. That same month Congress also approved a Natural Fibers Revolving Fund (PL 820) totaling $150 million that eventually was used to support massive exports of American raw cotton to Japan—a pump-priming program with obvious sectional appeal in Congress, although it did not reflect the emerging emphasis on promoting growth in Japan's nontextile sectors.[22]

As NSC 13 revealed, by 1948 the question of the future military disposition of Japan was being addressed on three levels: Okinawa, post-treaty U.S. bases in the rest of Japan, and Japanese rearmament. Okinawa by this time was explicitly identified as the primary forward base in U.S. nuclear strategy in the Far East. While the importance of continued U.S. access to the airfields in the rest of Japan was publicly discussed by top officials such as Draper, no formal decision had been made on this. And the issue of Japanese rearmament had been raised but shelved, emerging only obliquely in NSC 13 in the context of strengthening Japanese police forces against potential internal subversion.

Many formerly classified documents confirm that by 1948 the defense establishment was pushing fairly firmly in the direction of long-term U.S. bases in Japan and Japanese rearmament. As early as the spring of 1947, the Joint Chiefs of Staff (JCS) had identified Japan as the one country in Asia capable of holding the "ideological opponents" of the United States at bay while a major offensive was waged in the West. For that reason, the military planners observed, "of all the countries in the Pacific area Japan deserves primary consideration for current United States assistance designed to restore her economy and her military potential." Secretary of Defense James Forrestal requested a study of limited military rearmament for both Japan and Germany in February 1948, and by May had received a lengthy and extremely frank response under the name of Secretary of the Army Kenneth Royall, in which the army planners not only supported post-treaty bases and constitutional revision that would permit future Japanese rearmament but also went on to emphasize the importance of developing new markets and sources of raw materials for Japan abroad. Nonetheless, when this document came before the JCS in October (accompanied by a copy of MacArthur's views opposing rearmament), the rearmament of Japan was rejected as impractical under present circumstances. The rearmament policy was not approved until early 1950 and not actually urged upon the Japanese government until June 22 of that year—three days before the outbreak of the Korean War.

Certain military officers did openly proclaim their desire to enlist the Japanese as an active military ally from an early date. For example, in 1948 General Robert Eichelberger, commander of the Eighth Army in Japan (who had described the Japanese enemy as "monkeys" in his wartime letters), publicly called for a Japanese army of 150,000 men. Such men, he said, would be the sort of military force every commander dreams of leading—an appalling and terrifying remark to the rest of Asia. In the internal documents of this period, however, even those who were advocating "limited military rearmament" for Japan took care to emphasize the necessity of controlling and restraining whatever remilitarization might be allowed. Distrust of Japan remained a conspicuous feature of this second stage of U.S. planning.[23]

In what ways, then, was the Cold War policy of this second stage "soft" in comparison with the eventual San Francisco settlement? In the case of long-term bases in Japan and Japanese rearmament, the answer is obvious: neither policy had yet been adopted by the U.S. government, and both still had strong and persuasive critics (including Kennan and most of his State Department colleagues, as well as MacArthur and many of his key aides). In addition, despite the fact that Japan was now identified as the future "workshop" of Asia—and despite vague references to a Marshall Plan for Asia—the soft policy did not offer a coherent vision of regional anticommunist economic integration in Asia. On the contrary, it was assumed until 1950, and in some U.S. and Japanese circles even later, that Japan would and should establish substantial economic ties with China, no matter what regime controlled the mainland. No positive steps were taken to integrate Japan and Southeast Asia until much later; and no concrete, systematic attempt to stabilize the Japanese economy and to gear industry for export production was actually undertaken until January 1949, when the Detroit banker Joseph Dodge arrived in Tokyo to initiate the famous (or, to some, notorious) "disinflation" policy known as the Dodge Line. Although reparations policy began to be watered down beginning in 1947, the formal "postponement" of this program, which was so inhibiting to prospective Japanese investors and entrepreneurs, did not occur until May 1949. Indeed, NSC 13 itself was not approved by President Truman until October 1948 (as NSC 13/2), and well into the spring of 1949 policymakers in Washington still were lamenting that there had been virtually no progress in its actual implementation.[24]

Perhaps most striking, the soft Cold War policy minimized the overt threat of Soviet aggression against Japan and instead emphasized the possibility of Japan's "going communist" because of its own internal instability. As Kennan and others were quick to emphasize, Japan appeared extremely precarious economically and thereby politically precarious as well. Inflation was out of hand; lingering uncertainty over Occupation policy in the areas of reparations and economic deconcentration stifled capital investment; foreign trade, stymied by Occupation controls, hardly existed; and labor, caught in the inflationary spiral, appeared to be moving in an increasingly radical direction. In one of the more ideologically entertaining vignettes from this period, the "liberal" Kennan visited Japan in early 1948 and concluded that the "conservative" MacArthur was promoting policies conducive to communism. It was this vision of Japan as economically unstable and thereby ripe for communization *from within* that motivated the abandonment of some of the initial democratic and reformist policies of the Occupation and the adoption instead of policies conducive to capitalist stabilization and reconstruction.[25]

This nervous and occasionally even apocalyptic vision of Japan as economically vulnerable, politically unstable, and ideologically unreliable was especially unsettling because it coincided with the enunciation in U.S. circles of an absolutely fundamental thesis: that Japan was the key to the balance of power in Asia. Beginning around 1948, this balance-of-power argument was developed roughly as follows: (1) Japan, with its skilled manpower and great industrial and war-making potential, was the critical power in Asia. (2) In grand global terms, however, Asia ranked neither first nor even second in strategic importance to the United States. On the contrary, the European theater took priority, followed by the Near and Middle East. In military terms, this called for a "strategic offense in the West and strategic defense in the East." (3) In this global scheme, Japan was more important to the Soviet Union than to the

United States. (4) Consequently, the primary U.S. objective where Japan was concerned was not to make Japan a part of the U.S. offensive capability but rather, more simply, to keep Japan out of the Soviet sphere.

This concept of the *negative* importance of Japan (the need to "deny" it to the enemy) meant that even apart from any positive contribution to U.S. objectives, the United States never could conceive of "writing off" Japan, for this would mean incalculable gain for the Soviet Union. John Foster Dulles later became fond of citing a phrase attributed to Stalin in 1925 to buttress this line of thinking ("The way to victory over the West is through the East"), and the concept was repeated again and again in the U.S. policy papers prior to 1950. As late as December 1949, for example, one of the basic papers pertaining to Asia (NSC 48/1) observed that "if Japan, the principal component of a Far Eastern war-making complex, were added to the Stalinist bloc, the Soviet Asian base could become a source of strength capable of shifting the balance of world power to the disadvantage of the United States." Even more succinctly: "The Asian power potential is more valuable to Russia than to the United States." An analysis by the Central Intelligence Agency dated May 1949 spelled the same thesis out in fuller detail:

> Control of Japan's industrial machine would be more valuable to the USSR than to the US, not only because the USSR has more immediate need of the products of Japan's industry but also because the USSR will be in effective control of the area (chiefly northern China, Manchuria and Korea) whose natural resources Japanese industry can utilize most efficiently. For this reason, long-range US security interests dictate the denial of Japan's capacity, both economic and military, to USSR exploitation. . . . The difficulties and cost to the United States of making Japan the center of a Far Eastern war-making complex, and the fact that Japan's industry—measured in terms of realizable steel production—is only 5 percent of US, probably would make denial of the Japan complex to the USSR, rather than full exploitation of Japanese industry as an auxiliary to US war production, the dominant US strategic consideration. Japan's industrial plant would be of much greater positive value to the USSR than to the US; it would,

in fact, be for the Soviet Union the richest economic prize in the Far East.[26]

To call such a policy "soft" is not meant to minimize either its dynamics or its impact on the attentive public. The British and Chinese (of all political persuasions), as well as the Soviets, voiced concern about the specter of Japanese remilitarization beginning in early 1948, and before the end of that year the Soviets were citing Western press accounts in their denunciations of what they termed the U.S. military policy of surrounding China with a "defensive ring" stretching through Japan, Taiwan, the Philippines, Siam, Burma, and India. In the United States, a small, well-organized, and highly effective "Japan lobby" had emerged by 1948 under the name of the American Council on Japan, with excellent access to government, Congress, business and financial circles, and the media. And in Japan itself, the shift from reform to reconstruction was signaled by antilabor actions beginning in 1947 and, in 1948, the near-abandonment of one of the central announced policies of the demilitarization and democratization agenda: enforcement of a vigorous program of economic deconcentration.

Because of a variety of technical and political complications, the policy of democratizing the Japanese economy by eliminating excessive concentrations of economic power was almost stillborn. The basic enabling legislation for deconcentration was not even enacted until December 1947, by which time it already was wreathed in controversy. Although 325 companies were designated for investigation and possible reorganization in February 1948, by mid April the policy had been almost completely reversed and Occupation authorities were instructed that banks were to be totally excluded from the purview of the law and, in the words of a confidential internal memorandum, "no more than twenty companies were to be subject to reorganization under the law and these were to be chosen on the basis that they were interfering with Japanese economic recovery." By July, 225 of the 325 designated firms had been removed from designation, and eventually only eleven of the original 325 companies were ordered to split and another eight to make minor organizational changes. One of the members of a Deconcentration Review Board composed of U.S. businessmen sent to Japan in May 1948

178

to terminate the program expressed the prevailing sentiment in a memorandum that described the antitrust legislation as "bordering on (if not actually) the methods used by so-called communist States today." In the words of one of the original supporters of the program, written as these events unfolded, "Facts of the last war faded . . . and conjectures on the next war took their place."[27]

Although the archival record concerning the decision to abandon the economic democratization program contains the usual good portion of blunt and colorful confidential quotations, it is more important to keep in mind that this reversal of policy was plain for all to see. It flew in the face of Acheson's old "will to war" hypothesis concerning the structural roots of Japanese aggression, while giving concrete meaning to his more recent vision of the Japanese "workshop." And, every bit as much as the specter of a remilitarized Japan, it caused alarm and protest through most of the rest of Asia.

THE HARD COLD WAR POLICY, 1949–1951

The reconsideration of policy toward Japan obviously occurred at a time when U.S. officials were becoming profoundly pessimistic about trends elsewhere in Asia. In essence, they were envisaging the old Greater East Asia Co-Prosperity Sphere (including Japan itself) turning Red and being harnessed to the Soviet Union: references to a "Communist Co-Prosperity Sphere" or to communist-influenced "Pan-Asiatic tendencies" actually appear in U.S. documents from this period.[28] At the same time, U.S. officials now also were beginning to think explicitly of Japan's role in a future global conflict between the United States and the Soviet Union—and from this it was only a short step to the logical next stage in strategic planning: the notion that it was not only necessary to deny Japan to the enemy but also essential to incorporate Japan in a positive manner in the U.S. Cold War strategy. When this step was taken, it marked the end of the soft Cold War policy.

The "hard" or "positive" Cold War policy line involving Japan can be dated from June 1949, when, shortly after Secretary of Defense Louis Johnson had called for a coordinated policy "to contain communism" in Asia, the Joint Chiefs of Staff submitted a strong and controversial

179

statement of U.S. security needs in Japan to the National Security Council. In this document, NSC 49, the Joint Chiefs declared that America must maintain strategic control of an "offshore island chain" in Asia, with all of Japan playing a pivotal role in this chain as a forward staging area from which U.S. military power could be launched against the Soviet Union. NSC 49 also endorsed the creation of a Japanese military and indicated that eventually this military could be expected to play a significant role in the event of a global war between the United States and Soviet Union. In such a conflict, Japan would tie down the Soviets on their eastern front and thus prevent them from concentrating their forces against the United States and Europe in the west (unlike World War II, when the Soviet-Japanese neutrality pact had freed Russia in the east). This argument that Japan must play an *active* role in U.S. military policy—in contrast to the soft Cold War policy, with its relatively passive emphasis on denying Japan to the communist enemy— was concisely expressed in a basic JCS document of November 1949 that declared Japan "will be not only oriented toward the United States but also be actively allied with us in event of global war" (JCS 1380/75). Such thinking had indeed surfaced earlier, but now the Pentagon was placing it at center stage.[29]

After the outbreak of the Korean War one year later, the concept of the "offshore island chain" became a hotly debated issue in connection with a famous speech given by Secretary of State Acheson on January 12, 1950. On that occasion, Acheson had spoken of a defense perimeter in Asia that extended from the Aleutians through Japan and the Ryukyus to the Philippines. Because he left out South Korea, the secretary was later criticized for having invited the communist attack. It is understandable that this point of omission has attracted retrospective attention, but this has tended to obscure the positive thrust of the speech: the fact that the secretary's strategic line explicitly included Japan and Okinawa. At the time Acheson spoke (a matter of months after the Soviet Union had become a nuclear power and the People's Republic of China had been established), the United States was concretely building up its military capability on Okinawa and the four main islands of Japan.[30]

This does not mean that there was unanimity in U.S. decision-making circles at this time. Following the presentation of NSC 49, the Pentagon and the State Department fell into a quarrel over policy toward Japan which was not resolved until September 1950, although both sides were in general agreement before then on the necessity of Japanese rearmament and long-term U.S. military bases in Japan. The more subtle aspect of the disagreement concerned how to appraise and respond to the psychological and political inclinations of the Japanese. Could Japan be incorporated most effectively in the anticommunist camp by prolonging the Occupation indefinitely, it was asked, or would a contrary policy of granting a peace treaty in the near future be more effective? In the view of the JCS, U.S. strategy in Asia now required exclusive and extensive control of airfields throughout the Japanese archipelago, plus the cautious development of Japanese forces for self-defense. At the same time, however, the military frankly acknowledged that they were not confident that Japan would remain democratic or was sincerely committed to the anticommunist cause. Because they needed Japan but could not trust the Japanese, talk of a peace treaty was premature.

State Department officials did not challenge their military colleagues' skeptical view of the Japanese, as a circular cable to diplomatic posts abroad from the secretary of state himself in May rather crudely revealed. "Japs will either move toward sound friendly relations with non-Commie countries," Acheson suggested, "or into association Commie system in Asia." As the diplomatic wing of the bureaucracy saw it, however, indefinitely prolonging the Occupation might simply provoke the Japanese to the point where they would indeed become more favorably disposed to aligning with the "Commie system."

In its first formal response to NSC 49 (NSC 49/1 of September 30, 1949), the State Department reiterated its misgivings about the reliability of Japan's pro-Western orientation, concurred that the Japanese would have to develop their own self-defense capacity, rejected the argument that it was premature to start planning for a Japanese peace treaty, and expressed grave misgivings about the vast network of bases that the Pentagon wished to maintain indefinitely in Japan. General MacArthur, while backing off from his earlier idealistic stance, argued that adoption of the Pentagon's positive policy would threaten the communist countries and imperil Japan. "In any war," the general commented in January 1950 in response to the general thesis advanced in NSC 49, "regardless of what happened their [the Japanese] islands would be destroyed."

Thousands of pages of "secret" and "top-secret" arguments were devoted to these issues, but it should be noted (1) that the general principles (if not numbers) of long-term U.S. bases in Japan and Japanese rearmament had been agreed on by the first part of 1950, and (2) that the whole world was aware of the direction of the debate. By February 1950, several multimillion-dollar construction projects funded by congressional appropriations were under way to enlarge airfields and lengthen runways in Okinawa and Japan proper (and, as an attractive by-product, simultaneously to stimulate Japanese economic recovery through construction contracts). At the same time, a series of well-publicized official U.S. missions visited Okinawa and Japan, including, from January 31 to February 10, the Joint Chiefs of Staff. The JCS Chairman, Omar Bradley, was quoted in the *New York Times* as observing that "the former enemy appeared to be not only the strongest bastion but just about the only tangible thing left of the fruits of victory in the Pacific." Privately, the quotations were even pithier. In January 1950, when making the case for economic aid to Japan before the National Advisory Council, Joseph Dodge described Japan as a "springboard and source of supply." An investigative report to the Committee on Appropriations of the House of Representatives that same month identified Japan as the "west coast" of the United States.[31]

In Japan, prominent intellectuals organized against these trends as early as January 1950 by forming a Peace Problems Symposium (*Heiwa Mondai Danwakai*), which became the vanguard of the postwar Japanese peace movement. The Japanese government, conversely, sought to reassure the Americans of the wisdom of an early peace treaty by taking two bold initiatives, one secret and the other public. On May 2 the Japanese secretly offered to support post-treaty U.S. military bases in Japan, having concluded that the Americans would never end the Occupation without such a guarantee. The Japanese informed the Americans that they had consulted leading legal authorities and been assured that post-treaty U.S. bases would not violate the Japanese constitution. Then, on June 1, the Foreign Ministry issued a white paper that expressed Japan's willingness, if necessary, to accept a peace treaty not signed by all belligerents—in other words, to accept a "separate peace" without the participation of the Soviet Union.

The Japanese government was not at that point willing to undertake rearmament, however, as the conservative prime minister, Yoshida Shigeru, made emphatically clear to John Foster Dulles on June 22. Dulles had been brought into the Truman administration in May as a special adviser to help resolve the deadlock between the Pentagon and the State Department and to prevent the peace-treaty issue from becoming embroiled in partisan politics. He chose to urge the Japanese to rearm as virtually the first item of business on his first visit to Tokyo. Yoshida enlisted MacArthur's support in turning the request aside, and MacArthur, in turn, urged Dulles to consider rehabilitating Japan's idle war-related factories instead. Thus, when the North Koreans launched their blitz across the thirty-eighth parallel, post-treaty bases, Japanese rearmament, and now even Japan's industrial remilitarization were all already on the table.[32]

Actually, there was even more on the table. In the final days of 1949 the National Security Council had distributed a lengthy summary paper on "The Position of the United States with Respect to Asia" (NSC 48/1). This, plus a wealth of prior and subsequent documents, carried projections concerning Japan's future economic role in the containment of communism in Asia to a new level of thinking. NSC 48/1 offered a succinct three-part summation of the strategic importance of Asia to the United States: Control there would enhance the war-making potential of the Soviets; development of indigenous anticommunist forces would reduce Soviet influence, save the United States money, and provide forces in the event of war; and certain raw materials available in Asia (especially tin and rubber) were of value to the United States. The catch phrase of basic military policy remained "a strategic offense in the 'West' and a strategic defense in the 'East.' "

NSC 48/1 was the master statement both of the balance-of-power thesis pivoting on Japan and of U.S. anxiety concerning Japan's political and ideological propensities. Traditional social patterns "antithetical to democracy" remained strong in Japan, it was stated, and the country might easily veer to the political right or left. The United States could only hope to hold it to a middle-of-the-road course. The paper acknowledged that the Soviet Union did not pose a direct military threat to Japan or to the rest of Asia for the foreseeable future, and it also recognized potential sources of friction between the Soviet Union and China. As prior position papers had argued, Japan was expected to have to engage in substantial trade with China in the future. Indeed, such

Sino-Japanese trade, subject to restrictions on strategic materials, could serve U.S. purposes by making important Chinese commodities (such as tungsten, antimony, tung oil, and bristles) available to the United States, while drawing China closer to the capitalist economies. Although not mentioned in NSC 48/1, it is apparent from other archival sources that as of this date planners such as Kennan also looked forward to "the re-entry of Japanese influence and activity into Korea and Manchuria" as being "in fact, the only realistic prospect for countering and moderating Soviet influence in that area."[33]

Beginning in the latter part of 1949, however, and with mounting intensity thereafter, planners in Washington began to look to Southeast Asia rather than China as the critical area for Japan's future economic expansion. NSC 48/1 concluded with a general reference to the desirability of accelerating the integration of the Japanese economy with that of South and Southeast Asia; an earlier draft had noted even more precisely "the mutually beneficial character of trade of a triangular character" linking the United States, Japan, and Southeast Asia. The triangular metaphor became a key one in the months and years ahead, although this "triangle" actually had four corners: Southeast Asia, as other documents made clear, in good part meant the European colonies. Indeed, when the emerging blueprint of trilateral U.S.-Japanese-Southeast Asian integration was spoken of as an Asian version of the Marshall Plan or European Recovery Program, as also was frequently done, this too was somewhat misleading. In the first place, the United States did not regard the countries of Southeast Asia as in any way equivalent to the shattered but industrially advanced nations of Western Europe; only Japan had this advanced capitalist potential. More subtly, given the colonial structure of Southeast Asia and its perceived economic importance to Europe, U.S. promotion of the security and economic development of the area could more accurately be seen as a supplement—but also possibly a detriment—to the European Recovery Program, rather than simply a "little Marshall Plan" for Asia. As a report on the subject prepared in mid 1948 pointed out, the dollar earnings of Malaya, Indochina, and Indonesia played an important role in alleviating the dollar gap in transatlantic trade that plagued the British, French, and Dutch. The question that arose repeatedly in interagency discussions of promoting Japanese economic integration with Southeast Asia was whether this, too, would help the European nations by strengthening the Southeast Asian economies, or harm them by giving Japan a decided competitive edge in the southern reaches of its old "coprosperity sphere."

Like the issues of Japanese rearmament and post-treaty bases, recommendations to promote the integration of the Japanese and Southeast Asian economies can be traced back to early 1947 but were not lifted to the level of "hard" policy until mid 1949. The State Department introduced the concept of a "great crescent" of containment extending from Japan through Southeast Asia to Australia and India in March 1949 (PPS 51); the National Security Council distributed (but did not formally adopt) this concept the following July as NSC 51. Background commentaries on the concept made it clear that Southeast Asia would function primarily as a market and source of raw materials for both Japan and Western Europe. Even as Kennan was contemplating checking Soviet influence in Northeast Asia by promoting Japan's economic reintegration with Korea and Manchuria, he was simultaneously giving attention to "the terrific problem of how the Japanese are going to get along unless they again reopen some sort of empire to the south." At precisely the same time (October 1949), the CIA was talking about subsidizing the return of Japanese investors and trading companies to Southeast Asia, where their pre-1945 experience would serve them in good stead. On a parallel line, at least in the symbolic sense of resuscitating the architects and technocrats of the Japanese empire, even as the Joint Chiefs of Staff and State Department were arguing that the United States could not afford to intervene militarily to save the Chinese Nationalists on Taiwan (a policy stated in NSC 48/1 and reiterated in basic NSC policy papers for China in March 1950), former Japanese military officers who had fought in the China War secretly were being sent to Taiwan to advise Chiang Kai-shek on how to retake the mainland.[34]

Tracy Voorhees, Draper's successor as undersecretary of the army, quickly identified the Japanese–Southeast Asia nexus as crucial to future anticommunist regional integration of Asia and devoted much of his time from the beginning of 1950 to designing an integrated military and economic aid package that would promote such interdependence. His proposals, too, made clear, again prior to June 1950, that the Japanese workshop now was being viewed as a potential arsenal for noncommunist Asia, with military items being among the capital goods that Japan could export to its neighbors in the south. The first of many overlapping U.S. missions to study the feasibility of such anticommunist regional integration was dispatched to Southeast Asia and Japan in January 1950; and the first U.S. commitment of military aid to Indochina, Indonesia, Thailand, and Burma, made in early 1950 under the Military Assistance Program, was undertaken in the context of these broader considerations. Shortly before the Korean War began, the State Department tentatively approved the creation of a huge "special yen fund" that was to be integrated with U.S. aid programs in a manner that would make the raw materials and markets of Southeast Asia more readily accessible to Japan.[35]

As in other critical areas of postwar U.S. planning (such as NSC 68 of April 1950, which called for tripling the U.S. military budget), the great significance of the Korean War insofar as Japan was concerned was that it facilitated and accelerated the implementation of policies that already had been introduced and largely agreed upon at the highest levels. Japanese rearmament was initiated in July. The State-Defense deadlock over a peace treaty was solved by September, with the Pentagon agreeing that Japan's allegiance could be best secured by an early peace treaty. The Japanese economy, which had been "disinflated" under the Dodge Line but appeared to be heading for a recession or even a bona fide depression, was pulled out of the doldrums by a dramatic "Korean War boom" (which coincided with the introduction of quality-control techniques by the American statistician W. Edwards Deming); and extremely ambitious plans were made, though not always carried out, for the long-term industrial remilitarization of Japan.

Domestically, the hard Cold War policy was reflected in numerous areas of Occupation policy, most notably actions designed to weaken the labor movement and more radical Left. This accelerated internal "reverse course" also was clearly in train well before the Korean War began. Legislation enacted earlier in the Occupation to protect organized labor was watered down beginning in the latter part of 1948. Starting at the end of 1949, Occupation authorities and the Japanese government collaborated in a "Red Purge" of public employees that resulted in dismissal of some eleven thousand workers by June 1950; the great majority of these victims of Occupation-style "McCarthyism" were union activists. In the wake of the Korean War, the Red Purge was extended to the private sector and resulted in the firing of almost exactly the same number of activist workers. While the Red Purges were being directed against the political Left, the "depurge" of persons who hitherto had been prohibited from holding public or corporate office on the grounds of alleged militaristic or ultranationalistic activities was initiated. In a fitting symbol of the swiftly changing political climate, the Japanese bureaucratic apparatus that had been created at the start of the Occupation to handle the investigation and purge of persons deemed culpable of having contributed to repression and aggression before Japan's surrender was redirected to focus on persons associated with the political Left from 1949.[36]

In April 1951, the CIA summarized Japan's place in American strategic planning as follows:

> Because of the strategic location of Japan, its industrial capacity, and its large pool of trained civilian and military manpower, Japan's ultimate political alignment will be a decisive factor in the balance of power in the Far East. If the Communists controlled Japan, they could:
>
> a. Safeguard the Communist controlled territory in Northeast Asia;
> b. Breach the US defense line in the western Pacific;
> c. Strengthen the industrial and military power of the Soviet bloc, particularly in respect to shipping and sea power with the Far East;
> d. Facilitate Communist aggression in South and Southeast Asia; and
> e. Free Communist forces for deployment elsewhere.
>
> If, on the other hand, Japan were to be rearmed and aligned with the West:
>
> a. The West would benefit from the fact that the industrial and military resources of the nation were retained in friendly hands;

b. Japan would provide a potential base for Western military power in Northeast Asia;

c. The US would be able to protect its defense outposts in the Western Pacific;

d. Other non-Communist countries would be encouraged in their fight against the spread of Communism.[37]

The CIA study went on to speak of the theoretical capability of Japan to raise an army of up to a half-million within six months or a year after the country had agreed to rearm. Furthermore, the agency concluded that there were "enough trained workers in Japan to operate an industrial plant as large and productive as that maintained during World War II .... We estimate that within 12 to 18 months, a considerable portion of Japan's former capacity to produce weapons and ammunition for the use of ground and naval forces could be restored." The report also observed that South and Southeast Asia could "contribute significantly toward meeting Japanese requirements for food and such raw materials as iron ore, rubber, bauxite, tin, and cotton, and, to a lesser degree, petroleum," provided the area did not come under communist control.

Other internal reports not only accepted such projections but also urged something close to their full realization within the near future. Thus, the JCS reports in the months prior to the San Francisco conference made it clear that the military deemed it essential "to use Japan as a base for military operations in the Far East, including, if necessary, operations against the mainland of China (including Manchuria), the USSR, and on the high seas, regardless of whether such use is under United Nations aegis." At the same time, the U.S. government looked forward to the establishment of a Japanese army of 300,000 to 325,000 men in ten fully equipped combat divisions by 1953. General Matthew Ridgway, who succeeded MacArthur in the spring of 1951, declared emotionally, "Upon such an Army, in the final analysis, the entire Far East will be dependent for stability and protection." The creation of such a force, Ridgway went on, "with fighting spirit and ability equivalent to that displayed by Japanese Forces in World War II," was "paramount" over any other long-range project in the Far East. As a matter of course, it was assumed in all confidential U.S. documents from this period that

Japanese remilitarization should and soon would be preceded by revision of Article Nine.[38]

THE INTEGRATED COLD WAR POLICY, 1951–1952

Almost two years elapsed between the outbreak of the Korean War in June 1950 and end of the Occupation of Japan in April 1952, and it was not until fairly well into 1951 that U.S. policy toward Japan and Asia actually transcended the "nation by nation" approach lamented by so many policymakers and assumed more or less integrated form. The centerpiece of this coordinated regional policy was the peace treaty signed with Japan at San Francisco in September 1951, along with the three security treaties that accompanied this and linked the United States militarily with Japan, with the Philippines, and with Australia and New Zealand. Later the United States also would make security arrangements with South Korea (1953), the Nationalist regime on Taiwan (1954), and key countries of Southeast Asia (1954). Overall, these military pacts formed a patchwork pattern; there was no counterpart in Asia to the integrated structure of NATO.

The peace treaty that Japan signed with forty-eight nations in San Francisco followed the prescriptions set down by Kennan and his Policy Planning Staff in 1947: it was concise and nonpunitive, free of any provisions for post-treaty controls, and designed to give Japan every opportunity to emerge as a stable and prosperous member of the family of noncommunist nations. No one at the time, of course, anticipated how greatly Japan would prosper under its regained sovereignty. On the contrary, in the early 1950s both U.S. and Japanese officials remained generally pessimistic about the future prospects of Japan's "shallow economy." At the same time, no one really foresaw exactly how the bilateral military relationship between the United States and Japan would unfold. It was not until the early months of 1952 that the actual details of the post-Occupation U.S. presence in Japan were worked out, and the extensiveness of the military installations demanded by the Americans far exceeded Japanese expectations. For understandable reasons, neither the U.S. nor the Japanese government publicized the fact that Japan's status under the bilateral security treaty and its enabling "administrative agreement" was less equitable than the status of any other nation that entered into a postwar security agreement with the United States—a condition that persisted until the security treaty was revised in 1960.

The U.S.-Japan security relationship also did not develop precisely as expected on another, more consequential front: Japanese rearmament. Although the United States initially assumed that its goal of a 300,000-man Japanese ground force would be met by 1953, the conservative Japanese government resisted pressure for such rapid remilitarization and continued to do so over the ensuing decades. This resistance is well known, but the full range of reasons that Japanese leaders offered from the start is generally less well appreciated. In addition to arguing that the Japanese public would not tolerate such rapid remilitarization and that the economy could not support it, Prime Minister Yoshida also confided that he feared the United States would expect Japan to send troops to Korea if a large army suddenly materialized. (Japanese mine-sweepers did in fact participate secretly in the war.) Moreover, much like the queasy State Department and Pentagon advisers who worried about Japan's ideological propensities, the prime minister also worried that too-rapid expansion would enable the new military to become infiltrated by "Reds." Furthermore (in marked contrast to his American allies), Yoshida was acutely sensitive to the terror and hostility a suddenly revived Japanese army would provoke throughout the rest of Asia, especially among those erstwhile anticommunist allies who still bore the physical and psychological scars caused by the debauchery of the Imperial forces and their civilian camp followers. Finally, then and thereafter, Japan's leaders also argued that such blatant and extensive militarization as the Americans demanded would require constitutional revision. Article Nine could be reinterpreted as permitting the maintenance of "national police" or "self-defense" forces, they argued, but not the immediate creation of an army one-third of a million men strong; and it would be political suicide for the ruling conservatives to attempt to force constitutional revision on a public that already was leery about how far the "reverse course" might go. As they had ever since the prospect of Japanese rearmament was first seriously broached in 1947–48, U.S. officials agreed that Japanese remilitarization on the scale desired required that the constitution be revised. They were not convinced, however, that this was actually as far beyond their capabilities as the conservatives claimed.[39]

Militarily, the Occupation thus did give way to a "fortress Japan" much as many Pentagon planners had hoped from mid 1949—but a fortress in which the Japanese garrison never became the substantial force Washington desired. As U.S. policymakers had predicted ever since the "separate peace" concept was first mentioned in 1947, the linking of the "generous" peace treaty to the bilateral U.S.-Japan security treaty was unacceptable to the Soviet Union, which attended the San Francisco conference but did not sign the peace treaty. The relationship between the San Francisco settlement and Japan's relations with China was less predictable and more convoluted, but ended in Japan's isolation from China—against the wishes of most Japanese, including the conservative leadership. If the Japanese government's successful resistance to pressure for more massive remilitarization showed the limits of U.S. power, Japan's inability to pursue an independent China policy, despite its desire to do so, revealed the coercive and seductive power of the new Pax Americana in Asia.

The containment of communist China represented the critical negative face of the integrated Cold War strategy in Asia. The evolution of this policy, culminating in 1951–52, can be only briefly summarized here. Until early 1950, both military and civilian U.S. planners generally assumed that Japanese trade with mainland China was inevitable, was essential to helping Japan escape the dollar gap and attain economic stability, and might even be valuable in the Cold War context (by reintroducing Japan into Manchuria and North China as a "buffer" against the Soviet Union and by helping to "wean" the Chinese communists away from the Soviets and toward the capitalist camp). Much of this line of thinking was embodied in NSC 41 of March 1949 and reiterated in NSC 48/1 and 48/2 the following December. In the months prior to the Korean War, as the U.S. position toward China hardened, the Japanese were required to follow a stricter list of embargoed goods in their trade with China; nonetheless, Sino-Japanese trade showed a conspicuous upturn in 1950, even after the Korean War began.

Although occupied Japan naturally was forced to adhere to the full embargo on trade with China following China's entry into the war in November 1950, it still was assumed in many quarters that Sino-Japanese relations would and should be resumed once the Korean War ended. Given the political volatility of the China issue within the United States and disagreements on the subject between the United States and its leading allies of the time, neither the communist nor the Nationalist Chinese were invited to the San Francisco peace conference. The Japanese attended the conference, however, with the understanding that they later would be able to decide on their own what policy they wished to pursue toward China. This also was the British understanding of the situation. By December 1951, however, it had been brought home to the Japanese that if they did not commit themselves to relations with the regime in Taiwan, they faced probable rejection of the peace treaty in the U.S. Congress—and thus an indefinitely prolonged occupation.

During the final months of the Occupation, the Japanese therefore negotiated an independent peace treaty with the Chiang Kai-shek regime, along the lines of the San Francisco treaty. While this was taking place in Taipei, U.S. officials secretly were preparing the ground for locking Japan firmly into the economic containment of China. This policy culminated in September 1952 in the creation of CHINCOM (the "China Committee"), an adjunct to the secret CG ("Coordinating Group") and COCOM ("Coordinating Committee") mechanism whereby the United States and its allies planned trade controls against the Soviet bloc. Under the CHINCOM arrangement, Japan did not simply agree to adhere to the lists of embargoed items that the other nations agreed upon; it actually was forced to agree to much more extensive restrictions on trade with China than any of America's other allies.[40]

With the China market thus abruptly cut off, first by China's entry into the war in Korea and then by fiat from Washington, the long-contemplated plan of integrating the Japanese and Southeast Asian economies suddenly became a matter of urgent concern in both Washington and Tokyo. Viewed from this perspective, the integrated policy can be said to have been introduced to the world in the early months of 1951, when it was publicly christened with the somewhat misleading formal name of "U.S.-Japan economic cooperation." This concept became the keynote of much top-level Japanese economic planning over the next several years, and it was understood by all concerned that U.S.-Japanese collaboration in the promotion of economic development in Southeast Asia was a critical part of the cooperative policy.

The first Japanese economic mission to the nations to the south was dispatched by Occupation authorities in mid 1951, and the prospects of a revived coprosperity sphere (but now one that replaced rather than included China) taxed the imagination and energies of innumerable Japanese officials. In one of the revealing small touches of the San Francisco peace settlement, John Foster Dulles reintroduced the issue of the suspended reparations program, but with a twist. Japan, it was agreed, would pay reparations to its recent victims, but out of current production and with the primary objective of using these payments as an entering wedge for penetrating the Southeast Asia economies.[41]

As it turned out, Southeast Asia did not materialize as an immediate replacement for the closed-off China market, partly because of the weakness of these nations' economies and partly because the Southeast Asians nursed bitter memories and the reparations negotiations were protracted. What did materialize was an unexpected and immensely dynamic form of Cold War economic integration sparked by the conflict in Korea: the sudden burst of U.S. "special procurements" in Japan after June 1950 and, what was even more significant, the routinization of such military-related purchases under the rubric "new special procurements" beginning in mid 1951. In the ten years from 1951 through 1960, military procurements and expenditures pumped some $5.5 billion into the Japanese economy. This contributed greatly to military, economic, and technological integration among Japan, the United States, and the rest of the noncommunist world; and although the planners worked it into shape, the decisive impetus was unplanned. As Yoshida Shigeru, the doughty conservative leader, put it, for Japan the war in Korea was an unexpected "gift of the gods."[42]

A half decade after being devastated by war, Japan was redeemed by war in its former colony, and Truman's erstwhile "savages" and "beasts" had been reidentified as America's best hope in Asia.

NOTES

1 On the Japanese as savages, see "Today Has Been a Historical One: Harry S. Truman's Diary of the Potsdam Conference" (introduced by Eduard Mark), *Diplomatic History* 4 (Summer 1980): 324; also Robert H. Ferrell, ed., *Off the Record: The Private Papers of Harry S. Truman* (New York: Harper and Row, 1980), pp. 55–56. Truman's comment on having "to deal with a beast" was made in a letter dated 11 August 1945 and is

quoted in Barton J. Bernstein, "The Atomic Bomb and American Foreign Policy: The Route to Hiroshima," in Barton J. Bernstein, ed., *The Atomic Bomb: The Critical Issues* (Boston: Little, Brown, 1976), p. 113. The policy of low-level incendiary bombing of Japanese urban areas began with the devastating air raid against Tokyo on March 9–10, 1945, and had been extended to more than sixty Japanese cities by the time the atomic bombs were dropped.

2 An excellent annotated guide to the earlier literature is Robert E. Ward and Frank Joseph Shulman, eds., *The Allied Occupation of Japan, 1945–1952: An Annotated Bibliography of Western-Language Materials* (Chicago: American Library Association, 1974). Shulman also compiled a listing of "Doctoral Dissertations on the Allied Occupation of Japan, 1945–1952" for the 1978 MacArthur Memorial conference cited below. For a more succinct and recent list of basic published sources as of the early 1980s, see John W. Dower, *Japanese History and Culture from Ancient to Modern Times: Seven Basic Bibliographies* (New York: Markus Wiener Publishing, 1986), pp. 199–222.

For general historiographic appraisals of Japanese as well as English scholarship on the Occupation, see John W. Dower, "Occupied Japan as History and Occupation History as Politics," *Journal of Asian Studies* 34 (Feb. 1975): 485–504; and Carol Gluck, "Entangling Illusions: Japanese and American Views of the Occupation," in Warren I. Cohen, ed., *New Frontiers in American–East Asian Relations: Essays Presented to Dorothy Borg* (New York: Columbia University Press, 1983), pp. 169–236. Short essays by Dower, Edwin O. Reischauer, Eiji Takemae, and Rinjirō Sodei in Harry Wray and Hilary Conroy, eds., *Japan Examined: Perspectives on Modern Japanese History* (Honolulu: University of Hawaii Press, 1983), pp. 331–63, convey some of the interpretive diversity in the field today.

Among the most notable earlier influential accounts of the Occupation are the various editions of Edwin O. Reischauer, *The United States and Japan* (Cambridge, Mass.: Harvard University Press, 1st ed., 1950); Kazuo Kawai, *Japan's American Interlude* (Chicago: University of Chicago Press, 1960); Frederick S. Dunn, *Peacemaking and the Settlement with Japan* (Princeton: Princeton University Press, 1960); and Robert E. Ward, "Reflections on the Allied Occupation and Planned Political Change in Japan," in Robert E. Ward, ed., *Political Development in Modern Japan* (Princeton: Princeton University Press, 1968).

I myself have dwelled in earlier writings, with more extensive notations, on some of the more revisionist themes mentioned here. See *Empire and Aftermath: Yoshida Shigeru and the Japanese Experience, 1878–1954* (Cambridge, Mass.: Council on East Asian Studies, Harvard University, 1979), pp. 305–492; "The Eye of the Beholder: Background Notes on the U.S.-Japan Military Relationship," *Bulletin of Concerned Asian Scholars* 2 (October 1969): 15–31; "Occupied Japan and the American Lake, 1945–1950," in Edward Friedman and Mark Selden, eds., *America's Asia: Dissenting Essays on Asian-American Relations* (New York: Pantheon, 1974), pp. 146–206; and "The Superdomino in Postwar Asia: Japan In and Out of *The Pentagon Papers*," in Noam Chomsky and Howard Zinn, eds., *The Senator Gravel Edition of the Pentagon Papers*, vol. 5 (Boston: Beacon Press, 1972), pp. 101–42. Howard Schonberger has made extensive use of government archives and private papers to illuminate U.S. decision making and the Cold War context of the Occupation in a series of influential revisionist articles, among them the following: "Zaibatsu Dissolution and the American Restoration of Japan," *Bulletin of Concerned Asian Scholars* 5 (Sept. 1973): 16–31; "The Japan Lobby in American Diplomacy, 1947–1952," *Pacific Historical Review* 46 (Aug. 1977): 327–59; "American Labor's Cold War in Occupied Japan," *Diplomatic History* 5 (Summer 1979): 249–72; "General William Draper, the 80th Congress, and the Origins of Japan's Reverse Course," paper presented to the International Conference on the Occupation of Japan, Amherst College, August 1980; "The General and the Presidency: Douglas MacArthur and the Election of 1948," *Wisconsin Magazine of History* 57 (Spring 1974): 201–19; "U.S. Policy in Post-war Japan: The Retreat from Liberalism," *Science and Society* 46 (Spring 1982): 39–59; and "John Foster Dulles and the China Question in the Making of the Japanese Peace Treaty," in Thomas W. Burkman, ed., *The Occupation of Japan: The International Context* (Norfolk, Va.: MacArthur Memorial, 1982), pp. 229–54. Most of these essays, plus others, have been collected in Schonberger's "biographical history" of the Occupation, *Aftermath of Empire: Americans and the Remaking of Japan, 1945–1952* (Kent, Ohio: Kent State University Press, 1989).

For detailed analysis of the emergence of a broad regional approach in U.S. economic planning toward Japan and postwar Asia, see William Borden, *Pacific Alliance: United States Foreign Economic Policy and Japanese Trade Recovery, 1947–1955* (Madison: University of Wisconsin Press, 1984); and Michael Schaller, *The American Occupation of Japan: The Origins of the Cold War in Asia* (New York: Oxford University Press, 1985). Schaller's book is an elaboration of his incisive article on pre–

Korean War proposals to integrate the Japanese and Southeast Asian economies: "Securing the Great Crescent: Occupied Japan and the Origins of Containment in Southeast Asia," *Journal of American History* 69 (Sept. 1982): 392–414.

The major forum in the United States for studies of occupied Japan has been the symposia sponsored by the MacArthur Memorial in Norfolk, Virginia. Symposia with published proceedings include *The Occupation of Japan and Its Legacy to the Postwar World* (1975); *The Occupation of Japan: Impact of Legal Reform* (1977); *The Occupation of Japan: Economic Policy and Reform* (1978); *The Occupation of Japan: Education and Social Reform* (1980); and *The Occupation of Japan: The International Context* (1982). For the proceedings of a 1977 conference on occupied Japan and occupied Germany, see Robert Wolfe, ed., *Americans as Proconsuls: United States Military Government in Germany and Japan, 1944–1952* (Carbondale: Southern Illinois University Press, 1984).

3　Recent studies in English dealing with U.S. policy toward other parts of Asia in the first postwar decade and providing an important complement to the Japan-centered emphasis of this present essay include Akira Iriye, *The Cold War in Asia: A Historical Introduction* (Englewood Cliffs, N.J.: Prentice-Hall, 1974); Yonosuke Nagai and Akira Iriye, eds., *The Origins of the Cold War in Asia* (New York: Columbia University Press and University of Tokyo Press, 1977); Bruce Cumings, "Introduction: The Course of Korean-American Relations, 1943–1953," in Cumings, ed., *Child of Conflict: The Korean-American Relationship, 1943–1953* (Seattle: University of Washington Press, 1983), pp. 3–55; idem, *The Origins of the Korean War: Liberation and the Emergence of Separate Regimes, 1945–1947* (Princeton: Princeton University Press, 1984); idem, "The Origins and Development of the Northeast Asian Political Economy: Industrial Sectors, Produce Cycles, and Political Consequences," *International Organization* 38 (Winter 1984): 1–40; William Whitney Stueck, Jr., *The Road to Confrontation: American Policy Toward China and Korea, 1947–1950* (New York: Columbia University Press, 1981); Dorothy Borg and Waldo Heinrichs, eds., *Uncertain Years: Chinese-American Relations, 1947–1950* (New York: Columbia University Press, 1980); Robert M. Blum, *Drawing the Line: The Origin of the American Containment Policy in East Asia* (New York: W. W. Norton, 1982); Nancy Bernkopf Tucker, *Patterns in the Dust: Chinese-American Relations and the Recognition Controversy, 1949–1950* (New York: Columbia University Press, 1983); Robert J. McMahon, *Colonialism and Cold War: The United States and the Struggle for Indonesian Independence, 1945–1949* (Ithaca: Cornell University Press, 1981). The maiden issue of *The Japanese Journal of American Studies*, published in 1981, was devoted to "United States Policy toward East Asia: 1945–1950."

4 The most concise introduction to disagreement (as well as agreement) on Occupation policy among the allies of the United States is an early official publication: U.S. Department of State, *The Far Eastern Commission: A Study in International Cooperation, 1945–1952* (Washington, D.C.: D.O.S. Publication 5138, 1953). In 1982, the government of New Zealand published a mammoth (almost 1,800 pages) collection of pertinent documents as volume 2 of *Documents on New Zealand External Relations*, edited by Robin Kay and subtitled *The Surrender and Occupation of Japan*. British attitudes toward occupied Japan are closely examined in Roger W. Buckley, *Occupation Diplomacy: Britain, the United States, and Japan, 1945–1952* (Cambridge: Cambridge University Press, 1982). Australia's position was the subject of an earlier monograph by Richard N. Rosecrance, *Australian Diplomacy and Japan, 1945–1951* (Cambridge: Cambridge University Press, 1962). The published proceedings of the fifth of the MacArthur Memorial conferences, cited in note 2, contain many papers on the international aspects of the Occupation.

Although the Japanese Ministry of Foreign Affairs has adopted a policy of selective declassification of archives pertaining to the Occupation, scholars are still greatly hampered in gaining access to basic primary materials scattered throughout the Japanese bureaucracy. Petitions calling for more open and convenient access have been presented to the government by Japanese and non-Japanese specialists on the Occupation—notably in 1980 and 1983—but thus far the response has been essentially tokenistic; numerous materials have been made available on microfilm, but most of this is of little or no interest to scholars. The Soviet archives on the period are presumedly in the process of being made more accessible, and certainly will contribute to future revisionism in critical areas; as yet, they have not influenced Occupation scholarship. With certain minor exceptions such as the Wellington Koo papers at Columbia, the internal Chinese record is also inaccessible to researchers.

5 For Kennan and Rusk, see Committee on International Relations, House of Representatives, *Selected Executive Session Hearings of the Committee, 1943–50*, vol. 8 (United States Policy in the Far East, part 2), pp. 160, 512; cf. ibid., 242, for Dean Acheson on the same problem. Louis Johnson's famous blast at the lack of a coordinated policy was delivered on June 10, 1949, when the Defense Department adopted a hard stance on Asian policy in the form of the famous "NSC 48." See Kenneth W. Condit, *The Joint Chiefs of Staff and National Policy, 1947–1949*, vol. 2 of

the official *The History of the Joint Chiefs of Staff* (Wilmington, Del.: Michael Glazier, 1979), p. 516; also U.S. Department of Defense, *United States-Vietnam Relations, 1945–1967*, vol. 8, pp. 217–18.

6 For presurrender planning, see U.S. Department of State, *Foreign Relations of the United States*, 1944, vol. 5, pp. 1186–1289; and 1945, vol. 6, p. 497ff. (hereafter this series is cited as *FRUS*). Hugh Borton, a central figure in the State Department group that drafted most of the presurrender plans for Japan, has written two informative essays on this subject: "Preparation for the Occupation of Japan," *Journal of Asian Studies* 25 (Feb. 1966): 203–12; and *American Presurrender Planning for Postwar Japan* (New York: Occasional Papers of the East Asian Institute, Columbia University, 1967).

Some of the public discussion concerning postwar U.S. bases is summarized in J. W. Dower, "Occupied Japan and the American Lake"; the archival record on this is introduced in Melvyn P. Leffler, "The American Conception of National Security and the Beginnings of the Cold War, 1945–48," *American Historical Review* 89 (April 1984), esp. pp. 349–56. The song title is recorded in Colin Shindler, *Hollywood Goes to War: Films and American Society, 1939–1952* (Boston: Routledge and Kegan Paul, 1979), p. 35.

7 The formal policy of unilateral U.S. control of the nominally "Allied" Occupation was set forth in State-War-Navy Coordinating Committee (SWNCC) 150/2 ("United States Initial Post-Defeat Policy Relating to Japan") of 12 August 1945; *FRUS* 1945, vol. 6, pp. 609–12. International participation eventually took the form of a multinational Far Eastern Commission that met in Washington and a four-delegate (United States, China, U.S.S.R., and Commonwealth) Allied Council in Tokyo. Neither was a control commission.

8 Much of the *FRUS* volume for 1945 is devoted to these issues. The Soviet attempt to equate its own position in Eastern Europe with the American sphere in Japan and the Pacific emerges most strongly in the cables of the U.S. ambassador to Moscow, Averell Harriman. President Truman acknowledged the essentially moderate Soviet position in his *Memoirs: Year of Decisions* (New York: Signet, 1955), esp. p. 490.

9 On the "staging area," see Harold Issacs, *No Peace for Asia* (Cambridge, Mass.: MIT Press, 1947, rep. 1967), pp. 39, 119. See Mark Gayn, *Japan Diary* (New York: William Sloane Associates, 1948), pp. 42 (diary entry for Dec. 20, 1945), 119 (February 21, 1946), 212 (May 10, 1946), 237–40 (May 27, 1946); James Forrestal, *The Forrestal Diaries*, edited by Walter Millis (New York: Viking, 1951), p. 56 (May 1945); *FRUS* 1946, vol. 6,

pp. 285–86, 301–304, 337–39 (for the *place d'armes* memo and related discussion). Michael Schaller offers numerous other early U.S. statements concerning using Japan as an anti-Soviet base or ally in chapter 3 of *The American Occupation of Japan*, the most striking of which are the report of a meeting between General MacArthur and presidential envoy Edwin A. Locke in October 1945 and a February 1946 report from Tokyo by U.S. Treasury Department envoy D.R. Jenkins.

10 Roosevelt and Churchill spoke vaguely of the future disarmament of the Axis in the Atlantic Charter of August 1941, and on January 7, 1943, Roosevelt told Congress that Germany, Italy, and Japan "must be disarmed and kept disarmed," a declaration cited by many publicists; see William C. Johnstone, *The Future of Japan* (New York: Oxford University Press, 1945), p. 31. For Senator Vandenberg's speech, see the *New York Times* for January 11, 1945. There was indeed some ambiguity as to whether U.S. policy called for "permanent" disarmament of Japan, but the Potsdam Declaration of July 26, 1945, stated that the Japanese military would be "completely disarmed," and SWNCC 150/2 of August 12 stated that U.S. policy was "to accomplish the permanent and complete disarmament and demilitarization of Japan." The revised instructions sent to MacArthur on August 29 and made public on September 22 similarly said that "Japan will be completely disarmed and demilitarized." See *FRUS* 1945, vol. 6, pp. 552, 610; also Government Section, Supreme Commander for the Allied Powers, *Political Reorientation of Japan, September 1945 to September 1948* (Washington, D.C.: U.S. Government Printing Office, 1949), vol. 2, pp. 423–24, 431.

11 On SWNCC and the Borton-Blakeslee group, see citations in note 6 above and the analysis in Akira Iriye, *Power and Culture: The Japanese-American War, 1941–1945* (Cambridge, Mass.: Harvard University Press, 1982). The basic SWNCC (later SANACC) documents are available on microfilm in thirty-two reels under the title *SWNCC (State-War-Navy Coordinating Committee)/SANACC (State-Army-Navy-Air Force Coordinating Committee) Case Files, 1944–1949* (Wilmington, Del.: Scholarly Resources, 1977).

12 MacArthur's "President Rosenfeld" habit is recounted in an irreverent reminiscence by the general's former military secretary, Faubion Bowers, in "The Late General MacArthur, Warts and All," *Esquire* (Jan. 1967), 90ff. The initial demilitarization and democratization policies are covered at length in a variety of official sources. The best-known of these is the invaluable two-volume narrative summary and documentary collection prepared by MacArthur's headquarters and published in 1949 as *Political*

Reorientation of Japan, September 1945 to September 1948. Two volumes authored by State Department officials were published under nongovernment imprints while the Occupation was still under way: Edwin M. Martin, *The Allied Occupation of Japan* (New York: American Institute of Pacific Relations, 1948), and Robert A. Fearey, *The Occupation of Japan, Second Phase: 1948–50* (New York: Macmillan, for the International Secretariat, Institute of Pacific Relations, 1950). Between 1950 and the end of the Occupation in early 1952, MacArthur's staff also prepared a useful and often overlooked official history that eventually included fifty-five monographs about specific aspects of the Occupation; the series is available on microfilm from the National Archives under the collective title *History of the Non-Military Activities of the Occupation of Japan.* A neglected source on the military aspects of repatriation and demilitarization is *MacArthur in Japan: The Occupation: Military Phase,* "Volume 1— Supplement" of *Reports of General MacArthur* (Washington, D.C.: U.S. Government Printing Office, 1966).

The following nonofficial studies also are useful for specific aspects of Occupation policy: Richard Minear, *Victor's Justice: The Tokyo War Crimes Trial* (Princeton: Princeton University Press, 1971); Phillip R. Piccigallo, *The Japanese on Trial: Allied War Crimes Operations in the East, 1945–1951* (Austin: University of Texas Press, 1972); Hans H. Baerwald, *The Purge of Japanese Leaders under the Occupation* (Berkeley: University of California Publications in Political Science, 8, 1959); Meirion and Susie Harries, *Sheathing the Sword: The Demilitarization of Postwar Japan* (New York: Macmillan, 1987); Ronald Dore, *Land Reform in Japan* (New York: Oxford University Press, 1959); Eleanor Hadley, *Antitrust in Japan* (Princeton: Princeton University Press, 1970); Eleanor Hadley, "Zaibatsu" and " Zaibatsu Dissolution," *Encyclopedia of Japan* (Tokyo: Kodansha, 1983) vol. 8, pp. 361–66; T.A Bisson, *Zaibatsu Dissolution in Japan* (Berkeley: University of California Press, 1954); Chitoshi Yanaga, *Big Business in Japanese Politics* (New Haven, Conn.: Yale University Press, 1968); Chalmers Johnson, *MITI and the Japanese Miracle: The Growth of Industrial Policy, 1925–1975* (Stanford, Calif.: Stanford University Press, 1982); Martin Bronfenbrenner, "Occupation-Period Economy (1945–1952), "*Encyclopedia of Japan,* vol. 2, pp. 154–58; Miriam Farley, *Aspects of Japan's Labor Problems* (New York: Institute of Pacific Relations, 1950); Joe B. Moore, *Japanese Workers and the Struggle for Power, 1945–1947* (Madison: University of Wisconsin Press, 1983); Solomon Levine, *Industrial Relations in Postwar Japan* (Champaign: University of Illinois Press, 1953); Solomon Levine, "Labor," *Encyclopedia of Japan,* vol. 4, pp. 343–49; John M. Maki, transl. and ed., *Japan's Commission on the Constitution: The Final Report* (Seattle: University of Washington Press, 1980); Theodore Cohen, *Remaking Japan: The American Occupation as New Deal*, ed. Herbert Passin (New York: Free Press, 1987); Justin Williams, Sr., *Japan's Political Revolution under MacArthur: A Participant's Account* (Athens: University of Georgia Press, 1979); Alfred C. Oppler, *Legal Reform in Occupied Japan: A Participant Looks Back* (Princeton: Princeton University Press, 1976); "Legal Reforms in Japan during the Allied Occupation," special reprint volume of *Washington Law Review* (1977); Kenzō Takayanagi, Ichirō Ohtomo, and Hideo Tanaka, eds., *Nihonkoku Kempō Seitei no Katei* (Tokyo: Yuhikaku, 1972—volume 1 of this two-volume work on "The Making of the Constitution of Japan" contains basic English-language documents pertaining to constitutional revision from the papers of Milo E. Rowell, covering the period from December 1945 to the end of February 1946); Kurt Steiner, *Local Government in Japan* (Stanford, Calif.: Stanford University Press, 1965); Robert Ward and Yoshikazu Sakamoto, eds., *Democratizing Japan: The Allied Occupation* (Honolulu: University of Hawaii Press, 1987).

For case studies of prewar-postwar continuities in the political economy of Japan, see J. W. Dower, *Empire and Aftermath*; Johnson, *MITI and the Japanese Miracle*; Andrew Gordon, *The Evolution of Labor Relations in Japan: Heavy Industry, 1853–1955* (Cambridge, Mass.: Council on East Asian Studies, Harvard University, 1985); Sheldon M. Garon, "The Imperial Bureaucracy and Labor Policy in Postwar Japan," *Journal of Asian Studies* 43 (May 1984): 441–57. See also Chapter 1 of the present volume.

13 Continuities in military staffing are best summarized in Ikuhiko Hata's Japanese-language monograph *Shiroku—Nihon Saigunbi* (1976: Bungei Shunjū). In English, the Navy carryovers are documented in James E. Auer, *The Postwar Rearmament of Japanese Maritime Forces, 1945–71* (New York: Praeger, 1973). On the "Hattori clique" in the Occupation's G-2 Section, see Dower, *Empire and Aftermath*, p. 387.

For "Unit 731," which has received considerable publicity in Japan in recent years, the basic analysis in English is available in two articles by John W. Powell: "Japan's Germ Warfare: The U.S. Cover-up of a War Crime," *Bulletin of Concerned Asian Scholars* 12 (Oct.-Dec. 1980): 2–17, and "Japan's Biological Weapons: 1930–1945," *Bulletin of the Atomic Scientists* 37 (Oct. 1981): 43–53. Powell shows conclusively that Occupation authorities agreed not to prosecute Japanese scientists and officers who had engaged in lethal experiments with POWs in exchange for

201

technical information about the results of the experiments. Some of the lesser figures associated with Unit 731 were captured by the Russians when they invaded Manchuria in August 1945 and placed on trial in the so-called Khabarovsk war-crimes trials, the results of which were publicized in 1949 and published in a lengthy English-language summary in 1950 (*Materials on the Trial of Former Servicemen of the Japanese Army Charged with Manufacturing and Employing Bacteriological Weapons*, Foreign Languages Publishing House, Moscow). During the Korean War, when the communists accused the United States of experimenting with bacteriological warfare, it also was suggested that Ishii Shirō, the former head of Unit 731, was actively collaborating with the Americans.

The retention, abuse, and indoctrination of hundreds of thousands of Japanese POWs by the Soviet Union was widely publicized from around 1947 to 1949 and is generally well known. Less attention has been given to the retention—and frequently anticommunist military deployment—of Japanese in China and Southeast Asia. For a corrective to this lacuna, see Donald G. Gillin with Charles Etter, "Staying On: Japanese Soldiers and Civilians in China, 1945–1949," *Journal of Asian Studies* 42 (May 1983): 497–518. On Japanese POWs under British control in Southeast Asia as late as 1947, see *FRUS* 1947, vol. 6, pp. 192–93, 255–56.

14 The origin of Article Nine has been most attentively addressed by Theodore McNelly. See "The Renunciation of War in the Japanese Constitution," *Political Science Quarterly* 77 (Sept. 1962): 350–78; his more recent speculations (in both Japanese and English) in *Hōritsu Jihō* 51 (May 1979): 178–81, 256–60; and his comments in the *Daily Yomiuri* of May 3, 1980. On the draft disarmament treaty, see *FRUS* 1946, vol. 8, pp. 150–55, 227–28 (G.B.), 236 (China), 253–54, 326–32, 348–49, 356, 376. The basic "Draft Treaty on the Disarmament and Demobilization of Japan" was made public on June 21 and submitted to the Far Eastern Commission on June 24. The United States continued to reaffirm its support of a long-term disarmament treaty into 1947 (*FRUS* 1947, vol. 6, pp. 237, 450–53, 478–79), but this had become a dead issue by midsummer, when George Kennan et al. brought about a reconsideration of Occupation policy, as discussed in the following section on the soft Cold War policy.

15 On Okinawa and the Ryukyus, see James F. Schnabel, *The Joint Chiefs of Staff and National Policy, 1945–1947*, vol. 1 of *The History of the Joint Chiefs of Staff* (Wilmington, Del.: Michael Glazier, 1979), p. 335; Condit, *The Joint Chiefs of Staff and National Policy*, p. 495 (on JCS 1619/24 of September 1947) and ch. 9 (on the " Broiler," "Halfmoon," and " Fleetwood" plans); and *FRUS* 1947, vol. 6, pp. 495–96, 537–43.

16 For MacArthur's statements, see *Political Reorientation of Japan*, vol. 2, pp. 756, 765–66. The peace-treaty debate is extensively documented in *FRUS* 1947, vol. 6. On the "separate peace" concept, see ibid., 476–77, 479–85, 489–502; also *Department of State Bulletin*, August 24, 1947, p. 395.

17 The 1947 Japanese initiatives are described in various Japanese sources, including the valuable "insider" account by Nishimura Kumao, *San Furanshisuko Heiwa Jōyaku* (1971: vol. 27 of the Kajima Kenkyūjo Shuppankai series *Nihon Gaikō Shi*). In English, see Martin Weinstein, *Japan's Postwar Defense Policy, 1947–1968* (New York: Columbia University Press, 1971), ch. 2. The emperor's role was first made public by Shindō Eiichi in the April 1979 issue of the Japanese monthly *Sekai*. Takemae Eiji, the "dean" of Japanese specialists on the Occupation, among others, has called attention to Okinawa and the "semidivided" nature of post-1945 Japan.

18 MacArthur's comments on security matters appear at great length in the *FRUS* volumes and the files of the Joint Chiefs of Staff in the Modern Military Records branch, National Archives. Many of the basic JCS documents are available in fourteen microfilm reels as *Records of the Joint Chiefs of Staff, part 2, 1946–1953, The Far East* (Frederick, Md.: University Publications of America, 1980). For the "Switzerland of the Pacific" statement, see the *New York Times*, March 2, 1949; this quotation appeared, it should be noted, in an interview in which MacArthur proposed an offshore island chain of defense in Asia very similar to that which Secretary of State Acheson described on January 12, 1950—including the Philippines, the Ryukyus, Japan, and the Aleutians, and neglecting Taiwan and Korea.

19 PPS 10 is printed in *FRUS* 1947, vol. 6, pp. 537–43. See also PPS 28 of March 25, 1948, the key transitional policy paper between PPS 10 and NSC 13; *FRUS* 1948, vol. 6, pp. 691–719.

20 NSC 13 is reproduced in *FRUS* 1948, vol. 6, pp. 775–81. The key documents in the series are NSC 13 (June 2, 1948), NSC 13/1 (Sept. 24, 1948), NSC 13/2 (Oct. 7, 1948; approved by President Truman two days later), and NSC 13/3 (May 6, 1949).

21 For the "Martin Plan," see *FRUS* 1947, vol. 6, pp. 184–86. This evolved into the State Department's SWNCC 381 of July 22, 1947, which the army criticized as too soft in SWNCC 384 of October 9; ibid., pp. 265–66, 302–304.

22 The Supreme Command for the Allied Powers (SCAP) study entitled *A Possible Program for a Balanced Japanese Economy* was sent to army author-

ities on March 27, 1947; SCAP Records (in the National Archives in Suitland, Maryland), RG 331, Box 6670. In the convoluted genealogy of these internal studies and recommendations, this evolved into the so-called "Green Book" of October 1947 (*Possibility of a Balanced Japanese Economy*), and eventually the influential "Blue Book" of November 1948 (*Program for a Self-Supporting Japanese Economy*); see SCAP Records, RG 331, Boxes 7689, 7692, 8361. The text of Acheson's famous "workshop" speech appears as an appendix in Joseph M. Jones, *The Fifteen Weeks* (New York: Harcourt Brace and World, 1955).

For closely documented studies of the early recovery program, see Borden, *Pacific Alliance*, ch. 2; Schaller, "Securing the Great Crescent" and *The American Occupation of Japan*; Schonberger, "General William Draper, the 80th Congress, and the Origins of Japan's Reverse Course"; and the *Foreign Trade* volume (Monograph 50) in SCAP's *History of the Non-Military Activities of the Occupation of Japan.*

23 Okinawa's key position was spelled out in the secret strategy code-named "Halfmoon." Draper discussed the airfields in a May 17, 1948, speech entitled "Japan's Key Position in the Far East" (MacArthur Memorial Collection). The "ideological opponents" reference appears in JCS 1769/1 of April 29, 1947; *FRUS* 1947, vol. 1, p. 745. See also Schaller, *The American Occupation of Japan*, pp. 90, 104. Royall's important long memorandum of May 18, 1948, entitled "Limited Military Rearmament for Japan," appears under JCS 1380/48 of October 25, 1948 in the JCS archives, RG 218 (Geographic File 1946–47), Box 127. Further opposition to Japanese rearmament by MacArthur's staff, tendered on December 23, 1948, appears as JCS 1380/54 of January 6, 1949. Eichelberger's notorious 1948 comment is cited by Kazuo Kawai in *Pacific Affairs* (June 1950): 119; for the "monkey" reference, see Jay Luvaas, ed., *Dear Miss Em: General Eichelberger's War in the Pacific, 1942–1945* (Westport, Conn.: Greenwood Press, 1972), pp. 8–9.

24 The Joseph Dodge Papers in the Detroit Public Library are a major resource for analyzing economic policy toward Japan from the beginning of 1949. Critical earlier "reverse course" economic missions, discussed in the standard literature, were led by Clifford Strike (producing the "Strike Report" of February 1947 and "Overseas Consultants Report" of February 1948, both calling for reduced reparations); Percy Johnston (resulting in the "Johnston Report" of April 1948); and Ralph Young (leading to recommendations for stabilization and a fixed exchange rate in June 1948). For the less-than-dynamic implementation of NSC 13, see *FRUS*

1949, vol. 7, pp. 724–27, 754, 808–12, 815; also JCS 1380/59 of February 10, 1949 in RG 218 (1946–47), Box 122.

25 Kennan's own *Memoirs 1925–1950* (Boston: Little, Brown, 1967) are very clear on this; see ch. 16.

26 Central Intelligence Agency, "The Strategic Importance of the Far East to the US and the USSR" (May 4, 1949), Modern Military Records, National Archives; "The Position of the U.S. with Respect to Asia" (NSC 48/1), reprinted in Thomas H. Etzold and John Lewis Gaddis, eds., *Containment: Documents on American Policy and Strategy, 1945–1950* (New York: Columbia University Press, 1978), pp. 252–69.

27 See *Soviet Press Translations* 4 (1949), pp. 615–16, for the Soviet response. The major article on the American Council on Japan is Schonberger's "The Japan Lobby in American Diplomacy, 1947–1952" (note 2 above). For economic deconcentration, see Hadley (note 12 above), especially *Antitrust in Japan*, pp. 166, 172, 174, 180.

28 For the fascinating revival of "coprosperity sphere" rhetoric, see Schaller, *The American Occupation of Japan*, pp. 145, 179–80, 201, 205.

29 NSC 49 (June 15, 1949) and 49/1 (Sept. 30, 1949) are reprinted in Etzold and Gaddis, *Containment*, pp. 231–36. For JCS 1380/75 (Nov. 30, 1949), see RG 218 (1946–47), Box 127.

30 Dean Acheson, *Present at the Creation: My Years in the State Department* (New York: W. W. Norton, 1969), pp. 355–58.

31 The position of the military is set forth in NSC 49, JCS 1380/75, JCS 1380/77 (Dec. 10, 1949), and NSC 60 (Dec. 7, 1949). For Acheson's cable, see *FRUS* 1949, vol. 7, pp. 736–37; see ibid., pp. 724–29, for a useful summary of the State Department's support of a bilateral treaty, U.S. bases in Japan, and eventual Japanese rearmament. MacArthur's January 1950 response to NSC 49 appears in *FRUS* 1950, vol. 6, p. 1110. The statement by Omar Bradley appeared in the *New York Times* on February 7, 1950. For Dodge's statement to the National Advisory Council, see the "Appropriations" file, Box 1, Joseph Dodge Papers for 1950. The House Appropriations Committee report (Jan. 16, 1950) is among the Dodge papers in the Japanese Ministry of Finance collection. For the resolution of the long bureaucratic impasse, see *FRUS* 1950, vol. 6, pp. 1278–82 (JCS 1380/89 of Aug. 18, 1950); 1282–88 (the State Department response); and 1293–96 (the joint Defense-State memo of September 7 to the president). NSC 60/1 of September 8, 1950, by which President Truman authorized the government to proceed with negotiations for a peace treaty with Japan, marked the formal end of the stalemate.

32 For activities on the Japanese side, see Dower, *Empire and Aftermath*; Nishimura, *San Furanshisuko Heiwa Jōyaku*; Michael M. Yoshitsu, *Japan and the San Francisco Peace Settlement* (New York: Columbia University Press, 1982); and Takeshi Igarashi, "Peace-Making and Party Politics: The Formation of the Domestic Foreign Policy System in Postwar Japan," *Journal of Japanese Studies* 11 (Summer 1985): 323–56.

33 NSC 48/1 (Dec. 23, 1949) and NSC 48/2 (Dec. 30, 1949) are reprinted in Etzold and Gaddis, pp. 252–76. Kennan's observation, made in October 1949, is quoted in Cumings, *Child of Conflict*, p. 23; see also 26, 35–37.

34 The earlier draft of NSC 48/1 is quoted in Cumings, *Child of Conflict*, p. 36. Both Schaller and Borden document the emergence of the trilateral policy in great detail; for a concise summary, see Schaller's "Securing the Great Crescent," especially p. 398ff., for references to the European dimension of the linkage and the global problem of the "dollar gap." Kennan's comments on reopening a Japanese "empire to the south" are quoted in Cumings, "The Origins and Development of the Northeast Asian Economy," p. 18. The use of former Japanese military men by the Chinese Nationalists in Taiwan is discussed in Hata, *Shiroku—Nihon Saigunbi*, pp. 162–65.

35 For Voorhees and the intensified activities of early 1950, see Schaller, *The American Occupation of Japan*, pp. 213–33; also Borden, *Pacific Alliance*, pp. 124–42. For the "special yen fund," see *FRUS* 1950, vol. 6, pp. 1223–27.

36 Deming, later honored as the "father" of statistical quality-control practices in Japan, was invited by the Union of Japanese Scientists and Engineers in 1949 to teach industrial statistics in Japan; he convened his first eight-day seminar on the subject in Tokyo in July 1950 (attended by 220 engineers). The outbreak of the war two weeks earlier fortuitously provided a setting of military-related mass production and rapid industrial reconstruction that permitted the "Deming method" to be adopted, as it were, at the ground floor. For aspects of the "reverse course" in domestic Occupation policy, see Dower, *Empire and Aftermath*, pp. 332–33 (the purge and depurge), 338–41 (labor policy), 365–66 (the "Red Purge").

37 Central Intelligence Agency, "Feasibility of Japanese Rearmament in Association with the United States" (April 20, 1951), *FRUS* 1951, vol. 6, pt. 1, pp. 993–1001.

38 *FRUS* 1951, vol. 6, pt. 1, pp. 1258–59 (Chairman of the JCS to Secretary of Defense, July 17, 1951); see ibid., 1432–36 (JCS to Secretary of Defense, Dec. 12, 1951). For Ridgway, see ibid., pp. 1451–53 (Dec. 20, 1951).

39 See Dower, *Empire and Aftermath*, esp. pp. 369–400.

40 Concerning Japan and the containment of China, see ibid., pp. 400–14; Schonberger, "John Foster Dulles and the China Question in the Making of the Japanese Peace Treaty"; and Yoko Yasuhara, "Myth of Free Trade: COCOM and CHINCOM, 1945–1952" (Ph.D. diss., University of Wisconsin at Madison, 1984). The issue is voluminously documented in *FRUS* 1951, vol. 6, pt. 1, and *FRUS* 1952–1954, vol. 14.

41 On the "U.S.-Japan economic cooperation" policy, see Borden, *Pacific Alliance*, pp. 143–65, and Dower, *Empire and Aftermath*, pp. 415–36. For reparations as a potential boon to the Japanese economy, see *FRUS* 1951, vol. 6, pt. 1, pp. 1315–16.

42 See Dower, *Empire and Aftermath*, p. 316, for "gift of the gods" (a common phrase in conservative circles), and Borden, *Pacific Alliance*, p. 230, for procurement figures.

6

Yoshida in the
Scales of History

SYMBOLIC POLITICS AND
PRACTICAL POLICYMAKING

Almost a half century has passed since the end of World War II, and
during this period over twenty men have served as prime minister of
Japan. Some have been leaders of exceptional skill and influence; certainly this can be said, for example, of Kishi Nobusuke, Ikeda Hayato,
Satō Eisaku, Tanaka Kakuei, and Nakasone Yasuhiro. In the eyes of
most Japanese and non-Japanese, however, Yoshida Shigeru clearly
stands head and shoulders above all others. Indeed, among Japanese
political figures of the post-1945 years, only the Shōwa emperor seems
to surpass Yoshida in visibility and stature, and in the historical memory
the two men seem destined to remain in this position for many years to
come—one in the shadow of the other, and both above the crowd.

This is surely very close to the image that Yoshida, as a proud and
devoted servant of the throne, desired to leave to history—and there is
more than a little irony in the fact that he has succeeded so well, for his
career was uneven and his reputation was not always so high. Although

Yoshida is now generally regarded as a symbol of the conservative hegemony that has governed Japan for almost all of the postwar years, for example, it was conservative politicians and businessmen themselves who drove him from office in 1954. His famous nickname "One Man" now is usually offered as an attractive indication of Yoshida's staunch individualism, whereas when he was prime minister it was most often invoked in reference to his dictatorial proclivities.

Along somewhat similar lines, influential conservative Japanese writers such as Kōsaka Masataka and Inoki Masamichi have laid great emphasis on Yoshida's political realism and (in his own favorite phrase) "diplomatic sense." Between the 1920s and the mid 1950s, however, when he actually was immersed in the hurlyburly of diplomacy and politics, Yoshida did not really enjoy a high reputation for political adroitness and astuteness. I vividly recall visiting the Public Records Office in London as a very young researcher to look into the Foreign Office records concerning Yoshida's tenure as ambassador to Great Britain in the mid 1930s. "Ah, Yoshida," the elderly archivist murmured upon hearing my request. "They wrote some strong things about him. Very harsh. Unusually harsh." Indeed they did, and Yoshida's postwar Anglo-American counterparts were no kinder in private ("disquieting," "indiscreet," "equivocal," "ambiguous and evasive," "philosophical double talk," "a puff ball performance" are among the typical responses to him, for example, in the confidential U.S. files). In innumerable ways, time has burnished old One Man's charisma.

To put the matter lightly, it can be said that Yoshida already has enjoyed three or four political resurrections. He was drawn into the postwar political scene in 1946 after close to seven years of retirement from a diplomatic career that was, by his own account, mediocre. After a turbulent first term as prime minister in 1946–1947, he surprised most observers by succeeding in returning to power in late 1948. Following his reluctant resignation in 1954, which only a small number of his contemporaries lamented, he lived long enough to gain veneration as an elder statesman—the last Genrō, as it were. And beginning sometime in the 1970s, as Japan's impressive economic accomplishments became clear to all the world, Yoshida was again resurrected, this time in memory, as the most conspicuous early "architect" of the postwar recovery. Recently it has been said that Japan's postwar emergence as a global superpower reflects persistent adherence to the "Yoshida Doctrine" of economic nationalism, restrained remilitarization, and close relations with the United States.[1]

The simple fact that Yoshida's tenure as prime minister occurred during Japan's first postwar decade obviously goes far in itself in explaining his special place in history, for in the recent affairs of most of the great nations it is the leaders of the 1940s and early 1950s who are best remembered. The reason for this is clear enough: not only were these men called upon to make decisions during times of crisis and great change, but they also performed symbolic roles and have come to exemplify some of the larger dynamics of their times. In Yoshida's case, this symbolic role was and remains outstanding—due in part to the milieu in which he was called upon to perform, in part to his distinctive personality and modus operandi, and in part to the uneven nature of postwar archival materials in Japan. It even can be argued that it is primarily Yoshida's exceptional visibility as a political symbol, more than his concrete decisions as a policymaker, that accounts for the weight he now carries in the scales of modern Japanese history.

The pages that follow address these more symbolic aspects of Yoshida's career in greater detail, before turning to certain concrete and controversial policy issues. It may be useful, however, to have a preview of this agenda. Briefly, Yoshida's symbolic role is of interest at three levels. First, he exemplified the survival and reconsolidation of a social class and cluster of ideas and values that we can identify loosely with the upper-class "civilian old guard" that had been pushed to the sidelines during the years of war. Second, Yoshida carefully cultivated a conservative and patriotic posture, which he deemed appropriate for the so-called New Japan of the postdefeat period—a posture that can be described, again loosely, as "ultrapaternalistic democracy." The third and related level at which he played—and still plays—a conspicuous symbolic role is his intimate association with the "San Francisco System," the special military and economic relationship between Japan and the United States which has shaped Japan's course to the present day. In all of these areas we still can evoke concrete pictures of Yoshida in our minds—wearing kimono and white *tabi*, puffing expensive cigars, building a private shrine to the Meiji oligarchs in his garden, throwing water at newspaper reporters, denouncing leftists as "lawless elements" and intellectual supporters of Japanese neutralism as "literary sycophants," sending flowers and fruits to General MacArthur's wife, signing the peace treaty in San Francisco and having the peace settlement reported to the shrine of the Sun Goddess in Ise, bowing as prime minister before the emperor while announcing himself as "Your loyal servant, Shigeru." No other Japanese politician since the Meiji era has left such a vivid and suggestive personal portrait.

Almost all of this unfolded, of course, in a war-shattered and occupied country that was nominally under the control of the wartime Allied powers and, until April 1952, actually was obligated to follow U.S. policy. In such a context, as Yoshida was acutely aware, gestures and dramatic actions loomed especially large in the eyes of both the defeated and demoralized Japanese people and the wary and still-hostile victor nations. There was, to be sure, ample room for political maneuver in this setting—increasingly so as the Cold War intensified and U.S. policy toward occupied Japan shifted from political and social reform to economic reconstruction—and Yoshida did not hesitate to speak his mind to Occupation authorities and U.S. officials, or to play factional politics among them. A major part of his political activity as Japan's leader in the first postwar decade inevitably was directed toward relations with the United States, and this too sets him apart from almost all other Japanese leaders of the modern era. This certainly suited his career training as a diplomat, and Professor Inoki's laudatory study portrays Yoshida as exceptionally astute in this regard.

In the area of concrete policymaking, I myself would offer a more qualified evaluation of Yoshida's contribution. Few commentators would disagree that his overriding objective as prime minister was to bring Japan back to a position of respect and security within the noncommunist international community, and in this regard he saw his goals achieved in considerable part. At the same time, it also is worth keeping in mind that Yoshida confessed to being rather lazy, and on this score he does not seem to have been unduly modest. While Professor Inoki, for example, emphasizes the importance of Yoshida's personal relationship with General MacArthur, MacArthur himself privately told the Canadian scholar-diplomat E. H. Norman that he regarded Yoshida as "monumentally lazy and politically inept." The distinguished agrarian economist Tōhata Seiichi, whom Yoshida courted unsuccessfully for a ministerial post in his first cabinet, commented more charitably in 1948 about Yoshida's idiosyncratic combination of stubbornness and "unrational" disorganization. And as already indicated, both before and after World War II, non-Japanese diplomats and officials who had occasion to deal professionally with Yoshida more often than not found him puzzling, erratic, and exasperating. Whatever they may have said later for the public record, to my knowledge few if any of them ever described Yoshida in private as politically suave or adroit.[2]

This combination of tenacity and disorganization characterized Yoshida's behavior even in the policy area with which he is most intimately associated, namely, the formulation of the "San Francisco System." On this most controversial and consequential of all policies, Yoshida was tenacious in leading his countrymen to accept a "separate peace" that aligned Japan with the United States in the Cold War, and he was equally obdurate in resisting U.S. pressures for massive Japanese rearmament. Concerning the "separate peace" in general, I myself am inclined to sympathize with the ideals of those who advocated that Japan adopt a position of constructive neutrality in the Cold War—but to agree, at the same time, that by 1949–1950 this was not really a viable option given the immensity of American influence over Japan. While the economic, military, political, and ideological leverage that the United States wielded vis-à-vis Japan made it virtually impossible for any responsible Japanese leader to contemplate seriously a decisive break with U.S. Cold War policy, however, the Americans on their own part were acutely sensitive to the fact that a prolonged occupation of Japan would alienate popular Japanese support and be counterproductive to U.S. interests in the long run. Thus, by 1949–1950, the issue was not really a "separate peace" or no peace treaty at all, as Yoshida himself phrased it at the time, but rather what sort of separate peace and post-treaty military and economic status Japan would agree to. From this perspective, the real question insofar as Yoshida's leadership is concerned becomes: How well did he bargain within the emerging framework of the Pax Americana? The answer, in retrospect, seems mixed.

On the positive side, there are two areas in which Yoshida bargained stubbornly and made a difference. On an important issue generally neglected by scholars and commentators, he appears to have played an important role in asserting Japan's "residual sovereignty" over the Ryukyu and Bonin islands, thus expediting the eventual return of Okinawa to Japan in the early 1970s. His most significant contribution, however, surely lies in shaping the postwar Japanese policy of slow and incremental rearmament. Had the United States had its way in the early 1950s, Japan would have been propelled along a course of insanely rapid remilitarization with potentially explosive consequences both internationally and domestically.

On another critical aspect of the San Francisco System, however—relations with the People's Republic of China—Yoshida's policy was at best desultory and lackadaisical, and his private actions belied his occasional public criticisms of the U.S. containment policy. It may be true that American hysteria on the China issue left little room for bargaining. The documentary record that is available on the U.S. and British side, however, suggests that Yoshida never really seriously tried to exploit internal Anglo-American differences on the issue of dealing with communist China, or to promote a moderately more independent policy even after Japan had regained sovereignty. In this regard, he was more timid than some of his own trusted lieutenants, such as Ikeda Hayato and Aiichi Kiichi.

In the process of all this, Yoshida came to play a symbolic role that was especially galling to a staunch patriot, for the rigid conformity to U.S. Cold War policy exemplified in the worldwide containment policy reinforced the impression that the San Francisco System really amounted not to genuine sovereignty for Japan but rather to a form of "subordinate independence" within the new postwar American imperium. As it turned out, this anomalous status provided the circumstances under which Japan proceeded on a course of economic nationalism that brought unimagined material prosperity within a few decades—but at an enduring psychological and ideological cost. Japan's ultimate role as a "great" nation—always the proud Yoshida's goal—remained cabined and contorted by the constrictions of this dependent independence. As a consequence, the international respect for Japan which Yoshida so passionately sought has remained qualified and condescending.

On all of these issues, a detailed evaluation of Yoshida's leadership during Japan's first postwar decade—and, indeed, of the role and policy-making processes of the postwar Japanese government in general—is impeded by the spotty nature of available Japanese resources. While official and formerly classified U.S. and British records for this period are generally available to researchers, the Japanese archives remain relatively inaccessible. In addition, there are no troves of private papers comparable to those in the West. And, for the postwar period, there are relatively few important memoirs—virtually none with the heft, detail, and documentary annotation usually expected in the autobiographies of public figures in the West. Yoshida's own four-volume *Kaisō Jūnen* (Memoirs of a Decade) is but a partial exception, for this is an engaging but uneven (and partly ghostwritten) work whose primary value lies in presenting Yoshida's views on various topics. This highly impressionistic recollection still remains the major source for many Japanese commentators on Yoshida, however, as Professor Inoki's own three-volume study reveals. Such a loose and anecdotal narrative approach to autobiography, political biography, and indeed the very stuff of political history itself quite naturally reinforces the more "symbolic" approach to old One Man.

THE OLD GUARD

The forcefulness of Yoshida's personality, his unusually vivid symbolic role, and the peculiar strengths and weaknesses in the documentary record that pertains to him—all have contributed to a curious balance (or imbalance) in the lengthy studies published by both Professor Inoki and myself. For in both of our works, the pages devoted to Yoshida's activities prior to his becoming prime minister are more numerous than those devoted to his postwar activities. After Yoshida's death in 1968, his old colleagues and acquaintances met regularly for several years to reminisce about him, and they too linge. 4 longest over episodes and anecdotes from the prewar years.[3]

These prewar details are attractive for many reasons. Yoshida's values and personality, to put it mildly, were well formed by the time he became prime minister for the first time, at the age of sixty-eight. The earlier incidents and activities make him come alive as an individual—and, at the same time, serve as a reminder that as historians of Japan, as of any other place, we are dealing not with "forces" alone, but with congeries of individuals. At the same time, however, we also can see emerging from this background portrait a fairly distinctive *type*, a certain class and kind of man which can be identified for convenience as the "civilian old guard." Having offered this label, I would hasten to emphasize that Yoshida, for all his intense patriotism, should not be viewed as being peculiarly Japanese. He exemplified a type of upper-class and cosmopolitan official familiar in many nations in the late nineteenth and early twentieth centuries, whose career was primarily devoted to furthering the interests of the state within an international milieu of spheres of influence, cooperation, and conflict among the imperialist powers.

From Yoshida's life and career prior to August 1945, it is possible to abstract a number of experiences, attitudes, and values that, taken together, go far to help illuminate his postwar activities as an elderly man suddenly possessed of unaccustomed authority and summoned to face new challenges. The first and most personal point of note in this regard is the loneliness and emotional austerity of his early childhood, and the second is his socialization as a young gentleman of Meiji. Few commentators have failed to relate these cold but elitist early years of his life to the haughty and aloof individualism of Yoshida's "one man" style. The fact that he was thirty-four years old when the Meiji period ended in 1912, thus in every respect a full-fledged member of the "generation of Meiji," also places the vehemence of his opposition to the sweeping early reforms of the Occupation in a proper temporal perspective. Yoshida never found cause to question the correctness of the path charted by the Meiji oligarchs; and by marrying the granddaughter of Ōkubo Toshimichi, one of the great founding fathers of the Meiji state, he was even symbolically wedded to the very mainstream of Meiji statesmanship and nation-building. It was inevitable that the premise of many of the early Occupation reforms—that the roots of Japanese aggression and repression traced back to the very nature of the Restoration and Meiji state—were anathema to Yoshida. At the same time, however, his capacity to bend to changing circumstances, coupled with his acute sense of Japan's vulnerability in the global order, are strongly reminiscent of Ōkubo's well-known pragmatism.

The third formative experience of Yoshida's early career was his professional involvement as a young foreign-service officer, beginning in 1906, in the "traditional diplomacy" of the early decades of the twentieth century, when Japan first successfully emerged as an imperialist and colonial power. Tactically, this fostered appreciation of balances of power and spheres of influence, secret negotiations, Realpolitik, and

Machtpolitik. Strategically, "traditional diplomacy" rested on distrust of Russia; alliance with Great Britain, the dominant Western power in Asia; and a close and dominant economic relationship with the Asian mainland. The first two features of this orientation, formalized in the anti-Russian Anglo-Japanese Alliance of 1902–1922, provided an unmistakable model for Yoshida's postwar receptivity to a bilateral and anti-Soviet alliance with the United States. The conviction that Japan could not survive without close ties to China, on the other hand, became a source of tension when the United States forced the Yoshida government to participate in the economic containment of the People's Republic of China. To an old practitioner of "traditional diplomacy" such as Yoshida, who had spent much of his career directly engaged in China affairs, the postwar American argument that Southeast Asia should and could replace China as a market and source of raw materials seemed patent nonsense.

Yoshida's well-known association with the "pro-Anglo-American clique" (*shin-Ei-Bei-ha*) within the Foreign Ministry can be taken as a fourth characteristic of his prewar orientation, but this requires qualification. Yoshida was, to begin with, more Anglophile than pro-American. On a number of occasions before World War II, he described the Americans as untrustworthy and unsophisticated in diplomacy, and in the postwar period his disenchantment was reinforced not only by the early reformist "excesses" of the Occupation but also by the later militaristic excesses of John Foster Dulles. Yoshida's Anglophilism, moreover, had relatively little to do with admiration for British liberalism or parliamentary procedures. It reflected, on the contrary, his esteem for the cosmopolitanism of British high society and the sophisticated manner with which Britain managed its far-flung empire. By Yoshida's own admission, there also was an element of cynical Realpolitik in his prewar affiliation with the pro-Anglo-American clique. It would be more accurate, he once told an acquaintance, to see him as belonging to the "clique that makes use of Great Britain and the United States" (*Ei-Bei riyō-ha*).[4]

However calculating his support of close ties with the Anglo-American powers may have been, Yoshida continued to promote this position with considerable courage even during the 1930s, when Japanese militarists and Pan-Asianists were denouncing such policies as treason. Espousal of such pro-Western sentiments eventually earned him the label

216

of being an "old liberal" within the Japanese context, but as the preceding comments suggest, such characterization was misplaced. Yoshida's emergence in the postwar period as considerably right of center in the political spectrum did not in any way reflect abandonment of earlier liberal principles, for he had never conspicuously cherished such principles or evinced much interest in parliamentary politics. Public opinion in general and political parties in particular, he made clear on numerous occasions, were noisome impediments to the professional conduct of affairs of state. Both by training and temperament, Yoshida's preferred modus operandi was bureaucratic and autocratic. This "bureaucratism" can be taken as the fifth characteristic he carried with him into the postwar period, and was a somewhat ironic prelude to his emergence as the leader of the dominant political party.

Much attention has been given to Yoshida's distrust of the military establishment, and this can be taken as an important sixth point of note. This too requires qualification, however, for on various occasions in the 1920s and 1930s, Yoshida's position was hawkish. His hatred of General (and later Prime Minister) Tōjō Hideki, whom he once described in private correspondence as the son of the devil,[5] was offset by a striking emotional affinity for a succession of generals who were commonly associated with hard-line policies: Terauchi Masatake, Tanaka Giichi, Mazaki Jinzaburō, and Obata Toshishirō. In the Occupation period, this intriguing personal attraction reemerged to a certain degree in Yoshida's admiration not only for General MacArthur but also for General Charles Willoughby, the fanatically antileftist head of Counter-Intelligence Section whom MacArthur himself once referred to as a "loveable fascist." During the war, Yoshida also subscribed to the conspiracy thesis which held that many top militarists actually were secret communists or "Red fascists" who were deliberately using the war crisis to promote state control over the economy (Yoshida helped write the famous "Konoe Memorial" of February 1945, in which this argument received consummate expression). This peculiar fear of "Red" influences in the military carried over to become part of Yoshida's rationale for resisting U.S. pressure for rapid, large-scale remilitarization in the early 1950s.

It is nonetheless true that Yoshida was generally consistent in opposing military meddling in affairs deemed properly the domain of the civilian elites. From as early as the 1920s, he castigated military initiatives as

217

bringing the curse of "double and triple diplomacy" upon Japan; and when some of the ex-officers of the Imperial army, led by Tōjō's former aide Hattori Takushirō, attempted to assert control over the new Japanese military in 1950, Yoshida moved swiftly and predictably to thwart them and to reaffirm the principle of civilian control. Yoshida's reputation as an old antimilitarist also helped to buttress the basic argument that the civilian old guard in general used to criticize the reformist agenda imposed on Japan by the United States during the first stage of the Occupation. The reform policy as a whole rested on a critical structural and institutional analysis of prewar Japanese society, whereas the Yoshida group simply dismissed the years of accelerated Japanese aggression beginning in the early 1930s as an "aberration" brought about by militarist conspirators.

Yoshida's devotion to the Japanese throne, a seventh distinctive feature of his Weltanschauung, was personalized by his marriage to the daughter of Makino Nobuaki, Ōkubo's son and one of the emperor's most intimate advisers. It was personalized at an even more intimate level in 1921 by an encounter with the Prince Regent, Hirohito, which left Yoshida deeply moved by his future sovereign's "inborn beautiful characteristics."[6] Abstracted, the idealized pater familias of the emperor may have fulfilled a psychological need for Yoshida, who had been given away at birth by his real father, and whose adoptive father died when Yoshida was ten. Most certainly, however witting or unwitting, his profound devotion to the emperor system also was an act of self-preservation— for defense of the emperor and the national polity (kokutai), as promoted by the old guard, in concrete practice meant preservation of the status quo and the hierarchies of privilege.

Yoshida's activities certainly confirm the thesis that the number-one priority of the old guard in the immediate aftermath of the war was the preservation of the emperor system. This fixation—almost catatonic in the immediate wake of the defeat—is crucial to understanding why the conservative elites were willing to dampen their opposition to many of the progressive reforms that U.S. authorities demanded in the opening stages of the Occupation. Their overriding concern was to save the throne (and also ensure that Emperor Hirohito escaped indictment for war crimes); and to expedite this, they were willing to be conciliatory on any number of lesser political changes.

The most consequential bargain struck in this regard was the new Constitution promulgated in 1946, which, on the one hand, retained the emperor as "symbol of the State and of the unity of the people" and, on the other, renounced war and guaranteed an extensive range of human rights. The former, in conservative eyes, was quid pro quo for the latter. In Yoshida's view, this new formulation of the "symbol emperor" not only saved the throne but even may have insulated it against future political threats by explicitly detaching the emperor from the formal realm of power and authority. Under the new Constitution, the emperor became—in a subtle, almost aesthetic way—more transcendent than ever.

The ultimate thrust of such thinking says a great deal about the political nature of the postwar state, for it implies that Japan remained first and foremost a monarchy, and only secondarily and subordinately a democracy. This certainly was Yoshida's position, and he conveyed this with great flamboyance in November 1952, a half year after the Occupation ended, by referring to himself as *Shin Shigeru* ("Your loyal servant, Shigeru") while making a formal presentation to the emperor in his capacity as prime minister. By any calculation, this signaled a great victory for the old guard, for in effect Yoshida was symbolically wedding loyalism and bureaucratism by this obsequious and defiant act—and simultaneously thumbing his nose at the Occupation's "democratization" agenda. To Yoshida, public officials remained servants of the emperor rather than servants of the people.

The obverse side of reverence for the imperial institution was repression of "dangerous thoughts," which can be singled out as an eighth concern that preoccupied Yoshida and the old guard from an early date. In a remarkable letter to his father-in-law in 1921, Yoshida described in ecstatic terms his first encounter with the then–Prince Regent Hirohito, and proceeded directly to denounce the "literary sycophants" (*kyokugaku amin*; Yoshida erred in his ideographs) in Japan who promoted ideological confusion "under the name of freedom of research and independence of scholarship." In 1927, Yoshida solicited a post in the Tanaka Giichi cabinet, which was responsible for enlarging the compass of the Peace Preservation Law, under which tens of thousands of liberal, left-wing, and communist critics of the Imperial state were repressed. He also established a relationship at that time with Ueda Shunkichi, Prime

Minister Tanaka's private secretary. Over twenty years later, Ueda emerged as attorney general under Yoshida and helped repress the "dangerous thoughts" of the postwar era in the notorious "Red purges" that began in 1949 and were the counterpart in occupied Japan of McCarthyism in the United States. In 1950, Yoshida also caused an uproar by castigating Nanbara Shigeru, the Christian president of Tokyo University and a prominent spokesman for Japanese disarmament and neutrality, as a literary sycophant (*kyokugaku asei*).[7] Clearly, time never softened this intolerance—nor, as the Red purges (conducted in cooperation with U.S. Occupation authorities) confirmed, did time prove such animus to be politically anachronistic. Anticommunism in general was, of course, one of the major rationales that prewar Japanese civilian as well as military leaders used to legitimize Japanese expansion in continental Asia, and carried over into the postwar period to provide the ideological cement of the Cold War U.S.-Japan rapprochement.

The ruling groups endeavored to repress "dangerous thoughts" for a simple reason: they believed that revolutionary upheaval was eminently possible in Japan. This fear of revolution intensified as the Pacific War neared its end, and carried over into the early years of the postwar period. It received its most formal and apocalyptic expression in the Konoe Memorial of February 1945, but the specter of revolution was evoked by Yoshida and his colleagues on countless occasions both before and after Japan's surrender. This fear constituted a ninth, and very traumatic and dramatic, aspect of the conservative consciousness.

The conservative premonition of impending revolution in Japan is fascinating, for it contradicts almost everyone's favorite ideological construct of a placid, obedient, homogeneous Japanese body politic. The alarmist conservative vision was, to begin with, elaborate and detailed, depicting a radical upheaval and transformation of society emanating from "above" (the renovationist elites) and from "outside" (the international communist movement), as well as from "below." In giving voice to their apprehension, the conservatives exposed themselves as men who saw Japanese society as unstable and riven with tensions, and who believed that in times of exceptional stress and social dislocation the Japanese people might be all too ready to repudiate the vaunted emperor system (*tennōsei*) and national polity (*kokutai*). The frantic intensity of these fears revealed the hollowness and near desperation that underlay ruling-class pronouncements extolling the "harmony" of the "family state" and the everlasting virtue of the polity.[8]

In the immediate aftermath of defeat, the radicalism of SCAP's early reforms coupled with the vigor of popular and left-wing activity merely served to confirm the fear that Japan was teetering on the edge of revolution. Indeed, the Occupation's American publicists proclaimed a "democratic revolution," and in this volatile atmosphere much conservative energy was devoted simply to holding tight and marshaling the forces of counterrevolution. By the time Yoshida established his second cabinet in 1948, however, counterrevolution and anticommunism had become common ground on which the Japanese conservatives and the one-time American reformers were able to come together. By holding firm to prewar ground, Yoshida found himself closer and closer to the mainstream of postwar American policy.

Yoshida's intense patriotism, the final major strain in his worldview, embraced many of the concerns described above. His particular brand of nationalism, moreover, enabled him to hold fast to his conservative ideals through war and occupation with an impressive measure of confidence and clarity. To begin with, it rested partly on genuine pride in the accomplishments of Japan's recent nonmilitaristic past, its rapid rise from feudal seclusion to "modernity" and Great Power status by World War I. Thus, Yoshida remained confident that the disasters of the 1930s and early 1940s were truly an aberration—the fault of global catastrophe coupled with human mischief—and that the Japanese state as it had developed in the Meiji and Taishō periods (1868–1926) was fundamentally sound. This sort of patriotism, very much in the late Meiji mode, a priori excluded institutional criticism of society and made it possible to reject almost offhand the necessity of fundamental structural reform.

Such nationalism contrasted with the Japanese ultranationalism of the post–World War I years in two conspicuous ways. First, many of the ultranationalists were in fact highly critical of the legacy of Meiji and Taishō: unlike Yoshida, they advocated the drastic transformation of the state. Indeed, the relationship between their "renovationist" ideals and the extensive institutional changes of the post-1945 period poses interesting questions concerning transwar commitments to drastic and ongoing change. At the same time, the prewar ultranationalists also deviated from Yoshida's Weltanschauung in their repudiation of close ties with the Western powers and fixation upon the establishment of an optimally autarchic bloc in Asia. Yoshida's nationalism was, on the contrary, always directed toward establishing Japan as a great and respected power in the comity of nations, with especially intimate ties with the Anglo-American powers. Thus, when it came to managing Japan's role during the Occupation, Yoshida never lost sight of the ultimate goal of restoring and maintaining Japan's good name internationally. On many specific issues of policy, this meant that he tempered his opposition to domestic reforms in order to enhance his country's image of being a genuine "democracy" in the eyes of the great Western powers.

In the final analysis, the heart of this patriotism was also the central element in Yoshida's conservatism: the well-being of the state was the ultimate concern.

THE NEW JAPAN

In retrospect, it is clear that almost all the values and attitudes described above must be taken into account in analyzing not just Yoshida's role as a postwar Japanese leader but also developments involving occupied Japan in general. At the same time, more potent institutional legacies naturally also carried over from earlier decades to influence the course of postwar events. Especially notable among these were the throne, the bureaucratic apparatus as a whole, and the concentrated but immensely complex structures of monopoly capitalism.

While such legacies may seem overwhelming at first glance, they did not stifle accelerated change under the Occupation in the realms of law, landholding, politics, education, and labor organization. And in analyzing these post-1945 changes, it is essential to assess the relative importance of influences emanating from four directions: (1) U.S. policies as formulated in Washington and interpreted by the Supreme Command for the Allied Powers (SCAP) in Tokyo; (2) popular support for demilitarization and democratic reforms on the part of a wide range of Japanese people; (3) dynamic and ongoing structural changes in Japanese society, which often were stimulated by renovationist policies and "total war" mobilization beginning in the 1930s; and (4) input by Japanese leaders in politics, administration, private enterprise, and intellectual circles.

Each of these interlocking areas of influence can be elaborated upon at great length, but any discussion of leadership must in any case begin by acknowledging the constraints on Japanese initiatives at the policy-making level, especially during the first few years of occupation. For many reasons, including Washington's preoccupation with Europe, the Supreme Command for the Allied Powers in Tokyo did in fact find it possible to take the lead in initiating far-reaching reforms between 1945 and 1947; the personal input of General MacArthur and certain of his key personnel was crucial at this juncture, for they routinely interpreted Washington's guidelines in a liberal and even radical manner. The Japanese government was by contrast subordinate and subservient, be-fitting losers in a monumental game, and it is by no means easy to suggest important areas where Japanese officials *substantially* altered the course of events.

We can extend this generalization even to areas interpreted in contrary ways by other commentators, who often emphasize the personal influence of the emperor as well as Yoshida on MacArthur. Where the former is concerned, there seems no doubt that MacArthur found Emperor Hirohito personally acceptable and was pleased to have the Mikado visit him (MacArthur spent considerable time making clear to others that he was on close terms with Emperor Hirohito and Jesus Christ). His later effusions about the emperor's sterling character, however, should not obscure the fact that MacArthur was telling people before he arrived in Tokyo that it would be essential to retain the imperial institution in defeated Japan. His mind was made up on the crucial matter of the throne, including the need to eliminate its more esoteric spiritual trap-pings, long before he ever met Hirohito personally.[9]

In Yoshida's case, we already have seen that MacArthur regarded him as lazy and politically inept, although their relationship remained courteous. The extensive correspondence carried out in English between the Japanese prime ministers and SCAP contains exchanges and com-mentaries on a variety of issues where Yoshida frankly disagreed with SCAP's directives (concerning such fundamental policies as the purge, reparations, economic deconcentration, lèse majesté laws, economic stabi-lization policies, constitutional revision, police reorganization, tax policy, local autonomy, and so on). In almost every single case, however, Yo-shida's importuning failed to persuade MacArthur or his aides to modify their policies. Professor Inoki has emphasized the manner in which

Yoshida repeatedly evoked the threat of communism to persuade SCAP to modify its policies, but while the Red-baiting tactic is undeniable, the question of how effective it was remains moot. MacArthur and his staff did not have to be reminded of the virtues of anticommunism, and there is no evidence that they relied on Yoshida for advice on this.[10] In general, it seems fair to say that Yoshida was ideologically opposed to virtually all basic reforms associated with the early Occupation "democratization" agenda, essentially believing that a good purge of "militarists" would get Japan back on the right track. Thus, most reforms were introduced against his better judgment; and the survival of many of them after the Occupation ended, despite Yoshida's own fervent attempts to "rectify excesses" from 1952 on, derived from the support of the general populace.

This does not mean that Yoshida's role in the Occupation was insignificant prior to the negotiations pertaining to the peace and security treaties, although it seems obvious that had he not returned to power in 1948, his name would now be little more than an historical footnote of essentially the same minuscule order as the other Japanese who held the premiership between the ending of the war and 1948: Suzuki Kantarō, Higashikuni Naruhiko, Shidehara Kijūrō, Katayama Tetsu, and Ashida Hitoshi. Because he survived politically where others did not, his activities prior to the real onset of the "Yoshida era" in 1949 also have retained a place in Japanese political memory. They warrant passing attention.

First and foremost, Yoshida, from the first moments of defeat, struck a pose of confidence and national pride that was distinctive and, like a clever caricature, easy to remember (Japanese cartoonists, in fact, loved him). By gestures as small as his expensive cigars and immaculate white *tabi* socks, and as bold as his early blunt defense of the "old *zaibatsu*," he quickly came to personify the bedrock conservative argument that the war had been an aberration which had interrupted decades of admirable progress and accomplishments. "Militarist conspirators," in this simplistic historiography, had diverted Japan from the admirable course of modern nation-building which the Meiji oligarchs had established. The road to war had been an aberration, a "historic stumble"—but most certainly not a stumble over anything in the nature of deep-seated institutional or structural roots. (It was the American reformers and Japanese Left who cherished "root" metaphors, and thereby drove the old guard to distraction.) It followed from this line of thought that what

Yoshida's distinctive old-guard persona is captured in a cartoon by Shimizu
Kon published in January 1950. Here doughty old "One Man," wearing
patched-up traditional garb and smoking his omnipresent expensive cigar,
marches down the path to the "Seventh Diet" under the umbrella of
"making peace." His overgarment bears the insignia of "government," and
he has turned his back determinedly on the threatening snowstorm of
political groups opposing a Cold War peace settlement.

Japan needed was not so much "reform" as simply the opportunity to
get back on the right track. Thus, as clear alternatives to the reformist
agenda of "demilitarization and democratization" being advanced by
SCAP and supported by many Japanese, Yoshida articulated—and came
to symbolize—the more simple and pragmatic ideals of economic reconstruction and restoration of global respect for Japan.

In striving to restore Japan's credibility in the eyes of the world,
Yoshida embraced the advice of former prime minister Suzuki Kantarō,

Shimizu's February 1951 rendering of Japan's emerging military posture has Yoshida chiseling out a subordinate position of "self-defense" for Japan under the overarching structure of "collective security" fashioned by John Foster Dulles.

who served through the surrender, to the effect that Japan must be a "good loser." This accounts in part—but only in part—for his generally pragmatic acceptance of many early reforms that he personally found unpalatable. One accepted change because this is what the victors demanded. It is equally important to recognize, however, that Yoshida's acceptance of reformist policies also reflected his awareness of the depth of popular Japanese support for change. This aspect of Yoshida's "realism"—that is, this sensitivity to domestic resentments and aspirations—is as important to keep in mind as is the more commonly emphasized "realism" with which Yoshida viewed the international scene.

In March 1952, a month before the formal end of the Occupation, Shimizu offered this satirical speculation about what might happen to Yoshida's rickety parliamentary majority once it was no longer propped up by the General Headquarters of the U.S. Occupation authorities.

This pragmatism (the Ōkubo legacy" previously mentioned) is apparent in Yoshida's handling of the two most important reforms of the early Occupation, constitutional revision and land reform, both of which he opposed in principle but supported in practice. His ultimate support of the land reform was motivated primarily by fear that the countryside would explode in revolutionary upheaval if land redistribution were not carried out. This does not gainsay the fact, however, that once convinced land reform was unavoidable, Yoshida ensured its successful implementation by defying his own conservative partymembers and placing the program under the guidance of the relatively radical agronomist Wada

"The course of rearmament," which appeared in August 1953, conveys both Yoshida's tepid response to Dulles's vigorous plans for Japanese remilitarization and the posture of subordinate independence which Japan assumed after the Occupation ended in 1952. The caption at the top reads "Big gait, little gait?"

Hiroo, who had been purged for his "Red" inclinations in the "Cabinet Planning Board incident" of 1941.

Somewhat similarly, in early 1946, when General Courtney Whitney decided to shock then–Foreign Minister Yoshida and other figures in the Shidehara cabinet into realizing the necessity of drastic constitutional revision, his most effective threat was to imply that SCAP would turn the matter over directly to the Japanese people if the conservative government did not adopt a more progressive position. Yoshida was thunderstruck by this (his face, Whitney recalled, was a "black cloud"), but it turned out to be his own first cabinet that had to present the new charter drafted by the Americans as if it were a genuine Japanese creation. Yoshida introduced this distasteful draft to the Diet in 1946 with shrewd and pragmatic resolve, slipping in his own conservative interpretations where possible but ultimately bowing to the inevitability of a new constitutional order. Thus, on the one hand, Yoshida and his chief minister on these matters, Kanamori Tokujirō, dismayed Occupation authorities by repeatedly emphasizing that the new constitution did not alter the

228

old "national polity" in the slightest. Yoshida also won a remarkable little symbolic victory by having the new charter go into effect on the birthday of the Meiji emperor (May 3), thereby emphasizing fundamental continuity with the old Meiji constitution. On the other hand, however, as prime minister, Yoshida solemnly emphasized that the final version of the draft Constitution reflected serious give and take between Occupation authorities and the Japanese government. He also presented a strict pacifist interpretation of the most controversial clause in the new charter, the "no war" Article Nine. And even in later years, after being ousted as prime minister, he lent support to those who opposed hasty revision of the new Constitution. This was not a document Yoshida welcomed, but he bowed to both the ukase of the victors and the strong support the new Constitution received from the Japanese people at large.

Yoshida's early leadership of postwar political forces had lasting consequences of a more intended sort in the "bureaucratization" of conservative party ranks which began in 1948. The practice of bringing bureaucrats into the arena of parliamentary politics was already well established in the prewar period and undoubtedly would have recurred after the war no matter who headed the conservative parties. Yoshida, however, gave a peculiar thrust to the process simply by drawing into his own personal entourage ex-officials who possessed exceptional technocratic skills—the most notable among them being the later prime ministers Ikeda Hayato and Satō Eisaku. Under Yoshida, the general process of bureaucratization of the conservative parties thus assumed clearly defined personal and factional dimensions. The influence of the so-called Yoshida School that coalesced during the Occupation remained conspicuous in Japanese party politics into the 1970s. Although the Liberal Democratic party that has ruled Japan into the 1990s was formally established in 1955, the year after Yoshida stepped down, the roots of this extraordinary "one-party" conservative hegemony actually trace back to Yoshida's own majority electoral victory in 1949, upon which he based his strong third cabinet.

In none of these developments, however, was Yoshida's leadership as evident and decisive as it was to become beginning in 1949, when the dream of a peace treaty and end to the Occupation began to become a reality.

SUBORDINATE INDEPENDENCE

The peace treaty Japan signed with forty-eight nations in San Francisco in September 1951, along with the bilateral U.S.-Japan security treaty signed at the same time, defined the parameters of Japan's future as a sovereign nation, although consequential details concerning military bases in Japan, rearmament, and global economic relations remained to be worked out over the ensuing months and years. Yoshida's place in history depends in good part on how his contribution to the formulation of this "San Francisco System" is evaluated, and this is by no means a clear or simple task.

As a still-occupied nation, Japan was at a clear disadvantage in negotiating with the United States in 1949–1952, yet it did have several strong cards to play. U.S. officials regarded Japan's allegiance in the Cold War as absolutely essential, for without Japan, it was argued then, the "global balance of power" would shift in favor of the Soviet Union. In addition, after the Korean War began, the Americans recognized that they could not simply impose their terms on the Yoshida government. In January 1951, for example, following China's entry into the Korean War, John Foster Dulles informed Secretary of State Dean Acheson that the Japanese were beginning to question the wisdom of tight alignment with the United States. The conditions that the United States previously had deemed "vital," Dulles wrote, "now become matters to be negotiated for and obtained as fully as possible, rather than conditions which in September it seemed that we could obtain unconditionally merely by stipulating them."[11] Furthermore, within the U.S. government the State Department and military establishment were at loggerheads concerning Japan policy, and such factionalism could be exploited. Disagreement between the United States and other Allied powers, especially Britain, over proper policy toward Japan and Asia offered yet another area of uncertainty that a skillful bargainer might manipulate.

Beyond any question, Yoshida's most impressive accomplishment involved successfully opposing the United States on the speed and scale of Japanese rearmament. The Americans initially anticipated the creation of a Japanese army of some three hundred thousand men in ten fully equipped combat divisions by 1953, and were irritated and chagrined by Yoshida's stubborn resistance to this plan. Yoshida rested his case against rapid rearmament on a doubly ominous argument, namely that the Japanese economy could not absorb heavy military expenditures, and that rapid remilitarization would provoke immense social unrest within Japan. Given the long-standing debate over constitutional revision in post-Occupation Japan, it is interesting to note that in their secret conversations with the Americans, Yoshida as well as his aides and successors frequently referred to popular Japanese support for the constitutional restraints on rearmament. The "spirit of Article Nine" was one of their most effective bargaining cards.[12]

It appears that Yoshida also had some influence in persuading the Americans to grant Japan "residual sovereignty" over the Ryukyu and Bonin islands. When Yoshida broached this to General MacArthur, the general opposed him in no uncertain terms, stating that he was "unalterably opposed to any arrangement which does not divorce Japan completely from these islands." Yoshida persisted, however, and there is some indication that his entreaties were influential in persuading Dulles to support the "residual sovereignty" formula.[13]

On other critical issues such as U.S. bases in Japan and Japan's relations with China, however, Yoshida appeared to the Americans to be more passive and irresolute. In early April 1950, for example, a member of the U.S. State Department in Tokyo reported a long conversation in which the prime minister avoided specific commitments but conveyed the clear "inference that he would be favorably disposed toward whatever practical arrangements the United States might consider necessary in order to assist Japan in the maintenance of her security in the post-treaty period." It is now fairly well known that shortly after this, over a month prior to the outbreak of the Korean War, Yoshida secretly took the initiative in inviting the United States to maintain bases in post-treaty Japan. Less well known is the fact that a number of U.S. officials at that time were still arguing that post-treaty bases in the four main islands of Japan were unnecessary. Subsequently, in August 1950, Yoshida caused some confusion among the Americans by seeming to retract his offer. William Sebald, the State Department's adviser in occupied Japan, speculated that this might have been Yoshida's way of trying to lay "the groundwork for future bargaining." By his prior attitude and actions, however, the prime minister already had cut away the ground for any such bargaining of a serious nature.[14]

The most damaging comment concerning Yoshida's approach to the peace and security treaties appears in the confidential U.S. account of Yoshida's meeting with Dulles when the latter visited Japan in January 1951. "Mr. Yoshida gave the impression," it was noted, "that the Japanese were so eager for a treaty that they would be willing to approve almost anything."[15]

That the peace treaty itself was generous to Japan does not really reflect successful negotiating on the Japanese side, since Dulles had decided on his own at an early date that a punitive peace would prove counterproductive in the long run; his decision in this regard was based in good part on recollection of the dire outcome of the harsh terms imposed on Germany after World War I. On the other hand, when discussing the security treaty and accompanying administrative agreements in private in 1951–1952, Dulles and Dean Rusk spoke frankly of "very important and unprecedented rights given to the United States by the Japanese," and characterized the treaty itself as "one-way." When the security treaty came up for revision and renewal in 1960, U.S. Secretary of State Christian Herter acknowledged in Senate hearings that "there were a number of provisions in the 1951–52 Security Treaty that were pretty extreme from the point of view of an agreement between two sovereign nations."[16]

However one may evaluate the Japanese performance concerning the security treaty and administrative agreement, it is undeniable that the Japanese government approached these highly technical matters with great care. The same cannot really be said concerning the issue of relations with the People's Republic of China, for on this controversial matter the documentary record reveals Yoshida as definitely conveying the impression that he was "willing to approve almost anything" the United States demanded. The record on this score is surprising, for it continues past the end of the Occupation up to the final moments of the last Yoshida cabinet in late 1954, and it does not coincide very closely with Yoshida's public version of events.

In his later years, Yoshida took pleasure in criticizing the shortsightedness of America's China policy, and during the Occupation he did make it clear to the Americans that Japan desired closer economic ties with China. At one point, he told Dulles directly that instead of trying to break the Sino-Soviet alliance by imposing hardship on China through economic containment, it made more sense to attempt to "wean" the communist regime away from the Soviet Union by granting economic concessions.[17] In actual practice, however, Yoshida never mounted a serious or sustained campaign to promote a more enlightened China policy by the United States.

In the spring of 1951, for example—when Britain was urging that the People's Republic of China be invited to the Japanese peace conference, and the majority of the Far Eastern Commission nations were clearly opposed to Kuomintang participation in the conference—Yoshida personally informed the Americans that he supported Kuomintang attendance. In June 1951, after the United States had decided to invite neither the Nationalists nor the Chinese communists, the Japanese government was informed that it would later be free to choose with which Chinese regime it wished to establish a bilateral peace treaty. Yoshida responded that he did not welcome having a choice in the matter, and the Americans in Tokyo cabled the secretary of state that "it is obvious Jap[anese] are most reluctant [to] have decision left to them." At the peace conference itself, Yoshida proposed to give a speech that was so harsh and provocative in its comments about Communist China that the Americans themselves persuaded him to discard it. As Dulles explained the situation to Herbert Morrison, the British Foreign Secretary, "Yoshida had thought of stating in his speech at San Francisco that he did not intend to do business with the Chinese Communists, and we had urged against any such public commital at this time."[18]

It is entirely true that in the months following the peace conference, the United States put great pressure on Yoshida to commit Japan to a pledge to establish relations with the Nationalist regime on Taiwan. Within the Senate, William Knowland initiated a petition that threatened to withhold ratification of the peace treaty if Japan did not give public assurances on this matter. Shortly thereafter, Dulles and several key senators flew to Tokyo to tighten the screws. This was the background to the famous "Yoshida Letter" dated December 24, 1951, and released in January, in which Yoshida formally declared that Japan had no intention of establishing diplomatic relations with the People's Republic of China. The letter actually was drafted by Dulles, and it did not commit Japan to recognize the Kuomintang as the sole government of all of China. On this latter critical point, there was never any disagreement between the U.S. and Japanese governments.

As British archives on this period reveal, it was widely recognized at the time that the Yoshida Letter had been dictated by the Americans. In British eyes, this violated a prior Anglo-American understanding that Japan would not be forced to take a public stand on China before the peace treaty came into effect. It also, as the British ambassador in Tokyo phrased it, regrettably placed "the stigma of being a lackey of the Americans" on the Yoshida government. While the British acknowledged the virtually irresistible pressures to which the Japanese had been subjected, they did not entirely exonerate Yoshida from personal responsibility for provoking these pressures. As the ambassador also opined to the Foreign Office in London, Yoshida "displayed considerable ineptitude in the handling of this affair," for on several occasions after the San Francisco conference he had made provocative public statements about establishing close economic ties with the People's Republic. Had he been more diplomatic in his public utterances, U.S. pressure for a public commitment to the Nationalist regime might have been less vociferous, and Yoshida might have been spared the "odium" (another of the British phrases at the time) of having to sign his name to a ghosted document.[19]

The matter does not rest there, moreover, for in fact Yoshida did make a personal contribution to the wording of the Yoshida Letter. Given his occasional statements about the desirability of Japan emerging as a "bridge" between East and West, one might have expected him to tone down the letter. On the contrary, he made the comments criticizing the Chinese communists even harsher than they had been in Dulles's original draft. It was Yoshida personally who added the statement in the letter that read: "the Sino-Soviet Treaty of Friendship, Alliance and Mutual Assistance concluded in Moscow in 1950 is virtually a military alliance aimed at Japan."[20] This is not the sort of contribution one would expect of someone who claimed to oppose containment and confrontation and to support a more conciliatory policy toward China.

Even after Japan regained sovereignty, Yoshida continued to handle the China issue with extreme caution in his dealings with the United States. This is readily apparent, for example, in the confidential records from the two major talks in Washington that the Yoshida government engaged in after the Occupation: the Ikeda-Robertson conversations of October 1953 and the Yoshida visit of November 1954. On these occasions, the Japanese side did express its continued unhappiness at being forced to participate in the rigid containment of China. Once again, however, Yoshida personally did not support these protests in a forceful or sustained manner, and U.S. officials easily brushed them aside. Under the so-called COCOM and CHINCOM mechanisms that the United States used to control trade with Communist China, Japanese trade with China actually became more restricted than that of any other country except Canada and the United States.[21] Indeed, when Japanese officials complained about being forced to adhere to this unusually severe embargo list, the Americans neatly retorted with the very portion of the "Yoshida Letter" which Yoshida personally had added. In the grotesque, cryptic language peculiar to overseas cables at the time, the State Department wired its Tokyo representative as follows: "If Japs refer fact their controls far more restrictive than most other countries, you might note Japa state security FE area greater than any other country, Japa realization as stated Yoshida's letter to Dulles that Sino-Sov treaty virtually military alliance directed at Jap and ask rhetorical question re effect Commie domination Korean Peninsular wold have in Jap." This was precisely the opposite of what Yoshida presumedly desired, and not exactly an elegant endorsement of his vaunted "diplomatic sense."[22]

In sum, the San Francisco system relegated Japan to second-class status as a global power both militarily and diplomatically. The bilateral U.S.-Japan security treaty of 1951–1952 was, until renegotiated in 1960, more inequitable than any other Cold War military agreement the United States negotiated. Okinawa became the one and only outright neocolony of the United States, and remained so until the 1970s. U.S. bases throughout Japan served the dual purpose of providing a forward line of defense against the communist bloc while simultaneously providing *in situ* U.S. military control over Japan. While Okinawa was openly nuclearized under U.S. control, the movement of nuclear weapons in and out of the rest of Japan effectively remained beyond the control or even knowledge of the Japanese government. Japan's own development of ground, sea, and air forces became completely subordinated to U.S. planning and procurement procedures. All this was done, moreover, in circumstances where most American and Japanese officials, including

Yoshida, did not take seriously the possibility of a direct Soviet threat to Japan. While later American critics would argue that Yoshida and his successors essentially obtained a military "free ride" from the United States, the U.S. military posture in Japan from the outset was dictated by perceptions of America's own global strategic interests. By a different ledger of accounting, moreover, the Japanese paid a high psychological price for such thoroughgoing abnegation of genuine sovereignty, for they became typecast as the loyal followers and eternal subordinates of the great white power across the Pacific.

Had this burden of national dependency and subordinate sovereignty been confined to military affairs, it may have been less psychologically onerous. The United States, after all, was a global military hegemon, and Japan was but one of many nations folded into Washington's strategic agenda. As the United States' China policy so vividly revealed, however, Japan's subordination carried over to broader reaches of diplomacy and international affairs, and Yoshida essentially set his country on an abject and acquiescent course of "containing" China which even many staunch Japanese anticommunists deemed neither wise nor necessary. In the years that followed the Yoshida era, no Japanese leader found it possible to become a forceful advocate, either privately or publicly, for a more enlightened and less militant U.S. policy in Asia. As a consequence, Japan was forced to endure conspicuous public humiliation two decades later, when in 1972 the United States secretly and abruptly decided to abandon the containment policy and establish relations with the People's Republic of China. Japanese leaders were neither consulted nor even informed about this dramatic diplomatic *volte face* beforehand. As then Secretary of State Henry Kissinger, the facilitator of the China policy somersault, scornfully saw them, the Japanese were mere "small and petty bookkeepers," hardly to be taken seriously on great affairs of global policy.[23]

Under the San Francisco System, Japan's Ministry of Foreign Affairs essentially functioned as a substation of the U.S. Department of State where large issues of policy were concerned, an odd legacy for a proud patriot such as Yoshida whose "true" career (before resurrection as a postwar politician) had been as a diplomat. Essentially, what took the place of an independent, autonomous foreign policy in post-Occupation Japan was the pursuit of what later became fairly labeled "economic nationalism." Yoshida and his successors did receive a payoff in the form of economic favors for hewing so closely to the U.S. containment policy in Asia: to compensate for the denial of the China market and simultaneously integrate Japan more tightly with other capitalist economies, Japan was allowed to pursue protectionist policies domestically and at the same time was given privileged access to U.S. technological licenses and patents.

At the time, no one dreamed that less than three decades hence Japan would be regarded as an economic superpower that possibly threatened America's own economic well-being. Indeed, much of the energy of the Yoshida government in its final few years, before old One Man was forced to step down in late 1954, was directed to frantic efforts to shore up Japan's "shallow economy." This was the essence of the so-called Yoshida Doctrine: one nestled under America's wings, military on the one side and economic on the other, and concentrated—not on democracy, not on diplomacy, not on rearmament, certainly not on global leadership and statesmanlike initiatives—but on economic growth.

Materially, this intense sense of vulnerability and consequent preoccupation with economic security paid off handsomely for Japan. As wedded to the legacy of "go-slow" rearmament that Yoshida initiated in response to popular opinion, moreover, these fixations produced an economic system admirably focused on mobilizing talent and resources behind civilian rather than military productivity. That the postwar Japanese economy flourished so spectacularly without heavy reliance on defense production or military-related exports is singular and commendable. All this was accomplished at immeasurable cost in terms of national purpose and international image, however, for it locked Japan into the psychology and behavior of a neomercantilist nation perpetually inclined to leave great issues of global leadership and statesmanship to other powers. The "Yoshida Doctrine" earned Japan wealth, but only grudging respect.

Yoshida's proudest accomplishment was to have led Japan to sovereignty and a generous peace treaty under the San Francisco System, and in the process wedded his country firmly to U.S. Cold War policy. No more than anyone else at the time did he foresee the remarkable economic prosperity that his successors would attain within only a few decades under this system; nor could he really have anticipated, on the other hand, that the conundrum of subordinate independence inherent in his policy would not become dissipated as time passed. His legacy nonetheless lies in such contradictions.

NOTES

1 Kōsaka Masataka, *Saishō Yoshida Shigeru* (Tokyo: Chūō Kōronsha, 1968); Inoki Masamichi, *Hyōden Yoshida Shigeru*, 3 vols. (Tokyo: Yomiuri Shimbunsha, 1978–1981). Many of the points in this present essay are developed and annotated at length in J. W. Dower, *Empire and Aftermath: Yoshida Shigeru and the Japanese Experience, 1878–1954* (Cambridge, Mass.: Council on East Asian Studies, Harvard University, 1979); translated into Japanese by Ōkubo Genji under the title *Yoshida Shigeru to Sono Jidai* (Tokyo: TBS Britannica, 1981; Chūō Bunko no. 860, 1991).

See also John W. Dower, "Shigeru Yoshida in the Eyes of Westerners," published in three installments in *Asahi Evening News*, November 20 and 27, and December 4, 1981; this essay originally appeared as "Ei-Bei Dōjidaijin kara Mita Yoshida Shigeru," *Bungei Shunjū*, September 1981, pp. 212–22. The typical American comments cited here appear in Department of State, *Foreign Relations of the United States*, 1950, vol. 6, p. 1271; *Foreign Relations of the United States*, 1951, vol. 6, pt. 1, pp. 832, 1389–93, 1420. Henceforth, this documentary series is referred to as *FRUS*.

The term "Yoshida Doctrine" is of recent coinage, although emphasis on Yoshida's potent legacy has been common since the 1960s. For perhaps the earliest use of "Yoshida Doctrine," see Kenneth Pyle, "Nakasone's Grand Design," *Journal of Japanese Studies* 13, no. 2 (Summer 1987), pp. 246–47; in the same journal issue, see also T. J. Pempel, "Unbundling 'Japan, Inc.', " pp. 276–77.

2 Norman's comments appear in his internal memoranda to the Secretary of External Affairs, available in the External Affairs archives of the Canadian government in Ottawa, and were provided to me by Ōkubo Genji; see Norman's memo no. 110 of April 13, 1948, and memo no. 11 of January 8, 1949. On Tōhata, see Inoki, *Hyōden Yoshida Shigeru*, vol. 3, pp. 327–28.

3 Reminiscences of Yoshida by former colleagues were presented on a regular basis for several years at the monthly meetings of retired Foreign Ministry officials, and published in their privately distributed newsletter *Kasekikai Kaihō* between October 1967 and April 1971.

4 Mazaki Ryū, "Yoshida Shigeru-san o Shinobu" [Remembering Yoshida Shigeru], *Kasekikai Kaihō*, no. 271, p. 14.

5 *Nihon Keizai Shimbun*, Nov. 19, 1975; Inoki, *Hyōden Yoshida Shigeru*, vol. 3, p. 61.

6 Letter of June 10, 1921 from Yoshida to his father-in-law Makino Nobu-aki, included among the Makino papers in the National Diet Library, Tokyo.

7 Ibid. for the 1921 use of *kyokugaku amin*. For the attack on Nanbara, see Tōyama Shigeki, ed. *Shiryō: Sengo Nijūnen Shi*, vol. 6 (Tokyo: Nihon Hyōronsha, 1966), p. 100. The classical Chinese origins of the "literary sycophant" phrase, and Yoshida's ideographic error, are noted in Dower, *Empire and Aftermath*, p. 508, n. 43.

8 See the earlier essay in this present volume on "Sensational Rumors, Seditious Graffiti, and the Nightmares of the Thought Police."

9 The importance of retaining the emperor was emphasized in psychologi-cal reports prepared in MacArthur's Southwest Pacific military com-mand; see the papers of Bonner Fellers, former head of the psychological warfare section, at the Hoover Institution, Stanford University. Ac-cording to one source, on August 29, 1945, while stopping over in Okinawa on his way to Yokohama to begin the Occupation, MacArthur made clear to his top aides that all their policies were "to be implemented through the Emperor and the machinery of the Imperial government"; Frazier Hunt, *The Untold Story of Douglas MacArthur* [1954] (New York: Signet, 1964), p. 360.

10 Yoshida's English-language correspondence with SCAP appears in sev-eral interesting files in Government Section materials in Record Group 331 at the National Archives, Suitland, Md.: "Correspondence between MacArthur, Whitney and Prime Minister" (box 2974), "Correspondence between General Whitney and Prime Ministers" (box 2974), and "Prime Minister [1946–1951]" (box 2993). Other Yoshida letters to MacArthur (usually addressed to "My dear General") are held by the MacArthur Memorial in Norfolk, Virginia; see Record Group 10, "VIP file: Yoshida, Shigeru."

11 *FRUS* 1951, vol. 6, pt. 1, p. 783.

12 Emphasis on the popular and legal, as well as economic, constraints on rapid rearmament received strong emphasis, for example, in the "Ikeda-Robertson talks" in Washington in October 1953; see Dower, *Empire and Aftermath*, pp. 449–63. It is fair to say that because they feared the negative effects of rapid rearmament on both public opinion and their then precari-ous economic situation, the Yoshida conservatives welcomed the constitu-tional constraint as one more argument to buttress their "go-slow" policy.

13 *FRUS* 1951, vol. 6, pt. 1, pp. 821–22, 1235, 1269–70. The other side of this coin is the fact that neither Yoshida nor any other responsible Japanese official ever seriously attempted to persuade the United States to treat the Ryukyus as a totally equal part of Japan. From an early date, in fact, beginning under the Katayama cabinet in 1947, the Japanese government expressed willingness to trade off Okinawa in order to hasten the restoration of sovereignty to the rest of Japan.

14 *FRUS* 1950, vol. 6, pp. 1166–71, 1262–64, 1271.

15 *FRUS* 1951, vol. 6, pt. 1, p. 828.

16 U.S. House of Representatives, Committee on Foreign Affairs, *Selected Executive Session Hearings of the Committee, 1951–56*, vol. 17 ("U.S. Policy in the Far East"), pt. 1, p. 46, for Dulles and Rusk. The frank executive session discussions that took place in both the House and Senate, now declassified, tend to be neglected by researchers on the peace settlement. Herter's comments appear in U.S. Senate, Committee of Foreign Relations, *Treaty of Mutual Cooperation and Security with Japan*, 86th Congress, 2d session (June 7, 1960), p. 27; see also ibid., pp. 11–12; 30–31.

17 *FRUS* 1951, vol. 6, pt. 1, pp. 1438–39; see also ibid., pp. 827–28.

18 Ibid., pp. 1045, 1050, 1052, 1162, 1242, 1344. On Yoshida's San Francisco speech, see also William J. Sebald with Russell Brines, *With MacArthur in Japan: A Personal History of the Occupation* (New York: W. W. Norton, 1965), pp. 278–79; and the interview with Yoshida's former aide Shirasu Jirō in Andō Yoshio, ed., *Shōwa Seiji Keizai Shi e no Shōgen* (Tokyo: Mainichi Shimbunsha, 1966), vol. 3, pp. 409–10.

19 On the China issue and "Yoshida Letter" in general, see Dower, *Empire and Aftermath*, pp. 400–14; Howard Schonberger, "Peacemaking in Asia: The United States, Great Britain, and the Japanese Decision to Recognize Nationalist China, 1951–52," *Diplomatic History* 10, no. 1 (Winter 1986), pp. 54–73; and the interesting account (including diary excerpts) in William Sebald's interview in the oral history portion of the John Foster Dulles papers at Princeton University.

The British quotations appear in Foreign Office documents dated January 28 and February 4, 1952 from FO 371/FJ10310; these were kindly provided me by Howard Schonberger. Foreign Secretary Herbert Morrison aired the British grievances concerning the U.S.-Japan-China imbroglio in parliament; see *Parliamentary Debates, House of Commons*, Fifth Series, vol. 496, p. 946ff. (Feb. 26, 1952).

20 U.S. House of Representatives, Committee on Foreign Affairs, *Selected Executive Session Hearings*, vol. 17, pt. 1, p. 43; *FRUS* 1951, vol. 6, pt. 1, pp. 1446–47.

21 Basic documents from the Ikeda-Robertson talks and Yoshida visit are included in the Suzuki Gengo papers in the archives of the Ministry of Finance, Tokyo, but are not accessible to the public. On export controls under COCOM and CHINCOM, see Yōko Yasuhara, "Japan, Communist China, and Export Controls in Asia, 1948–52," *Diplomatic History* 10, no 1. (Winter 1986), pp. 75–89; Katō (Yasuhara) Yōko, *Amerika no Sekai Senryaku to COCOM, 1945–1992* (Tokyo; Yūshindo, 1992); Gunnar Adler-Karlsson, *Western Economic Warfare 1947–1967: A Case Study in Foreign Economic Policy*, vol. 9 in *Acta Universitatis Stockholmiensis, Stockholm Economic Studies*, New Series (Stockholm: University of Stockholm, 1968), esp. pp. 6–8 and ch. 16, on CHINCOM; Haruhiro Fukui, *Party in Power: The Japanese Liberal-Democrats and Policymaking* (Berkeley, Calif.: University of California Press, 1970), pp. 228–30. Japanese trade with the People's Republic of China did develop, but under severe restrictions.

22 State Department to SCAP (U.S. POLAD), February 23, 1952; Box 6800, National Archives, Suitland, Md. I am grateful to Katō (nee Yasuhara) Yōko for this document.

23 See "Fear and Prejudice in U.S.-Japan Relations" in the present volume.

7

Japanese Artists and
the Atomic Bomb

LATE ONE EVENING in Kyoto in 1975, I turned on the television at random and found an extraordinary drawing on the screen before me. It was an amateur's sketch of a hand against a blue-gray background, palm forward, thumb to the left, the four fingers burning like candles.

A woman was speaking. This, she said, is one of the sights I have never been able to forget: a corpse on its back, hand reaching toward the sky, fingers burning with a blue flame and already shortened to one-third of their former length. A dark liquid dripped from the fingers to the ground. Then as now, the woman went on, she could not help thinking that this hand might have embraced a child only a short time earlier.

UNFORGETTABLE FIRE

The woman was a survivor of Hiroshima, and the burning hand was one of more than two thousand paintings, drawings, and sketches that were submitted to Japan's national broadcasting corporation (NHK) after the television network solicited such personal recollections of the atomic bombs in 1974. These graphics, done three decades after the events depicted, stunned the general public who saw them in Japan; and this happened in a small circle later in the West as well, when 104 of the pictures were published in 1981, under the title *Unforgettable Fire*.[1] John Hersey, whose 1946 essay "Hiroshima" was the first intimate account of atomic-bomb victims, expressed a common response when he described *Unforgettable Fire* as being more moving than any photographs could be, "because what is registered is what has been burned into the minds of the survivors."

That was surely my own response when, following the television program, I located a small exhibition in Kyoto in which a selection of these survivors' pictures was displayed alongside photographs of the Hiroshima and Nagasaki catastrophes. Photography, by its nature, often holds the viewer at arm's length. We have become so saturated with the camerawork of war, from World War II and all the sanguinary conflicts since then, that it becomes easier and easier to block out the full import of what the glossy print is showing and look upon wanton death and destruction as little more than clichés. By contrast, these pictures by Japanese survivors—ranging in technique from rough to skilled, with explanations attached and captions often written on the painting or drawing itself, and always telling a personal story—these pitiful graphics are infinitely varied and incomparably intimate. These pictures have voices. They draw the reader in. Death and grievous emotional and physical pain become individual and personal here, and the human dimension is restored to our retrospections and prognostications about war.

More than this, the survivors' art collected by NHK illuminates the unique nature of nuclear war in a terse, memorable way. There is nothing comparable to this anywhere else—except in Japan itself, where the amateur graphics of the survivors of Hiroshima and Nagasaki are complemented by two other notable artistic depictions of the atomic-bomb experience: the general genre of children's picture books, and the monumental mural art of the husband-and-wife team Maruki Iri and Maruki Toshi.

Of the several illustrated children's books devoted to the atomic-bomb experience, by far the most famous is *Barefoot Gen* by Nakazawa Keiji, who was seven years old in Hiroshima when the city was destroyed. His blunt cartoon story of a feisty boy who (like Nakazawa himself) lost his father, sister, and brother in the bombing was originally serialized in the early 1970s in *Shūkan Shōnen Jampu*, a weekly comic magazine with a circulation of over two million. The series ran to over a thousand pages before being terminated by the publisher, later reemerging as an animated cartoon and in several book-length volumes. A later remarkable children's book by Kinoshita Renzō and Kinoshita Sayoko, titled *Pica-don* after the flash (*pica*, or *pika*) and blast (*don*) of the bomb, relies on illustrations without any text at all to introduce residents of Hiroshima before and after the bomb was dropped on August 6, 1945. In this instance, the book followed a prize-winning animated film of the same title. Another striking presentation for young people is Maruki Toshi's *Hiroshima no Pika*.[2]

Like Nakazawa Keiji, the Marukis too had firsthand experience of the atomic devastation, having rushed to Hiroshima, where they had relatives, as soon as they received news of the bombing. In a collaborative undertaking that has no parallels in its marriage of painterly talents, and few in its wedding of high art and political consciousness, these two artists, both famous in their own right, produced fifteen huge panels between 1950 and 1973 depicting various aspects of Hiroshima and nuclear war; since then, they have turned their joint talents to other powerful social and political subjects.[3] An average panel is roughly twenty-five feet wide and six feet high; the common medium is traditional india ink along with watercolors; and the artistic conventions as well as themes have differed in each monumental mural.

From this atomic-bomb art as a whole, amateur and professional together, emerge overpowering images that capture the transcendent horrors of nuclear war.

HELL SCENES

The overarching metaphor is hell. To a people familiar with Buddhist art and eschatology, this association was natural and almost uncannily precise. From at least the time of the tenth-century monk Genshin, the Japanese possessed terrifying prose descriptions of the excruciating tortures of the underworld; with this, in their painterly tradition, came an unsparingly detailed depiction of hell as a fiery inferno peopled with monsters and naked, tormented bodies. And this was almost exactly what the witnesses of Hiroshima and Nagasaki saw—a raging inferno; nakedness, as most clothing was stripped away by the terrific blast; streets full of monstrously deformed creatures; excruciating pain, without medicine and without surcease. The flames of hell, indeed, blossomed twice: once when the atomic bombs ignited the cities, and then a second time a few days later, when the corpses of scores of thousands of dead were cremated. "It was like hell" is the most common refrain among the words of the survivors. "Fire" is the motif of one of the Marukis' earliest panels. "Unforgettable Fire" is the title chosen for the survivors' art collected in the 1970s.

After the flames, nakedness, and mutilation, the most familiar and haunting image in this world of the damned was the procession of ghosts. In Japanese iconography and folktales, ghosts and ghouls shuffle forward in a manner much like the Western version of the living dead, with heads bowed, shoulders slouched and arms half-extended in front, the wrists loose and hands flopping down. When the indescribably bright flash of the atomic bombs occurred, Japanese in the streets instinctively covered their eyes, and as a consequence suffered severe burns on their arms and the backs of their hands. The pain was extreme, and best eased by holding one's hands out exactly as the ghosts were said to do. People fell into line in this posture; stunned and mute, they staggered forward. Thus, the byways of hell became filled with "processions of ghosts."

Many other scenes also were imaginable only in hell. Outlines of bodies were permanently etched as white shadows in a black nimbus on the streets or walls, but the bodies themselves had disappeared; outlines of grasses and mechanical objects remained, but no longer the objects themselves. And, just the opposite, there were innumerable corpses without apparent injury. Parts of bodies held their ground, like two legs severed below the knees, still standing. Many of the dead were turned into statues, some solid and others waiting to crumble at a touch. A soldier who was knocked unconscious while in the infirmary rushed out to see his comrades who were still standing on the drill field when he regained his senses; he touched one and saw him break into little pieces before his eyes. A more solid, blackened statue seen in Hiroshima a day after the bomb was dropped was a woman carrying a child, still upright, frozen in the posture of running. In another place a mother had thrown

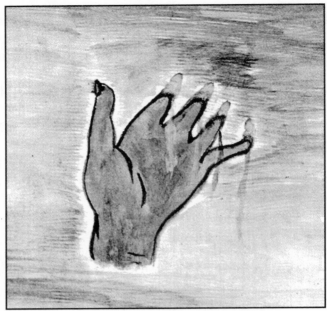

At age fifty-one, Takakura Akiko recalled this scene from
Hiroshima three decades earlier: a corpse on its back, hand
lifted to the sky, fingers burning with blue flames. The
fingers had been shortened to about a third of their length,
and Takakura remained possessed by the thought that
"this hand must have embraced a child before."

herself on the ground over her baby; both were totally charred but still
clearly formed, and the mother's hair stood on end. This also—hair
standing on end—was a not-uncommon sight among the living as well
as the dead; many survivors drew this, and one explained that he had
always thought this was a colorful cliché for utter terror, never dreaming
it really happened.

Through this macabre landscape stumbled the blinded, the demented,
and the horribly deformed. People who extended a hand to others often
found themselves holding skin that had peeled off (as so many said)
"like a glove." From every direction came cries for water, and the rivers
and cement water tanks for fire-fighting became choked with bodies.
Large flies appeared, and within a few days maggots began to swarm in

八月七日午前八時頃の旧広島放送局（上流川町）前の路上。

学校へ行くため両親と別々に被爆した私は翌七月七時半すぎ比治山越え借町の私の家の焼跡へ向った。焦土に残る数は少なく、一面の焼野原で人影をまばらに真黒に焼け爛れた死体を見た。旧放送局入口橋の水槽の中に折り重なる真黒な教徒だった。それから四五十米縮景園よりの路上に私は異様な女性らしき真黒げの片足を上げた走る姿のままの死体！近づいて見ると赤ちゃんをしっかり両手に抱いたろうとして京とした。この二人は一体誰だろうか。現在もなお鮮明に私の脳裏に残さるる無残……

広島平校専東浦町八一五

山県康子

At age forty-nine, Yamagata Yasuko drew this picture of a scene she witnessed three decades previously, almost exactly twenty-four hours after the bomb was dropped, in front of where the Hiroshima radio station had been. "Since I was at school in Ujina," she explains beside the drawing, "I had been exposed to radiation separately from my parents. The next morning at 7:30 I started from school toward the ruins of my house in Nobori-cho. I passed by Hijiyama. There were few people to be seen in the scorched field. I saw for the first time a pile of burned bodies in a water tank by the entrance to the broadcasting station. Then I was suddenly frightened by a terrible sight on the street forty to fifty meters from Shukkeien Garden. There was a charred body of a woman standing frozen in a running posture with one leg lifted and her baby tightly clutched in her arms. Who on earth could she be? This cruel sight still vividly remains in my mind."

the wounds of the living as well as in the cadavers. Horses on fire staggered through the ruins, while birds with their wings burned off hopped on the ground. Hours after the Hiroshima bomb, black rain fell. Days after the bombings, in both cities, people who thought they had escaped found their hair falling out and began to vomit blood, as the symptoms of radiation poisoning appeared.

247

ART AND POLITICS

All this can be seen in Japan's atomic-bomb art, and once seen it is difficult to forget. In the context of contemporary Japan this makes such art highly political indeed, for the policies of Japan's conservative leaders (and the Westerners who encourage them to remilitarize and deploy troops overseas under the United Nations) fare better when the past is forgotten or rendered benign. Thus, the atomic-bomb pictures tell us of times present as well as times past in Japan, and offer correctives to the currently fashionable Western impression of Japan as a harmonious hive of obedient and productive workers.

Among other issues, the political debate in Japan involves a struggle to shape the historical consciousness of the young, who have no personal recollection of war. From the conservative perspective, the pressing ideological task of the present day is to push aside recollections of the dark years of the China and Pacific wars and persuade the Japanese people to love their country, to accept more rapid remilitarization, to trust their leaders and trust the United States as well, and to take shelter as a more advanced military partner under America's nuclear "umbrella." To all this, the atomic-bomb art says "No!"

That the ruling groups look with disfavor and trepidation upon such art was made clear in August 1981, when the Ministry of Education withheld certification from a school textbook that contained an illustration from one of the Maruki panels: a famous scene depicting a woman and child lying on a litter carried by two men. The illustration had not been challenged in previous years, but the ministry now felt bold enough to contend that it was "too cruel" for youngsters to see. Years earlier, *Barefoot Gen* had been abruptly dropped from serialization because, it was explained, the publishers concluded it was "too harsh."

No one can deny the inherent harshness and cruelty of this subject, but the interpretation of the atomic-bomb experience as developed in a sustained manner by artists such as Nakazawa Keiji and the Marukis goes far beyond this. Japan's militaristic and ultranationalistic wartime leaders fare badly in the opening pages of *Barefoot Gen*, for example; and the greater part of this comic book story depicts not the immediate horrors of the atomic bomb but the subsequent struggles of Gen to cope with his traumatic experience and help build a better world out of the

Nakazawa Keiji's *Barefoot Gen,* the famous
cartoon rendering of Hiroshima and its aftermath,
was serialized in a popular children's magazine
and subsequently made into an animated film and
also published in a multivolume collection.

debris. In Japanese, Gen carries the meaning "root" or "source," and
Nakazawa has explained that he chose this name because he wanted his
young protagonist to become "a root or source of strength" for a generation who could tread Hiroshima's charred earth barefoot and find the
strength to say "no" to war and nuclear weapons. "I myself would like
to live with Gen's strength," Nakazawa has said, and in this sense his
own creation has become his model.

When the Maruki panels are viewed in their entirety, a panorama of
three decades of devoted thought and work, the range of impressions is
breathtaking. Both what the artists see and the style in which they render
this change constantly. As early as the fourth panel, titled "Rainbow"

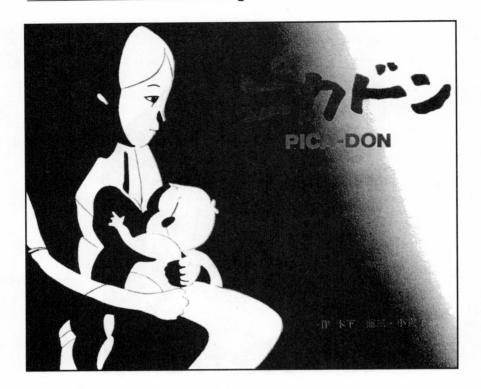

and completed in 1951, shackled American POWs are shown among the Hiroshima victims; and the torture and slaughter by frenzied citizens of Hiroshima of those POWs who survived the blast is the subject of the thirteenth of the panels, done in 1971 ("We trembled," the Marukis wrote in the text that accompanies this panel, "as we painted the death of the American prisoners"). In 1972, "Crows," the fourteenth panel, depicted the maltreatment Korean victims of the Hiroshima bomb experienced at the hands of their Japanese fellow sufferers—a staggering commentary on humankind's capacity for inflicting hurt that is also introduced in *Barefoot Gen*.

In "Rescue" (1954), the eighth of the Maruki panels and one of the most powerful, on the other hand, resolution and compassion are conspicuous even in the midst of grief and agony; and in the two panels that followed this in 1955—"Bikini Atoll" and "Petition"—common folk are depicted as people of strength and dignity. The twelfth and

The direct manner in which the human destructiveness of the atomic bombs is presented to Japanese youngsters is well represented in this sequence from a powerful textless children's book, *Pica-don,* published in 1983 by Kinoshita Renzō and Kinoshita Sayoko. In the initial graphic, used on the book's cover, the flash (*pica*) of the bomb illuminates a mother nursing an infant. Succeeding drawings illustrate the mother's transformation into a grotesque corpse as the blast (*don*) reaches them and she instinctively tries to shield her child. The book derived from a prize-winning animated film.

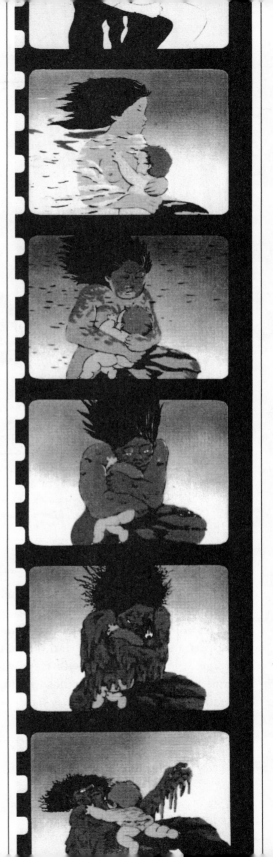

In this often-reproduced detail from the Marukis' 1950 mural "Water," a naked mother who has fled the flames finally pauses to give her breast, only to discover that her child is dead.

most brilliant of all the panels—"Floating Lanterns," completed in 1969—links the August bombings with the traditional August festival of Bon, when the souls of the dead are said to return to earth. In this richly colored montage, at once real and surreal and abstract, the symbols of past and present, birth and death, traditional reverence and modern tragedy, are interwoven with surpassing beauty. The anger, complexity, and humanism of these visions is unparalleled in the Japanese artistic tradition; and, indeed, one is hard pressed to find counterparts in the non-Japanese traditions of high art.

"Two sisters held each other's transformed bodies," the Marukis wrote in reference to this detail from their 1951 mural "Boys and Girls." "Other young girls lay dead without a scratch on their bodies."

Despite the shadings of this perception of victims and oppressors, both the Maruki panels and *Barefoot Gen* speak primarily, and hopefully, to and about the common people. They suggest in quite unmistakable ways that those in authority are not necessarily to be trusted—and that the average men, women, and children who were brutalized in the past must clarify their own values and take control of their own lives to ensure that neither they nor anyone else will ever be such victims again. It is this populist message, every bit as much as the more obvious antimilitarist and antinuclear dimension of the atomic-bomb art, that

253

makes these expressions so heretical in the eyes of those who believe in the "realism" of nuclear deterrence and the manifest destiny of technocratic elites.

In this way, the atomic-bomb art has become part of a larger manifestation of struggle and advocacy in contemporary Japan, a struggle that challenges both the myths and realities of what is commonly portrayed as Japan's well-regimented "vertical" society. It is a unique art form, with a particular place in the political as well as social and cultural history of modern Japan. But above all, it commands attention because it transcends national boundaries to speak with passion and eloquence of a world we hope never to experience again.

"Floating Lanterns," the twelfth of the Marukis' murals, painted in 1969, captures the conjunction of life and death, ritual and memory, in the practice of floating paper lanterns inscribed with the names of the dead, or with hopes for peace, on the anniversary of Hiroshima. The practice coincides with the traditional summer *Bon* observances, when the souls of the dead are said to return to earth. At the same time, the floating lanterns also replicate the rivers clogged with corpses after the atomic bomb was dropped on Hiroshima. In this detail, a young girl holds a lantern amidst images of both death and peace, and we cannot tell if the young couple with a child belongs to the living or the dead.

NOTES

1 Japan National Broadcasting Corporation, ed., *Unforgettable Fire: Pictures Drawn by Atomic Bomb Survivors* (New York: Pantheon, 1981).

2 The original *Barefoot Gen* serial (*Hadashi no Gen* in Japanese) has been reissued in a multivolume black-and-white edition in Japan by the Shō-bunsha publishing company. Over six hundred pages of this have been translated into English and are available from New Society Publishers (Philadelphia) in three volumes: *Barefoot Gen: A Cartoon Story of Hiroshima*, *Barefoot Gen: The Day After*, and *Barefoot Gen: Life After the Bomb*. Nakazawa also published a short, dramatic colored version of *Hadashi no Gen* in 1980.

The Kinoshitas' animated film *Pica-don* won a number of international prizes in 1978–1979 and became the basis for a 1983 book published by Dynamic Sellers Publishing Co. of Tokyo. Maruki Toshi, who is one of Japan's best-known illustrators of children's books, published *Hiroshima no Pika* in 1980. This has been translated into a number of languages, including an English version (under the same title) published by Lothrop, Lee Shepard Books (New York, 1981).

3 For reproductions in full color of all the major Maruki murals (including non-atomic-bomb subjects such as Auschwitz, the Rape of Nanking, the Battle of Okinawa, and the mercury-poisoned town of Minamata), see John W. Dower and John Junkerman, eds., *The Hiroshima Murals: The Art of Iri Maruki and Toshi Maruki* (New York: Kodansha International, 1986). A documentary film on the Marukis coproduced by Junkerman and Dower and titled *Hellfire: A Journey from Hiroshima* is available from First Run Films, New York, and deals with the artists' going beyond preoccupation with Hiroshima and Nagasaki (and the nationalistic victim consciousness this often involves) to place the atomic bomb experience in the broader context of twentieth-century atrocity and destructiveness, including Japan's own atrocities.

8

Race, Language, and War in Two Cultures

WORLD WAR II transcends our imaginative capacities. It is simply impossible to grasp what it means to say that fifty-five million individuals, perhaps more, were killed in a prolonged frenzy of violence. It is even difficult for any single individual to imagine all the different wars subsumed by that oddly detached phrase, "World War II." Germany's early expansion in eastern Europe, Italy's in Ethiopia. The Berlin-Rome Axis versus the Anglo-Americans. The German invasion of the Soviet Union. The Nazi war against the Jews and other *"Untermenschen."* The antifascist partisan wars and resistance movements of the West. In Asia: the China War and Pacific War and what the Japanese called the "Greater East Asia War," embracing Southeast Asia. And also in Asia, the anticolonial war within the war. In both East and West, the war between the Axis and Allies enfolded a multilayered struggle between communists and anticommunists. For African Americans, World War II, under the rallying cry "Double Victory," was simultaneously the onset of an all-out domestic struggle for civil rights.

For most Americans, the war always has involved selective consciousness, and now even these memories are fading. The hypocrisy of fighting with a segregated army and navy under the banner of Freedom, Democracy, and Justice was never frankly acknowledged and has been all but forgotten. In Asia, Japan was castigated for subjugating the native peoples of Dutch Indonesia, British Hong Kong and Malaya and Burma, America's Philippines, French Indochina—and neither then nor later did the anomaly of such condemnation sink in. Consciousness and memory have been deceptive in other ways as well. If one asks Americans today in what ways World War II was racist and atrocious, they will point overwhelmingly to the Nazi genocide of the Jews. When the war was being fought, however, the enemy perceived to be most atrocious by Americans was not the Germans but the Japanese, and the racial issues that provoked greatest emotion among Americans were associated with the war in Asia.[1]

With few exceptions, Americans were obsessed with the uniquely evil nature of the Japanese. Allan Nevins, who twice won the Pulitzer Prize in the field of history, observed immediately after the war that "probably in all our history, no foe has been so detested as were the Japanese." Ernie Pyle, the most admired of American war correspondents, conveyed the same sentiment unapologetically. In February 1945, a few weeks after being posted to the Pacific after years of covering the war in Europe, Pyle told his millions of readers that "in Europe we felt that our enemies, horrible and deadly as they were, were still people. But out here I soon gathered that the Japanese were looked upon as something subhuman and repulsive, the way some people feel about cockroaches or mice." Pyle went on to describe his response upon seeing Japanese prisoners for the first time. "They were wrestling and laughing and talking just like normal human beings," he wrote. "And yet they gave me the creeps, and I wanted a mental bath after looking at them." Sober magazines such as *Science Digest* ran articles entitled "Why Americans Hate Japs More than Nazis." By incarcerating Japanese Americans, but not German Americans or Italian Americans, the U.S. government—eventually with Supreme Court backing—gave official imprimatur to the designation of the Japanese as a racial enemy. They did so, of course, in the most formal and judicious language.

It is not really surprising that the Japanese rather than the Germans and their decimation of the Jews dominated American racial thinking. In the United States, as in Britain and most of Europe, anti-Semitism was strong and—as David Wyman among others has documented so well—the Holocaust was wittingly neglected, or a matter of indifference. Japan's aggression, on the other hand, stirred the deepest recesses of white supremacism and provoked a response bordering on the apocalyptic. As the Hearst papers took care to editorialize, the war in Europe, however terrible, was still a "family fight" which did not threaten the very essence of Occidental civilization. One Hearst paper bluntly identified the war in the Pacific as "the War of Oriental Races against Occidental Races for the Domination of the World."

There was almost visceral agreement on this. Thus Hollywood formulaically introduced good Germans as well as Nazis, but almost never a "good Japanese." In depicting the Axis triumvirate, political cartoonists routinely gave the German enemy Hitler's face, the Italian enemy Mussolini's, but rendered the Japanese as plain homogeneous "Japanese" caricatures: short, round-faced, jug-eared, buck-toothed, myopic behind horn-rimmed glasses. In a similar way, phrasemakers fell unreflectively into the idiom seen in the *Science Digest* headline: of Nazis and Japs. Indeed, while the German enemy was conflated to bad Germans (Nazis), the Japanese enemy was inflated to a supra-Japanese foe—not just the Japanese militarists, not just all the Japanese people, not just ethnic Japanese everywhere, but the Japanese as Orientals. Tin Pan Alley, as so often, immediately placed its finger on the American pulse. One of the many popular songs inspired by Pearl Harbor was entitled "There'll Be No Adolph Hitler Nor Yellow Japs to Fear." Pearl Harbor and the stunning Japanese victories over the colonial powers that followed so quickly in Southeast Asia—coupled with Japan's own rhetoric of Pan-Asianism—seemed to confirm the worst Yellow Peril nightmares.

World War II in Asia was, of course, not simply or even primarily a race war. Alliances cut across race on both the Allied and Axis sides, and fundamental issues of power and ideology were at stake. Where the Japanese and Anglo-American antagonists were concerned, however, an almost Manichaean racial cast overlay these other issues of contention. This was true on both sides. The Japanese were racist too—toward the white enemy, and in conspicuously different ways toward the other Asians who fell within their so-called Co-Prosperity Sphere. Thus, the war in Asia offers an unusually vivid case study through which to examine the tangled skein of race, language, and violence from a comparative perspective—not only with the luxury of retrospect, moreover, but also at a time when U.S.-Japan relations are very different and yet still riven with racial tension.

The war exposed core patterns of racist perception in many forms: formulaic expressions, code words, everyday metaphors, visual stereotypes. Such ways of thinking, speaking, and seeing were often vulgar, but their crudeness was by no means peculiar to any social class, educational level, political ideology, or place or circumstance (such as the battlefield as opposed to the homefront as opposed to the corridors of power and policymaking). On the other hand, in many instances the racist patterns of perception and expression were just the opposite: indirect, nuanced, garbed in the language of empiricism and intellectuality. This too was typical. Ostensibly objective observations often are laced with prejudice.

That racist perceptions shape behavior may seem obvious, but the war experience calls attention to how subtly this occurs, and at how many different levels. Myth, in this case race myths, almost always overrides conclusions drawn from sober, rational, empirical observation—until cataclysmic events occur to dispel or discredit the myth. It required Pearl Harbor and Singapore to destroy the myth cherished by Caucasians that the Japanese were poor navigators and inept pilots and unimaginative strategists, for example, and it required a long, murderous struggle to rid the Japanese of their conceit that the Anglo-Americans were too degenerate and individualistic to gird for extended battle against a far-away foe. We have become so mesmerized by the contemporary cult of military intelligence-gathering that we often fail to recognize how extensively unadulterated prejudice colors intelligence estimates, causing both overestimation and underestimation of the other side. Beyond this, in its most extreme form, racism sanctions extermination—the genocide of the Jews, of course, but also the plain but patterned rhetoric of exterminating beasts, vermin, or demons that unquestionably helped raise the tolerance of slaughter in Asia.

Given the virulence of the race hate that permeated the Pacific War, it seems at first glance almost astonishing that Americans and Japanese were able to move toward cordial relations so quickly after the war. At the state-to-state level, the Cold War abetted this, but postwar amity also rested on personal feelings of goodwill and mutual respect. This tells us something about the uniqueness and artificiality of hatred fueled by war and propaganda, perhaps, but it does not mean that racism simply disappeared. Rather, what we see here is the extraordinary nuance of racial stereotyping. Patterns of perception that abet killing can, with but a small twist, foster paternalism (or acquiescence to it) in more stable times. Damning stereotypes can be transferred, with minor adjustment, to new enemies.

This—after the patterns of racist perception, and the multiple links between perception and behavior—is the third broad area where the war in Asia offers insights into racial thinking in general. Put simply, racist stereotypes are as a rule malleable or flexible, capable of provoking contempt and violent oppression in one circumstance and paternalistic patronage in another. For the weaker side, this may translate into fear and defiance or, alternatively, acquiescence in an inherently unequal relationship. At the same time, beneath the surface specificity of preoccupation with "ethnic peculiarities," the basic patterns and idioms of racial stereotyping often tend to be free-floating, easily transferred from one target of prejudice to another. The very notion of "white supremacism" implies this, of course, but it is still sobering and illuminating to confront in concrete cases the ease with which fundamentally identical stereotypes have been transferred from one nonwhite group to another. What Americans said about the "uniquely" reprehensible Japanese during World War II, for example, was in considerable part a formulaic reiteration of invectives employed against Amerindians in the genocidal Indian wars, against Negroes ever since the slave trade, against Chinese since the opening of regular contact in the mid nineteenth century, against Filipinos in the American conquest of the Philippines at the turn of the century. Many of these same formulas, moreover, were subsequently applied to the Korean, Chinese, and Indochinese enemies in the wars of the post-1945 period.

Going a step further, the metaphors of racial difference are fundamentally even more free-floating. Ultimately they are codewords of power and domination, and overlap with the vocabularies associated with discrimination based on gender and class. For example, "childishness" is one of the most common terms used by whites to describe nonwhites. This can be buttressed with pseudo-scientific explanations (nonwhites being lower on the evolutionary scale, and thus biologically equivalent to children or adolescents vis-à-vis the "mature" white races) or pseudo-social-scientific equations (the "less developed" peoples of "less developed" nations, for example, or peoples alleged to be collectively blocked at a primitive or immature state psychologically by indigenous cultural practices or mores). The image of the child can convey contempt (as in *Newsweek*'s wartime reference to "the child mind of the Jap conscript") but can also evoke a paternalistic sense of obligation (such as the depiction of Japanese after the surrender as "MacArthur's children," or as the beneficiaries of a student-teacher relationship with Americans). This same metaphor of childishness is also integral to the rationale of male domination and rule by elites. To describe women as childish or childlike is one of the most familiar ways by which men traditionally have signified both the inherent inferiority of women and their own obligation to protect or at least humor them. Similarly, dominant social and political classes commonly affirm their privileged status and inherent right to rule by dismissing the masses as irrational, irresponsible, and immature. In its softer guise, the elite sense of noblesse oblige masks class inequalities with a paradigm of parent-to-child obligations.

Because the patterns of perception reflect not merely racial prejudice but also equations of power, the issue of racism in U.S.-Japanese relations becomes of even greater interest when the analysis is carried from the war years to the present day. Why? Because Japan's emergence as an economic superpower is inseparable from America's decline as the hegemon of the capitalist world. For the first time in modern history, a nonwhite nation has challenged the West by the very standards of wealth and power which for over four centuries have been associated with Western—and white—supremacy. This unprecedented development has been accompanied by rising tensions on both sides, and it is important to recognize that these tensions are rooted in the transformation of power relationships in the contemporary world. They are not irrational. They do not derive from "cultural differences." They are not fundamentally racist. Rather, the fear and tension we see today exists because the United States and Japan are competitors in a high-stakes, high-tech global economy that no one really understands or controls anymore. Still, race matters. The structures of institutionalized inequality that took the form of student-teacher, client-patron relations between Japan and the United States after 1945 have crumbled; and in this uncertain milieu of destabilized power, racial stereotyping and outright expressions of race hate have reemerged on both sides of the Pacific.

In this, we see the full implications of the malleability of racial metaphors and of the free-floating nature of these ways of denigrating others. The racist perceptions that were rendered soft can become harsh again. The contempt and hatred that was floated to other enemies can come back on the turn of the tide. Racism is not, in the end, an imaginative mindset. The patterns of perception are subtle and flexible, but limited, and in the current U.S.-Japanese conflict the racist words and images are eerily familiar. They are the spawn of the war years, and of centuries of racist thinking before then. How this is so is the subject of the pages that follow.

Five categories subsume the racist perceptions of the Japanese which dominated Anglo-American thinking during World War II. The Japanese were subhuman. They were little men, inferior to white Westerners in every physical, moral, and intellectual way. They were, as a collectivity, primitive, childish, and mad—overlapping concepts that could be crudely expressed but also received "empirical" endorsement from social scientists and old Japan hands. At the same time, the Japanese also were portrayed as supermen. This was particularly true in the aftermath of their stunning early victories, and it is characteristic of this thinking that the despised enemy could be little men and supermen simultaneously. Finally, the Japanese in World War II became the nightmare come true of the Yellow Peril. This apocalyptic image embraced all others and made unmistakably clear that racial hatreds, and not merely war hatreds or responses to Japanese behavior alone, were at issue.

Dehumanization of the enemy is desirable among men in combat. It eliminates scruple and doubt from killing, the reasoning goes, and this contributes to self-preservation; the enemy, after all, is simultaneously dehumanizing you and trying to kill you. Among Allied fighting men in the Pacific, this attitude emerged naturally in the ubiquitous metaphor of the hunt. Fighting Japanese in the jungle was like going after "small game in the woods back home," or tracking down a predatory animal. Killing them was compared to shooting down running quail, picking off rabbits, bringing a desperate and rabid beast to bay and finishing it off. The former sportsman turned GI was now simply "getting *bigger game*." One put the cross hairs behind the shoulder of the crouching Jap, just like in deer hunting back home.

The kill did not remain confined to combat zones, however, nor did the metaphor of dehumanization remain fixed at this general, almost casual level. In the United States, signs appeared in store windows declaring that it was "Open Season on Japs," and "Jap Hunting Licenses" were distributed in the midst of the hysteria that accompanied the incarceration of Japanese Americans. The psychology of the hunt became indistinguishable from a broader psychology of extermination that came to mean not merely taking no prisoners on the battlefield but also having no qualms about extending the kill to the civilian population in Japan. Here, the more precise language and imagery of the race war became apparent. The Japanese were vermin. More pervasive yet, they were apes. These metaphors had little to do with the battlefield per se. They exemplified the dehumanization of the entire race.

Vermin was the archetypal metaphor that the Nazis attached to the Jews, and the appalling consequences of that dehumanization have obscured the currency of such imagery in the war in Asia. On Iwo Jima, the press found amusement in noting that some Marines went into battle with "Rodent Exterminator" stenciled on their helmets. Incinerating Japanese in caves was referred to as "clearing out a rat's nest." Soon after Pearl Harbor, the prospect of exterminating the Japanese vermin in their nest at home was widely applauded. The most popular float in a day-long victory parade in New York in mid-1942 was titled "Tokyo: We Are Coming," and depicted bombs falling on a frantic pack of yellow rats. A cartoon in the March 1945 issue of *Leatherneck*, the monthly magazine for Marines, portrayed the insect *"Louseous Japanicas"* and explained that while this lice epidemic was being exterminated in the Pacific, "before a complete cure may be affected the origin of the plague, the breeding grounds around the Tokyo area, must be completely annihilated." *"Louseous Japanicas"* appeared almost simultaneously with initiation of the policy of systematically firebombing Japanese cities, and accurately reflected a detached tolerance of annihilationist and exterminationist rhetoric at all levels of U.S. society. As the British embassy in Washington noted in a weekly report, Americans perceived the Japanese as "a nameless mass of vermin."

The perception of the Japanese as apes and monkeys similarly was not confined to any particular group or place. Even before Pearl Harbor, Sir Alexander Cadogan, the permanent undersecretary of the British Foreign Office, routinely referred to the Japanese as "beastly little monkeys" and the like in his diary. Following Japan's capitulation, U.S. General Robert Eichelberger, alluding to the Japanese mission en route to the Philippines to arrange the surrender procedures, wrote his wife that "first, monkeys will come to Manila." Among Western political cartoonists, the simian figure was surely the most popular caricature for the Japanese. David Low, the brilliant antifascist cartoonist working out of London, was fond of this. The *New York Times* routinely reproduced such graphics in its Sunday edition, while adding its own commentary at one point that it might be more accurate to identify the Japanese as the "Missing Link." On the eve of the British debacle at Singapore, the British humor magazine *Punch* depicted Japanese soldiers in full-page splendor as chimpanzees with helmets and guns swinging from tree to tree. *Time* used the same image on its cover for January 26, 1942. The *New Yorker* also found the monkeymen-in-trees conceit witty. The *Washington Post* compared Japanese atrocities in the Philippines and German atrocities in Czechoslovakia in a cartoon pairing a gorilla labeled "Japs" and a Hitler-figure labeled simply "Hitler."

This ubiquitous simian idiom of dehumanization came out of a rich tradition of bigoted Western iconography. Only a few decades before they put the Japanese in trees, *Punch*'s artists had been depicting the Irish as apes. And generations of earlier white cartoonists had refined the simian caricature while working on Negroes and various Caribbean people. The popular illustrators, in turn, were merely replicating a basic tenet in the pseudo-science of white supremacism, namely, the argument that the Mongoloid and Negroid races (and for Englishmen, the Irish) represented a lower stage of evolution. Nineteenth-century Western scientists and social scientists had offered almost unanimous support to this thesis, and such ideas persisted into the mid twentieth century. President Roosevelt, for example, was informed by a physical anthropologist at the Smithsonian Institution that Japanese skulls were "some 2,000 years less developed than ours."

In the world outside the monkey house, the Japanese commonly were referred to as "the little men." Their relatively short stature contributed to this, but again the designation was essentially metaphorical. The Japanese, it was argued, were small in accomplishments when compared to the West. No great "universal" achievements were to be found in their traditional civilization; they were latecomers to the modern challenges of science and technology; they were imitators rather than innovators, ritualists rather than rationalists. Again, the cartoonists provided a good gauge of this conceit. More often than not, in any ensemble of nationalities their Japanese figures were dwarfish.

Such contempt led, among other things, to a pervasive underestimation of Japanese intentions and capabilities by British and American observers at even the highest levels. Prior to Pearl Harbor, it was common wisdom among Westerners that the Japanese could not shoot, sail, or fly very well. Nor could they think imaginatively; as a British intelligence report carefully explained, this was because the enormous energy required to memorize the ideographic writing system dulled their brains and killed the spark of creativity. There can be few better examples of the power of myth and stereotype over the weight of objective analysis than the unpreparedness of the Westerners when Japan attacked. Almost everything was a shock: the audacity of the Pearl Harbor attack and ability of the Japanese to bring it off, the effectiveness of the Zero aircraft (which had been in operation in China for over a year), the superb skills of the Japanese pilots, the esprit and discipline of the Japanese ground forces, the lightning multipronged assault against the European and American colonial enclaves. Equally shocking, of course, was the Western side of the coin: the unpreparedness in Hawaii, the debacle at Singapore, the humiliation in the Philippines. In the long view, despite Japan's eventual defeat, the events of 1941–1942 exposed the dry rot of the old empires and shattered the mystique of white superiority.

These Japanese victories—coupled with the spectacle of Japanese brutality and atrocity—set whole new worlds of racial thinking in motion. The little men suddenly became supermen; and at the same time, more elaborate versions of the little-men thesis were developed. A remarkable intelligence report circulated by psychological warfare experts within General Douglas MacArthur's command in mid 1944, for example, masticated the old thesis with excruciating thoroughness:

266

And yet in every sense of the word the Japanese are *little people*. Some observers claim there would have been no Pearl Harbor had the Japanese been three inches taller. The archipelago itself is a land of diminutive distances. Japanese houses are artistic but flimsy and cramped. The people, tiny in stature, seem to play at living. To a Westerner they and their country possess the strange charm of toyland. Centuries of isolation have accentuated the restrictive characteristics of their outlook on life.

Being *little people*, the Japanese dreamed of power and glory, but lacked a realistic concept of the material requirements for a successful world war. Moreover, they were totally unable to envisage the massive scale of operations in which the United States is now able to indulge.[2]

At the same time, the little-people thesis also was elaborated upon in ways that shed harsh light on racist bias in the academic disciplines by revealing the extent to which Western social sciences could be used to support popular prejudices. The war years witnessed the emergence of anthropologists, sociologists, psychologists, and psychiatrists as the new mandarins of theories of "national character," and as a whole they performed a valuable service in repudiating the old theories of biological determinism. What the social scientists did not dispel, however, were the racial stereotypes that had been associated with biological determinism. On the contrary, they essentially reaffirmed these biases by offering new cultural or sociopsychological explanations for them.

This is most clearly seen in three of the most influential themes that the social scientists introduced to explain Japanese behavior. The Japanese, it was argued, were still essentially a primitive or tribal people, governed by ritualistic and particularistic values. The influence of the cultural anthropologists was particularly apparent here. Furthermore, it was argued, Japanese behavior could be analyzed effectively by applying Western theories of child or adolescent behavior. Here the Anglo-American intellectuals turned to Freudian-influenced theories concerning toilet-training and psychic blockage at various stages of immaturity (the British social anthropologist Geoffrey Gorer was extremely influential on this theme), and also extolled the value of applying insights gained from American studies "of individual adolescent psychology and of the behavior of adolescents in gangs in our society, as a systematic approach to better understanding of the Japanese" (the quotation is from the minutes of a large 1944 symposium involving, among others, Margaret Mead and Talcott Parsons). Finally, in the third great preoccupation of the new mandarins, it was argued that the Japanese as a collectivity were mentally and emotionally unstable—neurotic, schizophrenic, psychotic, or simply hysterical.

In the final analysis, the "national character" studies amounted to a new way of explaining what the presumedly discredited biological determinists had concluded long ago: that the Japanese as a people displayed arrested development. While this was not inherent in their genes, it was the inevitable consequence of their peculiar history and culture. All of this was expressed with considerable erudition, and many of the insights of wartime social scientists concerning social pressures and situational ethics remain influential today. For the proverbial man from Mars, given access only to the wartime writings of these social scientists, however, it would be reasonable to conclude that imperialism, war, and atrocity had been invented in Asia in the twentieth century by developmentally retarded Japanese. They were unique, sui generis, and very peculiar indeed.

At the same time that Japan's attack on the West was inspiring this new racial "empiricism" among the Anglo-Americans, it also revitalized an old fantasy world. It is characteristic of the paranoia of self-designated master groups that even while dismissing others as inferior, they attribute special powers to them. The lower classes may be contemptible to the elites, but they also are perceived to possess a fearsome potential for violence. Women may be irrational in male eyes, but they are also said to have special intuition, and the Jezebel potential of becoming castrators. Where Western perceptions of the Japanese and Asians in general are concerned, there is in fact an intriguing congruence between the female mystique and the Oriental mystique as expressed by white male elites. Thus, in the war years, as now, the "femininity" of Japanese culture was emphasized. Traits attributed to the Japanese often were almost identical to those assigned to women in general: childishness, irrationality, emotional instability, and "hysteria." And also intuition, a sixth sense, even

268

an exceptional capacity to endure suffering. Put negatively, these latter qualities could be equated with nonrationality and simply integrated into the argument of arrested development. Positively framed, they became suprarational powers—impossible to explain, and all the more alarming to contemplate.

Because nothing in the "rational" mindset of Western leaders prepared them for either the audacity and skill of Japan's attack or the debacle of Euro-American capitulations to numerically inferior Japanese forces that followed, it was natural to look to nonrational explanations for these developments. Scapegoating helped to obfuscate the situation— the U.S. commanders at Pearl Harbor were cashiered, and the West-Coast Japanese Americans were locked up—but this was not enough. It also became useful to think of the Japanese as supermen. Graphic artists now drew the Japanese as giants on the horizon. Rhetorically, the new image usually emerged in a more serpentine or back-handed fashion. Thus, the U.S. print media from December 1941 to the end of the war featured a veritable "between-the-lines" subgenre debunking the new myth of the supermen. Battle A proved they could be beaten at sea, Battle B that they could be beaten in the jungle, Battle C that they were not unbeatable in night fighting, Battle D that the myth of the "invincibility of the Zero" was finally being destroyed. The *New York Times Magazine* took it upon itself to address the issue head-on with a feature article entitled "Japanese Superman: That Too Is a Fallacy." Admiral William Halsey, the most blatant racist officer in the U.S. high command, later claimed that he deliberately belittled the Japanese as "monkeymen" and the like in order to discredit "the new myth of Japanese invincibility" and boost the morale of his men.

The myth of the superman was never completely dispelled. To the end of the war—even after most of the Japanese navy and merchant marine had been sunk; after Japanese soldiers in the field, cut off from support, had begun starving to death and being killed by the tens and hundreds of thousands; after the urban centers of the home islands had come under regular bombardment—Allied planners continued to overestimate the will and capacity of the Japanese to keep fighting. There are surely many explanations for this, but prominent among them is a plainly racial consideration: the superman image was especially compelling because it meshed with the greatest of all the racist bogeys of the white men, the specter of the Yellow Peril. Hatred toward the Japanese derived not simply from the reports of Japanese atrocities, but also from the deeper wellsprings of anti-Orientalism. *Time* magazine's coverage of the American response to Pearl Harbor, for example, opened on this very note. What did Americans say when they heard of the attack, *Time* asked rhetorically; and the answer it quoted approvingly as representative was, "Why, the yellow bastards!" At one time or another, almost every mainstream newspaper and magazine fell into the color idiom. In poster art and every other form of anti-Japanese illustration, yellow was by far the dominant color. Among the music makers, we already have encountered Tin Pan Alley's revealing counterpoint of Hitler and the "Yellow Japs." Other song titles included "We're Gonna Find a Fellow Who Is Yellow and Beat Him Red, White, and Blue" and "Oh, You Little Son of an Oriental."

Spokesmen for Asian allies such as China were aghast at such insensitivity, and the war years as a whole became an agonizing revelation of the breadth and depth of anti-Asian prejudice in the United States. In the very midst of the war, these revelations actually prompted a year-long congressional hearing to consider revision of the notorious "Oriental Exclusion Laws," the capstone of formal discrimination against all peoples of Asian origin. What the Japanese attack brought to the surface, however, was something more illusive and interesting than the formal structures of discrimination, namely, the concrete fears that underlay the perception of a menacing Orient. Since the late nineteenth century, when the Yellow Peril idea was first expressed in the West, white people had been unnerved by a triple apprehension—recognition that the "hordes" of Asia outnumbered the population of the West, fear that these alien masses might gain possession of the science and technology that made Western domination possible, and the belief that Orientals possessed occult powers unfathomable to Western rationalists. By trumpeting the cause of Pan-Asianism and proclaiming the creation of a Greater East Asia Co-Prosperity Sphere, Japan raised the prospect that the Asian hordes might at last become united. With their Zero planes and big battleships and carriers, the Japanese gave notice that the technological and scientific gap had narrowed dramatically. And with the aura of invincibility that blossomed in the heat of the early victories, the Japanese "supermen" evoked the old fantasies of occult Oriental powers. All this would be smashed in August 1945, when Japan capitulated. And all this would resurface three decades later, when Japan burst upon the scene as an economic superpower and other Asian countries began to emulate its so-called miracle.

———

Racism also shaped the Japanese perception of Self and Other—again in patterned ways, but patterns different from those of the West. History accounts for much of this difference. Over centuries, Japan had borrowed extensively from India, China, and more recently the West; and had been greatly enriched thereby; and acknowledged these debts. And over the course of the last century, the Japanese had felt the sting of Western condescension. Even when applauded by Europeans and Americans for their accomplishments in industrializing and "Westernizing," the Japanese were painfully aware that they still were regarded as immature and unimaginative and unstable—good in the small things, as the saying went among the old Japan hands, and small in the great things. Thus, Japanese racial thinking was riven by an ambivalence which had no clear counterpart in white-supremacist thinking. Like the white Westerners, they assumed a hierarchical world; but unlike the Westerners, they lacked the unambiguous power that would enable them to place themselves unequivocally at the top of the racial hierarchy. Toward Europeans and Americans, and the science and civilization these peoples exemplified, the national response was one of admiration as well as fear, mistrust, and hatred. Toward all others—that is, toward nonwhites including Asians other than themselves—their attitude was less complicated. By the twentieth century, Japan's success in resisting Western colonialism or neocolonialism and emerging as one of the so-called Great Powers had instilled among the Japanese an attitude toward weaker peoples and nations as arrogant and contemptuous as the racism of the Westerners. Koreans and Chinese began to learn this in the 1890s and early 1900s; the peoples of Southeast Asia learned it quickly after December 7, 1941.

For Japan, the crisis of identity came to a head in the 1930s and early 1940s, taking several dramatic forms. Behind the joy and fury of the initial attacks, and indeed behind many of the atrocities against white men and women in Asia, was an unmistakable sense of racial revenge.

271

At the same time, the Japanese began to emphasize their own destiny as a "leading race" (*shidō minzoku*). If one were to venture a single broad observation concerning the difference between the preoccupations of white supremacism and Japanese racism, it might be this: whereas white racism devoted inordinate energy to the denigration of the Other, Japanese racial thinking concentrated on elevating the Self. In Japanese war films produced between 1937 and 1945, for example, the enemy was rarely depicted. Frequently it was not even made clear who the antagonist was. The films concentrated almost exclusively on the admirable "Japanese" qualities of the protagonists. The focus of wartime propaganda for domestic consumption was similar. In its language and imagery, Japanese prejudice thus appeared to be more benign than its white counterpart—by comparison, a "soft" racism—but this was misleading. The insularity of such introversion tended to depersonalize and, in its own peculiar way, dehumanize all non-Japanese "outsiders." In practice, such intense fixation on the self contributed to a wartime record of extremely callous and brutal behavior toward non-Japanese.

The central concept in this racial thinking was that most tantalizing of cultural fixations: the notion of purity. In Japan, as elsewhere, this has a deep history not merely in religious ritual but also in social practice and the delineation of insider and outsider (pure and impure) groups. By turning purity into a racial ideology for modern times, the Japanese in effect were nationalizing a concept traditionally associated with differentiation within their society. Purity was Japanized and made the signifier of homogeneity, of "one hundred million hearts beating as one," of a unique "Yamato soul" (*Yamato damashii*, from the ancient capital of the legendary first emperor). Non-Japanese became, by definition, impure. Whether powerful or relatively powerless, all were beyond the pale.

The ambiguity of the concept enhanced its effectiveness as a vehicle for promoting internal cohesion. At a superficial level, this fixation on the special purity or "sincerity" of the Japanese bears resemblance to the mystique of American "innocence." Whereas the latter is a subtheme in the American myth, however, the former was cultivated as the very essence of a powerful racial ideology. Like esoteric mantras, a variety of evocative (and often archaic) words and phrases were introduced to convey the special racial and moral qualities of the Japanese; and like esoteric mandalas, certain visual images (sun, sword, cherry blossom, snow-capped Mt. Fuji, an abstract "brightness") and auspicious colors (white and red) were elevated as particularistic symbols of the purity of the Japanese spirit.

Where Westerners had turned eventually to pseudo-science and dubious social science to bolster theories of the inherent inferiority of non-white and non-Western peoples, the Japanese turned to mythohistory, where they found the origins of their superiority in the divine descent of their sovereign and the racial and cultural homogeneity of the sovereign's loyal subjects. Deity, monarch, and populace were made one, and no words captured this more effectively than the transcendent old phrase resurrected to supercede plain reference to "the Japanese": *Yamato minzoku*, the "Yamato race." "Yamato"—the name of the place where Jimmu, grandson of the grandson of the Sun Goddess, was alleged to have founded the imperial line in 660 B.C.—was redolent with the archaic mystique of celestial genetics that made Japan the divine land and the Japanese people the chosen people. In *Yamato minzoku*, the association became explicitly racial and exclusionary. The race had no identity apart from the throne and the mythic and religious (Shintō) traditions that had grown up around it, and no outsider could hope to penetrate this community. This was blood nationalism of an exceptionally potent sort.

Many of these themes were elaborated in the ideological writings of the 1930s and early 1940s, and the cause of blood nationalism was elevated by the fact that 1940 became the occasion for massive ceremony and festivity in celebration of the 2,600-year anniversary of the "national foundation day." At the same time, the racial ideologues took care to emphasize that purity was not merely an original state, but also an ongoing process for each Japanese. Purity entailed virtues that needed to be cultivated, and preeminent among these were two moral ideals originally brought to Japan from China: loyalty and filial piety (*chūkō*). Why these became a higher expression of morality in Japan than elsewhere, higher even than in China, was explained by the fact that in Japan loyalty and filial piety had their ultimate focus in the divine sovereign. Purity lay in transcendence of ego and identification with a greater truth or cause; and in the crisis years of the 1930s and early 1940s, this greater truth was equated with the militarized imperial state. War itself, with all the sacrifice it demanded, became an act of purification. And death in war, the ultimate expression of selflessness, became the supreme attainment of this innate Japanese purity. We know now that most Japanese fighting men who died slowly did not pass away with the name of the emperor on their lips. Most often, they called (as GIs did also) for their mothers. Still, they fought and died with fervor and bravery, enveloped in the propaganda of being the divine soldiers of the divine land, and this contributed to the aura of a people possessed of special powers.

Both the Western myth of the superman and the bogey of the Yellow Peril had their analogue in this emphasis the Japanese themselves placed on their unique suprarational spiritual qualities. In Western eyes, however, this same spectacle of fanatical mass behavior also reinforced the image of the little men, the Japanese as a homogeneous, undifferentiated mass. There is no small irony in this, for what we see here is the coalescence of Japanese indoctrination with the grossest anti-Japanese stereotypes of the Westerners. In the crudest of Anglo-American colloquialisms, it was argued that "a Jap is a Jap" (the famous quotation of General John De Witt, who directed the incarceration of the Japanese Americans). In the 1945 propaganda film *Know Your Enemy—Japan*, produced by Frank Capra for the U.S. Army, the Japanese were similarly described as "photographic prints off the same negative," a line now frequently cited as the classic expression of American contempt for the Japanese. Yet in essence, this seen-one-seen-them-all attitude was not greatly different from the "one hundred million hearts beating as one" indoctrination that the Japanese leaders themselves promoted. Homogeneity and separateness *were* essential parts of what the Japanese said about themselves. In their idiom, this was integral to the superiority of the Yamato race. To non-Japanese, it was further cause for derision and contempt.

The rhetoric of the Pure Self also calls attention to the potency of implicit as opposed to explicit denigration. In proclaiming their own purity, the Japanese cast others as inferior because those others did not, and could not, share in the grace of the divine land. Non-Japanese were, by the very logic of the ideology, impure, foul, polluted. Such sentiments usually flowed like an underground stream beneath the ornate paeans to the "pure and cloudless heart" of the Japanese, but occasionally they burst to the surface with extraordinary vehemence. Thus, in a book of

274

war reportage entitled *Bataan*, Hino Ashihei, one of the best-known Japanese wartime writers, described American POWs as "people whose arrogant nation once tried to unlawfully treat our motherland with contempt." "As I watch large numbers of the surrendered soldiers," he continued, "I feel like I am watching filthy water running from the sewage of a nation which derives from impure origins and has lost its pride of race. Japanese soldiers look particularly beautiful, and I feel exceedingly proud of being Japanese."[3] These were the American prisoners, of course, whom the Japanese soldiers brutalized in the Bataan death march.

As a rule, however, the Japanese turned to one particular negative image when referring directly to the Anglo-American enemy: the demon or devil. "Devilish Anglo-Americans" (*kichiku Ei-Bei*) was the most familiar epithet for the white foe. In the graphic arts the most common depiction of Americans or British was a horned Roosevelt or Churchill, drawn exactly like the demons (*oni, akuma*) found in Japanese folklore and folk religion. As a metaphor of dehumanization, the demonic white man was the counterpart of the Japanese monkeyman in Western thinking, but the parallel was by no means exact. The demon was a more impressive and ambiguous figure than the ape, and certainly of a different category entirely than the vermin. In Japanese folk renderings, the demon was immensely powerful; it was often intelligent, or at least exceedingly crafty; and it possessed talents and powers beyond those of ordinary Japanese. Not all demons had to be killed; indeed, some could be won over and turned from menaces into guardians. Here again was an intriguingly malleable stereotype, one that would be turned about dramatically after the war when the Americans became the military "protectors" of Japan.

During the war years, however, this more benign potential of the demonic Other was buried. For the Japanese at war, the demon worked as a metaphor for the enemy in ways that plain subhuman or bestial images could not. It conveyed a sense of great power and special abilities on the part of the adversary, and in this respect captured some of the ambivalence that always had marked Japan's modern relationship with the West. At the same time, the demonic Other played to deep feelings of insecurity by evoking the image of an ever-present outside threat. Unlike apes or vermin, the demon did not signify a random presence.

In Japanese folklore, these figures always lurked just beyond the boundaries of the community or beyond the borders of the country—in forests and mountains outside the village, on islands off the coast. In origin, they exemplified not a racial fear, but a far more basic fear of outsiders in general.

Contrary to the myth of being a homogeneous people, Japanese society was honeycombed with groups suspicious of one another, and the blue-eyed barbarians from across the seas were absorbed into patterns of thinking that had emerged centuries earlier as a response to these tense and threatening insider-outsider relationships. The Westerners who suddenly appeared on Japan's horizon in the mid nineteenth century were the most formidable of all outsiders, and the response to them mobilized nationalistic and racist sentiments in unprecedented ways. Symbolically, however, the demonic Other already was present to be racialized. There was, moreover, a further dimension to this complicated play of symbolic representation, for it was but a short step from the perception of an ever-present "demonic" threat to the consciousness of being an eternal victim. This too is a sentiment that recurs frequently in the indigenous Japanese tradition, and in the modern world this "victim consciousness" (*higaisha ishiki*) became inextricably entangled with the perception of foreign threats. From this perspective, modern Japanese racism as exemplified in the demonic Other reflected an abiding sense of being always the threatened, the victim, the aggrieved—and never the threat, the victimizer, the giver of grief.

Where images and actions came together most decisively, however, demon, ape, and vermin functioned similarly. All facilitated killing by dehumanizing the enemy. The rhetoric of "kill the American demons" and "kill the British demons" became commonplace not only in combat but also on the homefront. A popular magazine published in late 1944 conveyed the fury of this rhetoric. Under the title "Devilish Americans and English," the magazine ran a two-page drawing of Roosevelt and Churchill as debauched ogres carousing with fellow demons in sight of Mt. Fuji, and urged all Japanese to "Beat and kill these animals that have lost their human nature! That is the great mission that Heaven has given to the Yamato race, for the eternal peace of the world!" Another magazine, reporting on the decisive battle in the Philippines, declared that the more of the American beasts and demons "that are sent to hell, the cleaner the world will be." Iwo Jima was described in official newsreels as "a suitable place to slaughter the American devils."

Demonization was by no means an essential precondition for killing, however. The most numerous victims of Japanese aggression and atrocity were other Asians, who were rarely depicted in this way. Toward them, the Japanese attitude was a mixture of "Pan-Asian" propaganda for public consumption, elaborate theories of racial hierarchy and Japanese hegemony at official and academic levels, and condescension and contempt in practice. Apart from a small number of idealistic military officers and civilian officials, few Japanese appear to have taken seriously the egalitarian rhetoric of Pan-Asian solidarity and genuine liberation of colonized Asian peoples. Never for a moment did the Japanese consider liberating their own Korean and Formosan colonies, and policy toward Southeast Asia—even where "independence" was granted—always was framed in terms that made Japan's preeminence as the "leading race" absolutely clear. The purity so integral to Japanese thinking was peculiar to the Japanese as a race and culture—not to "Oriental" peoples in general—and consequently there was no "Asian supremacism" counterpart to white supremacism in Japanese thinking.

Prior to the 1930s, the Japanese did not have a clearly articulated position vis-à-vis other Asians. The rush of events thereafter, including the invasion of China and decision to push south into Southeast Asia, forced military planners and their academic supporters to codify and clarify existing opinions on these matters. The result was a small outpouring of studies, reports, and pronouncements—many of a confidential nature—which explicitly addressed the characteristics of the various peoples of Asia and the appropriate policy to adopt toward them. That these were not casual undertakings was made amply clear in 1981, when a hitherto-unknown secret study dating from 1943 was discovered in Tokyo. Prepared by a team of some forty researchers associated with the Population and Race Section of the Research Bureau of the Ministry of Health and Welfare, this devoted over three thousand pages to analysis of race theory in general and the different races of Asia in particular. The title of the report provides an inkling of its contents: *An Investigation of Global Policy with the Yamato Race as Nucleus.*

The *Investigation* was a serious intelligence report, and its style was academic. In its way, it was a counterpart to the "national character" writings of the Anglo-American social scientists who mobilized in support of the Allied war effort (and found the Japanese "national character" best explained by theories concerning adolescent behavior and juvenile delinquency among Westerners). The Japanese researchers called attention to Western theories of race and, while attentive to Nazi ideas, surveyed the gamut of racial thinking beginning with Plato and Aristotle. In the modern world, they noted, racism, nationalism, and capitalist imperialism had become inseparably intertwined. And while modern scholarship had repudiated the notion of biologically pure races, blood still mattered greatly in contributing to psychological unity. In this regard, as Karl Haushofer had observed, Japan was fortunate in having become a uniform racial state. (Haushofer, the geopolitician whose writings influenced the Nazis, had done his doctoral work on Japan.) At the same time, overseas expansion should be seen as essential, not merely for the attainment of military and strategic security but also for preserving and revitalizing racial consciousness and vigor; on this point, the Japanese again quoted Western experts, including not merely the Germans but also the British. Looking ahead, it was predictable that the second and third generations of overseas Japanese might face problems of identity, and thus it was imperative to develop settlement policies that would thwart their assimilation and ensure that they "remain aware of the superiority of the Japanese people and proud of being a member of the leading race."

The focus of this massive report was on Asian rather than Western peoples, and its dry language provides insight into how racial inequality in Asia was rationalized. The central metaphor was the family. The critical phrase was "proper place"—a term that had roots in Confucian prescription for domestic relationships but was carefully extended to cover international relations beginning in the late 1930s. The family idiom is another example of the malleable social construct, for it suggests harmony and reciprocity on the one hand, but clear-cut hierarchy and division of authority and responsibility on the other; and it was the latter that really mattered to the Japanese. The authors of the *Investigation* were emphatic in condemning false consciousness concerning equality. "To view those who are in essence unequal as if they were equal is in itself inequitable," they observed. And it followed from this that "to treat those who are unequal unequally is to realize equality." The family exemplified such equitable inequality, and the Japanese writers made clear that Japan was not merely the head of the family in Asia now but was destined to maintain this position "eternally." Whether the Yamato race also was destined to become the head of the global family of races and nations was left unanswered, although passing comments suggested that this was the ultimate goal. The opening pages of the study flatly declared that the war would continue "until Anglo-American imperialistic democracy has been completely vanquished and a new world order erected in its place." And as the *Investigation* made amply clear, the Japanese-led imperium in Asia would assume a leading role in this new order.

Despite their Confucian overtones, the family metaphor and proper-place philosophy bore close resemblance to Western thinking on issues of race and power. The Japanese took as much pleasure as any white Westerner in categorizing the weaker peoples of Asia as "children." In their private reports and directives, they made clear that "proper place" meant a division of labor in Asia in which the Yamato race would control the economic, financial, and strategic sinews of power within an autarchic bloc, and thereby "hold the key to the very existence of all the races of East Asia." A secret policy guideline issued in Singapore at the outset of the war was equally frank: "Japanese subjects shall be afforded opportunities for development everywhere," it stated, "and after establishing firm footholds they shall exalt their temperament as the leading race with the basic doctrine of planning the long-term expansion of the Yamato race." Despite their detailed country-by-country, race-by-race summaries, the Japanese were interested in other Asians only as subordinate members of the family who could be manipulated to play roles assigned by Japan. For other Asians, the real meaning of Japan's racial rhetoric was obvious. "Leading race" meant master race, "proper place" meant inferior place, "family" meant patriarchal oppression.

There are two interesting questions to ask concerning racism in the postwar U.S.-Japan relationship. How did the racial hatreds dissipate so quickly after Japan's capitulation? And in what forms has racism reemerged in recent years, as economic frictions have mounted between the two countries?

The answer to the first question is a story in itself, and begins with the commonsense observation that intimate face-to-face contact for purposes other than mutual slaughter enabled each side to rehumanize the other. Although the American-dominated Occupation of Japan, which lasted from 1945 to 1952, was ethnocentric and overbearing in many respects, it also was infused with goodwill and—in its early stages—a commitment to "demilitarization and democratization" that struck a responsive chord. Contrary to the wartime stereotypes of propagandists in both the Allied and Japanese camps, the majority of Japanese were sick of regimentation, indoctrination, and militarism. At the same time, the Cold War facilitated a quick diversion of enmity, and anticommunism became a new mission uniting the two former antagonists at the state level. Enemies changed, enmity did not.

On both sides, this abrupt metamorphosis was cushioned psychologically by the ability to use old patterns of perception in new ways. For the Americans, the vermin disappeared but the monkeymen remained for a while as charming pets. The September 1945 cover of *Leatherneck*, for example—the first issue of the Marine monthly to appear after Japan's capitulation—featured a cheery cartoon of a Marine holding a vexed but thoroughly domesticated monkey wearing the cap, shirt, and leggings of the Imperial Army. *Newsweek*, in its feature article on what sort of people the Americans might expect to find in Japan when the Occupation commenced, ran "Curious Simians" as one subtitle. Other racist stereotypes traveled from war to peace in comparable ways. While defeat temporarily extinguished the superman mystique, it reinforced the perception of the Japanese as little or lesser people. Stated conversely, victory over Japan reinforced the conceit of inherent white and Western superiority. The more precise associations of Japan's "lesser" stature, however—the primitive nature of social relations and attitudes; the childishness of the populace both psychologically and politically; the collective neurosis—all this now provoked a paternalistic response. The American overseers of Occupied Japan thought in terms of a civilizing mission that would eliminate what was primitive, tribal, and ritualistic— an old but idealistic colonial attitude indeed. They would guide an immature people with backward institutions toward maturity. The Japanese "children" now became pupils in General MacArthur's school of democracy, learners and borrowers of advanced U.S. technology, followers of U.S. Cold War policies. Where the Japanese psyche was tortured, the Americans would be healers.

These were not frivolous attitudes, any more than paternalism itself is necessarily frivolous. At the individual level, moreover, countless Japanese and Americans collaborated equitably in pursuit of common goals. Neither democracy nor demilitarization nor—later—economic reconstruction and remilitarization were ethnocentric U.S. goals forced upon an unwilling, defeated people; on all of these policies, there was a gamut of opinion among the Japanese themselves. The overall relationship, however, was inherently unequal and patronizing on the part of the Americans, and it is here that racist attitudes survived. U.S. policymakers at the highest level also were not above cynically manipulating Japanese racism to serve U.S. purposes. In 1951, when Japan's allegiance in the Cold War was still not entirely certain, for example, John Foster Dulles recommended that the Americans and British take advantage of Japanese feelings of "superiority as against the Asiatic mainland masses" and play up the "social prestige" of being associated with the Western alliance. (In a fine example of a truly free-floating stereotype, Dulles, tapping a deep-rooted Euro-American tradition emphasizing the fundamentally Slavic or "Oriental" nature of the Russian people and culture, also liked to emphasize that the Soviet menace could be better understood if one remembered that the Russians were an Asiatic people.)

On the Japanese side, defeat was bitter but peace was sweet, and certain attitudes associated with wartime racial thinking also proved adaptable to the postsurrender milieu. Proper-place thinking facilitated acceptance of a subordinate status vis-à-vis the victorious Allies, at least for the time being. In this regard, it is helpful to recall that the "leading race" rhetoric of the war years was a relatively new ideology in Japan, whereas for most of their modern history the Japanese had played a subordinate role in the world order. The militarism of the 1930s and early 1940s arose out of a desire to alter that insecure status, and ended in disaster. To seek a new place in more modest new ways after 1945 was in fact the continuation of a familiar quest.

281

In fascinating ways, the wartime fixation on purity and purification proved adaptable to this commitment to a new path of development. Individuals who had been exhorted to purge self and society of decadent Western influences before the surrender now found themselves exhorted to purge the society of militarism and feudalistic legacies. This sense of "cleansing" Japan of foul and reactionary influences was truly phenomenal in the early postwar years, and while this tapped popular aspirations for liberation, it also politicized the militarists' ideology of the Pure Self in undreamed-of ways. Universal "democratic" values now became the touchstone of purity. And the guardians at the gates, to cap these astounding transmogrifications, were the erstwhile American demons. The U.S. assumption of a military role as protector of postwar Japan was a hard-nosed rational policy, but from the Japanese perspective it had a subtle, almost subconscious logic. The fearsome demons of Japanese folklore, after all, frequently were won over and put to use by the ostensibly weaker folk.

These transitional adaptations of proper place, purity, and the demon more or less deracialized the wartime fixations. They did not, however, eliminate the racial tensions latent in the structure of institutionalized inequality that has characterized postwar U.S.-Japan relations until recently. So long as Japan remained conspicuously inferior to the United States in power and influence, the structure and psychology of what is known in Japan as "subordinate independence" could be maintained. When relations of power and influence changed dramatically, however, neither side could be expected to rethink these fundamental relationships without trauma. The great change came in the 1970s, when it became apparent—abruptly and shockingly for almost everyone concerned— that Japan had become an economic superpower while America faced formidable problems. In this situation, war talk has become fashionable again: talk of trade wars; ruminations on who really won the Pacific War; doomsday warnings of a new "yen bloc," a seriously rearmed Japan, a "financial Pearl Harbor." Much of this is political grandstanding and yellow journalism, but the fears are real. The United States and Japan are mistrustful allies and serious competitors now, and they are capable of destabilizing the global political economy if unable to redefine their relationship. It is in this context of enormous stakes and high tension that the old vocabularies of racial pride and racial hatred have reemerged ominously on both sides.

■

The idioms of race are like hands: we can make a fist and strike others with it, or show the back of the hand in contempt, or offer the palm in friendship. That both Americans and Japanese have begun to withdraw the proffered hand in recent years is obvious. Thus, on the American side, Japan's success has rekindled the idioms of dehumanization with scorn for the "economic animal" and "robotlike" salaryman. The image of the little people has persisted even as the country's economic power becomes enormous. Henry Kissinger reportedly referred privately to the Japanese as "little Sony salesmen" and "small and petty bookkeepers." Lee Iacocca, one of the harshest critics of Japanese economic practices, falls back on an archetypical racist metaphor in offering advice on how to deal with Japan in his memoirs: "It's time for our government to call the kid in after class and ask him to explain his behavior."[4] In journalistic circles, the single most popular adjective for contemporary Japan is probably "tribal," a notion straight out of the national-character studies of the war years, and hardly adequate for analyzing the second largest capitalist economy in history. The madman image has resurfaced in countless forms, from commentaries on compulsive work habits to fears that Japanese financiers may throw the global economy into chaos on a whim to visions of a suicidal nuclear-armed Japan. The superman has been resurrected as the superpower, and again it is suggested that occult powers lie behind this accomplishment—miracle men, secrets of success, an inscrutable Zen of management, an indomitable and inimitable Japanese spirit. And overriding this, for Americans and most of the Western world, is the reincarnation of the Yellow Peril in the form not merely of Japan alone, but also the "four dragons" or "four tigers" that are coming on fast in Japan's wake: South Korea, Taiwan, Singapore, and Hong Kong. What the optimists refer to as the "Pacific Century" is, in the pessimists' phrase, the impending "Asian Century."

To most Japanese, the attacks on their success ring of sour grapes, and more. They confirm the old fears of an ever-present threat from outside, and rekindle the sense of being an eternal victim. The practitioners of Japan bashing are the new demonic menace, they are again mostly Americans and Europeans, and their numbers seem legion. They refuse to acknowledge the decline of the West, as it were, and Japan's new place in the world order.

What that place is, of course, is the nub of the problem. The rhetoric of "Japan as Number One" was first popularized in 1979 by an American scholar, Ezra Vogel, and has provoked pride among Japanese and fear and uncertainty everywhere, including in Japan itself. For it captures a central fact of our times—not that Japan is in fact "number one," but rather that the structure of global power and influence is in the midst of a historic transformation, and no one can foresee what the outcome will be. "Proper place" means different place now, a restructuring of established hierarchies, in some instances almost a complete inversion of the former teacher-student and leader-follower relationships.

For many Japanese, especially those who lived through the war and endured the long decades of humiliation built into the postwar structure of subordinate independence, there is an understandable and only thinly disguised sense of racial revenge in these developments. There is also a frightening tendency on the part of the more fervent new nationalists to attribute Japan's success to peculiarly Japanese qualities that are essentially the same as those emphasized in the blood nationalism and leading-race rhetoric of the war years. In explaining why the Japanese are winning the trade war, for example, the head of Nippon Telephone and Telegraph Corporation explained several years back that the superior quality of Japanese manufactures reflected the fact that the Japanese were racially pure and not "mongrelized" as were Americans. The prime minister of Japan spoke similarly in 1986, and provoked a violent outburst of anti-Japanese sentiment in the United States in return. Such remarks do more than reveal the persistence of the mystique of Japanese homogeneity and purity, and the special contempt that many Japanese still hold toward "nonwhites" (the targets in this case were primarily Afro-Americans and Hispanics). They also reveal an insular hostility toward pluralism which is incompatible with the global responsibilities their new power has thrust upon the Japanese.

The roads being traveled in global relationships today are unfamiliar paths to unknown destinations, but the racial language that has emerged as the United States and Japan jockey for position on these paths is familiar. No comfort can be taken in that.

NOTES

1 This essay summarizes some of the themes developed at length in my *War Without Mercy: Race and Power in the Pacific War* (New York: Pantheon, 1986), where full annotations can be found. Here I have sharpened the focus on racial language in comparative perspective.

2 "Answer to Japan," p. 20 (italics in original). This report appears in several archival collections at the Hoover Institution, Stanford University. See "Bonner Frank Fellers Collection," Boxes 1 and 15; also "U.S. Army Forces in the Pacific, Psychological Warfare Branch," Box 1.

3 From Hino's 1942 book *Batān Hantō Kōjōki*, as quoted in Haruko Taya Cook, "Voices from the Front: Japanese War Literature, 1937–1945," unpublished M.A. thesis in Asian Studies, University of California, Berkeley, 1984, pp. 59–60. In numerous ways, Hino can be seen as a Japanese counterpart to Ernie Pyle, quoted at the beginning of this essay. Both men were immensely influential in interpreting the war for their countrymen; and both obviously responded with similar visceral racial repulsion to first encounters with the enemy.

4 These quotations, and the brief observations in these concluding remarks in general, are annotated in the fuller treatment of contemporary racial idioms which appears in the essay which follows on "Fear and Prejudice in U.S.-Japan Relations."

9

Graphic Others/Graphic Selves: Cartoons in War and Peace

In war and peace, past and present, Anglo-American political cartoonists routinely resort to one of the most fundamental of all Western attitudes toward the Japanese and other Asians by portraying them as "little people" or "little yellow men," small not only in stature but also in accomplishments. Such condescension has contributed, among other things, to persistent underestimation of Japanese ambitions and capabilities.

Figure 1, drawn by the widely sydicated cartoonist David Low in November 1941, on the eve of Pearl Harbor, mocked Japanese complaints that they were being encircled and economically strangled by the U.S.-led Western powers (Low's caption read, "Japan Protest against Encirclement! Yes-No?"). Figures 2 and 3 were reproduced in the *New York Times* on the occasions, respectively, of Japan's surrender in August 1945 and the end of the Occupation and the restoration of Japanese sovereignty in the spring of 1952. Both graphics are examples not merely of the perception of the Japanese as exotic little people, but also of the counter perception of oneself (America, the West) as transcendent and all-powerful—as literally, in the artist's rendering, the "hand of God."

Fig. 1

Fig. 2

Fig. 3

Fig. 4

THE LITTLE PEOPLE   (*continued*)

Even Japan's emergence by the 1980s as the second-largest industrial economy in the world did not dispel the Western view of the Japanese as little men, an alien and lesser people. Danziger's March 1989 cartoon for the *Christian Science Monitor* about U.S. pressure on Japan to assume a larger military role is harsh on both sides, but relies on an archetypal depiction of the Japanese as childish and immature, perhaps even retarded (Figure 4). Oliphant's 1990 comment on corporate Japan's response to the Gulf War (Figure 5) was widely reproduced at the time, and nicely meshes the little men with another conventional Western image: the Japanese herd, devoid of individuality. The depersonalized, robotized, seen-one-seen-them-all image is captured in Figure 6 as well, which accompanied a feature story on Japanese white-collar workers in the *Washington Post* (September 1987) titled "Is It a Nerd? Is It a Brain? No, It's Salaryman!" The *Post*'s debunking of the myth of the Japanese superman, meant to be witty, tapped another familiar idiom of dehumanization.

Fig. 5

Fig. 6

THE JAPANESE SUPERMEN

Contempt for racially and culturally different peoples does not preclude fearing them, and thus racial stereotyping commonly involves contradictory images. Anglo-American depictions of the Japanese exhibit this with evocations of supermen—and the larger bogey of the "Yellow Peril"— alongside caricatures of a dwarfed, stunted, childlike people. "Little men" and "supermen" coexist in the Western imagination about the Japanese, and about Asians in general. What apparently is most difficult to imagine is a shared humanity.

The image of the Japanese superman became immensely popular in the aftermath of Pearl Harbor and Japan's sensational early military victories in World War II. This is conveyed in Figure 7, a British graphic that was reproduced in the Sunday *New York Times Magazine* in May 1943. Forty-four years later, the Sunday *Times* evoked a new Japanese Goliath in the form of a giant sumo wrestler looming over Wall Street (Figure 8). *Business Week*'s counterpart the very same month (September 1987) was a monster samurai seizing Wall Street. The superman comes and goes as Japan's power waxes and wanes. However, Japanese capitalism almost invariably is portrayed by such unique, traditional, even precapitalist representations—even at the peak of economic expansion in the 1980s.

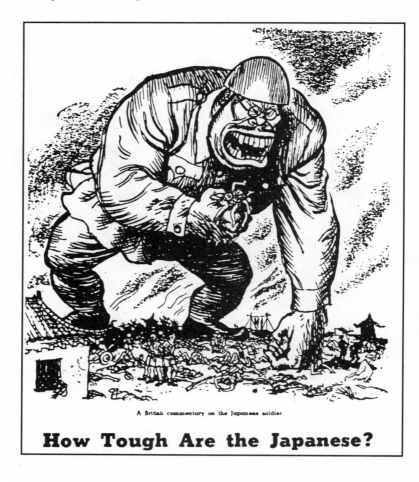

A British commentary on the Japanese soldier.

How Tough Are the Japanese?

Fig. 7

Fig. 8

293

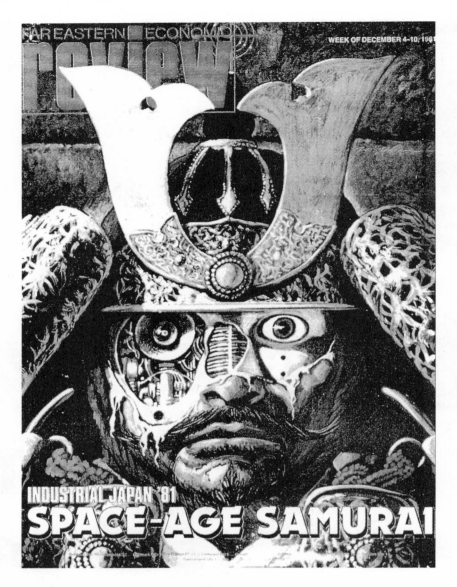

Fig. 10

HIGH-TECH YELLOW PERIL

Contemporary Western fears about Japan have historical roots in turn-of-the-century apprehensions concerning the "Yellow Peril" of Asian peoples, with their huge numbers and presumed occult secrets. Until Japan emerged as an economic superpower, however, it was assumed that Western mastery of science and technology would keep the Yellow Peril at bay.

The sophisticated economic and technological accomplishments of the Japanese, and of other Asian peoples close behind them, have shattered Western complacency and thereby effectively ended the half millennium of

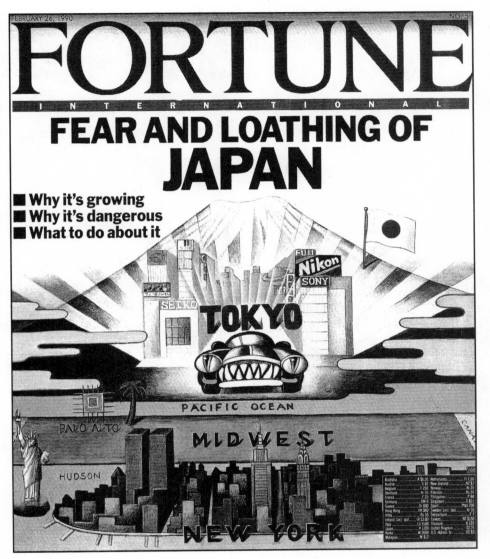

Fig. 11

Western global hegemony. As Figures 10 and 11 illustrate, Asian mastery of science and technology has given rise not to perceptions of East-West convergence but rather to an apocalyptic new vision of a high-tech Yellow Peril. The stunning image of the robotic samurai is triply evocative in this regard: it simultaneously dehumanizes the Japanese, brands them as culturally unique and backward, and calls attention to their mastery of cutting-edge technologies, hitherto the exclusive province of Euro-Americans.

Fig. 12

THREATENING AMERICANS

As a "late developer" on the world scene,
the Japanese characteristically have
viewed Euro-Americans as the bearers of
both gifts and threats. The threats—
manifested as economic and military
imperialism, colonialism, neocolonialism,
racism, unbridled capitalism, cultural
inundation, and so on—came to a head
in World War II. The militarized visage
of President Franklin Roosevelt in Figure
12, which appeared in a January 1943
publication, illustrates the demonized
image of the United States which
prevailed in Japan during the war.

Forty-nine years later, in the midst of
"trade war" conflicts, the *Asahi Shimbun*
ran the comparably mechanized
rendering of U.S. President George Bush
shown in Figure 13 (the caption, a
takeoff on earlier postwar Euro-
American denigration of Japan's leaders
as transistor salesmen and the like, had
the tiny Japanese prime minister
stammering "Welcome, Mr. 'Car and
Parts Salesman' President"). Figure 14,
the cover of a pamphlet published during
the Gulf War, evokes lingering Japanese
perceptions of the demonic nature of
"war-loving" America more explicitly.
The title is "Scary America."

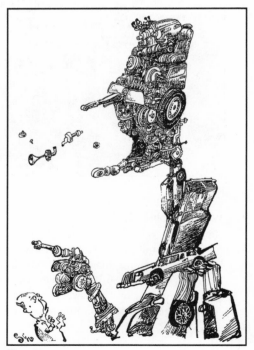

Fig. 13

296

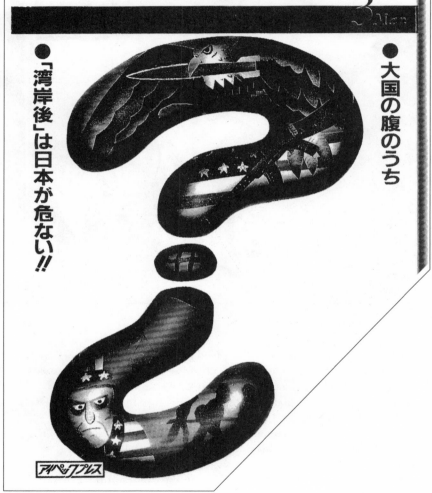

Fig. 14

Fig. 15

POOR, PURE JAPANESE

As counterpoint to perceptions of a threatening America, Japanese commonly dwell on their own vulnerability as a small and resource-poor nation, as well as on the sincerity of their actions and purity of their intentions. Like Westerners, albeit with entirely different meaning, they thus also tend to depict themselves as small and vulnerable.

Figure 15, drawn by the famous cartoonist Katō Etsurō and included in a book of political cartoons published a few months before Pearl Harbor, depicts Uncle Sam and other Westerners restraining little Japan in its noble attempts to introduce a racial-equality clause in the charter of the new League of Nations after World War I. Much the same aggrieved sense of being dominated and abused by the "hairy barbarians" (a traditional anti-Western idiom) emerges in contemporary graphics by Yamada Shin in the *Asahi* newspaper. In Figure 16, Prime Minister Kaifu Toshiki is pressured to contribute cash to the U.S.-dominated Gulf War. Figure 17, a graphic 1987 rendering of "Japan bashing," has President Ronald Reagan beating up Prime Minister Nakasone Yasuhiro in a dispute over customs duties.

Fig. 16

Fig. 17

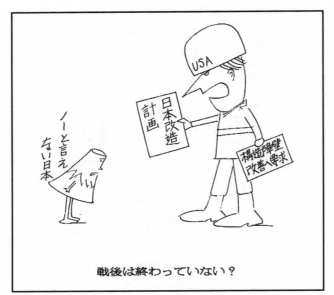

Fig. 18

In Figure 18, a March 1990 cartoon by the *Asahi*'s Yokoyama Taizō, a militant USA demands structural reform from poor little Japan, represented by Mount Fuji, the quintessential symbol of Japanese purity. In a witty takeoff on a best-seller titled *The Japan That Can Say No*, Fuji is labeled "The Japan That Cannot Say No." The caption, alluding to America's domineering posture vis-à-vis Japan ever since the Occupation, plaintively asks, "Isn't 'postwar' over?" Figure 19, by Yamanoi Norio, similarly conveys the sense of Japan being a small and vulnerable outsider in the community of militarized great powers, as the diminutive Japanese prime minister (Kaifu) gazes wistfully at the leaders of Germany, France, the United States, and Great Britain.

Fig. 19

10

Fear and Prejudice in
U.S.-Japan Relations

IN HIS 1942 book *Capitalism, Socialism, and Democracy*, Joseph Schumpeter coined a vivid phrase to describe the dynamic and contradictory nature of capitalist development. He called it a process of "creative destruction."[1] Neither Schumpeter nor anyone else living in those days, however, was capable of imagining how drastically capitalism would change in the years following World War II. We have, quite simply, entered a world of hitherto undreamed-of technological innovation, stunning transformations in the forces of production, whole new dimensions of fiscal and economic activity. Yet the characterization "creative destruction," now a half-century old, seems more appropriate than ever. Both spectacular accomplishments and appalling failures characterize the global capitalist economy today.

Schumpeter's phrase is actually effective in a double way. Not only does it convey a sense of objective contradictions within the economy, but it also suggests the subjective tensions and angst that accompany this economic turmoil. Creativity is exhilarating. Destruction is terrifying. And when these two phenomena come together with dizzying speed, as is occurring everywhere one looks today, the psychological result can be a pervasive feeling of uncertainty and fear.

This is nowhere more apparent than in present-day U.S.-Japan relations, for no two countries are more deeply involved in the process of creative destruction that is now taking place. At both the national and international levels, we have a sobering reminder of the poverty of economic prediction, for until the 1970s virtually no one inside or outside Japan really anticipated the occurrence (to say nothing of the speed) of Japan's emergence as a genuine economic superpower—victorious in sophisticated industrial and technological competition; dominant as a global trader and investor; preeminent, almost overnight, as the creditor of the capitalist world; bestriding the globe in tandem with its erstwhile American mentor and benefactor.

Among the many consequences of these unanticipated developments is one that longtime supporters of the U.S.-Japan partnership presumably should welcome. Not only has Japan become successful beyond anyone's dreams, but the two countries now are bound together by a web of economic, financial, and personal ties that is every bit as dense and intimate as the military bonds that hitherto linked them together. Many Americans and Japanese, even apart from private interests from which they may benefit personally, sincerely applaud this new density of interpenetration. The interests of the United States and Japan are vastly more inseparable now than was the case a half-century ago, on the eve of Pearl Harbor—and that is no small consideration in these times of mounting uncertainty. Yet despite this new bilateral intimacy, one would be hard-pressed to find anyone who argues that it has contributed to a more stable world order. On the contrary, the prevailing sentiment in Japan as well as the West appears to be one of abiding pessimism.

There are many explanations for this, some more immediately apparent than others. Obviously, if one treats the bilateral U.S.-Japan relationship—or global capitalism in general—as a zero-sum game, then Japan's gains become interpreted as others' losses. To most contemporary observers, it is impossible to separate astonishment at Japan's sudden emergence as an economic superpower from shock at the spectacle of America's relative decline. More generally, however, it is helpful to return to Schumpeter to understand why the current situation seems so threatening. Simply put, both the creative and destructive aspects of capitalism have become magnified in unprecedented ways. Today's advanced capitalism is not only "high-tech" but also high-speed and high-impact. What happens between Japan and the United States has quick and discernible consequences in the rest of the capitalist world; and to many observers, the situation appears close to being out of control.

This pessimism does not emanate from any particular political or ideological quarter. It comes from all directions, including longtime supporters of the U.S.-Japan relationship, and has assumed an increasingly apocalyptic tone. In 1984, for example, Robert Christopher, a former *Time* and *Newsweek* editor with close ties to Japan, observed that it was "disturbingly easy" to envision a "pessimistic scenario" concerning the future of U.S.-Japan relations. Since then, doomsday visions have indeed come one on the heels of the other. A massive study published by the Harvard Business School in 1987 carried the blunt zero-sum title *America Versus Japan*, for example, while a typical article in the Australian press the same year carried the banner headline, "The Coming Clash of the World's Economic Titans." Clyde Haberman, the able Tokyo correspondent of the *New York Times*, called attention in the spring of 1987 to a "growing sense that, deep down, neither side truly understands the other." In an article on "The Coming U.S.-Japan Crisis" published in the winter 1987 issue of *Foreign Affairs*, George Packard, dean of the School of Advanced International Studies at Johns Hopkins and a former aide to Ambassador Edwin Reischauer in Tokyo in the early 1960s, concluded that "if one examines closely the existing governmental agencies for managing the United States-Japan relationship, the situation appears nearly hopeless."

Lester Thurow, a liberal economist who frequently has expressed admiration for Japanese industrial and management practices, joined this gloomy chorus of the late 1980s with an extraordinarily pessimistic long-term prediction to readers of the *Washington Post*. Anticipating deep recessions in both Japan and West Germany, Thurow went on to argue that Japan, Germany, and the United States all appear to be incapable of submerging national sovereignty in the cause of larger global interests. As a consequence of this collective political failure, the capitalist world in all likelihood faces "a prolonged period of economic stagnation." Clyde Prestowitz, a former trade negotiator with Japan in the Reagan administration, is even bleaker about the probable outcome of

U.S.-Japan competition than Thurow, although that hardly seems possible. "It used to be that we could say America should be moving into the future," he told *Time* in April 1987. "Now we are finding out that we don't have a future." Prestowitz's influential book on this crisis is titled *Trading Places: How America Is Giving the Future to Japan.*[2]

Japanese commentators whose opinions reach the Western world almost unanimously appear to share these dark presentiments. Following the U.S. imposition of trade sanctions against Japan in March 1987, former Foreign Minister Abe Shintarō told American reporters that "the trade relationship between Japan and the U.S. is at its worst since the war. Should it worsen, I'm afraid it could cause a schism in our alliance." Management consultant Ohmae Kenichi, a ubiquitous commentator in the U.S. press, told *Newsweek* around the same time that Japan and the United States simply "cannot communicate with one another." In the summer 1987 issue of the *Journal of Japanese Studies*, the leading Western academic journal on Japan, Professor Haruhiro Fukui of the University of California at Santa Barbara published a gloomy analysis of opinions among officials in the Japanese Foreign Ministry. "The issues that confront the two governments now are already intractable," Fukui concluded, and "those to arise in the next decade will probably be even more contentious and unmanageable." Based on his in-depth interviews, Fukui predicted a steady rise in U.S.-Japan tensions "until a crisis point is reached."[3]

Such emotional language reveals one of the most striking anomalies of the current situation. On the one hand, we live in a world of immense sophistication, where technology and economics have become the provinces of highly specialized experts. Few people really understand what a semiconductor is, for example, or how the exchange rate or debt financing really operate. At the same time, however, this is also a world where elaborate and complex relationships can be drastically affected by subjective and irrational influences of the sort everyone understands— by stereotypes and catchphrases and all the simplistic images that the politicians and mass media love to offer.

This does not mean that emotional and irrational attitudes comprise the essence of current tensions between the United States and Japan. On the contrary, the heart of the problem lies in real conflicts concerning money, power, and influence in a rapidly changing world. It is only in this setting that the psychological dimensions of the U.S.-Japan relationship assume their full significance. Thus, entirely rational fears concerning economic well-being are involved on both sides. National pride enters the picture at an unusually intense level—as is only to be expected in a situation where the two nations are portrayed as competing to determine which is really "number one." Cultural differences also affect economic attitudes and behavior, although the influence of "cultural values" is usually grossly exaggerated in discussions of modern Japan.

At the same time—and this is the focus of the pages that follow—two areas of contention and uncertainty that contribute greatly to the tension in current U.S.-Japan relations deserve far more attention than they are generally given. The first is the vexing issue of capitalism itself—that is, the theoretical and ideological uncertainty that has arisen concerning capitalist growth at national as well as international levels. The second great source of tension involves race or racism in ways that do not arise in America's relations with European nations. Like all the other points of contention between the two powers, racism is a two-way street; and it seems especially sad and ironic (although hardly surprising) that at the very moment Japan has emerged as a more truly international power, we find protagonists on all sides resurrecting Kipling's hoary dictum that East is East and West is West and never the twain shall meet. Such sentiments have no legitimate place in today's world—but if they continue, they have the terrible potential of becoming a self-fulfilling prophesy.

THE CAPITALISM PROBLEM

No one denies that we are now witnessing a historic transformation, signaled by the rise of Japan as an economic colossus and the decline of the United States as the hegemonic power that has held the postwar capitalist system together up to now. At the same time, it is difficult and indeed implausible to envision Japan replacing the United States as economic hegemon—although more than a few analysts have argued that this is taking place. There are many reasons why this will not happen, at least in the foreseeable future. Despite its problems, the

United States remains militarily dominant, economically enormous, and politically hostile to the prospect of relinquishing world leadership. And despite its economic accomplishments, Japan still lacks the charisma, and as yet also the vision and will, to lead.

The best-case scenario that seems to be emerging for the future is thus something unprecedented in the modern world: some sort of "shared hegemony" involving the United States, Japan, and Germany, or even a bilateral capitalist hegemony dominated by the United States and Japan. These ideas are in the air in various forms, as noted below, but many things must fall into place for shared hegemony to work. One must assume, for example, that U.S. and Japanese capitalisms are compatible "market-oriented democracies," that both economies are viable, and that both countries can reconcile cooperation and capitalist competition in ways that are more constructive than destructive.

When such preconditions for a stable new capitalist order are scrutinized closely, it becomes apparent that there are formidable obstacles to success all along the line. That, at least, is the sentiment that comes through most strongly in the commentary of most serious analysts of the U.S.-Japan relationship, whose worst-case scenarios are generally far more persuasive than their best-case projections. That such views come from non-Marxists who profess faith in the capitalist system simply intensifies the impression of impending crisis. The essence of the capitalism problem as it emerges in current literature emphasizes three points: (1) Japan and the United States actually represent different and possibly incompatible models of capitalism; (2) the capitalist systems of both countries, Japan as well as the United States, face unprecedented problems; and (3) the psychological as well as institutional obstacles to creating a harmonious U.S.-Japan condominium are immense.

MODELING CAPITALISM

What the "Japanese model" implies for theories of capitalism is a complex and controversial subject. Where the psychological implications of this debate are concerned, however, it is appropriate to speak in terms of metaphors and shorthands, for in the final analysis this is what tugs at the emotions and boils the blood. Here Adam Smith is the central metaphor or icon, and the argument that the Japanese do not venerate

Adam Smith has become a shorthand for saying that they do not believe in neoclassical economics. In the ideological milieu of 1980s and 1990s America, they practice an un-American kind of capitalism.

Leading Western experts on Japan are quite explicit on this. "We are only beginning to realize," Chalmers Johnson has written, "that Japan has invented and put together the institutions of capitalism in new ways, ways that neither Adam Smith nor Karl Marx would recognize or understand." Ronald Dore, writing in a similar vein in a study of Japanese industrial policy between 1970 and 1980, states that the Japanese "have never really caught up with Adam Smith.... They don't *believe* in the invisible hand." Daniel Okimoto emphasizes the same point:

> Instead of standing back passively and letting Adam Smith's "invisible hand" take its course, they [the Japanese govern-ment] prefer to play a more active role in shaping the directions that the market takes. In doing so, they routinely draw on a broader array of policy instruments than their American counterparts, including coordination of industry-wide consensus on major goals and administrative guidance on specific problems.... In summary, the mixture of market and organization in Japan is strikingly different from that in the United States.

The journalist James Fallows, in an article significantly titled "Playing by Different Rules," summarizes the difference of the two capitalisms more succinctly: "In the U.S. economy the consumer is sovereign; in the Japanese the producer is. It's a fundamental difference."

These observations would be fairly commonplace to Japanese readers. In the West, they have been more provocative—prompting political scientists to reconsider their development models and providing ammunition for the Japan bashers who wish to emphasize that Japan does not play the game "by the same rules" or on a "level playing field." The lexicon by which Japanese and Western capitalisms are distinguished is quite well established by now. Professor Johnson, well-known for his case study of industrial policy under the Japanese Ministry of International Trade and Industry (MITI), contrasts the "plan-rational" Japanese state to the "market-rational" Western model, and also has coined the phrase "capitalist development state" for Japan. Professor Dore refers to the Japanese model as "organized capitalism," or sometimes the "community model." Professor Okimoto and others distinguish between Japan's "relational capitalism" and the more orthodox "transactional capitalism" of the West. Others use other terms, such as "state capitalism," but all tend to agree that Japan is not a market economy in the American sense and that the differences in basic philosophy and practice are conspicuous. A further difference between the two capitalisms is that the U.S. economy is militarized and the Japanese is not.[4]

A standard response to criticisms of Japanese unfairness, endorsed by many Japanese and non-Japanese alike, is that this amounts to little more than scapegoating for America's own economic failures. The targets here are familiar, ranging from managerial greed and shortsightedness in the U.S. corporate structure, to shop-floor inefficiencies, to the huge debts and deficits that were built up under Reaganomics. Critics also point to a range of activities, from joint ventures and overseas investments to participation in economic summitry and competition in common markets, as evidence that in the final analysis there is more congruence than incongruence in the two systems. Still, even as the U.S. and Japanese economies become increasingly interdependent, the differences and antagonisms between them command increasing attention. Neither side seems capable of fundamentally revising its position on Adam Smith.

THE "COMING CRISIS" OF U.S. AND JAPANESE CAPITALISM

It is possible that the vision of American decline may be exaggerated, as more sanguine economists argue, but it is not possible to deny the pervasiveness of the pessimistic forecasts or the role the Japanese are seen playing as the deus ex machina of America's demise. For example, *Forbes*, which is published under the motto "The Capitalist Tool," nicely captured the shock at America's sudden status of dependency with an article entitled "In Japan We (Must) Trust." The article was accompanied by a drawing of the U.S. one-dollar bill in which the portrait of George Washington had been replaced by Mt. Fuji.[5] The cartoon is witty, but no one should underestimate the collective trauma experienced by Americans who woke up one morning to discover that they no longer controlled their own financial markets.

At the same time, however, it is by no means certain that Japan controls its own destiny either. While the admiration that Americans hold for Japan's economic accomplishments is great, and while there is now a cadre of Western experts who do call for abandoning doctrinaire veneration of Adam Smith and "learning from Japan" in a wide range of capitalist practices—industrial policy, management-labor relations, quality control, longer-term horizons, even a greater sense of reciprocal obligations in the Confucian sense—there is a contrary strain of thought which argues that Japanese capitalism too, like its Adam Smith cousin across the Pacific, may be facing a period of prolonged crisis. If this is so, then the question of differing models of capitalism gives way to a larger question of whether capitalism itself is out of control.[6]

Thus, in the very midst of visions of Japan taking over Wall Street and the U.S. Treasury, one also encounters the contradictory image of Japanese economic vulnerability. Lester Thurow's gloomy prognostication, cited earlier, is a representative sample of this. In 1987, for example, *Fortune* devoted a special issue to "Japan's Troubled Future." *Newsweek* concluded that "the outlook for Japan is anything but rosy." Under the large headline "Dark Clouds over Japan's Economy," the *New York Times* featured an article by Ohmae Kenichi devoted to the thesis that "the brilliance of Japan's economic progress could fade as quickly as it appeared." An article by management expert Peter Drucker, another well-known commentator on Japan, nicely captured the paradox of the situation under a headline asking, "Will Its Success Destroy Japan?" By the early 1990s, the bursting of Japan's "bubble economy," which rested on wildly inflated stock and property prices, was taken by many observers as confirmation of these dark scenarios. Like the United States under Reaganomics, staid Japan also was revealed to have gone on an irresponsible speculative binge in the 1980s, with still incalculable consequences for the future. Among other things, the bursting of the bubble revealed not only rampant political chicanery in Japan's ruling conservative party, but also unexpectedly deep involvement in the economy by organized crime.[7]

When one stops to ponder what is happening here, it is no wonder that a kind of psychic blockage appears to have set in on both sides of the Pacific. It was little more than a decade ago that it became commonplace to say that Japan had achieved a "miracle." Now the Japanese and the world at large are told that the miracle has produced a brood of monstrous offspring. Whole industrial sectors are being destroyed by technological advances, the high yen, and competition from the newly industrializing countries (NICs) in Asia. Major portions of the economy are being "hollowed out" as companies move offshore, raising the specter of rising unemployment at home. The giant banks hold loans secured with overpriced property. Security firms have been found to be secretly covering the losses of their richest clients, while ordinary investors see their net worth shrink. Gangsters and corrupt politicians have their hands in the till. And amidst all this, demographic trends are creating a highly gentrified society which soon will place exceptional strains on the economy. By the beginning of the next century, two out of every five Japanese will be on pensions, as opposed to one out of four Americans (U.S. immigration policies account for much of this difference).

All of these developments pose real threats to large numbers of individuals and enterprises, and in such circumstances it would appear to be only rational to try to restore and reinforce the basic virtues and practices that brought Japan success in the first place. Yet it is at precisely this moment that the economic experts appear on the scene with their own peculiar kind of "rationality," look at Japan's ever soaring trade surplus, and demand that the Japanese abandon emphasis on exports, encourage imports, work less, save less, and consume more. The experts may be correct, but common sense and a hitherto successful tradition of hard work and self-restraint insist otherwise.

OBSTACLES TO "JOINT HEGEMONY"

In a recent study analyzing the liberal system of world trade in terms of the "theory of hegemonic stability," Robert Gilpin describes the role of Great Britain and subsequently the United States as the stabilizers of the world system from the nineteenth century to the present. Concerning the present scene, he concludes that "never before has history depended so greatly on cooperation between two economic giants as it now does on continuing agreement between the United States and Japan." This is the basic assumption governing those who advocate the creation of a U.S.-Japan condominium to regulate the world economy, and the language employed in such proposals is sometimes strikingly reminiscent of Schumpeter. C. Fred Bergsten, for example, who has expounded in detail on the necessity of creating a "Group of Two," describes the global economic crisis as a race between "constructive adjustment" and "a highly destructive perhaps irresponsible trade disruption."[8]

To think in terms of "hegemony" in these practical ways instills a consciousness of standing on the hinge of history. We turn to the past for lessons not merely about earlier hegemonic structures, but more dramatically about the rise and fall of hegemonic powers. And we turn to the future with a sharp consciousness of entering a new stage of global power relationships unprecedented in nature, scale, and speed of transformation. Whether looking backward or forward, the vista is discomforting.

Four impressions emerging out of the retrospective view of earlier hegemonies shed particular light on the current U.S.-Japan relationship. First is a clearer historical awareness of the central importance of the Pax Britannica and its succession by a Pax Americana. Second is a keener appreciation of the manner in which Japan was able to exploit its status as a late developer in achieving rapid growth during the heyday of the British as well as American hegemonies. (With this awareness, of course, comes a sobering appreciation among the Japanese that they are no longer in a position to pursue catch-up strategies; on the contrary, henceforth newer late developers will be gaining on *them*.) Third is the general perception that the beginning of the end of the Pax Americana can be dated fairly precisely to the early 1970s. Fourth, and most compelling, is the awareness that in the last hegemonic turnover, stability under the United States was obtained only at a cost of horrendous disorder, upheaval, and conflict—nothing less than the Great Depression, the collapse of the global trade system and emergence of bloc economies, and the abyss of World War II.

Such impressionistic snapshots of past experiences in the creation of hegemonic "stability" call attention to the historical consciousness that makes current contemplation of a new "joint hegemony" so traumatic. In both Japan and the West, there appears to be an almost irresistible impulse to compare the present transitional situation to the 1920s and 1930s, when the stage was being set for the new Pax Americana. The observations of the Harvard-trained economist Nakatani Iwao are typical. "If worse comes to worst," Nakatani warned in 1988, "the whole world may have to endure again the nightmarish experience of the years following 1929. Fierce political confrontation would set nations against each other, curtailing trade across national borders. And should the free world find itself in such awful disarray, the East-West balance could be upset and world peace put at serious risk." In Japan itself, Nakatani continued, anger at U.S. scapegoating and procrastination in setting its own economic house in order could even lead to "the sort of mass hysteria that prevailed on the eve of the war that Japan forced on the U.S. almost a half-century ago."[9]

Nakatani's allusions may be hyperbolic, but they accurately convey the emotionalism that has gripped Japan in response to both trade tensions and the "Black Monday" U.S. stock market plunge of October 19, 1987. The Japanese mass media, for example, has responded to widespread fear of financial instability and protectionist trends in the United States by popularizing the phrase *kaisen zenya*, "the eve of war"— a euphemism that explicitly evokes the period just prior to Pearl Harbor. Fear of a destabilizing "new protectionism" has thus emerged as the negative counterimage to visions of a new hegemonic stability, and trends outside the U.S.-Japan relationship have exacerbated such fears on both sides of the Pacific. Plans for the creation of an integrated European Community for example, simply reinforce anxiety concerning a world once again broken up into protectionist enclaves—where Fortress Europe stands against Fortress America, and Japan in response attempts to mobilize the East Asian NICs into some new version of the old Greater East Asian Co-Prosperity Sphere.[10]

This morbidly fascinating scenario does not end with autarchy, but with militarization—including a substantial push toward independent military capability in Japan. Professor Nakatani's cautionary evocation of the "mass hysteria" of 1940–41 has been echoed by other Japanese who also are not generally associated with alarmism, such as Inoki Masamichi, the former civilian head of the Defense College in Japan. Former U.S. Secretary of Defense Harold Brown voices similar concerns that painful readjustments in the Japanese economy coupled with a sense of vulnerability regarding access to foreign markets and raw materials could "cause a significant Japanese movement toward increased and independent military strength, as happened to an extreme degree in the 1930s." The more popular sensationalist renderings of this scenario, exemplified by Daniel Burstein's widely advertised book *Yen! Japan's New Financial Empire and Its Threat to America*, do not hesitate to postulate a nuclearized Japan thrown into massive rearmament "in the tradition of Japan's many fanatical national campaigns."[11]

It is very easy to transgress the line that separates serious concern about the militarization of Japan from plain unadulterated alarmism. By the same token, it also is easy to misread the more subtle military implications of Japan's emergence as a leader in sophisticated technologies. Although Japan is expected to become the world's third largest military spender, the possibility that it will ever become a military superpower is actually slight: a host of political and psychological factors inside as well as outside Japan dictate against this. At the same time, however, Japan's eminence in critical high-tech areas already is viewed by American strategists as jeopardizing the military supremacy and autonomy hitherto enjoyed by the United States. Thus we find Harold Brown expounding in detail that, as Japan overtakes the United States technologically, Americans can look forward to "a further degradation of the economic base on which rests U.S. geopolitical and military strength, and the ability to operate in the international economic arena." Without privileged access to superior technology, Brown concludes, the very willingness of the United States to exercise international leadership might well decline. If present trends continue—with the United States protecting Japan militarily, the two countries competing in the global marketplace, and Japan assuming the lead in advanced technology— "enormous political, economic, and security tensions" are the only foreseeable result.[12]

These alarming visions of the unravelling of the Pax Americana are the reason that proposals for U.S.-Japan joint hegemony are invariably presented as demanding urgent consideration. Amaya Naohiro, the plain-spoken former MITI official, suggests that a "Pax Ameripponica" might follow a company model, with the United States serving effectively as president and Japan as vice president. *Time* magazine offers "Pax Amerippon" as its neologism, and has Japan serving as the world's banker and the United States as its policeman.[13] Virtually everyone who engages the issue of joint hegemony in depth, however, agrees that drastic structural reform in both countries is an essential prerequisite for creating this new partnership. Needless to say, this will entail great sacrifice. And here, in the ostensible solution to the current dilemma, lies a further crisis.

The sacrifices that both countries are being told they must endure to restore stability to the world economy are bizarrely symmetrical—almost mirror images of each other. The United States, it is argued, must produce more manufactured goods, export more, save more, and consume less. Japan must do the opposite: produce fewer manufactures, export less, save less, consume more. The United States should shake off the invisible hand to some degree and adopt an industrial policy for critical sectors, while Japan should abandon the collusion involved in industrial policy and embrace Adam Smith. The United States must maintain privileged access to superior technology for strategic purposes, while Japan should somehow share such technology.

Business Week has estimated that the U.S. standard of living might drop around 7 percent if proper austerity measures are introduced. In the Japanese case, Bergsten's "Group of Two" proposal calls for structural renovation which would lop $100 billion off Japan's annual trade balance, cause the growth rate of the GNP to drop approximately one percent a year for four or five years, cut the growth rate of the manufacturing sector in half, and force "the Sonys and the Nissans" to retool production for the domestic market or else expand offshore production. He hopes a "housing boom" would absorb much of the shock of this massive transformation.[14]

Creative destruction, it would appear, has begun to inspire its own unique genre of creative writing—for surely these are almost imaginary objectives, given the political and psychological realities of the situation. For the United States and Japan to institute even a diluted version of these draconian agendas would require governments committed to serious structural reform and capable of marshaling a consensus in both the private and public sectors. No one really believes this is possible in either country.

THE RACE PROBLEM

It is in this context of accelerated change in the structures of capitalism that ethnocentrism and racism demand attention. These are not the basic cause of tension and misunderstanding between the United States and

Japan, but neither are they inconsequential. They distort perceptions, inflame emotions, and poison the goodwill that is essential if the two countries are to come to grips with their common problems.

These prejudices have deep roots. The condescension that many Americans still reveal in their dealings with Japanese taps a tradition of white supremacism that has characterized Western expansion from its earliest days. During World War II, the hatred inevitable in war was intensified by anti-Oriental prejudices that had long been festering in American society. That this blatant hatred and contempt disappeared so quickly after Japan's surrender is remarkable and praiseworthy. At the same time, however, Japan's defeat and its subsequent dependence on the United States in a variety of critical areas reinforced the American sense of innate superiority. No reasonable observer can deny that the U.S.-Japan relationship since 1945 has rested on the assumption of in-equality—whether phrased as teacher and pupil, parent and child, leader and follower, or simply superior and subordinate.

For all practical purposes, moreover, Japan since the mid nineteenth century—with the conspicuous exception of the 1930s and early 1940s—has acquiesced in this subordinate status. Indeed, as "late developers" in the world system, the Japanese have had little choice but to acknowledge their country's inferiority to the West in wealth and power (and the knowledge behind these). The love/hate relationship with the West that constitutes such an intriguing pattern in Japan's modern history stems from the inherent ambiguities involved in catching up. Conversely, the condescension that the Japanese themselves frequently display toward other Asians, and nonwhites in general, can be dated fairly precisely from the turn of the century, when it first became clear that the Japanese were outstripping others in Western-style modernization.

Where current U.S.-Japan relations are concerned, Japan's new status as "number one" in the mass media poses a conspicuous psychological challenge, for it signals that both countries must redefine their position—in image and in reality—vis-à-vis one another. Americans cannot be expected to casually cast off the mantle of superiority they have worn for so long, and the Japanese appear to find it exceedingly awkward—and perhaps also frightening—to repudiate the role of subordination and dependency that they have acquiesced to for so long. While Japan is commonly described as a status-oriented or ascriptive society and

America as democratic and egalitarian, in fact both are accustomed to viewing the world in hierarchical terms, and neither is psychologically prepared to act on the basis of genuine equality.

ADMIRATION WITHOUT ENVY

While it is impossible to sum up American attitudes toward Japan in a few words, the phrase "admiration without envy" captures some of the ambivalence Americans and many other foreigners feel toward the Japanese. Nobody denies that there is much to admire in contemporary Japan, but rarely does one hear outsiders expressing a wish to be "like the Japanese." This is intriguing, for it is not a natural response to a Great Power that has been economically and socially successful in so many ways. When China was powerful, its neighbors sought to become "Sinified." During the palmy days of European expansion, non-Europeans often sought to emulate their Western overlords. Even now, in the midst of all its problems, a great many people still desire to become Americanized, or even naturalized Americans.

The other side of this coin is difficult to decipher. Many Japanese seem aware that outsiders tend to admire but not envy them; and in a myriad of different ways, they make it clear to foreigners that it would be futile and presumptuous to even try "becoming Japanese." To what extent this reflects genuine pride, and to what extent it is a defensive response, is difficult to say. For whatever reasons, there exists—like a great wall of glass—an impenetrable but almost invisible psychological barrier between Japan and the rest of the world. This does not mean that the admiration for Japan is shallow, or that foreigners feel there is nothing to learn from Japan. Obviously, the contrary is true. Ronald Dore recently coined the phrase "Japanolatry" to describe the current fascination with Japanese management practices in American business schools, and he and others have written at length about some of the Japanese values that foreigners might do well to emulate: respect for education and public service, for example, as well as a pervasive concern for what Dore calls "fairness and compromise."[15] Foreigners rarely hesitate to express admiration for the diligence and thriftiness of the Japanese, their superb aesthetic sense, the high quality of their products, the relative equality of their income distribution (although this is changing now), and the low crime rates of their cities. Japanese quality-control techniques and labor-management practices are indeed studied as models by non-Japanese.

The list of Japanese qualities that outsiders do not envy or choose to emulate is equally long, however, and might be loosely summarized as the "five withouts." The first of these would be wealth without joy— what Japanese cynics themselves refer to as the "rich country, poor people" phenomenon. The *Wall Street Journal* has conveyed this to its readers under a headline reading "Japan: So Much Yen, So Little Else." *Forbes* carried a similar article entitled "Japan's Economic Masochism." Former Ambassador Edwin Reischauer referred to this phenomenon as Japan's "unhealthy economic growth."[16] Wealth without joy is of course a reference to the concatenation of urban crowding, miserable overpriced housing, poor public facilities, outrageous prices for simple pleasures, and the immensely long commutes that many Japanese in the metropolitan areas have to endure. No middle-class Westerner would choose to live this way—but this is not the end of the matter. In Western eyes, it is not clear why the Japanese themselves do not feel that they now can afford to devote more resources to domestic spending that would alleviate some of these onerous living conditions.

The second "without" is political in nature, namely, the perception that Japan is a country that values equality without genuine freedom. Such criticism obviously reflects the more individualistic nature of Western democratic attitudes, and emerges as a negative response to values that Japanese conservatives extol as great virtues—encapsulated in the emphasis on harmony and group conformity. James Fallows, whose articles from Tokyo in the *Atlantic* attracted quite a bit of attention, argues that the equality of opportunity provided by Japan's educational system is possible largely because of the exclusion of foreigners and the emphasis on a kind of tribal purity in Japan. Japan's "material equality," Fallows points out, coexists with a "proudly hierarchical social system." In conversations among Westerners with considerable experience in Japan, moreover, it is increasingly common these days to hear the argument that Japan's take-off into high growth, beginning with the government of Ikeda Hayato in the early 1960s, has been accompanied by increasing social regimentation. What this might signify for capitalist concepts of bourgeois democracy would constitute a fascinating essay in itself.[17]

Westerners also tend to look upon Japan as a country that promotes education without creativity, and "familyism" without genuine family life. The creativity issue preoccupies Japanese educators themselves, and some of the most caustic comments of Japanese critics have made their way into the U.S. media. Fallows, for example, quotes the distinguished social critic Katō Shūichi to the effect that the Japanese educational system is "well designed to produce very good mediocre people. It's geared to a high level of mediocrity." Western scientists who have taken young Japanese into their laboratories frequently express astonishment and dismay at the seniority system in Japanese universities that stifles initiative and originality at the junior level. The recent award of the Nobel Prize in medicine to Tonegawa Susumu became a classic example to the Western public at large of the Japanese scientist who has to leave Japan to do truly original work.[18]

Where "familyism" without genuine family life is concerned, many Westerners simply find the circumstances under which the average Japanese salaryman is forced to work unacceptable. The company is trumpeted as a family, while the father is rarely able to spend much time with his wife and children. In Western eyes, Japan appears to be a country of formal marital stability but de facto "single-parent" families, where the mother-child relationship is emphasized almost to a point of unnaturalness, while the father is virtually an absentee parent. This seems a mildly amusing irony (or hypocrisy) in a country that talks so much about the "family system." Perhaps more significantly, it also intensifies the Western perception of the Japanese as a people who practice economic masochism and accumulate wealth without joy. From such a perspective, Japanese work habits begin to appear to the outsider to be not so much a virtue as a compulsion, and the accumulation of capital not so much a policy as an obsession.

The fifth and last of the "withouts" concerns Japan's current position in the world, where it enjoys Great Power status without exercising Great Power leadership. Here, perhaps, it would be more accurate to reverse the admiration-without-envy equation. Much of the rest of the world does indeed envy Japan's Great Power status and wealth, but it does not yet admire or even really trust Japan as a world leader. For Japan, this is an awkward and difficult situation. Ever since Japan regained sovereignty in 1952, the country has engaged in foreign relations without really having an independent foreign policy. In part, this reflects the continuing legacy of "subordinate independence" that derives from the peace settlement of 1951–1952 and is built into the uneven nature of the U.S.-Japan military relationship. Beyond this, however, there is a further restraint on Japan's ability to act, and be accepted, as a world leader: no one has forgotten the 1930s and 1940s.

RACIAL THINKING ABOUT JAPAN

It is difficult to gauge the depth of anti-Japanese sentiment among Americans, for public opinion polls tend to be misleading, and sensational quotations in the media do not necessarily reflect popular sentiment. In the late 1980s, for example, it was fashionable for a while for pollsters to ask Americans whether they regarded the Soviet military or Japanese economy as the greater threat to the United States, and responses generally were weighted against Japan. This, then, was headlined as signifying that the Japanese had replaced the Soviets as the primary enemy in American eyes, but a fairer interpretation might have been that this was an intelligent answer to a loaded query. When Americans are asked more open-ended questions concerning what they regard as the greatest problems or threats facing the United States, the focus is almost exclusively on domestic issues, and negative evocation of Japan is negligible. And if one asks ordinary Americans outside of areas conspicuously hurt economically by Japanese imports what they think of the Japanese, the usual response is positive and material: they make good products, they are impressively efficient. The primary reason for Japan's problematic trade surplus with the United States, after all, is that huge numbers of Americans wish to own Japanese products.

Despite current trade frictions between the two countries, there thus remains a reservoir of respect and goodwill toward Japan among ordinary Americans. It is a reservoir capable of being polluted quickly and easily by racial tensions, however, for the reservoir itself rests on historical ground poisoned by centuries of Euro-American prejudice toward Asians and other peoples of color. Here is where the full significance of changing hegemonies in our modern times resides—not just in the end of the Cold War or end of the shortchanged "American Century," but rather in the end of five centuries of Western and Caucasian global domination. The Colombian quincentennial of 1992, from this perspective, actually represented a rare instance in which a grand historical anniversary had serious contemporary meaning. It marked the closure, after a full half millenium, of white supremacism.

This is unsettling for everyone involved, but particularly for white Euro-Americans who never questioned their manifest destiny to dominate the global political economy. "Hegemony" is a benign term, a kid glove of a word that tends to hide the iron fingers of imperialism, colonialism, exploitation, and racial and cultural condescension. Whether rationalized idealistically (the "civilizing mission") or self-righteously (the "white man's burden") or paternalistically (obligation to "little brown brothers") or contemptuously (mocking, for example, the "little yellow men"), the Euro-American global domination that existed from the time of Columbus and his fellow captains to the present rested on the assumption that nonwhites and non-Christians are inherently inferior. This conceit—seemingly confirmed by the physical and material domination of the non-Western world—is not easily dissipated.

It is in this sense that the "Japanese challenge" to the last Western hegemonic power assumes fullest meaning. The contemporary crisis of capitalism coincides with the emergence to global stature not merely of Japan alone, but of a cohort of dynamic Asian economies (South Korea, Taiwan, Hong Kong, Singapore), none of which feels compelled to kowtow to the secular bible of Adam Smith. This is shocking at any number of psychological levels. The "feminine" East (a favorite Euro-American fancy) now threatens Western virility. The "little people" now demand a respect that centuries of condescension have ill prepared most Westerners to give. And in the deepest recesses of collective consciousness, the rise of the new Asian capitalisms inevitably evokes premonitions of the Yellow Peril, a fear which traces back to the Mongol invasions of Europe in medieval times and received its modern nomenclature (as the *Gelbe Gefahr*) from Kaiser Wilhelm II of Prussia in the 1890s.

Initially, nineteenth-century Westerners looked to China, which Napoleon had called the "sleeping giant," as the inevitable leader of a new menace from the East. Following China's humiliating defeat in the first Sino-Japanese war of 1894–1895, however, Japan emerged as indisputably the most dominant of Asian powers—virtually the only Asian nation, in fact, which was neither colonized nor made a virtual neocolony by the Western powers. By their accomplishments in both war and industrialization, the Japanese assumed the mantle of the Yellow Peril from the turn of the century; and by their aggression and rapacity in World War II, they came to graphically exemplify every mean and ominous trait that Westerners had long included in their composite profile of the yellow men. The Japanese economic superpower of the present day, in short, is fundamentally and inescapably different in American eyes than any other capitalist competitor could ever be, for it evokes both vague apprehensions of the Yellow Peril and concrete, hateful memories of the Pacific War.

The Pacific War memories are binational, of course, and politicians and the media in both countries today find it difficult to resist the suggestion that the real victor of that war only will be determined when the outcome of the current trade wars becomes clear. In the United States, however, war memories play a more subtle and pernicious role in shaping contemporary attitudes toward the Japanese. At a most general level, the Japanese can never entirely escape the shadow of Pearl Harbor: they carry the stigma, however strong or faint, of being untrustworthy and treacherous. Beyond this, moreover, it is clear that many of the demeaning racist images that burst so violently to the surface in the cauldron of war still permeate, in softer guise, contemporary American perceptions of the Japanese. These are not the mere metaphors of war, but rather archetypal idioms of anti-Asian racism which war summoned forth and trade wars now threaten to resurrect again. This is the poisoned ground that can all too easily destroy current reservoirs of goodwill between Americans and Japanese.

I have dealt with these idioms of racial hatred and war, on both sides, at some length elsewhere.[19] They tend, in brief, to be formulaic, involving on the Euro-American side depersonalization and dehumanization of the Japanese "Other"; the perception of them as both "little people" of negligible consequence and "supermen" of enormous capability; and the application to them of notions of retarded development, expressed in terms of primitivism, childishness, and mental and emotional instability. All of these archetypal metaphors of prejudice remain imbedded in current American commentary on the Japanese.

Depersonalization, for example, is sometimes done baldly. During the war, this facilitated killing and took the form of "besides they ain't people" jargon (a famous line in the 1943 Hollywood film *Guadalcanal Diary*, spoken by an older marine to the innocent "kid" who asks him how he feels about killing people). In girding for the contemporary trade war, the same crude approach characterizes the treatment of Japanese through the entire length of one of the most spectacular U.S. bestsellers of the early 1990s, Michael Crichton's *Rising Sun* (at a key moment, Crichton's Caucasian hero, an older detective who speaks fluent Japanese and plays the role of mentor to his young and inexperienced white colleague, explains that his Japanese friends "always ask me to remember that they are human beings first, and Japanese second. Unfortunately, in my experience that is not always true").[20]

In a comparable way, subhuman metaphors survive in references to Japanese group behavior as antlike, beelike, herdlike (this is called "team spirit" when done by Americans). Wartime monkeymen have returned as "economic animals" and "predatory economic animals," and animal images also are conveyed by indirect colloquialisms. In the late 1980s, for example, it was fashionable for a while to say, as C. Fred Bergsten phrased it, that the Japanese "only move when hit over the head by a two-by-four." To almost any American, this immediately suggests beating a mule.[21]

"Little yellow men" imagery also retains a relentless hold on the American consciousness, particularly among males of the World War II generation, and frequently spills out as purely instinctive rhetoric. This contributes to the vicious circle of racial contempt, of course, for Japanese who follow such utterances closely are naturally aggrieved and seek to reciprocate. In a perverse way, however, such contempt for the "little people" has served Japan's interests—or at least did so in the 1960s and 1970s—by causing even high-placed Americans to underestimate Japanese capabilities and intentions.

It is a grave mistake to dismiss the pejorative of "the little people" as casual rhetoric or a vulgarism of ignorant and parochial people. It is a classic expression of upper-class white supremacism and reflects the abiding belief that Asians and other peoples of color are inherently smaller in capability and accomplishment than Euro-Americans. Thus, the cosmopolitan Henry Kissinger, while serving in the Nixon administration during the very period when we now look back to see Japan taking off and America stumbling into decline, privately disparaged the Japanese as "little Sony salesmen" and "small and petty bookkeepers."[22] At virtually the same time, Chrysler Corporation's Lee Iacocca, subsequently one of Japan's most relentless critics, told an acquaintance in Texas not to accept a Toyota dealership in 1971 because "we're going to kick their asses back into the Pacific Ocean." Iacocca's hubris was perfectly consistent with the Western tradition of looking down on others, and unwittingly reminiscent of what another unprepared white man had said about the Japanese thirty years previously. When awakened and informed by phone that the Japanese had attacked Singapore, the British colonial governor there responded, "Well, I suppose you'll shove the little men off."[23]

The idiom of "little people" conveys a vague sense of potential for growth, although those who use the term do not usually think in this manner. To them, the little people are inherently dwarfed, permanently inferior. In theory, the capacity for growth is more explicit in another classic racist trope, namely, perception of the Other as a child. In World War II, this emerged as an expression of pure contempt (the "child mind" of the Japanese soldier), while during the Occupation period it evoked paternalistic attitudes on the part of most Americans; it was a rare cartoonist who could resist portraying the Japanese as infants in Uncle Sam's arms, babes in the playpen of Occupation, children in MacArthur's school of democracy, adolescents on the road to a peace treaty.

In present-day U.S.-Japan relations, the child has returned as a ubiquitous figure on both sides, and generally an awkward one, seemingly doomed to remain trapped in prolonged adolescence. Nukuzawa Kazuo of the powerful Keidanren business federation, for example, was quoted in the late 1980s as complaining that "Japan has become a big boy, so it shouldn't be kicked around by the teacher." Lee Iacocca, on the other hand, thought it should be. "We can't go on like this," he wrote about the U.S. relationship with Japan in his best-selling autobiography. "It's time for our government to call the kid in after class and ask him to explain his behavior." Karel von Wolferen, whose extremely critical journalistic writings on Japan have had considerable influence, replayed the same familiar theme when he told readers of *Foreign Affairs* that "it is time for Japan to grow up."[24] Like "little people," the idiom of the child is neither random nor benign nor original. It is one of the most overworked codewords in the lexicon of hierarchical relationships, and even has an explicit place in the so-called recapitulationist theory of pseudoscientific racism in the nineteenth century, whereby nonwhite peoples were declared to be developmentally inferior to whites as the child or infant is to the adult.

This same formulaic imputation of inherently retarded development, and thus permanently subordinate stature and status, also characterizes depiction of the Japanese as primitive and unstable. When making the famous propaganda film *Know Your Enemy—Japan* for the U.S. Army during World War II, Frank Capra instructed his filmmakers to "use the most fantastic Shintō stuff we have available."[25] Such evocations of exotica remain a staple of the contemporary U.S. media, serving to emphasize what is old and alien to Westerners in Japanese culture; as the cartoonists render it, these are really samurai in business suits, geisha with walkmen. This can be entertaining but is equally often misleading, for writers and readers, imagemakers and the consumers of images, are almost irresistibly attracted to what is quaint, curious, extreme, or even aberrant in contemporary Japanese culture. It is well known, for example, that when Emperor Hirohito died in 1989, the Western press corps waited eagerly and in vain for someone to commit suicide before the Imperial Palace. Had but a single person done this, he or she would have become *the* story of the Japanese response, and an icon of the people's primitive soul.

The witting implication of such emphasis on what is traditional or extreme is simple: fundamentally, the Japanese are a premodern people and culture. Or, as framed more academically, they are essentially tribal. Western journalists use the word "tribal" as if they were waving a master's degree in anthropology at their readers, and even writers sympathetic to Japan are drawn to the concept. The opening section of Robert Christopher's well-received book *The Japanese Mind*, for example, is titled "The Japanese Tribe." While it may be possible to pursue this notion with some pretense at scholarly rigor, however, in common usage depiction of the Japanese as tribal serves the specific function of identifying them, once again, as a less developed or less mature people. Such an approach privileges culture over economic and political dynamics in a manner that perpetuates a grossly oversimplified view of the Japanese as a comparatively backward, thoroughly homogeneous, strongly ritualistic (rather than rational) people who are, like any tribe, inherently hostile to outsiders.

This sociocultural caricature is compounded by depiction of the Japanese as also being psychologically unstable as a collectivity. These racial metaphors are all of a piece. The people are little, immature, mentally or emotionally stunted. Primitives behave irrationally, just as children have tantrums. In the racist folk beliefs of World War II, Westerners commonly characterized the Japanese as collectively neurotic, psychotic, schizophrenic, paranoid, fanatic, hysterical, and so on. Today, in the midst of the stress which all nations and societies are experiencing, it is again common practice for Americans to diagnose the Japanese as being subject to peculiar psychoses.

This too emerges at various levels. For example, virtues which Americans used to cherish as the Protestant "work ethic" or the great immigrant "catching up" story, and which are simply identified as a Confucian work ethic where other Asian societies are concerned, become treated as compulsiveness, obsessiveness, fanaticism in Japan. In the current state of affairs, where Japan has emerged as an economic superpower, however, the attributions of psychic instability are more dire. This is what Harold Brown was referring to in his previously quoted warning that the Japanese might attempt to break away from the world order and try to go it alone, as they did in the 1930s. The respected Cold War elder statesman George Ball, writing in the *New York Times* in 1972, was more blunt and colloquial when he warned that "you never know when the Japanese will go ape"—a double-barreled racial image indeed.[26] Once this premise has been accepted, Western imaginations can run wild. "Neo-Nazi" trends are seen bubbling to the surface. Rampant militarism is predicted, even while the same critics belittle Japan's "checkbook diplomacy" and "one-country pacifism." The prospect of Japan breaking away from the Western alliance and attempting to form an independent yen bloc becomes plausible. Japanese indignation at Western economic pressure, the diagnosis goes, may lead Japan's leaders deliberately to throw the capitalist order into disorder—to contrive a "financial pearl Harbor" or (the title of a *New York Times* essay) "economic Pearl Harbor." Henry Scott Stokes, a former *Times* correspondent writing in *Harper's* in the mid 1980s, warns that we should even contemplate "the terrifying prospect of a suicidal nuclear-armed Japan."[27] Clearly, the kamikazes still shriek across the Western consciousness, as they once screamed across Pacific skies, but it is by no means certain where the most dangerous fanaticism and instability really reside.

Even serendipity plays a role in the shaping of racial imagination, and this emerges in two striking ways where Western perceptions of the Japanese are concerned. One is the color yellow itself, which since ancient times has carried essentially negative connotations in Western culture, being originally associated with jaundice and hence symbolically attached to weakness and ipso facto cowardice and other weak traits of character. "I never met a Jap that wasn't yellow," said Popeye in a 1942 animation titled *Scrap the Japs*, and the American politicians and lobbyists who now let "little yellow men" slip from their lips are essentially, well, aping Popeye. The second serendipitous coincidence is the inherent English-language pun in "yen," whereby this becomes not merely Japanese currency but also and simultaneously an intimation of unbridled desire. The previously mentioned book by Daniel Burstein (*Yen! Japan's New Financial Empire and Its Threat to America*) thus represents not a random catchy title, but yet one more formulaic construct for suggesting that the Japanese are, to a greater or lesser degree, collectively unhinged. In this instance, they are lustful, and now have the money to back up their excessive desires and presumedly intend to do so at the expense of Americans and other innocents. In 1980s America, the double entendre on "yen" inspired such mass media titles as "Yen for Power," "A Yen for Your Company," "A Yen for New York," even "I Have a Yen for You."[28]

Preoccupation with this acquisitive yearning of the Japanese has obvious roots in both wartime and contemporary realities. In the war years, lust and possessiveness took the form of literal rape of women throughout Asia, and of the pillage and aggrandizement that Japanese propagandists romanticized as a Greater East Asia Co-Prosperity Sphere. "Yen" had no double meaning to Westerners then, for Japanese money had no meaning to them. Now, of course, Japan's status as an immensely wealthy nation has changed the picture drastically; and because the Japanese leadership has been inept in defining long-term objectives in broad and statesmanlike terms, legitimate questions have arisen concerning the country's ultimate intentions. Japan's voraciously creative capitalism, to return briefly to Schumpeter's phrase, seems to threaten a great deal of destruction to others.

It is at this point that the capitalism problem and race problem merge most forcefully; and when the hard realities of fierce capitalist competition are all accounted for, the fact remains that racial thinking colors the perception of the Japanese threat. The Japanese "superpower" evokes images of the wartime "supermen" who humiliated the Americans at Pearl Harbor and in the Philippines, and the British in Singapore, and seemed for a brief while to possess uncanny skills and unbridled ambitions. And the Japanese mastery of Western science and technology, coupled with the mystique of Asian "secrets" or "miracles" and compounded by the spectacle of dynamic capitalistic economies throughout non-Christian East Asia, summons forth the old bogey of the Yellow Peril. Asians still outnumber Euro-Americans. They still speak languages Westerners cannot speak, and practice social arrangements Westerners have difficulty penetrating or emulating. In Japan's case, they already have begun to pull ahead in certain areas of technology critical to military as well as civilian domination. A half millennium after the European navigators girdled the globe, Asia essentially has caught up with the West in terms of wealth and power; and to fearful Westerners, this is not a welcome attainment of global equality but rather a development full of menace.

RACIAL THINKING IN JAPAN

Where racism is concerned, the United States is the most paradoxical of nations: a country scarred by prejudice and racial conflict, but at the same time more hospitable than any other country to people of differing racial and ethnic backgrounds. In Japan, racial thinking takes very different forms. Where white supremacism is distinguished by its denigration of the other, Japanese racism is much more preoccupied with extolling the unparalleled virtues of being Japanese. The Japanese lexicon of racist epithets is impoverished compared to that found in the United

States—but, at the same time, within Japanese society itself, non-Japanese remain eternal "outsiders." While the language of intolerance may be softer, the practice of exclusion is more severe. This poses serious obstacles to the genuine "internationalization" of Japan.

In one respect, at least, the situation is comparable on both sides. In Japan, as in the United States, current tensions and insecurities have rekindled racial attitudes reminiscent of the war years. Three aspects of this are especially noteworthy: a fixation on the alleged homogeneity, purity, and uniqueness of the Japanese; a perception of Westerners as "demonic others," powerful and threatening but also potentially protective and beneficent; and a vision of a world order in which each race and nation must assume its "proper place." Of these, the first constitutes the most important and potentially harmful element in contemporary Japanese racial thinking.

Emphasis on purity and homogeneity is rooted in ancient ritual and religion in Japan (and elsewhere as well, although such comparisons are not part of the Japanese discourse). The modern fixation on this as a unique and quintessential aspect of the Japanese national character, however, is best understood as a defensive response to the material and psychological threat of the West. It is a product of ideological cultivation, rather than an inevitable cultural legacy, and was most sedulously pumped up in a veritable avalanche of nationalistic texts, exhortations, and slogans in the years between the Great Depression and Japan's surrender. Thus, the notorious official tract known as *Cardinal Principles of the National Entity* (*Kokutai no Hongi*), issued in 1937, took great pains to indoctrinate the Japanese about the "pure and clear state of mind that belongs intrinsically to us as subjects" and "our national character that is cloudless, pure, and honest." The code word that came to embody these sentiments was *Yamato*, referring to the mythohistoric site of the founding of Japan's imperial line by a purportedly divine descendent of the Sun Goddess. From this came the evocative wartime designation of the Japanese as the "Yamato race" (*Yamato minzoku*), imbued with a pure and indomitable "Yamato spirit" (*Yamato damashii*).

The connotations of these affirmations of purity always remained vague at the edges, and their emotional appeal was increased thereby. In ways impossible to fully articulate, it was implied that the Japanese as a people embodied a unique confluence of race, culture, history, and moral integrity that had its origins more than two and a half millennia earlier. This rendered the Japanese homogeneous. It made them, in the popular wartime phrase, a "leading race" (*shidō minzoku*). And it set them apart from all other peoples, including Westerners, whose selfish values of individualism and egoism made one's heart "filthy and impure." By this same line of argument, it should be noted, Japan's wartime propagandists also argued that the heterogeneous and degenerate West would ultimately be incapable of thwarting the divine mission of the Yamato race. Like the Allied intelligence operatives who disastrously underestimated the capabilities of the Japanese "little men" before Pearl Harbor, Japanese military planners, who subscribed to the view of a materialistic and undisciplined Anglo-American antagonist incapable of pulling together for the long fight, were soon, at tragic cost, disabused of this conceit.

Many of these same sentiments have resurfaced, with some cosmetic surgery, in contemporary Japan. They are most conspicuous in the so-called *Nihonjinron* phenomenon—the seemingly interminable "discussion of being Japanese" that has dominated pop-culture discourse for a decade or so. No matter what intellectual level they occur at, these discussions share the common feature of attempting to factor out what it is that sets Japan and the Japanese apart from all other countries, races, and cultures. The crudest claims to uniqueness have brought international ridicule upon Japan, although sometimes they are more crafty than dumb. At one time or another in recent years, for example, the Japanese have declared that their snow, intestines, baseballs, and soil all have unique qualities (thus rationalizing import restrictions on skis, beef, and baseball bats, and exclusion of foreign contractors on domestic construction projects). As a whole, however, the *Nihonjinron* preoccupation with national uniqueness is more serious and intellectually pretentious, and the list of Japanese/non-Japanese antonyms that has emerged from these "dialectics of difference" is quite extraordinary. As but one among many lists, for example, the Japan scholar Peter Dale has identified these Japan-versus-West "principles of indigenous efflorescence" in the *Nihonjinron* literature: particularity-uniqueness versus universality; homogeneity versus heterogeneity; relativism versus absolutism;

harmony and continuity versus rupture; nature versus artifice; phenom-
enalism and concreteness versus abstraction; receptive/reactive versus
denotative/active; closed versus open.[29]

While it is true that some contributions to these discussions are critical
of Japanese values and practices, the overall thrust is to emphasize what
makes the Japanese not merely fundamentally different from others but
superior as well. Once again, as happened in a less open and democratic
milieu a half-century ago, in the midst of intense expansion abroad the
Japanese have turned inward to examine and extol the national soul. It
is not really surprising to find them doing so. To take the phrase from
Schumpeter with which this essay began, the affirmation of unique
Japanese qualities can be seen as a psychological as well as intellectual
response to the creative destruction of the present day. On the one hand,
it reflects pride in the creativity that brought Japan from defeat and
destruction to a pinnacle of economic power. On the other hand, it is
unmistakably also a search for something unchanging in a wildly changing world, a search for permanent values in a materialistic and appall-
ingly destructive environment. More subtly, perhaps, it is also an attempt
to privilege "culture" in a world that now seems driven by almost
irresistible economic determinism—to dispel, as it were, the nagging
image of the "economic animal," while at the same time finding reassur-
ance that the "unique" qualities of the Japanese will enable them to rise
and never fall—to do, that is, what no other Great Power has ever done.

Such a quest for certainty is a familiar phenomenon in today's world,
where neonationalist and fundamentalist movements have erupted everywhere, but it imposes a sense of profound separation between Japan and
the rest of the world. And it shades easily into racist thinking. Toward
white Americans, and Caucasians in general, Japanese attitudes remain
ambivalent. Even during the Pacific War, the Caucasian enemy was
caricatured by an ambiguous symbol—the demon—which in Japanese
folklore is most often portrayed as a figure that can harm but also help
the community (just imagine the ferocious guardian deities in Japanese
temple gates). Westerners always have conformed to this image in the
Japanese consciousness, posing threats but also, often simultaneously,
bringing to the Japanese wonderful intellectual, cultural, and material
gifts. When the American demon of the war years became the guardian
of Japan's postwar recovery and security, the same huge formidable

figure remained: only the horns, as it were, were retracted. Now, with the rise of tensions and vogue of Japan bashing, the more demonic nature of white America draws attention. In response to this, the Japanese in turn fall back on another of their cherished self-caricatures by depicting themselves as innocent victims.

The truly virulent implications of the mystique of Japanese purity and homogeneity are exposed in Japanese attitudes toward the United States as a heterogeneous society. An unusually vivid expression of this appeared in the *Wall Street Journal* in 1982, when a Japanese official was quoted as stating that "the Japanese are a people that can manufacture a product of uniformity and superior quality because the Japanese are a race of completely pure blood, not a mongrelized race as in the United States." Since that time, Japanese disdain for ethnically pluralistic societies in general and peoples of color in particular has been exposed on numerous occasions. Some of this is rhetorical, as in the case of former Prime Minister Nakasone Yasuhiro's denigration of American blacks and Hispanics in September 1986. More sobering yet is evidence that these biases are also influencing Japanese overseas activities at the grass-roots level. A detailed study of employment patterns in Japanese auto firms in the United States, for example, reveals a fairly consistent pattern of discrimination against blacks in shop-floor representation, auto dealerships, and the selection of company sites. They are hardly alone in practicing discrimination, but that is small comfort.[30]

In 1942–43 a minor section in the Japanese bureaucracy produced a mammoth secret document, only discovered a short while ago, entitled *An Investigation of Global Policy with the Yamato Race as Nucleus.* The guiding concept in this document was "proper place," which in practice meant a global division of labor with the Japanese firmly ensconced as the "leading race" in Asia. The document was vague on the world beyond Asia (although it did project the Japanese in Australia, New Zealand, India, Afghanistan, Iran, Iraq, and the Soviet Union east of Lake Baikal), but it did make amply clear that (1) in Japanese thinking, de facto equality among peoples and nations was not feasible, and (2) wartime Japan's conception of long-term hegemony over Asia was dictatorial and exploitative, and bore only the most tenuous relation to the public rhetoric about "co-prosperity."[31]

Times have changed dramatically since then, but proper-place thinking remains central to today's problems. The phrase itself emerges vaguely in current Japanese comments on the future division of labor in the world economy, but what this really means is still anyone's guess. As yet, there is not much reason to believe that the Japanese or Americans or anyone else really have the vision and ability to redefine "proper place" in a way that will contribute to more genuine equality and reciprocity within the capitalist system. That remains the most formidable of the creative challenges.

NOTES

1 Joseph A. Schumpeter, *Capitalism, Socialism, and Democracy* (New York: Harper and Row, 1942).
2 Robert C. Christopher, *The Japanese Mind* (New York: Ballantine, 1984), p. 309; Thomas McGraw, ed., *America Versus Japan* (Cambridge, Mass.: Harvard Business School, 1987); *Sydney Morning Herald* (Aug. 13, 1987); *New York Times* (April 5, 1987); George Packard, "The Coming U.S.-Japan Crisis," *Foreign Affairs* 66 (Winter 1987/88), p. 364; Lester Thurow, "The Whole World Has That Tired, Run-Down Feeling," *Washington Post Weekly* (Aug. 10, 1987); *Time* (April 13, 1987), p. 32 for Prestowitz.
3 *Business Week* (April 20, 1987), p. 37 for Abe Shintarō; *Newsweek*, international edition (April 13, 1987); Haruhiro Fukui, "Too Many Captains in Japan's Internationalization," *Journal of Japanese Studies* 13, no. 2 (Summer 1987): 359–81.
4 See the following three contributions by Chalmers Johnson: "How to Think about Economic Competition from Japan," *Journal of Japanese Studies* 13, no 2 (Summer 1987): 420; "The Japanese Political Economy: A Crisis in Theory," *Ethics and International Affairs* 2 (1988): 79–97; and his widely cited monograph *MITI and the Japanese Miracle* (Stanford, Calif.: Stanford University Press, 1982). See also Ronald Dore, *Flexible Rigidities: Industrial Policy and Structural Adjustment in the Japanese Economy, 1970–1980* (London: Althone Press, 1987); Daniel Okimoto, "Outside Trading: Coping with Japanese Industrial Organization," *Journal of Japanese Studies* 13, no. 2 (Summer 1987): 383–414, esp. 396–97; James Fallows in *The Atlantic* (Sept. 1987): 22–32.
5 *Forbes* (Sept. 21, 1987), pp. 32–34.
6 Compare Robert L. Heilbroner, "The Coming Meltdown of Traditional Capitalism," *Ethics and International Affairs* 2 (1988): 63–77.
7 *Fortune* (March 30, 1987); *Newsweek*, international edition (April 13,

1987); *New York Times* (July 27, 1987); *Financial Review* (Australia; Sept. 10, 1987), for Drucker. On the bubble economy, see Christopher Wood, *The Bubble Economy: Japan's Extraordinary Speculative Boom of the 80's and the Dramatic Bust of the 90's* (New York: Atlantic Monthly Press, 1992).

8 Robert Gilpin, *The Political Economy of International Relations* (Princeton: Princeton University Press, 1987); C. Fred Bergsten,"Economic Imbalances and World Politics," *Foreign Affairs* 65, no. 3 (Spring 1987): 770–94, esp. 773–74.

9 Nakatani Iwao, "Walking the Tightrope," *Look Japan* (Jan. 1988), pp. 11–13.

10 See the several articles on this subject in the *New York Times* (Oct. 23, 24, 1988).

11 Inoki Masamichi is quoted in the *Sydney Morning Herald* (Aug. 13, 1987). For Brown, see *US/Japan Economic Agenda* (a newsletter issued by the Carnegie Council on Ethics and International Affairs, New York), vol. 6 (July 1987). Burstein's 1988 book was published by Simon and Schuster and promoted with a costly mailing campaign: the quotation is from the apocalyptic preface.

12 Brown, *US/Japan Economic Agenda*.

13 Amaya Naohiro, "America in Decline?" *Look Japan* (May 1988), pp. 4–6; "From Superrich to Superpower," *Time* (July 4, 1988), pp. 28–31.

14 "Wake Up, America," special issue of *Business Week* (Nov. 16, 1987); see also the "Can America Compete?" special issue of *Business Week* (April 20, 1987); Bergsten, "Economic Imbalances and World Politics," pp. 771 and 781–82.

15 Ronald Dore, *Taking Japan Seriously: A Confucian Perspective on Leading Economic Issues* (Stanford, Calif.: Stanford University Press, 1987); "Japanolatry" appears on p. 85.

16 The *Wall Street Journal* article is cited in James Fallows, "Playing by Different Rules," *Atlantic* (Sept. 1987), p. 29; *Forbes* (Sept. 21, 1987); for the Reischauer statement, see Packard, "The Coming U.S.-Japan Crisis," p. 350

17 James Fallows, "Gradgrind's Heirs," *Atlantic* (March 1987), pp. 16–24. For extended critiques of contemporary Japanese society, see Gavan McCormack and Yoshio Sugimoto, eds., *Democracy in Contemporary Japan* (Armonk, N.Y.: M. E. Sharpe, 1986); Rokurō Hidaka, *The Price of Affluence: Dilemmas of Contemporary Japan* (New York: Kodansha International, 1984).

18 Fallows, "Gradgrind's Heirs"; see also "Japan Asks Why Scientists Go

West to Thrive," *New York Times* (Nov. 8, 1987), relating the creativity issue to Tonegawa's Nobel Prize.

19 See the preceding essay on "Race, Language, and War in Two Cultures," and my *War Without Mercy: Race and Power in the Pacific War* (New York: Pantheon, 1986).

20 Michael Crichton, *Rising Sun* (New York: Ballantine, 1992), p. 371. Whereas Crichton's two protagonists, the wise cop and the novice, are both Caucasian, the ballyhooed Hollywood version of *Rising Sun*, in a brilliant racist stroke, casts the younger man as an African American—still learning from the white man, but clearly identified with him as an American and fellow "human being," and not with the Japanese as another people of color. The analogue to this in World War II Hollywood war films was the so-called multiethnic platoon, in which Americans of diverse racial and religious backgrounds—although almost never including Asian Americans—came together as comrades with a common purpose. Crichton's contrast of individualized "Americans," as opposed to the depersonalized and dehumanized Japanese, also follows World War II formulas in essentially excluding Japanese Americans from the "American" identity. In *Rising Sun*, Japanese Americans are virtually indistinguishable from the Japanese, and actively serve Japan in the vicious economic war against the United States. General John De Witt, the commander of the U.S. Western Defense Command, who successfully agitated for the incarceration of Japanese Americans after Pearl Harbor on the grounds that "a Jap's a Jap," would have been pleased.

21 See *Time* (April 13, 1987), p. 38, for Bergsten. For a statement by Sir Roy Denman, the European Community's ambassador to Washington, explicitly criticizing this "two-by-four" mindset, see the *New York Times* (Jan. 17, 1988).

22 Marvin Kalb and Bernard Kalb, *Kissinger* (New York: Little, Brown, 1974), p. 255; quoted in Kenneth B. Pyle, "In Pursuit of a Grand Design: Nakasone Betwixt the Past and Present," *Journal of Japanese Studies* 13, no. 2 (Summer 1987), p. 248.

23 For Iacocca, see David Halberstam, *The Reckoning* (New York: William Morrow, 1986), p. 511; for the Singapore episode, see Dower, *War Without Mercy*, p. 100.

24 *New York Times* (April 5, 1987) for Nukuzawa; Lee Iacocca, *Iacocca: An Autobiography* (New York: Bantam, 1984), p. 317; Karel G. van Wolferen, "The Japan Problem," *Foreign Affairs* 65 (Winter 1986/87), pp. 288–303, esp. 301.

25 William J. Blakefield, "A War Within: The Making of *Know Your Enemy—Japan,*" *Sight and Sound International Film Quarterly* 50, no. 2 (Spring 1983), p. 133.

26 Ball's comment appeared in the *New York Times* (June 25, 1972), and is quoted in Pyle, "In Pursuit of a Grand Design," p. 248. For Harold Brown, see notes 11 and 12 above.

27 Ian Buruma offers a hyperbolic commentary on "neo–Nazi" trends in Japan in "A New Japanese Nationalism," *New York Times Magazine* (April 12, 1987). The numerous examples of U.S. apprehension concerning Japanese militarism include Packard, "The Coming U.S.-Japan Crisis," pp. 353, 356–57; *Forbes* (Jan. 26, 1987), pp. 32–33; *World Press Review* (Nov. 1987), p. 47; Christopher, *The Japanese Mind,* ch. 14; Henry Scott Stokes, "Lost Samurai: The Withered Soul of Postwar Japan," *Harper's* (Oct. 1986), pp. 55–63. The *New York Times* approached the fiftieth anniversary of Pearl Harbor with an unusually long op-ed piece by Karel van Wolferen entitled "An Economic Pearl Harbor?" (Dec. 2, 1991).

28 "Yen for Power" was the dramatic cover story of the *New Republic,* Jan. 22, 1990. "A Yen for Your Company" was the cover of *Venture,* July 1988, in which "I Have a Yen for You" appeared. "A Yen for New York" was the cover story of the Jan. 16, 1989 issue of *New York* magazine.

29 Peter N. Dale, *The Myth of Japanese Uniqueness* (New York: St. Martin's, 1986), p. 51; "dialectics of difference" is Dale's phrase. For other extended critiques of *Nihonjinron,* see Ross Mouer and Yoshio Sugimoto, *Images of Japanese Society: A Study in the Structure of Social Reality* (London: Kegan Paul, 1986); also Harumi Befu, "Internationalization of Japan and Nihon Bunkaron," in Hiroshi Manari and Harumi Befu, eds., *The Challenge of Japan's Internationalization: Organization and Culture* (New York: Kodansha International, 1983), pp. 232–66.

30 *Wall Street Journal* (Nov. 19, 1982); Robert E. Cole and Donald R. Deskins, Jr., "Racial Factors in the Employment Patterns of Japanese Auto Firms in America," *California Management Review* 31, no. 1 (Fall 1988), pp. 9–22. A racial-distance survey conducted by the late Wagatsuma Hiroshi reveals that Japanese, like white Americans, rank people of color, including other Asians, as the least desirable neighbors and associates: Wagatsuma Hiroshi, *Nihonjin to Amerikajin—Koko ga Ōchigai* (Tokyo: Nesco, 1985), p. 246.

31 The document is analyzed in Dower, *War Without Mercy,* pp. 262–90.

11

Postscript: Two Reflections on the Death of the Shōwa Emperor

WHEN EMPEROR HIROHITO, monarch of the extraordinary Shōwa era, entered his final illness in 1987, all Japan became mesmerized by the death watch. The emperor's reign, which began on December 25, 1926, and finally ended on January 7, 1989, enfolded the lives of most of his subjects. Tens of millions of Japanese had first known him as their god emperor of war, the ramrod-straight young Son of Heaven riding his famous white horse. The sovereign in whose name one was asked to die. And tens of millions of other Japanese, born after 1945, knew him as a small, shuffling man in civilian suits who had witnessed a great deal, said precious little, and grown old as Japan grew wealthy.

When the emperor died, no Japanese under sixty-three years of age had ever known another monarch. His passing was not merely the end of an epoch that had embraced war, defeat, occupation, uncertainty, and prosperity. It also was an occasion that almost inescapably forced his subjects to reflect on their own lives, and what drastic changes they had witnessed and endured. When the emperor died, people saw their own lives passing before their eyes. This does not happen in countries with presidential elections every four years, and more than eight years of celestial reign forbidden.

The two pieces that follow were written for readers in Japan as the emperor lay dying. One (my files indicate) was sent on December 7, 1987, the other a day later. We Americans and Japanese seem to be trapped by our anniversaries.

The Emperor in
War and Peace:
Views from the West

WHEN EMPEROR HIROHITO visited the United States in 1975, he left behind several different impressions.

Many Americans, for example, were simply astonished to learn that one of the great leaders of World War II was still alive. After all, the war leaders Americans were most familiar with—Roosevelt, Truman, Churchill, Hitler, Stalin, DeGaulle, and Chiang Kai-shek—were already all gone from the scene.

At the same time, there was also a rather philosophical response to the emperor's visit at the popular level. There is a popular folk saying in English to the effect that "time heals all wounds," and the 1975 visit seemed to be a fine example of this. The same individual who had been the sovereign of a hated enemy thirty years earlier was now the honored leader of an indispensable ally.

Another, more personal impression called attention to the emperor's modesty, physical frailty, and middle-class tastes. When Emperor Hirohito visited Disneyland (and took pleasure in the receipt of a Mickey Mouse wristwatch), the contrast to the old image of the "god-emperor" Americans recalled from the war years became very vivid indeed.

Perhaps the greatest impression of all from the 1975 visit, however, concerned the emperor's most famous utterance. When asked by American reporters how Japanese values had changed in the thirty years since the war, he replied that fundamentally nothing had changed. The journalistic account of his response runs roughly as follows: "I realize that various people have advanced any number of opinions about this since the termination of the war. From the broadest point of view, however, I do not think there has been any change between the prewar and postwar periods" (*Sensō shūketsu irai, iroiro no hito ga ikutsumo no iken o nobeta koto o shōchi shite imasu. Shikashi hiroi kanten kara miru naraba, senzen to sengo no henka ga aru to wa omotte imasen*).

This is apparently the sort of vaguely mystical answer that pleases Japanese conservatives, but it had a divisive effect in the United States. To some Americans, the emperor's comments were intriguing. He himself, after all, was living proof of the enduring links between the presurrender and postsurrender periods. To others, the emperor's statement was irrational, for it ignored the significant differences between the militaristic values of the early Shōwa period and the more democratic and peaceful values of Japan after 1945. To yet others, the statement was ominous. If nothing had really changed, this could only mean that neither the emperor nor his subjects had learned anything from the repression and aggression of the first two decades of Shōwa.

Such splits in American opinion concerning the emperor are not new. Even during the bitter years of the Pacific War, Americans were divided in their views of Emperor Hirohito and the Japanese imperial institution in general.

The harshest Western critics of the emperor system during the war came from many different backgrounds. They included well-known scholars of Asia such as T. A. Bisson, William Johnstone, and the Englishman Owen Lattimore; lawyer-bureaucrats such as Dean Acheson; poet-bureaucrats such as Archibald MacLeish; missionary-writers such as Willard Price and Willis Lamott; and the great majority of the American and British media. As Professor Johnstone summarized the critics' position in 1944, the emperor was the ideological nucleus of all that was archaic, feudalistic, autocratic, and totalitarian in Japan. He was the "keystone of the militarist-imperialist system."

Willard Price, a prolific American writer who lived in Japan for almost twenty years before the war, was more slanderous. In a popular 1945 book entitled *Japan and the Son of Heaven*, Price wrote rather affectionately about Emperor Hirohito as an individual, but he devoted many pages to attacking the modern emperor system in general. Price argued that contrary to official propaganda, the imperial line had been "broken" many times in the course of history. Furthermore, the Japanese people had shown scant respect for their emperors prior to the Meiji Restoration. With considerable validity, Price pointed out that ultranationalistic emperor worship was a *modern* ideology in Japan. He also took pleasure in arguing that the propagation of the imperial line had involved a great deal of incest, and that both the Meiji and Taishō emperors were "illegitimate" offspring.

In the view of this widely read ex-missionary, the best way to destroy the imperial mystique in wartime Japan would be for the United States to bomb the imperial palace, the Ise Shrine, and Yasukuni Shrine. Many Christians—although by no means all—supported this position.

The media and general public in wartime America also supported a hard-line approach. *Fortune* magazine, one of the most sophisticated U.S. publications, stated the antiemperor position strongly in its issue of February 1942. "The world can never again be free from the fear of ambush unless the imperial throne is rooted out," *Fortune* declared, "and with it destroyed the sinister phenomenon of a people without a conception of their own slavery."

Public opinion polls in the United States during the war tended to focus more on Emperor Hirohito personally than on the throne in general. They reflected some popular confusion concerning the emperor's name as well as his role, but were generally severe concerning how he should be treated after Japan's defeat.

A poll conducted in April 1944, for example, found that over 44 percent of Americans believed that the emperor was "the only Japanese god." Nineteen percent responded that he was "only a figurehead, except in religion," 16 percent believed he was "the dictator" of Japan, and 6 percent stated that the emperor was to Japan "what the King is to England."

In a rather amusing poll conducted in May 1945, 54 percent of Americans were able to identify the emperor by name ("Hirohito"), but 40 percent believed his name was Chiang Kai-shek, Yokohama, Hara Kiri,

Fujiyama—or simply something unpronounceable. One percent thought Tito (which rhymes with Hirohito) was the emperor of Japan.

Less amusing were the views expressed about how Emperor Hirohito should be treated after Japan's surrender. From 1943 to 1945, a fairly consistent one-third of Americans polled supported the emperor's execution after the war. In a poll conducted on May 29, 1945, responses to the question "What do you think we should do with the Japanese Emperor after the war?" were as follows:

Execute him	33%
Let court decide his fate	17
Keep him in prison the rest of his life	11
Exile him	9
Do nothing, he's only a figurehead for war lords	4
Use him as a puppet to rule Japan	3
No opinion and miscellaneous answers	23

In an often cited Gallup poll of June 29, 1945, 70 percent of Americans favored the execution or harsh punishment of Emperor Hirohito.

In Great Britain, popular sentiment at war's end also was strongly hostile to the emperor. Immediately after the Japanese surrender, 67 percent of Britons polled agreed Emperor Hirohito should be deprived of his throne, and only 22 percent believed he should be allowed to remain as sovereign (the remaining respondents had no opinion).

More striking than such predictable antiemperor sentiments in the midst of a bitter war, however, is the persistence of proemperor sentiments in both American and British ruling circles. In both countries, for example, it was forbidden to attack the emperor in official propaganda. When the aerial bombing of Japan commenced, U.S. planners explicitly excluded the imperial palace and imperial shrines as targets (the palace was partially damaged by mistake). Leaflets urging the Japanese to surrender, which U.S. planes dropped on Japanese cities in the final months of the war, took care to attack the Japanese military "high command" rather than the emperor.

The rationale behind this cautious policy was threefold. Direct attacks on the palace or imperial shrines, it was believed, would simply increase the will of the Japanese to fight to the bitter end. A secret report prepared

by the U.S. Office of Strategic Services (OSS) in July 1944, even before
the air raids against Japan began, expressed this in the following terms:

> Because of the Emperor's position as the symbol of Japanese
> divinity, it is believed that an attack on the Palace, rather than
> creating panic, would stimulate an offensive spirit among the
> people and increase effort put into war production, since the
> attack would tend to outrage the loyalty to the Emperor felt
> personally by most Japanese and to decrease any existing
> tendency toward acceptance of defeat. This would reinforce
> the political position of fanatic leaders preferring to "fight to
> the death."

Following from this line of reasoning, the advocates of a more conciliatory policy toward the emperor also argued that the emperor commanded
such respect and obedience in Japan that his cooperation would be
essential in bringing about a surrender. Finally, it was argued that the
throne was a "neutral" force in Japan, capable of being manipulated for
peaceful purposes as easily as it had been manipulated for war.

In the United States, these arguments were most forcefully expressed
by former ambassador to Japan Joseph Grew and the so-called Japan
Crowd in the State Department, as well as by social scientists such as
Clyde Kluckhohn in the Office of War Information. In Great Britain,
the Foreign Office as a whole, led by the scholar-diplomat George
Sansom, was quite consistent in its support for the throne.

Conservatives in both Japan and the West tend to look back on these
wartime U.S. and British supporters of the throne as men of wisdom
and foresight, but in many cases their position was Janus-faced. On the
one hand, they argued that the emperor was the essential "stabilizing
power" in Japan. At the same time, however, they frequently spoke of
the emperor in disparaging terms as a "puppet," "tool," "figurehead,"
or "mouthpiece" of the dominant political forces.

This point is often forgotten: the defense of the Japanese imperial
institution by certain Anglo-Americans during and after the Pacific
War usually rested on the argument that the Japanese were politically
immature. Thus, in May 1945, when Ambassador Grew and the Japan
Crowd were attempting to persuade President Truman to make a state-

ment about preserving the throne after the war, Grew told the president that the throne was undeniably one of the "relics of feudalism" in Japan. "From the long range point of view," he continued, "the best we can hope for in Japan is the development of a constitutional monarchy, experience having shown that democracy in Japan would never work."

George Sansom and the British Foreign Office similarly opposed fundamental reformist policies before and after the surrender because they did not believe democracy had any real chance of taking root in Japan. The generally contemptuous attitude of British diplomats toward Japan was vividly expressed in an October 1945 dispatch about the Shidehara cabinet. "They are as little fitted for self-government in a modern world as any African tribe," the British representative in Tokyo reported, "though much more dangerous."

It was such ethnocentric arrogance as this which prompted Sansom to call the 1947 constitution "idiotic." Such Anglo-American officials, whose contacts in Japan were confined to upper-class circles, simply believed that the average Japanese was incapable of taking charge of his or her own life. More radical Westerners, such as Bisson and Lattimore, had greater faith in the ability of middle- and lower-class Japanese to govern themselves.

Despite wartime support for the emperor on the part of many U.S. and British officials, however, it was by no means certain that Emperor Hirohito personally, or the throne in general, would be supported by the Allies after Japan surrendered. Before and after the surrender, China, Australia, and New Zealand all demanded that the emperor be tried as a war criminal. An early postsurrender British document listed the emperor as a war criminal. The U.S. Senate and House of Representatives approved a joint resolution to this same effect in September 1945. As late as October 6, 1945, the official U.S. policy toward Japan still spoke of eventually bringing Emperor Hirohito to trial for war crimes.

It was in this context that two significant developments occurred. General Douglas MacArthur dramatically threw his personal support behind the emperor. And Emperor Hirohito became—contrary to almost everyone's expectations—personally and intimately associated with genuinely "democratic" developments.

General MacArthur's support of the emperor is well known, but usually in a highly romanticized form. The common story, which derives primarily from the general's own extremely unreliable memoirs (plus reminiscences by some of his less than trustworthy former aides) is that when MacArthur and the emperor met for the first time on September 27, 1945, the emperor volunteered to assume full responsibility for the war. The general was so impressed by this that he enthusiastically threw his full support behind Emperor Hirohito's continued reign.

This dramatic fable has two flaws. In the first place, MacArthur had resolved to conduct the occupation through the emperor well before he and Emperor Hirohito met. He told this to aides in both Manila and Okinawa before he even set foot in Japan at the end of August 1945. And second, the most trustworthy record we have of the September 27 meeting—which comes from the detailed summary of the emperor's own interpreter, Okumura Katsuzō—has MacArthur doing almost all of the talking, and makes no reference whatsoever to any magnanimous attempt by the emperor to assume responsibility for the war.

Indeed, where MacArthur personally is concerned, the policy of preserving the emperor can be found in recommendations prepared by his intelligence officers in the Southwest Pacific Command over a year before the war ended. A long and little-known confidential analysis dated July 1944, for example, concluded that "to dethrone, or hang, the Emperor would cause a tremendous and violent reaction from all Japanese. Hanging of the Emperor to them would be comparable to the crucifixion of Christ to us. All would fight and die like ants...." MacArthur's intelligence advisers concluded their July 1944 report with this scenario: "Once the Tokyo militarists are dead, once the armed forces are destroyed and a liberal government formed under the Emperor, the Japanese people—sadder, fewer, and wiser—can begin the reorientation of their lives."

The unreliability of MacArthur's famous memoirs is apparent in various errors pertaining to the emperor. The general incorrectly stated, for example, that Emperor Hirohito had been exonerated of war crimes by the United States prior to September 27. This is untrue. MacArthur's casual pontification is also apparent in his declaration that he met Emperor Hirohito's "father" during the Russo-Japanese War. It was Emperor Meiji, Emperor Hirohito's grandfather, whom he met—no small difference.

Even General MacArthur's avowals of respect for Emperor Hirohito must be taken with a grain of salt. There is no reason to doubt that the general liked the emperor as a person. He did not, however, exaggerate the emperor's personal qualities in private. On the contrary, in private conversations he was quite down-to-earth. For example, MacArthur privately did not even believe that the emperor had been a truly significant contributor to peace. Thus, in January 1946, George Sansom reported to the Foreign Office that MacArthur had confidentially expressed the opinion that the emperor

> had been from the beginning to the end a puppet, a "complete Charlie McCarthy" [the puppet of a very popular American ventriloquist], who had neither begun the war nor stopped it. At every point he had acted automatically on advice and he could not have done otherwise. The Cabinet meeting which ended the war was as much staged as those which began it, though the Emperor was certainly more enthusiastic about the former than the latter.

While MacArthur's veracity as a recorder of history may be dubious, however, his skill as a political manipulator is undeniable. For, by playing on the Japanese ruling groups' fears that the emperor might be indicted as a war criminal or forced to abdicate, the general succeeded in encouraging the emergence of the postwar emperor as a genuinely "democratic" symbol.

In part, to be sure, the unexpected "democratization" of the emperor was a result of his own personal activities. The emperor's famous "declaration of humanness" (*ningen sengen*) of January 1, 1946, was one aspect of this (the necessity of such a "renunciation of divinity" had been suggested in various wartime American writings, including popular writings by Christian spokesmen such as Willis Lamott). More effective by far in humanizing the "divine emperor," however, were Emperor Hirohito's unprecedented and exceedingly awkward visits among the common people. His very vulnerability in ordinary society made him an appealing and rather sympathetic figure—not only in Japan, but in the eyes of many Westerners as well.

The apogee of the emperor's metamorphosis from a militaristic to a democratic symbol, however, occurred with the promulgation of the new constitution in 1946. What the constitution did, in a single bold stroke, was associate the "symbolic" emperor with antimilitarism, as embodied in Article Nine, and with a highly idealistic guarantee of human rights. MacArthur's political genius lay in not only promoting this three-cornered linkage, but in correctly anticipating that it would gain the support of the great majority of Japanese people.

This intimate association of the emperor with the progressive reforms of the early postsurrender period gave the lie to most of the wartime American predictions. Not only the critics but also some of the supporters of the emperor miscalculated the extent to which he could become an integral part of meaningful "democratization." And once Emperor Hirohito became associated with the postwar reforms, the fear and hatred most Westerners had held toward him disappeared. After 1946, the emperor attracted little comment beyond Japan's shores.

In the years following the Occupation, the image of the emperor and imperial family became diluted in the West—in much the same way that it was diluted in Japan. He became, that is, less a symbol of democratic ideals and more of a symbol of bourgeois family life and middle-class pursuits. Thus it was that when the emperor visited the United States in 1975, he was perceived as an elderly and generally likable gentleman—with limited personal charisma, no great democratic idealism, and only a musty aura of past imperial glories.

It is in this sense that Emperor Hirohito's enigmatic 1975 words about an unchanging Japan ring true, at least insofar as he personally is concerned. Japanese conservatives like to describe the emperor as the "mirror of Japan," meaning that he is supposed to reflect the traditional virtues of the country. To more skeptical Westerners, however, the Shōwa emperor has been a "mirror" in a more literal sense—reflecting ultranationalism when the militarists were in power, democracy when genuine reformism was taking place, and uneventful bourgeois complacency during the era of economic growth and consumerism that marks the last two decades of Shōwa.

In Western eyes, this is quite fascinating—and ominous. It is fascinating because no other country in the world still has an emperor, to say nothing about a "bourgeois emperor." The very phrase, to use a fancy word, seems to be an oxymoron. And it is ominous because the emperor symbol obviously remains malleable, and thus still appears capable of being manipulated in dangerous directions by future ideologues.

To judge from recent developments surrounding the emperor's illness, the Japanese response to the end of the Shōwa period in the future may startle and even alarm many Western observers. There are two particular developments to look out for here.

First, when Emperor Hirohito passes away, it seems predictable that many Westerners will be surprised by the emotional intensity and highly religious and mystical nature of the funeral rites for the departed sovereign, the ascension ceremonies for his successor, the adoption of a new reign name (*gengo*), and so on. They will learn that the basic ceremonies that accompany the departure and ascension of the sovereign have not changed substantially since the prewar period, when the emperor was declared "sacred and inviolable." And from all this, they may well conclude that the Japanese sovereign is not just a secular ruler after all; that the declaration of humanness (*ningen sengen*) and middle-class image of recent years were deceptive; and that Japanese values indeed may not have changed all that much since the terrible years of the China and Pacific wars.

The second danger follows from this, and again depends on exactly how the Japanese government and media handle the end of the Shōwa period and transition to a new imperial era. Grief, ritual, and celebration are only natural in such circumstances—but these can easily become perceived in the West as yet one more reaffirmation of Japanese "uniqueness," "homogeneity," "spiritual purity"—and, implicitly, racial and cultural superiority vis-à-vis the rest of the world. The Western media today already depicts Japan as a country torn between "internationalization" and Nihonjinron-style affirmations of unique and superlative national characteristics. If official and popular responses to the "end of Shōwa" tend to reaffirm the impression of Japanese exceptionalism, this could have the exceedingly unfortunate consequence among Japanese and non-Japanese alike of stimulating a heightened impression of irreconcilable differences.

This would be a tragedy for everyone.

Shōwa as Past,
Present, and Future

THERE HAVE BEEN three truly momentous symbolic events in the history of twentieth-century Japan. The first was the death of the Emperor Meiji in 1912. The second, thirty-three years later, was Japan's surrender ending World War II. The third event is upon us now. It is, of course, the death of the Shōwa emperor after an extraordinary reign, through war and peace, of sixty-two years.

It seems fair to say that during the first two decades of his reign, from 1926 to 1945, Emperor Hirohito was revered in Japan and, as Japanese militarism intensified, despised outside of it. He was the god-emperor for whom Japanese were socialized to fight and die, and it was in his name that the Japanese military invaded China and Southeast Asia and took on the imperialist powers of the West. To Japan and the world at large, the Hirohito of early Shōwa was the uniformed figure on the white horse—ramrod straight, in the prime of life, and utterly unapproachable.

How different was the public persona of the emperor of the last four decades of Shōwa: shy and even vulnerable, always in civilian clothes, almost always on foot—and certainly never again seen on horseback. After 1945, as before, all this was carefully orchestrated by the emperor's

349

advisers, of course. Still, the emperor of postwar Japan quickly succeeded in impressing Japanese and many non-Japanese as well with his modest personal qualities. This is the figure that most Japanese now mourn.

In "proper" Japanese circles, many of the popular images of the postwar emperor are unmentionable. In the immediate aftermath of defeat, when the throne appeared in jeopardy and the emperor was encouraged to walk among the common people and show concern for their well-being, his awkward response to whatever he was told earned him the popular nickname "Mr. Ah So." Among irreverent young people, he was sometimes referred to as *Tenchan*, which translates roughly as "Little Emp." Following his much-publicized visit to the United States in 1975, it was widely rumored that his most treasured souvenir was a Mickey Mouse wristwatch from Disneyland.

I mention such anecdotes not out of disrespect but, on the contrary, because they suggest a level of familiarity which contrasts sharply with the highly formalized emperor worship of the presurrender years. As the emperor grew older, moreover, he seemed to earn the kind of affection mixed with solicitude that people give to an aging grandparent. He was frail and kindly, and people worried about his health. And in the final years and months of his life, there emerged a conspicuous new popular sentiment: pity.

The pity which the emperor garnered at the end of his life is extremely suggestive, for it rested on the growing popular perception that he was a prisoner, a pawn in the hands of callous advisers who were more concerned with manipulating the throne for their own purposes than they were with ensuring the well-being of their elderly sovereign. The emperor was less free during the final decades of his reign than he was during the middle decades, it was observed. As the saying went, he was being withdrawn behind the "chrysanthemum curtain" once again for vague political purposes. The most scandalous rumor of all concerned the emperor's final illness. He was ill and in pain for a long while, it was reported, before his shadowy managers within the Imperial Household Ministry finally agreed that it was permissible for him to have an operation.

These rumors were accepted as true by many well-informed Japanese, and at the simplest level they evoked a genuine sense of sympathy. "The poor man" (*okinodoku na kata*) was a common sentiment among many

Japanese during the emperor's final months. More than mere pity under-lay such a response, however. The emperor was transformed into some-one who, like most common Japanese, was manipulated by others. And, again consistent with a rather popular motif in Japanese popular con-sciousness, he also came to personify the trials and tribulations that the "suffering" Japanese as a whole had endured through the whole sixty-plus years of Shōwa.

These responses are particularly suggestive, I would submit, because they simultaneously reveal widespread Japanese cynicism concerning manipulation of the throne and (in the image of the Shōwa emperor and his subjects as victims) a susceptibility to such manipulation.

There are, of course, countless ways of thinking about the life and legacy of the Shōwa emperor, and the debate will continue long after the formal grieving is done and the new emperor has been installed on the throne. Much of what is said and done in the next few weeks and months, however, will shape both the popular memory of the Shōwa period and the course of future ideological politics in Japan. With this in mind, I would offer, as a modest contribution to the current discussion, three regrets concerning the recent past and three cautions concerning the future manipulation of the imperial symbol.

The first regret is that the Shōwa emperor did not use his immense power and prestige to attempt to check the rising tide of Japanese militarism and repression that culminated in the China and Pacific wars, or to press for an earlier end to World War II in Asia.

This, of course, is the most sensitive issue of all where the emperor is concerned. Indeed, in many circles, both in Japan and the West, any intimation of imperial war responsibility is virtually taboo. Yet, after all the disarming arguments concerning the emperor's conservative under-standing of "constitutional monarchy" and the like have been presented, the fact remains that prior to 1945 Emperor Hirohito was a young, vigorous, well-informed monarch who possessed real power, often made his preferences known, and actively allowed himself to be turned into the central icon of Japanese ultranationalism. We will never know exactly what he did or did not do between 1926 and 1945. In light of the death and destruction that was unleashed in his name beginning in the 1930s, however, it does not seem inappropriate to wish that he had been personally more forceful in working for peace.

This leads to a second and milder regret: that we will never even know what the emperor might have told us about the political workings of presurrender Japan. That he knew a great deal about the "secret history" of these years is incontestable, and there was a brief moment after Japan's defeat when he might have been persuaded to share at least part of his inside knowledge.

Politics, this time on the part of the Americans, thwarted this opportunity. While it is well known that General Douglas MacArthur personally intervened to prevent the emperor from being indicted as a war criminal after the war, it is less well known that the general simultaneously forbade the emperor from being used as a witness, or even interviewed, in conjunction with the war crimes trials. All this was part of the American decision that Emperor Hirohito could be used as a force for peace just as easily as he had been used as a rallying point for war. As so often happens at such moments of grand politics, the opportunity to clarify the historical record was sacrificed in the bargain.

My third regret involves history of a deeper sort, but is no less controversial because of that. It is essentially a cultural lament: that even after Japan's surrender, the mystique of the unbroken imperial line has prevented the Japanese from doing serious archaeological research on their own ancient past.

This is a delicate matter indeed, for what is at issue here are the great tumuli that date from around the fourth century and have remained unexcavated to the present day. In the wake of Japan's defeat, U.S. Occupation authorities made no serious effort to persuade the Japanese to unlock this buried past, presumedly in deference to the argument that this would desecrate the graves of the ruling family. And although recent scholarship suggests that the earliest and largest tombs (such as the gigantic tumulus of Nintoku, near Osaka) may belong to a different royal lineage that preceded the current imperial family, this is too heretical for most Japanese antiquarians to contemplate.

Thus, the hundreds of ancient tumuli designated as belonging to the present imperial family remain closed. It is possible that they were looted and cracked open to the atmosphere in ages past, and now contain only dust and debris. It is also possible that they would reveal only artifacts and decorations of a primitive sort, such as have been found in various nonroyal tombs. Then again, the burial chambers may have spectacular (but ideologically unsettling) contents in the manner of the small Taka-matsuzuka tomb excavated in 1972, which contained brilliant wall paint-ings that revealed in a dramatic way the immense Sino-Korean influence on the early Japanese nobility. The situation, in any case, is anomalous. The modern nation that takes most pride in its ancient and imperial past is also the nation that has steadfastly refused to seriously uncover that past.

Obfuscation can be functional, however, and much of Japanese politics in the modern period has revolved around the way the throne lends itself to reinterpretation and manipulation. This malleability has contrib-uted to positive accomplishments as well as disastrous abuses in the past, and it carries potential dangers for the future.

The first of these dangers is that the image of the Shōwa emperor which most Japanese will remember—indeed, the only image that Japa-nese under forty years old really know—will be that of the frail, gentle, and elderly civilian monarch. The taboos against criticism of the emperor have grown increasingly strong over the course of the postwar decades, and in the context of long and formal grieving these may become all but irresistible. This, of course, can only serve the purpose of those conserva-tive and right-wing revisionists who would romanticize the repressive nature of the prewar emperor system and sanitize the record of the "holy war" waged in the emperor's name.

At the same time, the death of the Shōwa emperor is the natural symbolic end of the era known as "postwar" Japan. As such, it offers the prospects for another sort of conservative revisionism—in this instance, closing the books on the democratic reformism of the early postwar years and intensifying the clarion call for substantial revision of the "Occupation-period" agenda. More specifically, the adoption of a new reign name and inauguration of a new imperial era will surely see heightened efforts by Japanese neonationalists to revise the constitution in a conservative manner and promote accelerated remilitarization. By no means do all Japanese share these impulses, but the more extreme conservatives have proven their mettle before in manipulating national symbols. This is the second danger that calls for vigilance in the months and years ahead.

The third danger follows from this and involves, more directly, the extraordinary mystique that continues to adhere to the throne. Much has been made of the emperor's "declaration of humanness" in 1946, and—as already emphasized here—his considerable personal appeal in the postwar years. In the formal Japanese scheme of things, however, he is not an ordinary mortal, nor is he simply a secular and symbolic monarch. The prolonged Shintō funeral ceremonies that mark the passing of the Shōwa emperor will reveal in striking ways the intimacy of church and state that still persists in Japan. So also will the elaborate rituals that will accompany the ascension of Emperor Hirohito's son and successor.

Why is this potentially dangerous? Because in subtle ways such rituals can be used to reinforce the cult of Japanese uniqueness and stimulate highly irrational nationalistic emotions. In the early Shōwa period, the most potent expressions of Japanese separateness, homogeneity, spiritual purity, and racial superiority were inseparable from emperor worship. Now, at a time when somewhat comparable racial and patriotic sentiments appear to be reemerging in Japan, the emperor's death raises the prospect of renewed expressions of imperial veneration and even deification. Within Japan, the event almost certainly will be presented as a uniquely spiritual moment which can only be truly appreciated by the Japanese people. It can easily become an unusually intense emotional occasion for affirming Japanese exceptionalism—and superiority.

Such considerations take us very far from the modest elderly man who has just passed away, and may well be unduly pessimistic. There are undeniably more promising countertrends in Japan, including the very secular personality of the new emperor as well as the sensitivity of many Japanese to how the throne has been manipulated in the past. Still, symbolic politics lies close to the heart of power in Japan; and, in death as in life, the Shōwa emperor remains the most ambiguous and enticing symbol of all.

Sources and Credits

ESSAYS

"The Useful War" originally appeared in the Summer 1990 special issue of *Daedalus*, devoted to "Shōwa: The Japan of Hirohito," and subsequently was reprinted in Carol Gluck and Stephen R. Graubard, eds., *Shōwa: The Japan of Hirohito* (New York: W.W. Norton & Co., 1992).

The original version of "Japanese Cinema Goes to War" appeared in the July 1987 *Newsletter* of the Japan Society of New York.

An earlier version of " 'NI' and 'F': Japan's Wartime Atomic-Bomb Research" was published under the title "Science, Society, and the Japanese Atomic-Bomb Project During World War Two" in *Bulletin of Concerned Asian Scholars* 10.2, April–June, 1978. The present essay includes new materials.

"Sensational Rumors, Seditious Grafitti, and the Nightmares of the Thought Police" derives from four unpublished draft chapters eventually compressed as a short section on "War, Polity, and Revolution" in J. W. Dower, *Empire and Aftermath: Yoshida Shigeru and the Japanese Experience, 1878–1954* (Cambridge, Mass.: Council on East Asian Studies, Harvard University, 1979), pp. 278–92.

"Occupied Japan and the Cold War in Asia" originally appeared in Michael J. Lacey, ed., *The Truman Presidency*, a Woodrow Wilson Center Series publication jointly published by the Woodrow Wilson International Center for Scholars and Cambridge University Press (1989).

"Yoshida in the Scales of History" originally was prepared for a November 1983 conference on "The Allied Occupation of Japan in World History" sponsored by Hosei University, Tokyo. A Japanese version titled "Yoshida Shigeru no Shiteki Ichi" appeared in the conference proceedings, which were published as *Sekaishi no Naka no Nihon Senryō* (Tokyo: Nihon Hyōronsha, 1985). The present essay includes new materials.

"Japanese Artists and the Atomic Bomb" appeared in slightly different form in the Wisconsin Humanities Committee publication *Perspectives* in Autumn 1982.

"Race, Language, and War in Two Cultures," which summarizes some of the themes in John W. Dower, *War Without Mercy: Race and Power in the Pacific War* (New York: Pantheon, 1986), originally was presented under the title "Group Defamation and the American-Japanese War" at an April 1988 conference on "Group Defamation and Freedom of Speech: The Relationship Between Language and Violence," sponsored by Hofstra University, New York. Conference proceedings edited by Eric Freedman and Monroe Freedman are scheduled to be published by the Greenwood Publishing Group.

"Fear and Prejudice in U.S.–Japan Relations" first appeared in English in *Ethics and International Affairs*, vol. 3 (1989). This was preceded by a longer two-part version of the essay in Japanese in the March and April 1988 issues of *Kokusai Mondai*.

"The Emperor in War and Peace: Views from the West" originally appeared in the March 1989 issue of the Japanese-language monthly *This Is*, published by Yomiuri Shimbunsha.

"Shōwa As Past, Present, and Future" was published under a different title in a commemorative retrospective on Emperor Hirohito and his times in the January 9, 1989 issue of the *Japan Times*.

ILLUSTRATIONS

Five Scouts (*Gonin no Sekkōhei*, p. 40), directed by Tasaka Tomotaka, was produced by Nikkatsu in 1938.

Fighting Soldiers (*Tatakau Heitai*, p. 41), directed by Kamei Fumio, was produced by Tōhō in 1939.

China Night (*Shina no Yoru*, p. 42), directed by Fushimizu Osamu, was produced by Tōhō in 1940.

The Story of Tank Commander Nishizumi (*Nishizumi Senshachō-den*, p. 43), directed by Yoshimura Kōzaburō, was produced by Shōchiku in 1940.

The Suicide Troops of the Watchtower (*Bōrō no Kesshitai*, p. 44), directed by Imai Tadashi, was produced by Tōhō in 1942.

The Loyal 47 Rōnin (*Genroku Chūshingura*, p. 45), directed by Mizoguchi Kenji, was produced by Shōchiku in two parts in 1941–1942.

Army (*Rikugun*, p. 46), directed by Kinoshita Keisuke, was produced by Shōchiku in 1944.

The Most Beautiful (*Ichiban Utsukushiku*, p. 47), directed by Kurosawa Akira, was produced by Tōhō in 1944.

The four cartoons of Yoshida Shigeru on pp. 225–228 are by Shimizu Kon and appeared in the *Asahi Shimbun* in January 1950, February 1951,

March 1952, and August 1953. The first three of these are reproduced from the Shimizu collection titled *Yoshida Shigeru: Fūshi Mangashū*, published by Hara Shobō in 1989.

The *hibakusha* drawings on pp. 246 and 247 are by Takakura Akiko and Yamagata Yasuko respectively. They were included in Japan Broadcasting Corporation, ed., *Unforgettable Fire: Pictures Drawn by Atomic Bomb Survivors* (New York: Pantheon, 1977), and are reproduced here courtesy of the Hiroshima Peace Culture Foundation.

The *Barefoot Gen* "cartoon story of Hiroshima" by Nakazawa Keiji (p. 249) is available in a multivolume English translation from New Society Publishers, 4722 Baltimore Ave., Philadelphia, PA 19143.

Pica-don (pp. 250–251), by Kinoshita Renzō and Kinoshita Sayoko, based on their animated film of the same title, is reproduced here courtesy of Dynamic Sellers Publishing Co., Ltd., Tokyo.

The three details from the collaborative atomic-bomb murals of Maruki Iri and Maruki Toshi (pp. 252–254) are reproduced courtesy of the Maruki Gallery for the Hiroshima Panels in Saitama, Japan.

David Low's November 1941 graphic (p. 288) was reproduced in David Low, *Years of Wrath* (New York: Simon and Schuster, 1946). Copyright Solo Syndication.

"Directive Is To Be Complied With Without Delay" (p. 289), by Quincy Scott of the *Oregonian*, was reproduced in the Sunday *New York Times* of August 19, 1945.

"Bon Voyage" (p. 289) originally appeared in the *Newark News* and was reproduced in the Sunday *New York Times* of May 4, 1952.

"Re-Arming Japan" (p. 290) by Jeff Danziger originally appeared on March 8, 1989. Copyright 1989, Christian Science Monitor and World Monitor News Service. Distributed by the Los Angeles Times Syndicate.

"Ah, So Sorry" (p. 291) is by Pat Oliphant, copyright Universal Press Syndicate. Reprinted with permission. All rights reserved.

The graphic at the bottom of p. 291 is by Dan Hubig and appeared in the *Washington Post National Weekly Edition* on September 7, 1987.

"How Tough Are the Japanese?" (p. 292) originally appeared in the *London Daily Mail* and was reproduced in the May 2, 1943 issue of the *New York Times Magazine*. Copyright Solo Corporation.

The sumo wrestler looming over Wall Street featured on the cover of "The Business World" supplement to the *New York Times Magazine* (p. 293) is by Joo Chung and appeared on September 20, 1987.

The "Japan on Wall Street" cover of *Business Week* (p. 293) was featured on both the regular and international editions of September 7, 1987.

"Space-Age Samurai" (p. 294) was the cover story of the December 4, 1981 issue of *Far Eastern Economic Review*, Hong Kong.

"Fear and Loathing of Japan" (p. 295) was the cover story of the February 26, 1990 issue of *Fortune*. *Fortune* is a registered trademark of Time Inc.

The threatening mechanized rendering of President Franklin Roosevelt (p. 296) appeared in the January 1943 issue of *Manga*.

The rendering of President George Bush as a "car and parts salesman" being addressed by Prime Minister Miyazawa Kiichi (p. 296) is by Yamada Shin and appeared in the January 6, 1992 issue of *Asahi Shimbun*.

The "Scary America" (*Soraosoroshii Amerika*) pamphlet cover on p. 297 is reproduced courtesy of IPEC Press, Tokyo.

The illustration by Katō Etsurō on p. 298 appeared in a June 1941 collection of patriotic cartoons titled *Taiheiyō Manga Tokuhon* [Pacific Cartoon Reader] compiled by the Kensetsu Mangakai [Association for

359

Constructive Cartoons] and published by Dai Nippon Sekiseikai Shuppankyoku.

The two cartoons by Yamada Shin on p. 299 appeared in the *Asahi Shimbun* on May 19, 1991 (top) and June 8, 1987 (bottom).

Yokoyama Taizō's cartoon on p. 300 appeared in the March 24, 1990 issue of *Asahi Shimbun*.

Yamanoi Norio's cartoon on p. 300 appeared in the Japanese magazine *AERA* in 1991.

While every effort has been made, it has not been possible to locate possible copyright holders, if any, for a few of the graphics. Persons with information about this should contact The New Press, 450 West 41st Street, New York, N.Y. 10036.

Index